# The Trial

## of

## Gilles de Rais

# THE TRIAL

OF

# GILLES DE RAIS

Documents Presented by

## GEORGES BATAILLE

*Translated by Richard Robinson*

Los Angeles

Amok Books edition
January 2004


ISBN 1-878923-02-1


The texts of the two trials of Gilles de Rais were based on the minutes and annotated by Georges Bataille.

The Latin text of the ecclesiastical trial was translated into French by Pierre Klossowski.

This book was originally published as Le Procès de Gilles de Rais, © 1965 by Jean-Jacques Pauvert, Paris

Cover Design: Tom Dolan

English Translation © 1991 Richard Robinson


Amok Books are available to bookstores through our primary distributor: SCB Distributors, 15608 South New Century Drive, Los Angeles, California 90248. Phone: (310) 532-9400. FAX: (310) 532-7001. Email: info@scbdistributors.com.

UK Distributors: Turnaround Distribution, Unit 3 Olympia Trading Estate, Coburg Road, Wood Green, London N22 6TZ. Phone: 0181 829 3000. FAX: 0181 881 5088.

To view the complete Amok Books catalog, please go to the Amok Books website at www.amokbooks.com.

# TABLE OF CONTENTS

# ACKNOWLEDGMENTS

The publishers would like to thank Matias Viegener for his extensive editing of the translation of Bataille's writings, and Nikki Halpern for her extremely thorough editing of the trial documents. Their contributions were integral to the shaping of this project.

We would also like to thank Melissa Hoffs for her painstaking proofreading and accomplished revisions of various drafts; Peter Wollen for his advice; Michael Intriere for his production expertise; and Sarah Koplin, Monica Moran and Michael Sheppard for their additional editorial assistance.

# FOREWORD

Abbot Bossard wrote that the trial of Gilles de Rais was "in all things the polar opposite of Joan of Arc's." But he adds that "together they compose the two most celebrated trials of the Middle Ages and perhaps also of modern times." We have known other exciting trials since then, but something here holds true. And if it is true that Abbot Bossard's book, the most important as yet dedicated to Gilles de Rais, is obsolete today, this is not the case with the trial documents: this is not the case with these most terrible documents. At one time published in a defective form, however, the texts are unobtainable today. One can see their republication here; they have been the object of a long and meticulous study, which we hope proves worthy of the exceptional interest of the document.

In the second part of the introduction we have held ourselves to saying whatever was known of this individual, as it seemed to us. We have added to this a certain number of historical facts, given in chronological order whenever possible.

N.B. — For place names, we have followed the current, officially designated usage. However, we have made an exception of *Rais*. We have not followed the currently accepted spelling, which is *Retz*. In fact this spelling involves an absurd pronunciation. In the 15th century it was most often written as *Rais*, or occasionally *Rays*. The pronunciation, always observed in the region, was *ray*. We have gotten rid of the *y*, which is nothing but an idle embellishment.

For the names of people, we have striven to give the most probable spelling, taking into consideration the incoherence and fancy of that given in the texts. Let us specify only that each time the texts give the spelling *cz* (*e.g.*: *Princzay*), or *cs*, we have written *c* (*e.g.*: *Princé*), which corresponds to the pronunciation.

# The Tragedy

## of

# Gilles de Rais

# THE TRAGEDY OF GILLES DE RAIS

## *The Sacred Monster*

Gilles de Rais owes his lasting glory to his crimes. But was he, as some affirm, *the most abject criminal of all time*? In essence, this speculative affirmation is barely defensible. Crime is a fact of the human species, a fact of that species alone, but it is above all the secret aspect, impenetrable and hidden. Crime hides, and by far the most terrifying things are those which elude us. On the night marked out by our fear, we are bound to imagine the very worst. The worst is always possible; and also, with crime, the worst is the last thing imaginable.

That is why — more than the actual crimes — legend, mythology, literature, and, above all, tragic literature set the standard of our fear. We can never forget that it is crime's legendary aspects alone that have ordained the truth of crime.

That said, we cannot enter upon the story of Gilles de Rais without granting him his privileged place. In the end, we cannot leave the evocative power held in everyday reality unmentioned. And faced with Gilles de Rais' crimes, we do get the sense, perhaps misleading, of a summit. His nobility, his immense fortune, his lofty achievements, and his execution in front of a scandalized crowd (which was perplexed, however, by his remorse and his many confessions and tears) consummate his apotheosis.

Undoubtedly, nothing completely vindicates the passion of the crowd that flocked to his execution. Gilles de Rais was simply a brutal man of war, a powerful nobleman without discretion, without scruples. Nothing designated him for the final sympathy of that crowd. His violence at least warrants the astonishment provoked by such an uncalculating and, as it were, bewildered passion. The violence of remorse corresponded, in effect, to the sick violence of vice, which brought this criminal to so many murders. Popular emotion was the consequence of the excess that had commanded a life never dominated by calculation. Gilles de Rais is a tragic criminal. The main constituent of tragedy is crime, and this criminal, more than any other perhaps, was a character of tragedy.

We must picture these sacrifices of dead children, which kept on multiplying. Let us imagine an almost silent reign of terror which does not stop growing, and for fear of reprisals the victims' parents hesitate to speak. This anguish is that of a feudal world, over which are cast the shadows of massive fortresses. Today, tourists are attracted to the ruins of these fortresses; then they were monstrous prisons, and their walls evoked torments of which they only occasionally muffled the cries. In the presence of Gilles de Rais' fairy-tale castles, which people will later call the castles of Bluebeard, we ought to recall these butcheries of children, presided over not by wicked fairies, but by a man drunk with blood. His crimes arose from the immense disorder that was unwinding him — unwinding him, and unhinging him. By the criminal's confession, which the scribes of the trial took down while listening, we also know that sensual pleasure was not of the essence. Ostensibly he would sit on the belly of his victim and, in this fashion, masturbating, come on the dying body; what mattered to him was less the sexual enjoyment than to see death at work. He liked to watch. He had the body cut open, the throat cut, the members carved to pieces; he relished seeing the blood.

However, only one last satisfaction was missing for him. Gilles de Rais fancied himself a sovereign lord. As Marshal of France, after the victory at Orléans and the consecration of Charles, he had himself bestowed with quasi-royal arms. He rode preceded by a royal escort, accompanied by an "ecclesiastical assembly." A herald of arms, two hundred men, and trumpeters announced him; the canons in his chapel, a kind of bishop, cantors, and the children in his music school made up his retinue on horseback, glittering with the richest ornaments. Gilles de Rais wanted to be dazzling, to the point of ruinous expenditure. In providing for the necessities that his delirium commanded, he liquidated an immense fortune without thinking. Some sort of dementia was at the heart of his propensity to spend money; he underwrote great theatrical performances accompanied by gifts of food and drink. He was compelled to fascinate people at all costs, but he lacked what a criminal quite often lacks on this order of things; this makes him recognize, in his confession, his excessive display of what necessarily should have remained hidden: *his crimes* . . .

Crime, obviously, calls for night; crime would not be crime without darkness, yet — were it pitch dark — this horror of night aspires to the burst of sunshine.

Something was lacking in the Aztec sacrifices, which took place at the same time as Rais' murders. The Aztecs did their killing in the sun atop pyramids, and they lacked the consecration that belongs to a hatred of the day, to a longing for the night.

Conversely, there dwells in crime an essentially theatrical capacity, demanding that the criminal be unmasked, wherein the criminal does not delight until finally unmasked. Gilles de Rais had a passion for theater; from the confession of his baseness, from his tears, from his remorse, he wrung the pathos of his execution. The crowd that assembled to see him die appears to have been paralyzed by the remorse and forgiveness that the tearful nobleman humbly begged of his victims' parents. Gilles de Rais wanted to die in front of his two accomplices; in this way he could display his hanging and burning to the bloody companions who had assisted him in his butcheries, of whom one at least had known his carnal embraces. For a long time they had been able to watch him wallowing in endless horror; for them he had long been the "sacred monster" that he became, in an instant, before the crowd.

During his life, Gilles de Rais' exhibitionism was appeased before a small number of witnesses, his accomplices: Sillé, Briqueville, Henriet, Poitou, and a few others. However, the spasmodic meaning of his death and confessions emerged when strangled, hanged, he appeared before the crowd through the executioner's flames.

Gilles de Rais is preeminently a tragic hero, the Shakespearian hero, whom perhaps this sentence from a judicial report evokes no less forcefully than the trial. (Published under the title of *Mémoire des Héritiers*, the text was edited after his death through the efforts of his family, who wanted to prove that he had dilapidated its fortunes lavishly — with reckless extravagance): "Everyone knew that he was notoriously extravagant, having neither sense nor understanding, since in effect his senses were often altered, and often he left very early in the morning and wandered all alone through the streets, and when someone pointed out to him that this was not fitting, he responded more in the manner of a fool and madman than anything else."[1] He was, moreover, conscious of this monstrous character. He said he had been "born under a constellation such that no one could understand without difficulty the illicit things he committed." One participant in these horrors heard him say "that there was no man alive who could ever understand what he did." Now he was moved by his planet to act as he did . . .

[1] Dom H. MORICE, "Mémoire des héritiers de Gilles de Rais pour prouver sa prodigalité," *Mémoires* . . . , Vol. II, col. 1338.

He doubtlessly developed a superstitious image of himself, as if he were of another nature, a kind of supernatural being attended by God and by the Devil. A victim of the profane world, of the real world, which had loaded him with advantages at his birth, but which had not supported him in the end. He was persuaded that the Devil, at his first beckoning, would run and fly to his aid. Through crime, as well as through a lasting devotion, he had a feeling of belonging to the sacred world, which might in no way refuse to support him. The Devil would make good the wrongs he had suffered, which in truth had come from his own imprudence! But this recourse to the Devil ended by impoverishing him; it left him at the mercy of charlatans who exploited his credulity. His tragedy is that of a Doctor Faust, but an infantile Faust. Before the Devil, in fact, our monster trembled. Not only did the Devil — our criminal's last hope — leave him trembling like a leaf, but Gilles de Rais was ridiculously, devotedly afraid of him. The Devil reduced him to begging. The monster was covered in blood, but he was a coward.

With astonishing impudence, Rais imagined saving himself to the end, despite his abominable crimes, and escaping Hell's flames, which for him were the object of a coal-seller's implicit faith. Even though he invoked the demon and expected from him the reestablishment of his fortune, up to the end he was naïvely a good and devout Christian. A few months before his death, still free, he confessed and approached the Sacred Altar. He even had a feeling of humility on this occasion; in the church at Machecoul, the common people moved aside, leaving room for the great lord. Gilles refused, asking the poor folk to stay beside him. This was a moment when anguish perhaps took him by the throat, when he wanted to renounce his orgies of blood. He decided then to go abroad, to go crying in front of the Holy Sepulcher in Jerusalem.

He dreamed of the endless voyage that would save him . . . But he contented himself with the intention. He was hardened, and during his last days of freedom he again began cutting children's throats.

This bedlam is not contrary to the truest Christianity, which is always — be it frightening! be it Gilles de Rais'! — ready to forgive crime. Perhaps Christianity is even fundamentally the pressing demand for crime, the demand for the horror that in a sense it needs in order to forgive. It is in this vein that I believe we must take Saint Augustine's exclamation, "Felix culpa!," Oh happy fault!, which blossoms into meaning in the face of inexpiable crime. Christianity implies a human nature which harbors this hallucinatory extremity, which it alone has allowed to flourish. Likewise, without the extreme violence we are provided with in the crimes of one Gilles de Rais, could we understand Christianity?

Perhaps Christianity is above all bound to an archaic human nature, one unrestrainedly open to violence? In his mad Christianity, no less than in his crimes, we see one aspect of the archaism of a man who, "leaving very early in the morning, wandered all alone through the streets . . ."

## Bluebeard and Gilles de Rais

It does not seem to me that Christianity above all requires the rule of reason. It may be that Christianity would not want a world from which violence was excluded. It makes *allowances* for violence; what it seeks is the strength of the soul without which violence could not be endured. Gilles de Rais' contradictions ultimately summarize the Christian situation, and we should not be astonished at the comedy of being devoted to the Devil, wanting to cut the throats of as many children as he could, yet expecting the salvation of his eternal soul . . . Whatever the case, we are at the antipodes of reason. Nothing in Gilles de Rais is reasonable. In every respect, he is monstrous. The memory that he left behind is that of a legendary monster. In the regions that he inhabited, this memory is in fact confounded with the legend of Bluebeard. There is nothing in common between Perrault's Bluebeard and the Bluebeard to whom the populations of Anjou, Poitou, and Brittany later attributed the castles of Machecoul, Tiffauges, and Champtocé. Nothing in Gilles de Rais' life corresponds to the forbidden room or the stained key of the legend, nothing to Sister Anne's watch at the top of the tower . . . In any case, we cannot expect any logic in the materials of legend. With little significance beyond the transfer of a real person into a legendary being — in conformity with a monstrous past that memory paints darker and darker — Gilles de Rais' castles and crimes were attributed to Bluebeard in popular imagination. We need not trouble ourselves here with what was, in its various, occasionally contradictory versions, the story of Bluebeard.[2] It hardly matters, in particular, to know whether the origin of the character goes back to Brittany. Michelet and some others believed so. But in speaking of Gilles de Rais, we need only consider the tradition concerning him. Abbot Bossard, from whom we have the most serious work on the criminal, wanted to establish this tradition and knew how to give it the precision it could eventually be given.

Bossard did his job so well that since his work, we can say that wherever he lived, Gilles de Rais was identified with Bluebeard. It is striking, even in a sense troubling, that such a diabolical memory would have found so suitable a

[2] The opinion that we express here on the resemblances between the history of Gilles de Rais and the story of Bluebeard has been given in precise terms by Charles PETIT-DUTAILLIS, who writes (in *Charles VII*, 1902, p. 183): "We do no want to say that Gilles de Rais was Bluebeard's prototype. The story of Bluebeard and his seven wives appears to be of ancient and popular source and is not in itself analogous to that of Gilles de Rais, who did not marry but once and left his wife to live a life apart; but it is certain that in Brittany and in the Vendée the people have amalgamated the story of Bluebeard and the history of Lord de Rais."

popular countenance. Is history effectively incommensurate with legend, which alone has the power to evoke that which, in crime, is not reducible to the limits of the familiar world? In attaching significance to the horror and excess in the figure of Gilles de Rais, we cannot do better than to attribute it to the name of Bluebeard, as the poor country folk did. I will not return to the specific facts before having insisted on one aspect which I should like to reveal as a primary truth: what interests us in the character of Gilles de Rais is generally what binds us to the monstrosity that a human being harbors since tender infancy under the name of nightmare. I spoke, to begin with, of the "sacred monster," but formerly and more simply, the poor folk called him Bluebeard . . .

Here is what Abbot Bossard was able to gather around 1880, methodically enough, from local tradition: "There is neither a mother nor a wet nurse," he tells us, "who, in their account, mistakes the places where Bluebeard dwelled: the ruins of the castles at Tiffauges, Champtocé, La Verrière, Machecoul, Pornic, Saint-Étienne-de-Mermorte, and Pouzauges, all of which belonged to Gilles de Rais, are noted as the spots where Bluebeard lived."[3] Abbot Bossard occasionally shows his naïveté, but on this point he wanted to proceed attentively. "Numerous are the old people we interrogated in the proximities of Tiffauges, Machecoul, or Champtocé; their accounts are unanimous; it is indeed the lord of Tiffauges, or the lord of Machecoul, or the lord of Champtocé, who was or is still for everyone the real Bluebeard." He finally says: "With the secret intention of shaking their conviction and troubling their belief, how many times did we try to confuse their memories and make them adopt an opinion that was not our own! 'You're mistaken,' we said, 'Bluebeard wasn't lord of Champtocé, nor lord of Machecoul, nor lord of Tiffauges.' To some we said, 'He dwelled in Mortagne or Clisson'; to others, 'Champtoceaux'; to others finally, some well-known ruin in the area. Everywhere, it was the same surprise at first, followed by the same air of disbelief and same response: that Bluebeard dwelled, for the people of the Vendée, at Tiffauges; for the people of Anjou, at Champtocé; for the people of Brittany, at Machecoul . . . We have listened to people over ninety years old; they affirmed that their accounts came from old people before them. In speaking only of the region of Tiffauges, whose traditions we are familiar with above all, the terrible baron lives there still; no longer, it is true, with the original features of Gilles de Rais, but with the somber and legendary physiognomy of Bluebeard. One day, while walking among the ruins of the castle on the broken dike of the pond of La Crûme, at the foot of the big tower, we came upon a group of tourists sitting on the grass, in the middle of which was an old, native woman talking about Bluebeard. This woman is still alive; she was born within the walls of the fortress, where her family dwelled for three centuries, until 1850,

---

[3] Abbot E. BOSSARD, *Gilles de Rais, maréchal de France*, 1st ed. (1885), p. 399.

at which point she retired to the village. Her sister, even older than she, has since confirmed all the information that we received that day, even the most precise details . . . Bluebeard had been the lord of this castle; her parents had always told her so and on the faith of their immediate ancestors — 'And hold on,' she suddenly added, 'let me take you to the very room where he usually cut the infants' throats.'

"We climb the formerly steep hill, diminished today by the rubble of collapsed towers; she leads us directly to the foot of the dungeon and points with her finger to a small door very high up in the corner of two immense stretches of wall: 'There's the room,' she says. — 'But once again, who told you?' — 'My old parents always said so, and they knew it well. A stairway led up to it in the old days, and I'd often climb it when I was young; but today the stairway is collapsed and the room itself is almost filled by the walls and vault caving in.' "

It thus seems that in the people's memory, Marshal de Rais existed in the form of a monster called Bluebeard. Sometimes this Bluebeard is a Gilles de Rais whose name alone has changed. Sometimes the Bluebeard of the most common legend bleeds onto Gilles: "The people of the Vendée," Abbot Bossard repeats, "imagine that the funereal room where the seven wives of Bluebeard were hanged still exists in a hidden spot of the castle at Tiffauges; only the steps of the stairway leading to it have collapsed with time, and woe to the curious tourist who stumbles upon the ruins by accident! He'd fall instantly into a deep abyss where he'd die miserably. In the evening, the common folk avoid these fatal ruins, haunted as on the worst days by Bluebeard's restless and evil shadow." Nevertheless, the classic legend seems only secondarily associated with this tradition in which essentially only the name of the character was changed. "At Nantes," Abbot Bossard says again, "the little expiatory monument piously erected by Marie de Rais at the place of the execution of her father was known and designated only as Bluebeard's monument. The old people in proximity of Clisson have told us how, while passing before this little edifice during their childhood, their parents would tell them, 'this is where Bluebeard was burned'; they did not say 'Gilles de Rais.' " As if so excessive a story was unable to have anything but a monster as its protagonist, a being outside common humanity for whom the only appropriate name was one charged with legendary miasmas. Bluebeard could not have been one of our own, only a sacred monster unbound to the limits of ordinary life. Better than the name of Gilles de Rais, that of Bluebeard lengthened the shadow that the poor folk's imagination harbored.[4]

---

[4] These poor folk were able to be led to this identification by the difficulty of speaking to their children about the scandalous story of Marshal de Rais. The name Bluebeard corresponds as well to the designated figure.

## Glaring Truth . . .

In accordance with the peoples of the Vendée and Brittany, who quickly stopped seeing what it was in Gilles de Rais that distinguished him from Bluebeard and naïvely confused the two, I at first wanted to describe the legend, the legendary monster, the fantastic being who exceeded accepted bounds.

It is time to go beyond these first considerations which, depicting things in their unity, represent them as the popular imagination and most attentive stories have done. There are also the pure details — more precise and more concrete, having little meaning in themselves — which permit us to understand this troubling figure a little less vaguely. I would like to evoke them successively, just as the documents specify them; I imagine that their truth is occasionally glaring, but they never contradict the "sacred monster" who has imposed himself from the beginning in every fashion with so much force.

Between Vannes and Nantes, in the little town of La Roche-Bernard, Gilles de Rais leaves the house where he has just passed the night. He is accompanied by a child whose mother, Peronne Loessart, made the mistake of entrusting him to one of the great lord's valets the day before. Occasionally Gilles de Rais is affable, he can be friendly, but Peronne Loessart's testimony at the trial depicts him at a moment of superb calm. He left with the child who was no doubt happy to have left the poverty of his home. Having seen them exit, the mother quickly overtakes them; perhaps she is devastated. She appeals to the man who will soon cut the throat of the small ten-year-old boy following them. *Not deigning to respond to the mother's humble plea*, and addressing himself to the servant who beats back the prey, Gilles de Rais speaks simply, tranquilly: the child, he says, is "well chosen"; he adds: "He is as beautiful as an angel." A few moments later, bobbing up and down on a pony, the innocent victim leaves in the ogre's escort, in the direction of the castle at Machecoul . . .

We would misunderstand the monster whose violence will soon be unleashed if we did not notice in him this apparent insensitivity, this nonchalant indifference, which to begin with places him well above the feelings of the average man. This calm in expectation of the worst, which Peronne Loessart's testimony illustrates with most genuine naïveté, would it have anything to do with what follows? The accumulation of blood, the violence of a wild animal! — it links blood to the truth and violence to the sovereign monstrosity of Rais, whose grandeur tramples those who confront him, who now and then naïvely laughs at seeing the jolts and contortions of children, their throats cut. Is there anything more glaring than this "beautiful as an angel," pronounced in front of the mother, and in front of the child who shall die — this boy of ten — pronounced by a man who, soon to be sitting on the belly of his victim, will lean forward the better to see, to bring to climax the joy drawn from his agony?

The murder of Peronne Loessart's child took place at Machecoul in September 1438. At this moment Gilles de Rais was not completely the tracked animal that he became a little bit more every day. But by the spring of 1440 he has no more money, the resources that remain are removed; public rumor grows, accusing him with deafening insistence. He is very much indeed the tracked animal who is blinded and attempts to forge his destiny: by force of arms he retakes the castle of Saint-Étienne-de-Mermorte from the man to whom he had sold it. This aberrant behavior is bound to attract dangerous reprisals, and any meaning it has descends from chaos and powerlessness.

Gilles de Rais, from then on having no other outlet for escape than death, loses his footing. He lets himself founder blindly. On the same day, he hides a company of sixty men-at-arms in the forest; at the close of High Mass, he brandishes a combat-axe and brutally enters the church with several of them. He hurls himself screaming on the buyer's brother, a clergyman charged with guarding the castle. Gilles de Rais is an energumen, a loose cannon in the church who roars: "Ha, ribald, you beat my men, and extorted from them; come outside the church or I'll kill you on the spot!"

The denouement of this tragedy is captured with almost perfect precision in the clerk-of-the-court exactitude of the trial record, reporting for us in this form, in French rather than Latin, the decisive aberrational outburst of this moment. We are unable to discover what triggered this abrupt anger in Gilles de Rais, suddenly refusing to tolerate the situation that resulted in the liquidation of his castles. But, violating the sanctity of the church, disdaining the ecclesiastic immunity of then-officiating Jean le Ferron, finally flouting the authority of the Duke of Brittany — the only support that he had left — he guaranteed his own ruin: his trial and execution follow shortly after the scene at Saint-Étienne-de-Mermorte. Gilles de Rais believed he had one trump; he imprisoned Jean le Ferron in a dungeon; first at Saint-Étienne, then at Tiffauges. But only his naïveté permitted him to see a way out where evidently he barely had a chance to catch his breath. Indeed, the Duke of Brittany was forced to run to the Constable of France, who alone had the power to act outside Brittany, at Tiffauges in Poitou. But this constable, Arthur de Richemont, was the Duke's own brother: the madman had bought himself a few weeks. The Saint-Étienne-de-Mermorte affair having occurred on May 15, 1440, Lord de Rais was executed on October 26th. Crimes that kept multiplying, desperate appeals to the Devil, finally the most foolish prank of all — there was nothing that did not work towards his rapid ruin.

One knows that at first he was disdainfully insolent in the presence of his judges. His attitude has nothing calculated, nothing cunning in it; he passes from rudeness to collapse without transition. But he is a fool in his insolence.

And if he reveals a grandeur beyond his baseness, it is in the calm of collapse. The courage and audacity with which he defies punishment and death are opposed to the panicked fear he has of the Devil. His courage and daring were proved in battle. But this tragic fear stands out if death alone is not in question, as it simply is in war: if crime and expiation call into play that which signifies tragedy, that which makes tragedy the very expression of destiny. In this sense the dialogue between judge and criminal, Pierre de L'Hôpital and Gilles de Rais, attains a rare degree of intensity. Dimly, the grandeur of this dialogue must have appeared from the shadows; that is why the scribe gives it in French, as he does every time that the proceedings, often encumbered with judicial pedantry, suddenly assume pathetic value.

Interrupting the ecclesiastical proceedings with an extraordinary interrogation, only decided upon at the last instant in front of a prepared torture rack, the high secular magistrate Pierre de L'Hôpital insists that Gilles tell "from what motives, with what intent, and to what ends" he had his victims killed. The latter had only just specified how he committed his crimes "according to his imagination and idea, without anyone's counsel, and following his own feelings, solely for his pleasure and carnal delight." Gilles is disconcerted and tells him, in response:

— Alas! Monsignor! you torment yourself and me along with you.

Pierre de L'Hôpital's retort is itself given in French:

— I don't torment myself in the least, but I'm very surprised at what you've told me and simply cannot be satisfied with it: I desire and would like to know the absolute truth from you for the reasons I've already told you often.

— Truly, there was no other cause, no other end nor intention, if not what I've told you: I've told you greater things than this and enough to kill ten thousand men.

What the secular magistrate is asking for is simple. It is what any man governed by reason wants to know. Why did Gilles kill? Following which instigations, which examples, why did he proceed in this manner, and in no other? The explanation of crime matters to a judge . . . Conversely, Gilles understood only a tragic, monstrous truth, of which he was the blind expression. This fatal need to kill, to kill without reason, which no words could clarify, which had possessed him as a gallop possesses an overexcited horse . . . It was not important to the guilty party to learn or reveal the origin of his

22

crimes. These crimes had been what he himself inherently was, what he was deeply, tragically, so much so that he thought of nothing else. No explanation whatsoever. Nothing appears commensurate with the immense delirium that he experienced except for expiation, which he is going to experience. Expiation then is the only word that corresponds, in Rais' mind, to what the judge would have wanted to know: "Enough to kill ten thousand men!" It is illogical, but it carries the spirit that is the life of the criminal; to the end this man must, I do not say live, but be drowned, immersed, in crime. The moment that the possibility of murder is taken away from him, in prison, confession binds him to what he does before everyone; and expiation, exposing his crimes to the crowd that is attracted by their enormity and the spectacle of his execution — confession, expiation, would continue to be his to the end. To the very last breath, he will live in crime and in the forgiveness that he will tearfully supplicate God to bestow on him while dying.

"Enough to kill ten thousand men!"

How could anyone display more pride or more humility?

In tears, Lord de Rais renews his remorse: what he cannot do is stop being monstrous. It is a monster who cries and a monster's repentance that he manifests. We must not deceive ourselves here. It is common to be moved by the piety of his last days. But these several words to follow, which the clerk of the court records, are troubling. They were addressed, at the end of a confrontation, to his young Florentine sorcerer, François Prelati. It is necessary to say here, without delay, that this Prelati was a cunning, cultivated comedian, but a lout; without a doubt, he seduced his master (by appearance, he was homosexual himself) and, to be sure, devoured him. To the end, he took advantage of Gilles' naïveté; one day he feigned having been mercilessly beaten with a stick by the Devil, howling and reappearing with wounds. But in the judges' presence, when the accused was before him again, at the moment when Prelati left the hall, he said to him between sobs:

— Goodbye! François, my friend! never again shall we see each other in this world; I pray that God gives you plenty of patience and understanding, and be sure, provided you have plenty of patience and trust in God, we will meet again in the great joy of paradise! Pray to God for me, and I will pray for you!

Few human beings have left behind traces permitting them, after five centuries, to speak thus! to cry thus! Such scenes are not the work of an author. *They happened:* somehow we have the stenography of them. But we cannot be surprised at being left in uncertainty: the tragedy of this farewell does not diminish its ridiculousness. And if we look for coherence in the story, in this character, and in the whole affair, we have the premonition of a primary truth: this monster who, however, is quite the legendary monster, the Bluebeard of those countrysides over which the ruins of feudal walls and towers at night spread terror, this monster before us is like a child.

We cannot deny the monstrosity of childhood. How often children would, if they could, be Gilles de Raises! Let us imagine the practically limitless power that he had at his disposal. Reason alone defines monstrosity, which we justifiably call monstrous from the fact that it belongs to man, to that being of reason. At bottom, neither the tiger nor the child are monsters, but in this world where reason rules, their apparent monstrosity is fascinating; they escape the necessary order.

But I would now be induced to say in what fashion, and to what degree, the monster who — under the name of Gilles de Rais, then Bluebeard, and who haunted the mournful land of Rais — was a child.

I cannot be content with the aspects that I have just now attributed to him. These aspects correspond to the power of fascination that permits me to evoke the figure after five hundred years. These aspects are relatively the most famous. This is not so with that foolishness, with that childishness, which I would like chiefly to render perceptible: foolishness and childishness have the habit of escaping attention. Wanting to illustrate the misunderstood aspects of Gilles de Rais, I must now link them to his whole life.

## *The Heir of Great Lords*

Gilles de Rais, who became in 1429 Marshal de Rais, is the great-grand-nephew of Constable Guesclin, the grandson of Jean de Craon, and the son of Guy de Laval. The house of Laval-Montmorency, from which his father comes; that of Craon, from which his maternal grandfather comes; or that of Rais, from which, indirectly, he received the heritage and name, number among the noblest, richest, and most influential houses of feudal society of their time.

What we know of Gilles' father or, generally, of his family members is vague; it is the same with representatives of the family of Rais, of which he was the heir and which died out in 1407 in the person of Jeanne Chabot, called La Sage. The only persons of whom we do know individual details are Pierre and Jean de Craon, Gilles' maternal great-grandfather and grandfather. We will speak of them, but first we ought to depict the world of the relatives of this bloody man who, during years of anguish, waited for the moment to throw himself on children, violate them, and cut their throats.

All of Gilles' near relations are powerful feudal lords, proprietors of vast rural estates, dominated by massive fortresses. Each of them possesses many, occasionally a great number, of these high positions, which wield violent power in fear and horror. A power in some way religious even. (The sovereign power of the King is supernatural in part, the power of a great lord resembles it, is the reflection of it.) Indeed, these feudal lords are not clearly conscious of the situation by which they profit, living in search of glory, but in comfortable luxury (if they do not have material comfort, a most genuine comfort is afforded them by the number of servants). Charity, religious terror, ambition, vain pleasures, and sordid interests share an opulent and fragile life, a life that at each moment death can terminate conclusively. In this world of great lords — who laugh, who chase and make war, who never stop thinking of the enemy, of the rival, but who rarely get bored and never work — nobody escapes for long the thought of a grimacing Devil, ruling over the eternal terror of Hell. Our life today, which is thought reasonable, is in part a fabric of contradictions. But unreservedly a great lord at the beginning of the 15th century, far from striving for reason, lived in a contradictory chaos of calculation, violence, good humor, bloody disorder, mortal anguish, and the absence of anxiety . . .

Speaking of Gilles de Rais' crimes, we alluded at first to the archaism of his character; we will see that this archaism stands out in many ways.

Gilles de Rais belongs primarily to his time. He is one of those unreasonable feudal lords, with whom he shares the pleasures of egoism, laziness, and disorder. He lives in the same way, in those heavy and luxurious fortresses, among the men-at-arms in his service, and in contempt of the rest of the world.

In all respects, his education identifies him with the whole of these mediocre and prestigious men. If he has military capabilities, it is in the degree to which he has been broken in by violent exercises; but of the art of war, he could have received the rudiments only (one did not train warriors back then; one possibility alone presented itself: life among those who had the experience of war). The family riches determined that Gilles would have two ecclesiastic tutors, who doubtless taught him how to read and write easily; he knew Latin, which he must have also spoken, but nothing proves that he had a true education. Some manuscripts, which are perhaps most likely handed down from him, do not suggest that he dedicated a significant part of his life to them.

Gilles de Rais, on the whole, is lost in the feudal masses of the time. But he is opposed in one respect (relating to his archaic character) to the one who received the charge of his education: his grandfather. As we have said, we know more about the life of this grandfather, Jean de Craon, than about any of his other relatives.

Gilles' mother, Marie de Craon, and father, Guy de Laval, died young, and one after the other in the course of 1415. Guy de Laval fears that, his own ancestors having disappeared, the tutelage of his children will fall to the maternal grandfather, whom he must not be on good terms with, or whose immorality he evidently fears. He wants to prevent what he justly holds to be disastrous. Notwithstanding how carefully he might have formulated them, his last will and testament had no effect. Gilles, at eleven years old, passes into the hands of this grandfather to whom, in certain regards, he is identical; to whom, at the same time, he is the opposite.

## The Maternal Grandfather: Jean de Craon

We have just alluded to Jean de Craon's immorality. This very great lord is in fact devoid of scruples: he is brutal, he is greedy; his methods depend on banditry. But he is to no extent anachronistic; his faults are not opposed to the character traits of his time. On the contrary, they accentuate them. Being a great lord, that he would have the outlook and the habits of a freebooter would not surprise anybody. What is more, he is precisely representative of feudal society in a period when the bourgeois ideal of management of interests and exploitation of goods prevails over the attention to traditional virtues bound to the notion of feudal honor. There is nothing romantic about the banditry of a Jean de Craon.

His fortune is considerable. Except for the ducal family, his is the richest feudatory in Anjou. But one preoccupation dominates him: to augment his riches. He constructs intrigues that involve him in the great politics of his day; he is avaricious and no profit is negligible to him. He regularly resides in a castle dominating the Loire, at Champtocé, an important garrison and the military key to neighboring Brittany. He exercises a right of toll on the ferrymen's commerce, but he uses violent means beyond the recognized rights; the ferrymen take him to court and the Parliament of Paris convicts him.

We do not know whether he possesses the known courtliness and seductiveness of his father, better known than himself, one of the relatives of the Duke of Orléans whom Jean sans Peur had assassinated. It is possible; but from him he gets the sense and taste for politics. The father passes for having paid the greatest attention to honor. It is possible that above all honor indicates a fastidious sense of feudal decorum. But if the son resembles him in this regard, it is to the degree that occasionally the most double-dealing of gangsters has a sense for the rules in his neighborhood. If one puts aside a totally exterior respectability, Jean de Craon has the outlook and the facility, if one likes, of a purse snatcher. He is responsible for Gilles; he has the charge of his education but he mocks it. He leaves his grandson free, in his own manner, to do all the evil he pleases. If the grandfather intervenes, it is to set an example; he instructs him to feel above the law.

We will see that it is not here that the young man is opposed to the old!

Later (pp. 73-74) we find the account of an act of banditry in which the grandfather involves Gilles at the age of sixteen.

It is a question of extortion by which a great lady, a relative, is abducted, imprisoned, and menaced with being put in a sack and drowned like a cat in the Loire. Three men, who come to reclaim her, are thrown into a dungeon, and one of them dies as a result of his stay there. Faced with Gilles and his grandfather, it is possible to imagine the brutalities of the Nazis . . .

## *The Grandfather and the Grandson*

But one difference quickly appears between the grandson and the grandfather. The latter, astute, manages his interests skillfully. The former occasionally profits by the calculations of the latter, but he does not calculate for himself. If Gilles is in agreement with the principle of reason which always, in an act, looks to the end result, that supposes another who guides and counsels him. He never acts on his own in the capacity of a shrewd man. Capable of base cruelties, he is incapable of calculation. Whatever reflection entered into his acts came from the intervention of another.

Jean de Craon does not hesitate in the face of crime, but what attracts him to crime is the result. He has no other concern but advantage. With Gilles it is different. The grandfather dead, he continues the crimes into which the old feudal lord initiated him. He will go even further, much further than the initiator, but only in response to his obsession, to his delirium. He acts feverishly. With Craon's death, he enters into the hallucinatory series of child murders. Occasionally going beyond the demands of his passion, he also surrenders himself to unprofitable, scandalous acts of violence. But he never knows how to put immorality to his advantage. If he is cruel and unscrupulous, he forgets to attend to his interests, and ignores or neglects them.

In this respect, the opposition between the grandfather and the grandson is most profound. It is perfect. Finally, the grandfather attempts to instill in Gilles an ambition conforming to his views. The rapacious old man imagines this impetuous young man, who will back down from nothing, becoming an influential man in the realm, augmenting the immense fortune that he is about to leave him. He will counsel him, he will set him on his way. Indeed, under these circumstances, Gilles' courage and impetuosity will take him to the very top of the heap. In 1429, at twenty-five years old, glorious Marshal of France, companion of Joan of Arc, and liberator of Orléans — these things foretell, it seems, an incomparable destiny. But the success is fragile; it is the annunciation, the beginning of ruin; it introduces the incomparable disaster. What the old man sordidly would have turned to profit Gilles turns to delirium, to disorder. He has in himself a delirium and inordinateness that places him at the antipodes of this insensitive old man and his rational deceit. After the death of his grandfather, he lapses into incredible expenditures that in a matter of years will drain one of the largest fortunes of a period when, the difference between rich and poor being greater, the riches possessed were worth more than today. From the beginning, Gilles de Rais' opulence is such that the greatest lords and the King were not equal to it. As Marshal of France he receives considerable wages; however, to him this post is above all — such is his propensity — the occasion for excessive expenditures. The need to shine makes his head swim: he cannot resist the possibility of dazzling spectators; he has to astound others through incomparable splendor. Others would have turned the glory that he originally had to their fortune's advantage. It succeeds, on the contrary, in driving him to his ruin; it plunges him into a state of increased extravagance. At all costs, he must dazzle others; but it is he himself, ahead of the others, that he dazzles. The impulse, which is not so rare, attains a sickly frenzy in Gilles. Gilles de Rais is not only the monstrous criminal, he is the mad prodigal: extravagance is like drunkenness. Jean de Craon had thought that by his becoming a man of the first rank he would know how to sober up, but the status he achieved actually served to intoxicate him more; he gave way without measure to his need to astonish through magnificent fairytale expenditures.

The conflict between the grandfather and the grandson first breaks out in 1424, when at the age of twenty Gilles demands the administration of all of his assets. The grandfather immediately reacts. It results in a violent tension between the two men.

Yet Craon cannot maintain a firm stand. How could this harsh grandfather, however indifferent, persist? He lost his only son in the Battle of Agincourt in 1415. And if he had hoped, by marrying again, that his wife would give him a direct heir, he must have finally gotten used to the idea that this grandson, with whom he was on bad terms, would inherit his great fortune.

He assumed responsibility for Gilles after the death of his father, the same year as the death of his son; he gave him a disastrous education. Not only did he give him his own bad example, but he foolishly abandoned him to the idleness and mayhem of childhood.

We know from the declarations of Gilles himself at the trial what characterized, from his eleventh year, this savage and violent childhood. Apparently the two clergymen, who had instructed him up to this point, quit. We know very little of his relationship with this pair. But twenty years later, in 1436, he has one of them, Michel de Fontenay, arrested; he has him thrown into prison (pp. 98-99), and we know what prison meant then . . .

His studies terminated, left to himself, a frightful development began. "On account of the bad management he had received in his childhood, when, unbridled, he applied himself to whatever pleased him, and pleased himself with every illicit act . . ." Such are Gilles' own words, which the scribe took down.

The scribe specifies: "He perpetrated many high and enormous crimes . . . , since the beginning of his youth, against God and His commandments . . . "

Morality, to tell the truth, was not Jean de Craon's business. Evidently the grandfather's avarice alone was at the bottom of one disagreement, which the grandson's impetuosity was necessarily fated to overcome.

Finally this grandfather introduces the young black sheep to the court. In 1425, Gilles is with Craon at the interview in Saumur where Charles VII and the Duke of Brittany, Jean V, consider an accord. The accord cannot resolve for long the difficulties that oppose the France of the "King of Bourges" to Brittany, which is divided between fear of an English invasion and the will to avoid French domination.

However, in 1427 an exceptional occasion presents itself. Jean de Craon receives the lieutenant generalship of the duchy of Anjou from his suzerain, Yolande d'Aragon, Charles VII's mother-in-law. She intends to be the mother of a true queen; this is why she has the interests of her son-in-law at heart. From time to time she overcomes the inaction of this erratic king. At court two years later she will effectively support Joan of Arc. In 1427 she takes the initiative in a limited, but judicious, action. The struggle against the English will resume in her domains. She comes to terms with Craon, her most powerful vassal, who will take charge of operations. But Craon is old, probably in his sixties. He cannot take part in the campaign. Whereas experienced captains lead the royal contingents, Gilles, at twenty-three years old, is placed at the head of an Angevin army. However, he is not alone. Jean de Craon entrusts him to a kind of mentor: Guillaume de La Jumellière, an Angevin lord, who appears under the name of Monsignor Martigné in Gilles' records. Gilles' military knowledge is limited; not so that of La Jumellière, apparently the only advisor in his hire who is what you would call respectable (the others unscrupulously live at the expense of his naïveté). Under these circumstances, Jean de Craon also facilitates for Gilles a certain disposition of his personal fortune; from the start, the future Marshal of France astonishes people by the number of spies he employs and the wages they receive.

As Gilles' good luck would have it, this prudently conducted campaign is an undeniable success. Charles VII's men seize many fortresses from the English. But Gilles does not distinguish himself simply by the abundance of his monetary resources. It is probable that from then on he gives proof of great courage, and that he shows when attacking a warlike fury, the memory of which lasts after his death. It is doubtless that this fury merited his being summoned by Joan of Arc, determined to force the outcome below the walls of Paris. In addition to the Duke of Alençon, Joan of Arc wants this young man, who harbors all the fury and violence of crime, beside her at this time. We mustn't forget that if a quarrel had not gone through her shoulder, the outcome that the Maid was hoping for would have been possible on this day. Evidently Gilles is a superb leader in battle. He belongs to that class of men thrust forward by the delirium of battle. If Joan of Arc wants him by her side at the decisive moment, it is because she knows this.

## Georges de La Trémoille and Gilles de Rais

But this impetuosity could never have been of service if it had not initially entered into the kind of calculations of which Gilles is not capable. If the grandfather had not put the grandson in touch with Georges de La Trémoille, their relative — if he had not become an intimate of this schemer — the madcap would never have seized the primary role in history that, in a lightning flash, he grasped.

On the occasion of Joan of Arc's arrival at Chinon, Gilles de Rais enters into calculations of great political consequence. He doubtless knows nothing of these calculations but he serves them and, in serving them, they give him what he did not have a chance of attaining by himself: an effectiveness. In April 1429 he binds himself by oath to the charlatan La Trémoille, who, having become Charles VII's favorite, is practically the Prime Minister. La Trémoille needs a man whose will is his own; he needs a blind and sumptuous armor for his army, the commanding appearance — and, when the moment comes, the valor — which corresponds to his interests.

La Trémoille, this cunning man, has many reasons for deciding upon Gilles de Rais. Kinship, first of all (I have already mentioned the family tie with the Craons). But most of all La Trémoille fears the influence of anyone other than himself on the King. He could have thought at first of Joan of Arc, but a woman cannot play a political role herself. That is not the case with a man of war who, benefiting from possible successes, would thereafter have access to the King. The choice by a man as calculating and prudent as La Trémoille ought therefore to fall on a man who was able militarily, but who at least must be incapable politically.

La Trémoille apparently did not hesitate. He knew what Gilles de Rais was all about from the start: Craon, the grandfather, was unscrupulous but cunning; Rais, the grandson, had no more scruples than the first, but when it came to ruses, calculations and intrigues, he was destitute; these things were beyond him. We do not know what La Trémoille thought of Gilles on the occasion of their first ties. But in 1435, after his disgrace, the rake is seen to reproach himself for having taken advantage of the Marshal's credulity (the two "friends" had the same financial affairs back then).

Abbot Bourdeaut specifies that it became "evident that La Trémoille was taking advantage of the credulity and mad extravagance of his cousin." La Trémoille must have always taken him for a fool; he finally expresses his opinion in an arresting form, the reproach couched as a joke. He responds without hesitation with this enormity: "It is good," La Trémoille affirms, "to encourage him to be bad"![5] Today these words leave us breathless, but how could this mediocre statesman, this cunning man, have imagined an opposition between foolishness and goodness — and between wickedness and intelligence? He apparently did not know Rais' hysterical cruelty until much later.

Gilles' wickedness was boundless. However, even he would have been unable to conceive of the calculations and bad faith of a La Trémoille. In the face of this bad faith and these calculations, he felt no repugnance. But if someone did not calculate in his place, he would not calculate. Under La Trémoille's aegis, he kept his place in Charles VII's entourage. Close to Joan of Arc in the decisive and very delicate affair of the liberation of Orléans, he played a primary role, evidently right after that of the Maid. Abbot Bourdeaut has shown that the "particular character" of this role had "not been elucidated"; still, in 1445, "when, at the trial to clear the name of Joan, Dunois gave his deposition in an age when nobody boasted of having rubbed elbows with the Marshal . . . , he put the sad Gilles at the top of the leaders of battle who had commanded the army of the liberation."[6] But the role of a leader of battle is limited in this period to the great lord's personal prestige and to the warrior's valor. Evidently, taking La Jumellière's advice, Gilles can speak in the councils before the battles. In these battles, above all, he can carry his own and strike.

La Trémoille pushed Gilles into the highest echelon but retained for himself, so far as calculation is concerned, all that was political. If young Baron de Rais had known how to scheme, La Trémoille would have prevented him from becoming a Marshal.

Without La Trémoille, the madcap would have never had a place in history. But if he had not been a fool, that madcap whom we know today — La Trémoille would have never made use of him.

## The Foolishness of Gilles de Rais

Usually one avoids noticing that in Gilles de Rais' monstrosity there is this strange thing: this Marshal of France is a fool!

But our character is bewitching.

At the opposite extreme, Huysmans saw in him one of the most cultivated

---

[5] A. BOURDEAUT, *Chantocé, Gilles de Rays et les Ducs de Bretagne*, p. 78.

[6] *Op. cit.*, p. 67.

men of his time!

Huysmans had one sustaining reason: Marshal de Rais, like him, was mad about church music and hymns. From there he draws foolish conclusions based on appearances that prove nothing.

But Huysmans only carried a common reaction to its conclusion. Generally the grandeur and, above all, the monstrosity of our character is imposing. There is a sort of majesty in his ease, one that he keeps even during the tears of confession. There is in the evidence of monstrosity a sovereign grandeur which does not contradict the humility of the wretched man proclaiming the horror of crime.[7]

Also this grandeur, in a sense, agrees with the foolishness of which I speak. Indeed, from the foolishness of Gilles de Rais to what one usually designates with this term, the difference is great. At its heart there lies a sovereign indifference which caused him to pay double for what pleased him . . . This indifference, this absence, made others laugh. But Gilles undoubtedly did not deign to know this.

I have already said how Prelati, who seduced him, took advantage of him. Gilles bore witness that, until the end, he would never withdraw his affection for him. Likewise, with regard to Briqueville, who odiously extorted power of attorney from him (p. 91), he kept a long-lasting loyalty.

The oddest thing is his relationship with La Trémoille, who mocked him and, without wanting to, deceived him! Who wanted to "encourage him to be bad."

But there are very few occasions in which an excessive indifference, a kind of absence followed by violent reactions, does not appear. A stranger to prudence, he seems to be at the mercy of impulses that reflection cannot control; look at the absurdity of the Saint-Étienne affair! In particular, his attitude at the trial is a result of this boyish brusqueness. First he insults the judges, then suddenly (though we are unable to know the reason for the change) he breaks out in tears; he confesses, exposing at length unspeakable infamies.

He has absolutely no skill in defending himself. He moves about violently from one impulse to another, which destroys him.

I insist: this is a child.

But this child had at his disposal a fortune that appeared inexhaustible to him and nearly absolute power.

Childishness, in principle, has limited possibilities, whereas by reason of this fortune and power, Gilles de Rais' childishness met with tragic possibilities.

In his crimes, in fact, Gilles is not fully the child that he is at his very core.

His foolishness attains, in blood, a tragic grandeur.

---

[7] Reciprocally, would not the ordinary man assume, in his conception of sovereignty, that it has an equivalence to crime?

## *Childishness and Archaism*

With Gilles de Rais, there is no longer a question of what we commonly designate as childishness. In effect, the question is of *monstrosity*. Essentially this monstrosity is childlike. But it involves the childishness to which the possibilities of adulthood belong and, rather than childlike, these possibilities are archaic. If Gilles de Rais is a child, it is in the manner of savages. He is a child as a cannibal is; or more precisely, as one of his Germanic ancestors, unbounded by civilized proprieties.

Joined to the god of sovereignty by initiatory rites, the young warriors willingly distinguished themselves in particular by a bestial ferocity; they knew neither rules nor limits. In their ecstatic rage, they were taken for wild animals, for furious bears, for wolves. The Harii of Tacitus augmented the fright provoked by their delirium by employing black shields and, wanting to surprise their enemies, to terrify them, rubbed their bodies with soot. This "funereal army," in order to augment the terror, chose "pitch-dark nights." Often the name of *Berserkir* ("warriors in bear skins") was given to them. Like the Centaurs of Greece, the Gandharva of India or the Luperci of Rome, they became animals in their delirium. The Chetti, whom Tacitus also describes, indulged in *scelera improbissima*: they struck, they executed and they skinned. They were slaughterers, and "neither iron nor steel could do anything against them." The fury of the *Berserkir* turned them into monsters. Ammien Marcellin, speaking of the Taifali, is indignant when describing their pederastic practices . . . They gave themselves up to drinking bouts that finally succeeded in taking away whatever humanity they still had.[8]

There was nothing in the Germans' religion that could offset this cruelty and these juvenile debaucheries. There was not, as with the Gauls or the Romans, a priesthood to oppose learning and moderation to drunkenness, ferocity, and violence.

During the first centuries of the Middle Ages, we should at least consider that something remained of these barbarous customs in the education of knights. In the first place, knighthood was apparently nothing but a continuation of the society of young German initiates. The Christian influence on the education of knights came later. It barely shows before the thirteenth century, the twelfth at a pinch, two or three centuries before Gilles de Rais . . .

It may be that nothing precise, nothing that we could speak about clearly, had survived of the distant traditions of which I have spoken. But we cannot imagine that nothing had subsisted. An atmosphere of violence and drinking bouts, the relish for terror, must have subsisted for a long time. As a rule,

---

[8] See Georges DUMÉZIL, *Les Dieux des Germains* (Paris, 1939), in 16mo, passim.

archaic traits continued to dominate the principles of knighthood and nobility, and these traits correspond precisely to aspects of the life of Gilles de Rais.

These traits played a much greater role in his life as he was naïve, and as he was no more familiar with the implementation of reason than with a rake's calculations. In fact, as for the formation of Gilles de Rais' character, the only elements that left traces are, on the one hand, warlike violence, dragging along with it, as in the time of the Germans, extreme courage and the rage of a wild animal; and, on the other hand, a habit of drinking that we have seen could be traditionally linked to the sexual excesses, homosexuality for instance. Apparently the boys of this time, who acquired vicious or cruel habits at an early age, saw themselves supported by tradition, even if those habits belonged only to limited groups. It seems to me, moreover, that certain of their more unspeakable proclivities could be developed and reinforced in common. Neither the distant past, to which the life of these boys gravitated, nor the necessity of brutal training practices could make them wiser. They had every chance to take almost unmerciful advantage of the young serfs, as well as the young female serfs of their parents: there is no reason to think that Christianity would have sensitively moderated their tendency to pay no more attention to the life of human beings than that of animals.

The principles of courtly love only slowly erected a barrier against the coarseness of a world of arms. As with Christianity, courtly love was relatively opposed to violence. The paradox of the Middle Ages was that it did not want men of war to speak the language of force and combat. Their parlance often became saccharine. But we ought not to deceive ourselves: the camaraderie of the old French was a cynical lie. Even the poetry for which nobles of the 14th and 15th centuries affected fondness was in all senses a deceit: the great lords chiefly loved war; their attitude differed little from that of the German *Berserkir*, who dreamed of terror and butchery. The famous poem by Bertrand de Born is, in other respects, a confession of their violent feelings. These feelings could go hand in hand with courtliness, but this poem permits us to see at what point their hunger for carnage and the horror of war continued burning. Gilles de Rais, more than anyone, must have had the sensibility of violence harkening back to the fury of the *Berserkir*. He also had the habit of drinking; he took strong drinks in order to whet his sexual excitement. For Gilles, as for the barbarians of the past, the goal was in breaking bounds; it was a question of living sovereignly.

The privilege of the German warrior was to feel himself above the laws, and from there to draw violent consequences. I do not say that all young nobles had the same frenzied outlook — even less traditionally were companions in arms inclined to homosexuality — but whether they became softened or not, the habits of these young men who brandished a sword or battle-axe were probably repugnant in part. I do not doubt that it very often accrued to one's honor to show oneself more hateful than one's counterpart. They could not help being hardened; they had one foot in the stirrup. Even though it had doubtless lost the character of ritual, homosexuality, without a doubt, must have facilitated things.

## *Sexual Life: War*

It appeared to me possible to situate the vices of Gilles de Rais in an ensemble of traditional cruelties and drinking bouts. Besides, we are informed, albeit imperfectly, on the actual development of his vices.

I have already spoken of the confessions Gilles de Rais himself made that "iniquitously . . . since the beginning of his youth," he had committed "high and enormous crimes." I have also cited what the trial said afterwards: that the origin of these crimes is attributed by the guilty party "to the bad management he had received in his childhood, when, unbridled, he applied himself to whatever pleased him, and pleased himself with every illicit act." From here it is difficult to become more explicit. From a vague tradition to begin with (we have to imagine the occasional stories: "this fellow's son did this, that one did something else"), violent habits, at least of precocious irregularity, could have thus perpetuated themselves. However, two distinct aspects are implicated in the confessions.

In the first place, during his childhood, inasmuch as it seems on account of the bad management of the grandfather, the grandson must have practiced the various illicit acts that were accessible to him slyly and unchecked. As we have seen, he was eleven years old in September 1415 upon the death of his father (which followed several months after the death of his mother). Still, the tutelage of the grandfather had a sense of total freedom for the child. But it was then a question of reprehensible acts — of unquestionably sexual, perhaps sadistic, perversions — but not of crimes.

The crimes, properly speaking the "high and enormous crimes," date from the "beginning of his youth."

On this point we cannot be more specific.

On the date of the first child murders, the trial gives two contradictory indications.

According to the bill of indictment, it all began around 1426, fourteen years before the trial: invocations of demons and murders of children. But according to the guilty party's confessions, which coincide with the first testimonies of the victims' parents, the first murders dated only from the year of the grandfather's death, that is from 1432.

The year 1426 would correspond to the beginning of his youth: twenty-two years old. This is the date, moreover, when the campaign into the Maine region begins. Gilles has asked, as of 1424, to take control of the administration of all his goods. In 1426, taking the field, he revels in an increased freedom in addition to his complete personal power.

One conjecture would resolve the difficulty; the "high and enormous crimes" of the beginning of his youth would be separate from the series of child murders that, as of 1432, must have had a certain continuity and given way to a sort of "fixation": the same procedure, same ceremony, finally, more and more, the same participants. As early as the "beginning of his youth" there would have only been, regarding the words *crime* and *enormity*, the conjury of demons and maybe those cruel brutalities that could then be associated with war.

It is doubtful in my opinion that this reveler who took so much pleasure in spilling blood would not, from the first campaign, have profited from war.

We ought not to lose sight of precisely what we know of Gilles de Rais, or what we know of the wars of this period.

We ought never to forget that in this period of incessant wars, the scenes of slaughter in towns and burning villages had a sort of banality to them. Pillage was then the inevitable means of feeding a voracious soldiery. In every sense, it is certain that war stimulated greed . . .

I cannot evoke *these fundamental aspects of human life* any better than by recalling how the King of Spain, Philippe II, vomited from his horse during the pillage of Saint-Quentin. But far from vomiting, Gilles evidently found some pleasure in watching the wretches be disemboweled. Faced with the spectacles of war, this pederast must have had occasions to bind his sexual excitement to these butcheries.

As for these butcheries, and the banality of these butcheries, we can refer to the text of the Archbishop of Reims, Juvénal des Ursins (in his *Epistles* of 1439 and 1440). The prelate contends that not only were such offenses an act of the enemy, but of "no one allied to the King"; locating their indispensable provisions in a village, the soldiers "seized men, women, and children, without distinguishing between age or sex, raping the women and girls; they killed husbands and fathers in the presence of their wives and daughters; they took wet nurses, leaving their babies who died for lack of nourishment; they seized and shackled pregnant women who, in their chains, gave birth to their offspring, which were left to die unbaptized, and they were then going to throw mother and child into the river; they took priests, monks, men of the Church, laborers, shackled them in various manners and thus tormented, beat them, by which certain of them died mutilated, others enraged or out of their senses . . . They . . . imprisoned them . . . , they put them in irons . . . , in pits, in disgusting places full of vermin, they left them . . . to die of hunger. Many died of it. And God knows the tyrannies that they did! They roasted one another; they pulled each other's teeth out, others were beaten with big sticks; they were never set free before having given more money than they possessed . . ."[9] In 1439, one of Gilles de Rais' captains just missed being hanged for acts of this very nature. But after 1427 Gilles himself probably had very few occasions in which to participate in these sadistic scenes; after the first campaign, he could have only fought two times: first, beside Joan of Arc, who was violently opposed to lawlessness; and second, in 1432 at Lagny, where it is probable that things did not drag on.

In any case, nothing proves that Gilles took part in actual butcheries. We only know that, at Lude, he insisted on hanging French prisoners who had fought with the English and who could have passed for having betrayed their country. It is likely that other captains, more anxious for money, would have preferred a ransom. In his own way Gilles also appreciated money, but he refused to appear to prize it.

Whatever the case, it is difficult to believe that, while he was making war in 1427, the "high and enormous crimes" of the "beginning of his youth" were far removed from the bedlam that the passing men-at-arms brought on. We will see that the sight of human blood and bodies cut open fascinated him. Later he must have only been interested in privileged victims, in children. His curiosity and excitement, however, could have been exhibited earlier on coarser occasions. He would have not spoken of crime, if crime itself had not cruelly intervened; if at that time he had done his killing with a taste for cruelty. It is not certain, but it is believable, and after everything has been said on the subject, it is probable. Doubtless he could have been speaking of crime when referring to invocations of the demon; without a doubt, these began during this period. But the murders which followed from 1432 on, did they have no antecedent? The abuse of children, it seems to me, had a greater chance of degenerating into murder if Rais at some point had had the opportunity to begin amusing himself with blood.

In speaking of this period (he is speaking of this period, apparently, if he is speaking of his youth), he says that he, "for his pleasure and according to his will, had done whatever evil he could"; he also says that at that time he had put "his hope and intention into the illicit and dishonest acts and things that he did." The opportunity to take pleasure in butchery was too good to pass up. What later became relatively dangerous was absolutely not inconvenient in the field.

## Sexual Life: The Child Murders

A description of the monster's sexual deviations does not, by itself, consti-

---

[9] G. DU FRESNE DE BEAUCOURT, *Histoire de Charles VII*, Vol. 3 (Paris, 1885), pp. 389-390.

tute the hallucinatory aspect of Gilles de Rais' life; it is, at the same time, the best known aspect. We are familiar with it not only by Lord de Rais' confessions, but by his valets' depositions. From various sides, the trial accumulates an abundance of suffocating details. Twice rather than once, what we come to know only rarely — the tastes, the fantasies, the caprices, the preferences of the monster — were noted with a meticulousness which defies decency.

From 1432 on, each of Rais' residences had a room worthy of the cruel imaginings of Sade, where pleasure was fused to the jerks of dying bodies. There was such a room reserved for horror in the enormous fortress at Champtocé. Maybe his grandfather had just died there? Maybe he finished dying a little later on? The practice of murdering began the year that this grandfather died. Right from the start, surrounded by his companions, Gilles abandoned himself to sensual pleasure. Things were arranged so that if he wanted to do the killing, he could do so himself. Or if he preferred, he prevailed upon Guillaume de Sillé or Roger de Briqueville, his accomplices and cousins, who came from noble families ruined by the war. Often Gilles did the killing himself, in the presence of Sillé and Briqueville; but if it was needed, one of these brigands would lend a hand. All of them lived at the master's expense; the master paid, but first they procured for him that which he desired.

To begin with, the company gave themselves up to excess; they gorged themselves on fine food and strong drink — but it seems the fanatics never abandoned Gilles to the solitude of blood.

After 1432, Champtocé probably had stopped being used; the house of La Suze at Nantes, the castles at Tiffauges and at Machecoul very quickly took over. Later the participants of these feasts were also completely changed; others entered into the secrets. At first there apparently were singers from the chapel: André Buchet from Vannes and Jean Rossignol of La Rochelle, both of whom apparently had the voices of homosexual angels, and both of whom Gilles made into canons of Saint-Hilaire-de-Poitiers. There was Hicquet de Brémont and Robin Romulart (or "Petit Robin"), who apparently died at the end of 1439. Finally, two valets going by the names of Poitou and Henriet made it into these bloody barracks. Other, younger singers, spared by the master, were used on the days when new victims could not be found; persuaded to keep quiet, they were probably introduced into the secrets . . . These libidinous abodes at Machecoul and Tiffauges were terrifying . . . Filled with people, they were terrifying. Even if we forget the frivolity of sorcerers who sought the Devil and priests who sang the Office, they were terrifying . . . These fortresses had the feeling of diabolical traps. They closed around those children imprudently waiting for alms at their portal. The greatest number of the juvenile victims were taken by this trickery. In this monstrous lawlessness was a suffocating preparation for the worst. Occasionally Gilles himself chose, sometimes he requested Sillés or others to choose. Once the child was brought into Gilles' room, things abruptly began. Taking his "virile member" in hand, Gilles "rubbed" it, "erected" it, or "stretched" it on the belly of his victim, introducing it between his thighs. He rubbed himself "on the bellies of the . . . children . . . , he took great delight, and got so excited that the sperm, criminally and in a way it ought not, spurted onto the bellies of the said children." With each child Gilles only came once or twice, whereupon "he killed them or had them killed."

But it was rare for the orgy to begin without the child first being abused. To begin with, there was a sort of strangling: the poor wretches were put on an abominable apparatus. Gilles wanted to "prevent their cries" and avoid their being heard. "Sometimes he suspended them by his own hand, sometimes he had others suspend them by the throat with cords and rope, in his room, on a peg or small hook." Thus, with their necks extended, they were reduced to death rattles.

At this moment, a comedy could intervene. Gilles, halting the suspension, had the child let down; then he caressed and cajoled him, assuring him that he had not wanted to "harm" him or "hurt him," but that, on the contrary, he only wanted "to have fun" with him. If he had at last silenced him, he could then have his way with him, but the appeasement did not last.

Having drawn violent pleasure from the victim, he killed him or had him killed. But often Gilles' enjoyment combined with the child's death. He might cut — or cause to be cut — a vein in the neck; when the blood spurted, Gilles would come. Occasionally, at the decisive moment, he wanted the victim to be in the languor of death. Or further, he had him decapitated; from then on the orgy lasted "as long as the bodies were warm." Occasionally, after decapitation, he sat on the belly of the victim and delighted in watching him die like this; he sat at an angle, the better to see his last tremblings.

He occasionally varied the method of killing. Here is what he himself said on the subject: — Sometimes he inflicted, sometimes the accomplices inflicted "various types and manners of torment; sometimes they severed the head from the body with dirks, daggers, and knives, sometimes they struck them violently on the head with a cudgel or other blunt instruments." He specifies that the punishment of suspension was added to these torments. When interrogated, the valet Poitou enumerates the manner of killing as follows: "Sometimes beheading or decapitating them, sometimes cutting their throats, sometimes dismembering them, and sometimes breaking their necks with a cudgel." He said also that there was a "sword dedicated to their execution, commonly called a *braquemard*" (p. 226).

But we are not at the end of this voyage to the limits of the worst.

Here is what we know from Henriet the valet. Gilles boasted in his presence of taking "greater pleasure in murdering the . . . children, in seeing their heads and members separated, in seeing them languish and seeing their blood, than he did in knowing them carnally" (p. 237). Thus he expressed, before the Marquis de Sade, the principle of libertines inured in vice.

What we know of the search for the "most beautiful heads" leads us to the aberration. We learn of it from the monster himself: when at last the children were lying dead, he embraced them, "and he gave way to contemplating those who had the most beautiful heads and members, and he had their bodies cruelly opened up and delighted at the sight of their internal organs" (p. 196). Henriet, who, of the two valets, reports it with the minutest of details, is for his own part not ignorant of this delirious aspect.

According to him, Gilles "delighted" in looking at the severed heads, and he showed them to him, the witness, and to Étienne Corrillaut . . . , "asking them which of the said heads was the most beautiful of those he was showing them, the head severed at that very moment, or that from the day before, or another from the day before that, and he often kissed the head that pleased him most, and delighted in doing so" (p. 237). In Gilles' eyes, mankind was no more than an element of voluptuous turmoil; this element was entirely at his sovereign disposal, having no other meaning than a possibility for more violent pleasure, and he did not stop losing himself in that violence.

No sexual confession is more pathetic, as it exceeds all bounds in the will to horrify.

The following words do away with the possibility of not trembling:

— "And very often," he said, "when the said children were dying, he sat on their bellies and delighted in watching them die thus, and with the said Corrillaut and Henriet *he laughed at them* . . ." (p. 196).

Finally, Lord de Rais — who in order to excite his senses as much as possible had gotten drunk — went out like a light. The servants cleaned the room, washing up the blood, and while the master slept, burned the cadaver in the fireplace. Long logs and a quantity of faggots allowed them to rapidly reduce it to ashes. They took pains to burn the clothes one by one, wanting, as they said, to avoid the stench.

The whole order of the feast had taken place according to plan: it did not correspond to the impulses of passion. Designed to serve the sensual pleasure of one sole man, it passed without anguish: these children of seven to twenty died with no more fuss than a kid goat.

If there was tragedy, it was not unceasing. Rather, what is the more remarkable in these horrors is the indifference of the participants.

They could not have conceived of the feeling that this unbending severity assumes for us: terror and indignation beyond bounds . . . In his day, Gilles de Rais was a very important man, and the little beggars whose throats he cut were worth no more than the horses.

It is difficult for us to evaluate the distance that then separated the man (magnified by birth and fortune) who did the crushing from the insect crushed between two stones.

More than a century later in Hungary, an eminent lady was killing her servants with no more difficulty than Gilles had killing children. This great lady, Erszebeth Bathory, was related to royalty, and she was not pursued until after having yielded to a desire to kill daughters of the lesser nobility. Gilles de Rais himself was not distressed until after a long pause, and that was not until after absurd blunders; probably public rumor finally grew to such a point that one could not easily close one's eyes. Without friends, without support, Gilles was unable to shake off the hostility and the general weariness. But with skill and moderation, his crimes would not have been profoundly shocking; without any other reason, one's first impulse might have been to close one's eyes.

## *The High Rank of Gilles de Rais*

In this blood-filled drama, we cannot forget what determines Rais' prominence more than anything else: he is not just any man in this world, but a noble; this man of war, this ogre who violated and killed little children, is primarily a privileged man. His fortune moreover is not his only privilege. His existence in itself is privileged; his existence itself, in itself, is fascinating. It radiates, it is glorious by itself; because of his birth, it is glorious as luxury and war are glorious.

Rais' prominence, of itself, is a force that seduces and dominates. It goes without saying that there is nothing seductive about cutting children's throats. But Rais' *nobility* is not noble in an adulterated sense. Rais is noble in the sense of the German warriors. His nobility has the ardor of a violence respecting nothing, and in the presence of which there is nothing that does not give way; like that of the *Berserkir*, such a violence places him whom it inspires outside this world. The nobility of Gilles de Rais is the distinguishing mark of the monster.

Occasionally his inherent nobility no longer distinguished itself from his terrifying aspect; it ends up possessing itself of the allure of night and the fear that night gives. One need only recall the German Harii and the soot with which they covered themselves, the better to belong to the terror of the night. Violence involves an ambiguity between seduction and terror. The noble warrior, the great lord, he who fascinates, is terrifying.

41

At the same time, Gilles de Rais trembled before the Devil. But the Devil fascinated him; indeed, he solicited an alliance with that which terrified him. Fundamentally, the supernatural world, that of the Devil or God, was — like him — of noble essence, of sovereign essence if one likes. The existence of God or the Devil had but one aim, what a noble held as an aim for the entire world of the nobility: a diurnal or nocturnal enchantment, similar to those very beautiful paintings that dazzle and fascinate the viewer. These tableaux can include bloody battles, they include martyrs (sexual themes having necessarily been transposed . . . ). But terror is always intimately joined to enticement.

On this level, Lord de Rais at least has this merit. He represents in a pure state the impulse that tends to subordinate the activity of men to enchantment, to the game of the privileged class. Men, on the whole, produce; they produce every kind of good. But in 15th-century society, these goods were destined for the privileged class, for those who among themselves can devour each other, but to whom the masses are subordinate. For the mass of men it is necessary to work so the privileged class can play, even if they also sometimes play at devouring themselves to their ruin. The goods that represent work to the masses mean nothing but a sense of game for the privileged class. The work that entered into the product cannot be noticed by them, because the noble, the privileged man, does not work and never ought to.

One often forgets, but the very principle of the nobility, what it is in essence, is the refusal to suffer degradation or disgrace — which would be the inevitable effect of work!

For an earlier society work was shameful in a fundamental way. It is the task of the slave or serf, one who, at the same time in his own mind, has lost his dignity; the free man could not work without falling from grace.

This is related to the fact that work could not be interesting in itself; it is a subordinate activity, a servile activity, which serves something other than itself. He who wants to escape the servile life cannot as a rule work. He must play. He must amuse himself freely, like a child; free from his duties, the child amuses himself. But the adult cannot amuse himself like the child if he is not privileged. Those who have no privilege are reduced to working. By contrast, the privileged man must make war. Just as the unprivileged man is reduced to working, the privileged man must make war.

War itself has the privilege of being a game. It is not, like others, a reasonable activity; it has no other meaning than the anticipated result. War indeed can be seen from the angle of utility: a city or a country can be attacked and must be defended. But without the turbulence of countries or cities which assail their neighbors without necessity, men could avoid war. War is, from the start, the effect of a turbulence, even if it is true that it is occasionally the inevitable result of the impoverishment of a region whose inhabitants must seek the means to survive elsewhere.

Most often, those who take the initiative of war were led to it by an exuberant, explosive impulse. That is why war for so long was able to have the feeling of a game; a terrifying game, but a game.

In Gilles de Rais' time, war is always the game of lords. If this game devastates populations, it exalts the privileged class. It has for the privileged class the *ultimate* meaning that *work* could never have for the poor folk. The interest of work is subordinated to its result; the interest of war is nothing but war. It is war itself which fascinates and which terrifies. Those who are like Gilles de Rais, who live in the expectation of these terrible battles leaving death, cries of horror, and suffering behind them, know nothing else that gives them this violent excitement. Present generations no longer know practically anything about the exaltation, even though death was the basis of it, that formerly was the least ridiculous meaning and aim of war, a fact that is likely to abandon us to a feeling of our powerlessness in the world. Are we not blinded at the very moment when the mad truth of another time is hidden from us?

Faced with as vain a question, what can we do, if not hide?

But we must continue the paradoxical quest, as given in the questions that his life and the world of his time posed for Gilles de Rais . . .

## The Tragedy of the Nobility

The fact that Gilles de Rais lived in a world of war linked to privilege does not prevent us from seeing that the world was changing at this time. In Gilles' eyes, war was truly a game. But this manner of seeing is less and less truthful, to the extent that it ceased to be even that of the majority of the privileged class. More and more, war is then a general misfortune; it is, at the same time, the *work* of many people. The general situation deteriorates and becomes more complex; misfortune reaches even the privileged class, who are less and less eager for war, and for play, who finally see that the moment has come to give way to the problems of reason. At this time, the technical and financial means of war involve such machinery that personal impetuosity and exaltation are limited. The heavy cavalry, essentially those arms that made war a luxurious game, succeeded during Gilles de Rais' lifetime in losing a great part of its importance to the advantage of infantry and archers, arrows and pikes. Likewise, armed bands and pillagers take the upper hand over prestigious combats of costumed horses and knights; the need follows to substitute regular and hierarchical armies for companies of old hands without discipline. Only hierarchy and discipline could maintain part of the place that the privileged class had in war.

Indeed, something subsists of the game that war is in its essence. In a strict sense, something subsists of it in our day. But discipline, strict orders, and scientific command stamp war with an essentially rational character, which has caused us to forget — in the fundamental debate between game and reason — that it has been very recently, and as a secondary consequence, that war moved to distinguish itself from individual impetuosity and violence, which had been the truth and heart of war, to the advantage of cold reason.

Things evolve slowly: one does not arrive right away at this enormous build-up of modern arms that has ultimately suffocated the violent spirit of play that transfigured war. But in the years following the death of Joan of Arc, Gilles de Rais, remaining Marshal of France, had ceased to be at home in the armies of his day, which were condemned to become regular. Since Constable Richemont had prevailed over La Trémoille in 1434, there was an embryo of the royal administration which resulted in the Estates General of Orléans in 1439.

Gilles de Rais still held the title of Marshal of France in 1434. But after La Trémoille's disgrace, he was no longer anything. He had been a "gallant knight of arms"; he knew how to mount an assault, to line up magnificent horses and superb knights. He knew how to drink, and evidently he enjoyed the worst confusion. Above all, he loved to fight, and beside Joan of Arc, he covered himself in glory at Tourelles, at Patay, and, even after the heroine's death in 1432, at Lagny.

The administration, being organized after the time when no rake was assuring him the favor of the King, saw to it that his military valor suddenly no longer held meaning. He was nothing on his own but a bungler; from this moment all that he was, his state of mind and his reactions, no longer suited the spirit of new necessities.

From 1432 on, from the day he abandons himself to the obsession of cutting children's throats, Gilles de Rais is nothing but a failure. Everything gets mixed up. In August 1432 at Lagny, he figures again as the glorious captain. His grandfather dies in November. The disappearance of this brutal force must free him, relieve him, and unhinge him at the same time. He is bound to badly handle a too complete, too sudden freedom, and a wealth that has become staggering. That following summer, La Trémoille falls. It must not be imagined that Rais took his disgrace lightly. I have spoken of his foolishness . . . But what I said of the game he played helps us see how he lived it, and how this game was confused with his life. The deprivation must have affected him all the more as he had just yielded to frightful habits . . .

I have spoken of his childishness. It is, in fact, in a childish manner — consequently the most entirely, the most madly — that he incarnates this spirit of feudal society that with all its vivacity originated with the game that the *Berserkir* had played; he was riveted to war by an affinity that marked a taste for cruel pleasures. He had no place in the world, if not that which war gave him. A society steeped in feudal war alone could provide what it expected of this privileged man, who could do nothing other than drink to the dregs of privilege. Not only his vanity was affected, but his passion was hurt by the disfavor that caught up with him. This worn-out feudal world put him on the shelf. Under the appearance of wealth, what he had as yet to live was, in advance, blighted. However, one thing opposed him to these miserable lords, all ready to possess what remained: this privileged man could never, in the face of death, accept a life that would no longer fascinate him.

In the tragedy of Gilles de Rais, there was at first a suffocation. There could be no question of admiring the wretch, or pitying him. But the tragedy took place upon the disappearance of the acquired conditions on which the life of the privileged class rested. What the feudal world had lived on disappeared. At the same moment, his castles began to smell of death. At Champtocé and Machecoul, bodies were drying up or putrefying at the bottom of certain towers (pp. 101 and 102). These castles were enormous masses of stone, inside of which the nooks could have been or very nearly were inaccessible, as deeply buried as burial vaults. These fortresses were the outward signs — or the sanctuaries — of ancient feudal wars, of which these lords were still gods. These wars insisted on drunkenness, they insisted on the vertigo and giddiness of those whom birth had consecrated to them. They insisted on rushing them into assaults, but occasionally suffocated them in dark obsessions. The game that these castles externalized was expected to be played to the hilt; possessing them, whoever resided in them could not have easily escaped. He could only do so if he rejected the spirit that these high, thick walls embodied. Whoever was effectively occupied with his interests — like Craon, managing his fortune with a bourgeois' calculation and greed — was able to stop playing this game if he wanted. But he who is dominated by his interests is compromised: he works in some way, he is enslaved. In contrast, it was Gilles de Rais' passion — far from giving in to the event — to be stubborn, to be obstinate to the point of ruin.

The decline of Gilles de Rais has the look of funereal magnificence.

His obsession with death is tangible: a man, little by little, locks himself up in the solitude of crime, of homosexuality and the tomb; in this profound silence, the faces that obsess him are those of dead children, whom he profanes with an abominable kiss.

Before the backdrop of fortresses — and tombstones — Gilles de Rais' decline takes on the appearance of a theatrical hallucination.

We cannot judge the monster's states of mind.

But it is from the bloody room where the children's heads stare at him that it evidently occurs to him early in the morning to wander through the village streets of Machecoul and Tiffauges.

Could a long, intolerable hallucination possess a profounder truth?

Gilles de Rais' character is bound to this tragic apparition. This apparition is linked to the decisive disgrace that comes from La Trémoille's fall.

It is linked to that disgrace in a way that exposes Rais' personal tragedy at the same time as it exposes the tragedy of a world to which a bloody figure is suited, who from the *Berserkir* to Proust's M. de Charlus in every respect betrays a cruel foolishness. The feudal world, in fact, cannot be separated from excess, which is the principle of war. But at the instant that royal politics or intelligence alters it, it is no longer the feudal world. Intelligence or calculation are not noble. It is not noble to calculate or to reflect, and no philosopher could have been able to embody what is essentially the nobility. These truths said in regard to Gilles de Rais have precisely the advantage of seizing on the impure source of his life. Tragedy is necessarily impure; it is all the more real as it is impure.

To what is this principle joined, which is no less sound for being misrecognized? That without the nobility, without the refusal to calculate and reflect (which is its essence), there would have been no tragedy; there would have been only reflection and calculation.

I will go so far as to say that the *tragedy of Gilles de Rais* — considered as tragedy through ponderous reflection, through reflection taking into account a world that refused reflection (which even, by such a refusal, became the point of departure for it) — is the tragedy of feudal society, the tragedy of the nobility.

But what does that affirmation mean?

That without the profound foolishness in Gilles de Rais that ordered — commanded — the brutal refusal, there would have been no tragedy.

We are not digressing from Gilles de Rais. These reflections would be meaningless if they could be separated from the character and all the blood clinging to him. But if it is true that only feudal society, which he embodies, renders him tragic, then feudal society, in this tragic game unquestionably and *naïvely* the force to bind the violence of life, does not differ from this *sovereignty* that is the principle not only of Greek tragedy but of Tragedy personified. *Tragedy is the powerlessness of Reason.*

That does not mean that the laws of Tragedy are contrary to Reason. A law cannot truly belong to what is contrary to Reason. Could a *law* be opposed to Reason? But human violence, which has the strength to fall afoul of Reason, is tragic and, if possible, ought to be suppressed; at least it cannot be ignored nor disregarded. I should say this in speaking of Gilles de Rais, who differs from all those whose crime is personal. The crimes of Gilles de Rais are those of the world in which he committed them. The convulsive tremblings of this world are what these slit throats expose. This world had sanctioned the cruel differences that left these throats defenseless. It had left free — or very nearly so — these tragic games: the games of an energumen, at the limit of his sovereign power! It is true that already afoot in this world was a deeper movement that would reduce these differences, that would slowly reduce them . . . This slow movement, in its turn, would at one time have the tragic abruptness, therefore, of an opposed violence . . .

## The Theatrical Ruin of Orléans

I have shown how this tragedy was that of the nobility, of this tragic, occasionally tragicomic if one likes, humanity that is the nobility. As for Gilles de Rais, the tragedy was prolonged during the years that followed his disgrace, from 1433 to 1440. Once having stopped making war, his life assumed the lamentable course laid out by his crimes and a series of feeble efforts.

Independently of his will, the last appearance of the Marshal on a field of battle felt like a vain parade (p. 87). On this day, under the direction of Constable Richemont, the French king's army measured itself against the English. But neither the French nor the English engaged in action. Having made their show of strength, the adversaries retired without fighting. It happened, nonetheless, that on the occasion of this day Gilles made himself noticed because of the splendor of his arms bearers! It is possible that it was decided by chance, but the men whom he had led into bloody combat must have only been of service to him henceforth in parades (with the exception of local affairs). From the beginning he loved to put his men-at-arms in formation, as others in our day love to put horses in formation. This resulted in excessive expenditures. This is why it occurred to him to sell some of his land in order to meet payments. At the time of Joan of Arc, these expenditures were justified. If they were large, they were still in proportion to an immense fortune. On the death of his grandfather, this fortune grew. But a short time afterwards, Gilles' credit tumbled. With La Trémoille in disgrace, his title of marshal no longer had meaning. Then the opposite of what would have logically been expected occurred. Far from getting better, the situation of his fortune becomes precarious. His expenditures, formerly of necessity, are expenditures of ostentation! But apparently the Marshal's decorous retinue is more burdensome than that of a captain engaged in war — as if he must compensate for lost prestige with a false front.

There are numerous records of Rais' mad expenditures. However, they are not precisely itemized; we are unable to explain what seems to have finally ruined him, or to what extent he was ruined. We see what happened, but we do not see the exact degree or cause of it.

We can only affirm that the expenditures multiplied; ruin was one of the nagging aspects of the tragedy of which I speak. Gilles de Rais' expenditures do not depend on any extravagance; they are the result of the *excessive* game that is the principle of primitive humanity. In comparison with war itself this game is in principle secondary, but it had a profound reality for a man whose every reaction is archaic. This violent man, to whom the game of war was lost, needed a compensation. He seems to have found it in the game of ostentatious expenditure. But would this game have a sufficient attraction if it did not threaten to drag the player into ruin?

When he wasn't anyone anymore, Gilles de Rais saw only one possibility of playing, of still playing. What could this feudal lord do in this world?

A feudal lord's privilege has only one meaning: freeing him from work, it consecrates him to the game. But war is the only game that gives full value to the privileged man. Could "ostentatious expenditure" justify an ardor comparable to the transports of war? The game of wild expenditures no longer mattered to Rais' peers. It appeared comical to them. It belonged to a world on its way to extinction. In this game cities openly confronted one another constructing tall cathedrals. But the 15th century was already engulfed in a profound transformation wherein reality was to prevail over appearances.

A Gilles de Rais could remain steeped in the reactions of the primitive world only through isolation, which 12th-century nobility understood thoroughly. On the occasion of a "court" held in Limousin, a knight in the 12th century had pieces of silver sown in a plowed field; another, in response to this challenge, had his meals cooked with church candles; another, "in boastfulness," ordered that all his horses be burned alive. We know today what this *boastfulness* means, corresponding so clearly to Lord de Rais' unintelligible expenditures.

In societies different from our own — we ourselves accumulate wealth with a view to continual growth — the principle has prevailed instead to squander or lose wealth, to give it away or destroy it. Accumulated wealth has the same meaning as *work*; on the other hand, wealth wasted or destroyed in tribal *potlaches* has the meaning of a *game*. Accumulated wealth has only a subordinate value; in the eyes of whoever squanders or destroys it, wealth squandered or destroyed has a *sovereign* value, for it serves nothing else if not this squandering itself, or this fascinating destruction. Its *present* meaning is in its squandering, or the gift that one makes of it. Its utmost reason for being is on account of that which can suddenly no longer be put off until later, being *of that instant*. But it is consumed *in that instant*. It can be with magnificence; those who know how to appreciate consumption are dazzled, but nothing remains.

Such is the meaning of the pieces sown and lost, the church candles for meals, and the horses roaring in the flames.

Such also is the meaning of the mad expenditures which Rais intensified when he ought to have renounced war.

In the spring of 1434, after the Sillé affair, he still has not definitively renounced war. He keeps in contact with La Trémoille. Having been duly charged to no longer appear at court, the ex-favorite attempts to marginally recover a dwindling activity; he profits by the fact that his friend, the Duke of Bourbon, is still at war with the Duke of Burgundy. He would like to come to the aid of Bourbon, whose city, Grancey, situated in Burgundy, is under siege by the Burgundians. Doubtless he figures that Charles VII will be pleased with this action. He therefore proposes to Rais to levy troops and come to the aid of Grancey. Rais seems at first to have accepted enthusiastically.

We are unable to understand exactly what followed, but nothing was arranged. As for the affair in question, it is possible that others threw sticks into the gears . . .

Indeed, Gilles obtained Charles VII's official order to free Grancey, but the very day when this city surrendered to the Burgundians we know that he was at Poitiers . . . He asked his brother René in advance to take charge of the troops he had effectively levied in Brittany.

However, the unemployed Marshal still has not abandoned the party.

He goes to Orléans: he has the intention of living there sumptuously, according to his demeanor, but La Trémoille goads him on from there. Gilles then agrees to follow him into Bourbon. Presently this is a question of aiding the Duke of Bourbon, but quite in vain.

The two men together are stubborn. They attempt, at the beginning of the following year, to attack Jean de Luxembourg. After the peace of Nevers, concluded between the Duke of Burgundy and the King (February 1435), Luxembourg remained at war with the French.

But La Trémoille and Rais have little money. What is more, they come to terms badly on this subject, inasmuch as Rais clearly wants to lead a royal life, a life of dazzling splendor.

He hesitates. He is not resigned to the chaos and disarray in which he founders, but Gilles senses that La Trémoille has overexcited him. He is offered insignificant affairs, without credits, without royal money. He clearly lets himself go. From then on he carries all the effeminate luxury of a Roman cardinal.

Surrounded by young singers, he has himself named canon of Saint-Hilaire of Poitiers. (Until then, only the dukes of Aquitaine had borne this title.) On this occasion he must have appeared in a sumptuous costume: half-Church, half-helmeted warrior. He then travels with his ecclesiastical retinue, a "collegiate church," whose seat as a rule was a chapel of the Saints-Innocents situated within the walls of Machecoul. This chapel had its canons and even a so-called bishop; it had singers, a music school analogous to those of cathedrals; every one of them was liturgically and sumptuously dressed: more than fifty people, and as many horses. Added to the ecclesiastical retinue was the military: two hundred horsemen, which a herald of arms and trumpeters preceded. We have said nothing of sorcerers, alchemists, armorers, an illuminator, and those who had the responsibility of carrying an organ on these travels . . . This man, walled up in a criminal solitude, could not dispense with a crowd that recalled a king's entourage. We know what comprises this crowd from the notarial records of Orléans, where he stayed more than a year. The same crowd, a little later, must have accompanied him to Poitiers. At Poitiers, this delirium had a scandalous aspect which ought to be underlined. Two young singers who had charmed him also accompanied him; later he will make them into criminals. One is André Buchet of Vannes, who was to lead victims to him at least twice. The other, Jean Rossignol of La Rochelle, to whom he made a grant of land at Machecoul, took part in the transfer of children's skeletons from Champtocé (see p. 103). On this day, in the church of Saint-Hilaire, he institutes two stipends in favor of these darlings. Apparently he was searching for veiled exhibitionism, which would assume the feeling of crime for him; he must have feverishly loved these voices of angels, these voices of corrupted ephebi, whom he joined in his orgies.

The journey to Poitiers at the end of the year, and the long stay at Orléans the year after, thus allow us to imagine the hellish retinue that Marshal de Rais led as of the day when he was no longer Marshal except in name only (the title was then revocable, but it was not withdrawn from him). Orléans, it seems, cost 80,000 gold crowns; an important part not of his revenues, but of his fortune. (In 1437 he only received 100,000 crowns for Ingrandes and Champtocé, his two most important properties, which Jean V of Brittany had prized above all.) On his return, his finances were so bad that he had to lie low for a while in his domains in Brittany.

He then establishes himself in the region of Rais, in the fortress of Machecoul.

He had not sown pieces of silver, he had not locked his horses in a furnace, but the expenditures to which he had just devoted himself had given the same feeling of an ostentatious game, "boastfulness" and unreasonableness, as the extravagances of the Limousin . . .

It is then that Guillaume de La Jumellière abandons him, this Angevin lord to whom Jean de Craon had entrusted him.

On all these campaigns La Jumellière had assisted him with his counsels. He was still accompanying Gilles when, at the end of 1434, he arrived at Orléans followed by his military assembly.

The blazing, unrestrained expenditure at Orléans signified, at the same time as a definitive renunciation of war, what was in no way another escape, but the recourse to the impossible; far from being a modest throwback of the Limousin extravagances, those at Orléans recall tragedy. Orléans, which in 1429 had foreshadowed Rais' glory, six years later consecrates his disgrace.

In effect, the stay — after which Rais clearly recognized that the glorious past he had previously lived in this city was dead — signifies that he remains connected to this place.

In the course of this ostentatious existence, he wants once again to be the young Marshal of France that he became beside Joan of Arc, throwing himself with an irresistible fury upon the English, delivering to his country an unexpected victory. This event had a different meaning to him than it did to everyone else. For Gilles de Rais, Joan of Arc was evidently unintelligible. How would he be interested in the destiny of a people? What was said about this was troublesome: he was only interested in himself. In a pinch he managed, in his childishness, to partake in the great emotions that he was incapable of understanding . . . But like every year, on May 8, 1435, Orléans celebrated its liberation; for Gilles this involves garnering for himself a part of the delirious popularity that Joan of Arc possessed from the first day at Orléans. The unfortunate Joan was now four years dead; she had died in the flames, survived by Rais himself, who by her side had had one of the great roles of the day, the greatest after her own perhaps. It was his second chance to relive that day in the enthusiasm of the crowd; but this time he was alone, and the liberation of Orléans, the battle of the Tourelles, became his personal triumph.

This commemoration of the liberation apparently lasted several days. On this occasion, Gilles let the gold flow. He was spending as one drinks liquor, to become giddy; the principle of the feast was, as it still is, the interminable procession that followed the first year the English departed, but the procession was set off with "mystery plays" presented along the way. In these mysteries, one represented episodes of the battle of 1429. We know that, this year, a performance took place at the moment when the procession reached the boulevard of the bridge: it had to do with taking the Tourelles, the fortress that commanded the bridge over the Loire. The City participated in the costs, but — as the municipal reports that we possess show — only assumed a portion of them. Rais had the mysteries performed quite often; he is said to have worked his ruin in this way. He multiplied the purchases of new and magnificent costumes, not wanting them to be used twice; it was possible for him to have the spectators served with wine, hippocras, and delicacies. We know moreover that four years later in 1439, in another performance of this same assault on the Tourelles, a standard and a banner came from him. We cannot doubt that, in this same year when he spent 80,000 crowns, an important part of this fortune went toward the considerable costs of these feasts.

But when he returned to Brittany, his coffers were empty.

His coffers were empty, and his indignant relatives had just obtained royal letters of prohibition against him. At Angers, Tours, Orléans, Champtocé, Pouzauges, and Tiffauges, this prohibition was blaringly announced. He could not have managed this delirium without selling a part of his property, but from then on nobody, in the realm at least, could enter into a contract with him.

It is probable that Gilles de Rais was then not as completely ruined as it might seem. But in addition to his moral disgrace, this prohibition made another disgrace apparent to everyone: his financial disgrace — which must have also depressed him.

A striking character trait ultimately emerges from these great expenditures at Orléans: that which must have sovereignly counted double for Gilles de Rais was to make of his life, and of himself, a spectacular blaze! With this purpose he had a sense of theater. In 1435 he was all washed up. But at Orléans he rediscovered in a theatrical form the grandeur that he had lost. And for that he knew how to ruin himself!

In 1435, at Orléans, he had known how to theatrically magnify the warlike fury that had beaten the English.

In 1440 he will unite an immense crowd into a different glory, a paradoxical and sinister one: that of the criminal! For this last blaze he will pay with his life. And at the end of these few pages, we ought to at least acknowledge the magnificence that he knew how to deliver.

## A Desperate Attempt: The Appeal to the Devil

But the prohibition contained in the letters of July 2, 1435, did not have full effect, inasmuch as the Duke of Brittany, Jean V, refused to ratify them in his domain . . . Yet the situation was no less serious. It was impossible for Rais to follow any course except that to which his disgrace had already led him.

To tell the truth, as of 1432 he went from one crisis to another. The aberration to which he surrendered in this unfortunate year literally withdrew him from the world. This aberration locked him in a tragic hallucination. Yet he had the feeling of being conveyed by a privileged destiny: finally the prodigy — or the monster — that he was would be saved. Such was his naïveté. I was going to say his stupidity. He had no doubt about his two contradictory recourses, one to God, the other to the Devil. This naïve, demonic man never entangled himself in anything; in the pact that he offered to the Devil, he exempted his soul and life. In any case, this privileged man could not have conceived that he would not be riding on everyone else's belly in the next world as in this one. One day he did manage, in his magnanimity, to ask the poor folk to congregate beside him at the Sacred Altar. This did not alter the exaggerated feeling that he had of himself. Worst of all is his certitude at the trial that he would rejoin Prelati, his accessory and accomplice, in paradise at the very hour the executioner hanged them . . .[10]

In truth, the presumptiousness at the source of all this drama is more generally the basis of that feudal superiority, insolence, and exploitation essential to the nobility.

The impulse that personifies tragedy can be accounted for by one formula: facing headlong into the impossible! The situation is untenable but it never belies the excessiveness of a Rais, who fights to the finish. This man is threatened with a rapid ruin; ceaselessly, at the limits of remorse, he marches into an abyss; yet for all this, he has an offhand bearing, an incongruous confidence, which makes the catastrophe inevitable.

Day in and day out, he waits for the Devil, his supreme hope . . . He awaits him for years. If he admits that he has "since his youth, committed and perpetrated high and enormous crimes," he thinks, at least partly, of his attempts at conjury. As soon as he could, he conferred with everyone who boasted of a power in these domains.

We cannot be sure, but one of the first contacts he had with an alleged Hereafter (which fascinated him) could be related to the meeting, doubtlessly at Angers in 1426, with a person about whom we know very little: he was an Angevin and a knight. Rais must have met him before fighting the English under Yolande d'Anjou's banner, when he recruited a company of Angevin men-at-arms; he was then twenty-two years old (this age corresponds to the expression "since his youth," which Gilles himself used). Versed in the arts of alchemy and invocation of the Devil, this knight was subsequently imprisoned: the Inquisition accused him of heresy. In the prison at the castle of the Dukes of Anjou, Gilles conversed with him. The knight possessed a manuscript examining the suspect arts; Gilles de Rais borrowed it from him and had it read aloud to several people in a room. We know moreover that the book was returned to the Angevin, but as to what befell the wretch, we know nothing. This visit to the prison and this reading of a manuscript suggest the initial steps. It is logical that at this period Gilles would have stayed for a long time in Angers, "fourteen years" before the trial in 1440.

At the same time, we must believe Rais' own affirmations that by 1440 he had practiced the art of conjury for "fourteen years."

It is possible in this way to think that his demonic initiation, dating from around 1426, began with this information drawn from a prisoner and a book.

---

[10] Indeed, Salomon Reinach, who did not possess but a cursory and incomplete knowledge of the documents, formerly attributed this extravagant certitude of salvation to his innocence! (cf. pp. 138-141).

Evidently numerous contacts followed, leading to the practices prescribed by professional conjurors.

As for these invocations, executed for "fourteen years," the trial informs us that they were sometimes done in the castles at Machecoul and Tiffauges, and sometimes in the house called La Suze at Nantes. There was one or several attempts at Orléans in the house called the Croix d'Or. The former are the first to be dated; Lord de Rais' stays in the house of the Croix d'Or at Orléans take place in 1434 and 1435.

We have, besides, a certain number of details about which conjurors were engaged or about such-and-such precise invocations.

We're told the names of a trumpeter named Dumesnil, of a "man named Louis," and of Antoine de Palerne from Lombardy. They may have been in Lord de Rais' service rather early on, some of them very early. At these invocations, the majority in which Gilles participated, "as much at Machecoul as at other places," "a circle" was traced "in the soil . . . of figure in the form of a circle"; whosoever wanted to conjure the Devil "where the intention is to see the Devil . . . , to speak and make a pact with him must, in the first place, trace this circle on the ground" . . . On this subject, Rais himself affirmed elsewhere that he was never able to see the Devil or speak with him, "although he did everything he could, to the point that it was not his fault if he could not see the Devil or speak with him."

In particular, we have the circumstantial account of certain invocations. Gilles de Sillé participated in one of them in addition to Lord de Rais. We do not know the name of the conjuror, but it took place in a room in the fortress at Tiffauges, without a doubt quite early on. The circle was traced on the ground, but on this day the two associates trembled. Rais, who "held in his arms an image of the Blessed Virgin Mary," is supposed to have entered the circle filled with apprehension "because the invoker had forbidden him to cross himself, because, if he did, they would all be in great danger; but he remembered a prayer to Our Lady that begins with *Alma*,[11] and at once the conjuror ordered him to leave the circle, which he immediately did while crossing himself; and he left the room promptly, leaving the invoker and locking the door behind him; then he discovered . . . Sillé, who told him that someone was beating and striking the invoker left alone in the room, which sounded as if someone were beating a featherbed; which he . . . (Rais) did not hear, and he had the door of the room opened and at its entrance he saw the conjuror wounded in the face and in other parts of his body, and having, among other things, a bump on his forehead so large he could barely stand up; and for fear that he might die in consequence of the said wounds, Gilles wanted him to be confessed and have the sacraments administered, but the

---

[11] It is a well-known hymn, the first verse of which is *Alma Redemptoris Mater . . .*

conjuror did not die, and recovered from his wounds." Imitating the noise that a demonic attack might have made and wounding himself to drive the point home, the conjuror is evidently employing a traditional ruse which Rais was the victim of at least twice.

Besides the excessive reaction of Rais, who earlier on could still be more frightened, there is one reason to believe that the date of this invocation is early: the role that Sillé plays in it and that he plays alone. Until about 1435-1436, so far as the conjurors and alchemists are concerned, Sillé seems at first to have been Gilles' sole procurer (during the same period he seems to have been the principal procurer of children, and it is he, as a rule, who did the killing when his master tired of doing so).

From 1435-1436 on, the priest Eustache Blanchet must have been, in his position, responsible for controlling the conjurors and alchemists (so far as the children are concerned, Henriet and Poitou assume the primary role, but Sillé does not disappear).

In the first place, Gilles de Rais had charged Sillé with seeking conjurors for him "in the region upriver," but apparently he had no occasion to be satisfied with them. Sillé reported to him that a female conjuror had told him that if his master did not turn his soul away from the Church, in particular from his chapel at Machecoul, he would succeed in nothing; another one, in different terms, had pretty much told him the same thing. A conjuror, whom he was to bring back, drowned. Another came but, as soon as he arrived, died . . .

Eustache Blanchet, who was subsequently expected to return from Italy with the young and prestigious Prelati, does not seem to have made the slightest mistake in the beginning. The conjuror that Blanchet had called in from Poitiers to Pouzauges stole from Lord de Rais. The latter had a castle at Pouzauges which he owned through his wife, like that at Tiffauges. But it is not in the castle that the invocation was performed. It occurred during the night in a forest nearby. Rais, Blanchet, Henriet, and Poitou were present. (Sillé must have been out of favor then.)

The conjuror, a physician named Jean de La Rivière, entered alone into the woods. He was armed. He had a sword and other arms, and he wore white armor. The participants suddenly heard a loud noise, as if La Rivière were fighting. Blanchet thinks that he was striking his sword against his armor with all his might. Upon his return, he had a "frightened and terrified" air. He said that he had seen in the woods "the Devil in the guise of a leopard." The demon had passed by him without saying a word, avoiding him. Gilles believed the conjuror without checking.

He paid him twenty gold royals on the spot. Everyone then returned to Pouzauges, where they held a feast and passed the night. Afterwards, La Rivière said that he was going to look for something he needed and would return as soon as possible, but he kept the twenty gold pieces and no one heard from him again.

Apparently it was around 1436 that this invocation took place. The business of the goldsmith from Angers might have taken place during the same period. The fact remains that Gilles must have passed through Angers that year. He attacks his ex-tutor there, who had made the mistake of taking sides with his family against him. Gilles could have been staying at the Lion d'Argent then, where Blanchet says he sent a goldsmith who professed to know alchemy. Gilles pays him a silver mark "to work." But, locking himself in a room, the goldsmith starts drinking. Gilles was indignant when he found him sleeping . . . He chased him, but the drunkard kept the silver.

However, the drunkard was perhaps honest as others were not: he was not a conjuror, but an alchemist. And alchemy — which the Church does not persecute as resolutely as sorcery or conjury, which occasionally it even tolerates — is basically the origin of chemistry . . . A little later, an alchemist in Rais' service is evidently honest. Like the one from Angers, he is a goldsmith; work with metals was preparation for alchemy, being in accord with it. We do not know when he came to Tiffauges to lodge with Lord de Rais, but he was there on May 14, 1439, when Prelati arrived; Prelati and Blanchet, arriving from Italy, were put in the same room with him on this day. We know just about everything we can say of him from Blanchet's testimony (p. 218); likewise, we have to think that the latter brought him to Gilles de Rais as he had brought the one from Angers. The second goldsmith was from Paris and answered to the name of Jean Petit.

He was still in Gilles' service in December 1439 when his master sent him to Mortagne in order to convince Blanchet, who had just escaped from Tiffauges, to return. But Blanchet refused. He told Jean Petit to repeat to Gilles and Prelati that public rumor was against them, that they ought to renounce their criminal life. When Jean Petit told him, Gilles, beside himself, had him led to the castle of Saint-Étienne-de-Mermorte, where he was thrown in prison; there he "remained a long time," according to Blanchet. We do not know the date on which he left Gilles' service, but he must have no longer been in it as of September 15, 1440, the date of the arrest. If on this date he had been at Machecoul, he would have been arrested, as was Prelati, with whom he had shared daily tasks for a long time. Prelati worked with him at the ovens that he evidently had installed before, perhaps even well before, the arrival of the Italian.

Such other alchemists as the Italians, Antoine de Palerne and Prelati, were not just alchemists but conjurors too. Antoine de Palerne seems to have been in Gilles' service early on, but he did not remain long; and when Gilles speaks of experiments with mercury, it is probable that Jean Petit was the initiator (the

Italians devoted themselves principally to conjury). Gilles was certain of succeeding at the transmutation of metals one day or another with Petit or Prelati, particularly with the both of them; he seriously believed that he was going to make gold. He remained convinced; if the unexpected visit of the future Louis XI, then Viennese Dauphin, had not obliged him to destroy his ovens (because an ordinance by Charles V prohibited alchemy) in December 1439, he would have fabricated gold! He would have regained his colossal fortune, and he would have been in possession of unlimited power and inexhaustible riches!

## *Prelati, Final Euphoria, and Catastrophe*

In fact the arrival of François Prelati, whom Blanchet brought back from Florence in the spring of 1439, ended by ruining him. Young, adorned with the marvels of magic, literature, and Italy, Prelati literally seduced Lord de Rais; his actual attainments and his charlatanic eloquence dazzled him.

Gilles no longer expected anything but the aid of the demon. He received this brilliant man like a savior who seemed to him, as no other, versed in knowledge that was going to return him to his former state of fortune. Insolent, audacious, coming from a city where homosexuality was rampant, Prelati appeared to come marvelously to terms with a master who himself must have seduced the unscrupulous — in addition, prodigiously corrupt — ambitious man. Gilles must have seduced him inasmuch as he continued to generously command a still appreciable wealth despite an actual fall from grace. Treated as a friend, maybe as a lover (though we cannot be certain), François Prelati escalated the number of invocations from the beginning, without concerning himself in the least with the obstinateness of a devil determined not to show. Easy lies, occasionally clumsy comedies, succeeded in passing off the deceptions. As an earlier conjuror had already done, he resorted to the simulated attack of a demon, and was given credit for having vigorously beaten him in the room in which he had taken the trouble to lock himself. Frightened, imagining his friend already dead, Gilles found him wounded; he intended to take charge of caring for him himself, not letting anyone else approach. But if the devil refused to appear to Gilles, he did not fail to provide François with reasons. In fact, when the latter was alone his personal demon, named Barron, sometimes graced the young and charming charlatan with his presence . . . It was easy to maintain his master's terrors and superstitions in this way. The lies of Prelati, in other respects, could demonstrate nothing: there managed to exist between the two men a sort of friendship, evidenced by Gilles' sublime goodbyes to François at the trial (p. 194), of which we have already spoken. Apparently these wayward souls stopped at nothing . . .

Despite their excessive corruption, it was possible for each of them to have certain sentimental capacities . . . the imbroglio of their feelings would have been constructed between one's deceit and the other's foolishness. We ought to recall no less the scene wherein the young comedian brutally landed a kick on the behind of his landlady who, crying over her dying husband, had disturbed him (p. 161). The kick would have made the miserable woman fall from her ladder if an old nurse had not caught her by the robe . . . This is the image with which it is appropriate to respond to the emotion that might have been warranted by the goodbyes that, on the threshold of the other world, the monster addressed his mystifier before the judges.

I will later provide in full (pp. 111 to 125) the details of what Gilles' confessions and Henriet's, Poitou's, and Blanchet's, not to mention Prelati's, testimonies permit knowing of the invocations that followed one another from the spring of 1439 to the arrest in September 1440. From rather numerous, rather precise descriptions we get a rich idea of the ritual of conjury of this period . . . I should only like to depict without further delay the atmosphere that was created in the castle at Tiffauges by these appeals to infernal powers. Prelati discovered, at the same time that he learned of his master's superstitious piety, the cruel murders that were impossible to do without; he was therefore going to make him live in the paradox that came from a vain expectation of a savior-devil and the demonic atmosphere that sprang from the children whose throats had been cut. To the evasions of this devil, for whom Rais kept waiting in the marvelous euphoria of inexhaustible gold . . . was answered only by the nightmare of bloody heads and the threat of final catastrophe, which it was each day a bit more childish to ignore.

In the first place, Prelati had his master drop the habit he had of participating at invocations. He attributed the devil's hesitation to some dissatisfaction or another; the devil, on the other hand, appeared each time the scrupulous Italian operated alone! From April to December 1439, the latter was able to maintain a kind of enchantment over this bloody man who was blindly forging ahead. But the situation became graver. Around July-August, Gilles went to Bourges, where he stayed long enough to have news and even a present sent to him from the devil: a "black powder on a slate stone" given to Rais by Barron, Prelati's personal demon. The Italian wrote to his master regularly at this time. At first Gilles carried the powder around his neck in a silver box. But after several days he admitted that it was not doing him any good . . . Probably after his return to Bourgneuf from Bourges, where Rais had encountered the Duke Jean V of Brittany, he must have forced Prelati to let him attend an invocation conducted on the premises, with the intention of obtaining from Barron the Duke's good graces. In vain. Deceived and depressed, Gilles immediately yields to his thirst for blood: a fifteen-year-old child, Bernard Le

Camus, loses his life on this day. But nothing does the trick; the criminal, apparently, cannot find appeasement: terror and remorse oppress him. Even at Bourgneuf he dreams of reforming himself, of going to cry before the Holy Sepulcher in Jerusalem. It is probably after this setback, which the crisis followed, that Prelati, divining the need to take his master in hand, proposes what could be a last resort: the irritated demon asked Gilles for a sacrifice! It was time to sacrifice an infant to the Devil. At first this proposition seems to have left Gilles in anguish. Prelati must have known in advance that this superstitious man would tremble; he knew the reticence of the criminal who never ultimately abandoned the hope and anxiety to save his soul; Gilles could not dissemble what was impardonable and repugnant in the sacrifice of an innocent, of a miserable child to the "unclean spirit." However, at bay, at all costs wanting to save, as with his soul and life, what was left of his riches, he appeared one evening carrying the hand, heart, and eye perhaps, of a child. He was so eager to see the devil! During the night, the Italian presented the horrible offering, but the devil did not come . . .

We can easily imagine Rais' state of mind during the period that followed. Spattered with blood, it is possible that this man was feverish. Would Prelati have been able from then on to maintain the spell under which he had attempted to keep him? Everything ought to have terrified him. His only outlet, it seemed, was in anger, violence . . . On Blanchet's request, Jean Petit had conveyed to him the public rumor that was mounting; he had requested that he not persevere in crime: the goldsmith went moaning into one of those terrifying prisons, from which, in order not to die, he needed to leave pretty quickly . . .

What ought to have put the finishing touch on Gilles' distress was the sudden visit of the future Louis XI, then the Viennese Dauphin. This sinister character was sent into Poitou by his father with the mission of putting an end to the mayhem of wars that had not stopped reigning in these regions. He came to Tiffauges, where it seems that Rais had just enough time to have the alchemical ovens destroyed. An old ordinance by Charles V prohibited, in effect, the practice of alchemy. The ovens being gone, the Dauphin — with whom so shabby a marshal as Lord de Rais in 1439 held no prestige — restricted himself to arresting the captain of men-at-arms at Tiffauges, guilty of pillages and "requisitions" in the countrysides of that region. The arrest was in response to the fact that Rais' men-at-arms often lived off the land . . . This hostile visit actually had a disastrous result: the destruction of the ovens announced to the criminal that he simply would not soon get his hands on that gold, which he sought in anguish for the possibility of avoiding ruin. It is true: by alchemy, if he had so desired, the demon would have granted his zealous servant the object of his request! But obstinately the demon refused to appear! For Gilles, Prelati's illusion and quackery were merely good for a few month's respite. The euphoria announced the catastrophe; the burst of life precipitated the definitive fall.

By the beginning of the year 1440, everything is theoretically played out. The Marshal's fortune and moral credit are at an all-time low. Everything fails at the same time. The Devil mocks him. If Prelati's seduction had not bewitched him, he might have sent packing the braggart who had succeeded at nothing. But Gilles could not have endured being alone in his misery. Prelati's company was precious. They could speak Latin together and, at any rate, the Italian's conversation was refined. Gilles' French companions were probably louts, cruel killers like Sillé; Briqueville was a vulgar profiteer; Henriet and Poitou, younger, perhaps had some charm: their depositions are lively . . . , and we know above all that Poitou, who had been Gilles' lover, was handsome. But these boys were bumpkins, and it is logical to suppose that Prelati, who perhaps on his own behalf offered himself to his master's embrace, granted him the satisfaction that came of his education. Growing tired of one orgy after another, it was impossible for Gilles to pass up on this handsome braggart. For lack of having saved his master by means of the Devil, Prelati at least knew how to amuse and distract him at a moment when his life was ending up sinking into the nightmare which his thirst for blood had confined him.

He came so far short of these last hopes; the sinister Marshal was now nothing more than flotsam. For a long time he was living in a hell, intersected by excessive joys, that is the eroticism of one who has abandoned a reasonable life.

In his depressed state an impulse of exasperation, of anger, blinded him. He had sold to Geoffroy Le Ferron, the Treasurer of Brittany, one of his last remaining castles, one of his castles in the Rais domain, Saint-Étienne-de-Mermorte. He learned that Lord de Vieillevigne, one of his cousins, would have voluntarily bought this castle because it had once been part of his family's endowment. Rais thought that Geoffroy Le Ferron would accept going back on the transaction. He was wrong. We do not know why Rais persisted. But he could not accept the treasurer's refusal. Against all wisdom, he decided to forcibly reseize the castle that had been sold. There was no garrison at Saint-Étienne-de-Mermorte. The treasurer had only installed his brother Jean, who was of the Church and who was protected by ecclesiastical immunity.

Not only did Gilles de Rais strike out against Jean V's treasurer, but this high officer was undoubtedly only a signatory for the Duke himself. Whatever his reasons were, there was a sort of dementia in the obstinacy of Gilles who, bearing arms, burst screaming into the village church where the treasurer's brother was attending to the Divine Office.

Threatened with having his head immediately cut off, the clergyman saw himself reduced to opening the doors of the castle for the energumen, who thereupon had him put in irons.

This impulse of rage pitched him violently against those who were going to bring him down, provoking at the same time the reactions of the Duke of Brittany and the Bishop of Nantes.

He struggled; he hoped to save himself by taking advantage of the multiplicity of powers. He transferred his prisoner Jean Le Ferron, who was answerable to the Duke of Brittany, from Saint-Étienne to Tiffauges, which was independent of the Crown.

He strove to negotiate with Jean V. But four months were enough. On the one hand, Jean V held an interview with Rais that made him believe in a possibility of appeasement. At just about the same time, the Duke got his brother, Charles VII's constable, to seize Tiffauges and liberate Jean Le Ferron, whom Rais was counting on as a hostage. On September 15th, Jean V's men seized Lord de Rais at Machecoul. They arrested him in order to lead him to the prison at Nantes at the same time as Prelati, Eustache Blanchet, Henriet, and Poitou.

Already the inquest into the murders of children was well advanced. It had been ordered on July 30th by the Bishop of Nantes, Jean Malestroit, Jean V's chancellor and right-hand man.

The absurd Saint-Étienne affair had set off legal proceedings that the starvelings, whose throats so great a lord had cut, would not have roused for a long time still.

## *The Spectacular Death*

It is only recently that the judicial execution of men ceased to be a spectacle intended for the entertainment and anguish of the crowd. There was no corporal punishment in the Middle Ages that was not spectacular. Death by corporal punishment was then, in the same capacity as tragedy is on the stage, an exalting and significant moment in human life. Wars and massacres, stately or religious parades, and corporal punishments dominated the crowds in the same capacity as churches and fortresses: thence was dictated the moral sense and generally the profound sense of every aspect of life (but maybe at the same time its little moral sense and, finally, its little sense). Before being judged and consequently executed, Gilles de Rais was thus destined for the crowd at the instant of his arrest; he was promised to them as is a choice spectacle on a theater bill.

Likewise, ten years earlier, Joan of Arc had been promised to the same anonymous crowd, the noise and fury of which continues to reach us through the ages . . .

Of all the victims offered to this crowd, Joan of Arc and Gilles de Rais, these companions in arms, are opposed to each other in the same way as are derided innocence and the crime that exhibits in the same breath the horror and tears of the criminal! In the case of both these victims, a single aspect lends itself to comparison: the *emotion* that this thundering mass could have had, before which Joan died in flames; the *emotion* that was evidently attached to this same anonymous thundering at the moment that Gilles, in his turn, appeared in the flames. As strange as it sounds to us, the fright that his crimes inspired (the innumerable children whose throats the assassin cut, spilling his seed on them, according to his confession) contributed, with the spectacle of tears, to the crowd's compassion. It contributed to it because in excessive social commotions it is always possible to obtain the best as well as to expect the worst; on this day the crowd had been invited to show up early in procession to the place of execution, praying to God for Gilles and his accomplices, who were being led to their death. Thus, that day the crowd could discover in their tears that this great lord who was to die, being the most infamous criminal, was like everyone in the crowd.

We know nothing of the reaction that Gilles de Rais must have had at the moment of his arrest.

It is possible that at first he believed in the possibility of extricating himself from the bad move that the Saint-Étienne affair had been. Initially he is the object of regard appropriate to his rank. He is given a high room in the castle that has nothing in common with the dungeons in which one locks the wretched (so little in common that an interrogation of the accused was done there in front of ten or fifteen people). Proceedings were begun before the ecclesiastical tribunal, over which the Bishop of Nantes and the Inquisitor of the Faith presided. The ecclesiastical proceedings alone had a dramatic aspect that gave the trial of Gilles de Rais the eminent place that it occupies among all criminal trials. (The secular trial proceedings were less important; the ecclesiastical proceedings are, on the other hand, the only ones of which a detailed record has come down to us.)

Of all the executions in the Middle Ages, as spectacular as they were, that of Gilles de Rais seems to have been theatrically the most moving. Likewise it appears that, in the beginning, his trial was at least one of the most animated and pathetic of all time.

This was a man accustomed to making men tremble who confronted the judges, a far more difficult accused party than those in our criminal courts.

Far from being a rake, Gilles de Rais had, as I have said, a genuine foolishness. It showed clearly in his first reaction, his insults, which were followed by his breakdown, his tears, and his inadmissible confession. Whatever fearfulness he still possessed beforehand inclined the judges to no less prudence. With his first appearance they avoided approaching the essential; doubtlessly they wanted the accused to acknowledge their competence before measuring the gravity of the accusation. This appearance took place on September 28th. Abandoning him to the depression of solitude, they waited until October 8th before making him appear again. But the accusation this time appeared in its true light: inexpiable. Gilles was no longer accused simply of having violated the immunity of the Church at Saint-Étienne; he had conjured the Devil, he had cut the throats of children and violated them, he had offered the hand, eyes, and heart of a child to the demon. Gilles understood and his anger was unleashed. He must have known from the beginning that he was lost. He exploded, challenging his judges. Evidently he thought of dragging the trial out, hoping for an intervention. But he immediately came up against the resolute firmness of the judges, who revealed their decision: they wanted to do away with him at once. When Gilles appeared again on the 13th, his powerless rage was unleashed; he insulted his judges as outrageously as he could, addressing them as ribalds and simoniacs, trying in vain to oppose them to the president of the secular tribunal, present at the proceedings. The judges reacted coldly; they excommunicated the madman at once.

In this day, excommunication had an overwhelming impact. Gilles de Rais managed, on the surface, to place himself above his judges. But the superstitious devotee — that he had not ceased being in spite of his crimes and satanic pursuits — broke down. Returned to the solitude of his room, he discovered again, more terrible than ever, the nightmare in which he raved.

One frightening way out remained, however, which suited the madman. To make a blaze of the disaster! An unquestionably disastrous but spectacular blaze, ultimately a delirious blaze; the crowd that would approach its glare would be fascinated . . .

In the course of the lengthy hallucination that he was living, the vain man that he had been came to a point where the violent movement of his thought exceeded its shabby limits. Succumbing definitively, his only authentic glory clung to his crimes. But he could only boast of these crimes under one condition:

He was going — crying, desperate, already nearly dying — to confess them, but, at the same time, to revel in their horrible grandeur, a grandeur that would make men tremble!

He was going to do what the Christian path had taught him, the path that, despite everything, he had always wanted to follow. While moaning, he would implore the forgiveness of God and all those who had suffered from the prodigious disdain that he had for others. He would implore while moaning, he would implore while dying; his tears, in this heavy apotheosis, would be authentic tears of blood!

But we have, however, only a remote understanding of what goes on in a fragile mind at the moment when the possibility of making a stand is stripped away, before our comprehending or divining, if possible, what leads it from one point to another. Likewise when we can discern nothing on a stormy night, the traces of lightning that escape us are dazzling . . . provided they escape us; and what is forced upon us, more than a comprehensible aspect, is the dizzying mobility wherein the possible aspects succeed one another. We must no less illustrate — or try to illustrate — by beginning with some trifling thing, what the documents inform us could have happened. We cannot to any extent forget that Gilles de Rais could never, unless vaguely — could not, in any case, but differently — have had the reactions which we impart to him. In their indecent precision what the statements suggest is the *turmoil* from which emanated these tears, these confessions, these entreaties that we are familiar with. But without the statements to suggest it, we would be no more familiar with the turmoil than we would be, asleep, with the storm that dazzled us. It is in this sense — only in this sense — that the commentaries add to the statement of facts. But need Lord de Rais' theatrical death appear, conclusively, limited by the poverty of these facts? Could the facts be separated from the incomprehensible lightning storm of the possible?

When on October 15, 1440, Gilles de Rais appeared again, the change that he had undergone in two days time in the solitude of his room was so great that it was comparable to death; only death might have brought about a more profound havoc . . . He was resigned; to his judges he came asking forgiveness for his insults; he was crying. He did not confess everything the first day, but if he denied what was the most serious thing to the clergymen, he immediately acknowledged the inadmissible: he had put children to death!

On his knees, in tears, "with great sighs," he pleaded to be absolved of the sentence of excommunication that the judges had pronounced against him. The judges, who had already forgiven him for the insults, absolved him as he requested. The hesitation of his first confessions is not necessarily significant. Doubtlessly, it is not unbelievable that at the outset profound reservations still stalled him. Would he have thought that a repentant great lord could be forgiven for putting to death poor children, whereas the conjury of demons warranted fire? It is possible.

It is difficult to believe, however, that the first leap, the most difficult, was superficial. I believe that the deep turmoil in which he struggled abandoned him again to tortuous thoughts. Though dimly, he must have been from the beginning no less open to the dizzying possibility that the confession of his repugnant crimes would fascinate those who heard them. Could he live without fascinating? Live without fascinating? Live without breathing! Whatever there was convulsing in him aspired to the moment when those who heard him would tremble. Fascinated, in their horror, they would tremble! The exhibitionism of criminals, compensating for the anxiety of dissimulation, generally has this aspect; it is on account of this that confession is the temptation of the guilty party who always, beginning from the disaster of crime, *has the possibility of a blaze, disastrous in itself.*

The decisive confessions, Gilles de Rais' inadmissible confessions, did not take place until October 21st, the date on which torture had been decided upon. These confessions could therefore have been the result of the threat. It seems to me less risky to believe that the threat facilitated what was a response to passion, but was not the cause of it. Threatened, Gilles de Rais beseeched the judges to grant him a postponement. He would reflect but, in advance, he promised to speak spontaneously in a manner that would satisfy them. He secured a hearing not by the ecclesiastical judges, but by the president of the secular tribunal — to whom the Bishop of Saint-Brieuc would be united. Torture deferred, Gilles entered upon the path of these unprecedented confessions, after which it became unthinkable to insist. The session of October 22nd was decisive: before the ecclesiastical judges, assembled in numerous attendance, Gilles exposed his depravities at length. He recalled the most dreadful thing. The decapitated heads that his accomplices and he himself examined in order to pick the most beautiful, which he then kissed. Finally the bursts of laughter that they had together on seeing the grimaces of the dying.

This violent exhibitionism was itself only possible under the condition of an ambiguity. Would it have been imaginable without the great lord's sobs? Or if the criminal who was crying had not been this great lord? In the moments of his confessions, there was a peak . . . They appeared in a sovereign, unusual light, from the fact of the criminal's grandeur (doesn't tragedy demand the criminal's sovereignty); at the same time he is offered for the horror, the criminal is offered for the terrified sympathy, for the compassion of those who see him cry, who cry with him.

What grips us in Gilles de Rais' death is the compassion. It seems that this criminal moved his audience to compassion; in part by reason of his atrocity, in part by virtue of his nobility and the fact that he was crying.

At the end of the secular trial, when the condemnation to death had been pronounced, and when the president of the tribunal and Gilles spoke together for several moments, the judge did not address himself like a judge to the accused; he bore him the deference that, under ordinary circumstances, a man has for another man. Doubtlessly, in his own eyes, the judge felt vindicated on account of the piety which Gilles de Rais gave proof of during these last moments. Doubtlessly the powerful family of the man he had just sentenced to death troubled him. I believe, above all, that the ignominy and the repugnant character of the butcheries — associated with this piety, these tears, and this grandeur — bewildered him; and that this judge had lost all possibility of discerning what opposed him to the criminal, what opposed him to his infamy.

At the same time I believe that the guilty party himself was obscurely conscious of the commotion that, under these conditions, would result from his death.

His naïveté on this day was on a par with the naïveté of the judges whom he had moved. It is thus that he requested that the president of the secular tribunal intervene on behalf of the Bishop of Nantes, who had presided over the ecclesiastical tribunal; the "excessive" desire of the criminal was that a procession of all the people, which the Bishop himself and the men of his church would arrange, would accompany him to the place of execution in order to pray to God for him and his accomplices, who were going to die after him.

The judge promised immediately to request this favor, which was accorded him.

He had previously requested and obtained a previous favor: since he was expecting to be hanged and, as soon as he was hanged, delivered to the flames, "before the flames could open his body and entrails," he would have liked to have been taken from the furnace, placed in a coffin, and led into the church of the Carmelite monastery at Nantes.

So well had they arranged things that his death was the occasion of a theatrical pageant.

Leaving the castle of La Tour Neuve, where the convict had been judged, the procession of an immense crowd chanting prayers and songs accompanied the miserable wretch, who had brought to the end his contempt for these little people who followed him and who were now supplicating God for him. The procession arrived at a meadow beyond the Loire that overlooked the city.

The church songs that he always loved to distraction lent to his death the resplendence that he could never get enough of in his lifetime. It seems that as soon as possible, "women of noble lineage" took care to pull out of the flames the dead man who, from the end of a rope, had appeared for one instant engulfed in the flame's bewildering splendor.

Then they placed him in a coffin, and solemnly the body was carried to its last resting place in the church, where the peaceful solemnity of the funeral service awaited him.

# Analysis

# of

# Historical

# Facts

# ANALYSIS OF HISTORICAL FACTS

*The first part of the introduction — which has preceded — considers the*
*problem of Gilles de Rais in its entirety.*
    *In this second part, we have assembled the* details *of his life, their immediate*
*consequences, and various related questions.*

## The Historical Facts in Chronological Order

**1400**

By a series of circumstances, before he is even born, a colossal fortune
is piled on the head of the abominable Gilles de Rais.

On the verge of dying heirless, the last descendant of the house of
Rais, Jeanne la Sage, decides to adopt Rais' future father, Guy de Laval
II of the house of Montmorency-Laval, and make him her heir.

This Guy de Laval is the nephew of Constable Du Guesclin.

If he accepts Jeanne la Sage's proposition, he is expected to renounce
the title and arms of Laval, at the same time assuming for himself and his
descendants the title and arms of Rais.

**1401**

Guy de Laval II accepts the inheritance of the barony of Rais and the    September 25
conditions that Jeanne la Sage had posed to him.

**1402**

For a moment, the combination of circumstances leading up to    May 14
Gilles' immense fortune and destiny is apparently compromised. For
reasons unknown to us, Jeanne la Sage renounces the appointment of
Guy de Laval as her lawful heir. She leaves everything to Catherine de
Machecoul, Pierre de Craon's widow. But, by a twist of fate, destiny
nicely reestablishes what was decided upon earlier. It requires an alliance
between the houses of Laval and Craon. The Craons were then the most

**(1402)**

powerful feudal house in Anjou (after the descendants of Louis I (1339-1384), Jean le Bon's youngest son, to whom his father had given the appanage of Anjou).

**1404**

*February 5*

In fact, Guy de Laval II secures Jeanne de Rais' inheritance in spite of everything; he marries Marie de Craon, the granddaughter of Catherine de Machecoul and Pierre de Craon, and the daughter of Jean de Craon.

After a trial period, harmony between the interested families foreshadows the fortune of the new couple's heir. Marie de Craon abandons, by contract, all rights to the inheritance of the house of Rais to her husband, Guy de Laval. Therefore Guy de Laval and his descendants will definitively possess, along with the fortune, the name and arms of Rais.

*Near the end of the year*
*Gilles de Rais is born*

Gilles de Rais is born on the banks of the Loire, in the Black Tower of the castle at Champtocé, the vast fortress and home of Jean de Craon. "All the neighboring nobility" are invited to his baptism in the village church: everyone takes part in the ceremony, "holding a candle."[1]

**1407**

Jeanne la Sage dies in the fortress of Machecoul, where she is buried. After her death, Gilles and his parents reside at Machecoul.

*Around 1407*

The birth of René, Gilles' brother.

**1415**

*Near the*
*beginning of the year*

The death of Marie de Craon, Gilles' mother. She is buried in the chapel of Notre-Dame, in the Buzay abbey at Rais.

*September 28*
*Death of his father*
*Gilles' education*
*is entrusted to*
*Jean de Craon*

Dying, Guy de Laval of Blaison draws up his testament; in it he entrusts the education of his children to Jean Tournemine de La Hunaudaye, his cousin. He asks, at the same time, that the two tutors — two priests to whom he entrusted Gilles — Georges de La Bossac and Michel de Fontenay, continue his education. Guy de Laval is buried in the same tomb as Marie de Craon.

However, the testament has no effect on the tutelage. Jean de Craon alone, in fact, assumes charge of raising Gilles and René and administering the older son's property. At this time, he is not yet sixty years old. Violent and unscrupulous, he abandons Gilles, who is motherless, to passions that nothing can curb. He is responsible for an important part of the completely lax education to which Gilles himself attributes the origin of his monstrosity during his trial.

---

[1] A. BOURDEAUT, *Chantocé, Gilles de Rays et les Ducs de Bretagne*, p. 46.

At the disastrous Battle of Agincourt, the death of Amaury, Jean de Craon's son, succeeds in making Gilles, then only eleven years old, one of the richest heirs in the realm.

October 25

**1417**

Gilles is engaged by his grandfather to Jeanne Peynel (the daughter of Foulques, Lord de Hambye), a very rich heiress of Normandy. For Jean de Craon, it has to do with getting his hands on an orphan's estate while paying the debts of her tutor. The greedy Jean de Craon is not interested simply in Gilles' future, but in the management of his property during his youth. But the parliament of Paris, alerted, forbids his marriage to Jeanne Peynel before her majority.

January 14

**1419**

Companions of the Dauphin Charles stab Jean sans Peur, the Duke of Burgundy, on Montereau bridge during negotiations that some had thought might put an end to the civil war and draw partisans of the future Charles VII and the Burgundians together against the English. Double-dealing by Jean sans Peur is undoubtedly at the bottom of the assassination, which would widen the gap between the opposing parties for a long time to come.

September 10

Jean de Craon engages Gilles a second time; he gives his hand to Béatrice de Rohan, the niece of Jean V, the Duke of Brittany. We do not know why this transaction, which was contracted and dated in Vannes, fell through.

November 28

**1420**

King Charles VI, who has lost his sanity, disinherits the Dauphin Charles; Joan of Arc's dream will later restore to him a realm that might well have seemed lost.

January 17

Jean V, the Duke of Brittany, of the house of Montfort, is ambushed by his enemies the Penthièvres. He is imprisoned at Champtoceaux. This episode begins a new phase in the war between the Montforts and the Penthièvres. Jean de Craon then sides with the Montforts. Because of this, his and Gilles' fiefs are preyed upon by bands in the Penthièvres' service. Mothe-Achard is occupied. But the Penthièvres are defeated. Jean V is freed. Jean de Craon "and his son de Rays" are indemnified for losses and recompensed.

February 13

But Gilles de Rais himself does not seem to have participated in these feudal combats. Abbot Bossard assumed that he did and Roland Villeneuve followed his opinion, but he was only sixteen years old then; the

**(1420)**

documents are silent; it is not likely, and we do not even know whether he was present at Jean V's triumphal return to Nantes.

May 20

By the Treaty of Troyes, Henry V, the King of England, becomes heir to Charles VI; the kingdoms of England and France are expected to be united under the same crown. The University of Paris and a semblance of the Estates General recognize the treaty. The Duke of Brittany recognizes it in turn but, after Charles VI's death, he will change his mind several times; this whimsical character, who never keeps his word, answers to the English crown one day and to the Dauphin's camp the next.

September 28

Jean V grants Jean de Craon and his grandson one hundred pounds in annuity, taken from one of the Penthièvres' partisans. This one hundred pounds is, by all accounts, the equivalent of nearly one million of our own money (1959).

November
Gilles' marriage

With Jean de Craon's approval, Gilles abducts Catherine de Thouars, his cousin, the daughter of Milet de Thouars and Béatrice de Montjean. Catherine's property in Poitou adjoined the barony of Rais, which it complemented. It is difficult to understand the reason for the abduction, which is followed by a quiet wedding ceremony. Perhaps their relatively close relation necessitated putting the deed, rather than the proposition, before ecclesiastical authorities and families. In any event, Gilles de Rais and his grandfather benefited from the fact that Milet de Thouars had just "died at Meaux of a high fever."[2]

Around 1420

Jean de Craon's wife dies. After several weeks, he marries a second: Anne de Sillé, Catherine de Thouars' grandmother, a relative of probably the most ferocious of Gilles de Rais' future companions in debauchery.

**1421**

March 22

Near Saumur, at Baugé, the future Charles VII, who is given the title of regent on account of Charles VI's insanity, wins a victory over the English troops.

Around 1421

Her period of mourning observed, Béatrice de Montjean marries a young knight, Jacques Meschin de la Roche-Aireault. This able young man had been chamberlain in the Dauphin's court; he was able to give his wife the support without which she could never have opposed the

---

[2] A. BOURDEAUT, *op. cit.*, p. 52.

brutality of Jean de Craon and Gilles de Rais; they had already seized Catherine's possessions, her mother's dowry, and the fortresses at Tiffauges and Pouzauges in Poitou.

**1422**

April 24

Public marriage, with Rome's authorization, of Gilles de Rais and Catherine de Thouars. Jacques Meschin interferes — he will live to regret it — to obtain a settlement on behalf of Béatrice de Montjean.

August 31

Death of Henry V of England. His son and successor, Henry VI, is now ten months old.

October 21

Death of Charles VI. His succession will oppose the Dauphin, Charles VII — the King of Bourges — against the regent of France for the English, Bedford, Henry V's brother, who represents the rights of young Henry VI.

**1423**

June 14

Bedford disposes, in favor of an English lord, of the castles of Ambrières and Saint-Aubin-Fosse-Louvain, which belonged to Jean de Craon.

**1423-1424**

Abduction of the mother-in-law

In Jean de Craon's service, the captain of the garrison of Tiffauges, Jean de La Noe, forces Béatrice de Montjean and her younger sister to follow him to Louroux-Bottereau, where he imprisons them. From there they are led to Champtocé, where Gilles and his grandfather threaten to sew Béatrice in a sack and throw her into the river.[3] Catherine's mother is called upon to renounce her dowry at Tiffauges and Pouzauges. But the husband lays claim to his wife. He will never see her again, he is told, unless she renounces her dowry (not to mention other demands). A short while later, Jean de Craon has three of Jacques Meschin's messengers, including his brother, Gilles Meschin, thrown into a deep pit. At the request of his wife, Anne de Sillé, he sends Béatrice back to her husband but keeps the messengers. Béatrice's sister has meanwhile married Girard de La Noe, the son of the captain who had abducted the two women. Finally Jacques Meschin must yield to the demands of the rapacious men at Champtocé, who wield a much greater power than his own. He pays the messengers' ransom, but one of them, Jacques' brother, dies from his horrible stay in the pit; his companions recover badly. Later the affair comes before the royal parliament, then sitting at Poitiers. There is an amicable settlement, but royal authority is so weak then that it is

[3] A. BOURDEAUT, *op. cit.*, p. 54.

**(1423-1424)**

unable to have the sentences enforced. Béatrice de Montjean's dowry, protected to the limit, is assigned in Limousin. The choice is given to Meschin and Béatrice between Pouzauges and Tiffauges. But Gilles holds on to them both; Pouzauges under the pretext that his wife goes by that "name in the world."[4]

When the president of parliament, Adam de Cambray, comes to Pouzauges to see that the settlement signed before parliament is observed, he is brutally assaulted by Gilles de Rais' men. For this, Jean de Craon and Gilles are fined for *lèse-majesté*, but in 1443 (Gilles has already been dead for three years) the fine is still unpaid. After the disaster at Agincourt, the royal authority is mocked by the great feudal lords, especially if they aid the King with their military forces. This is the case with Gilles and his grandfather.

**1424**

At twenty years old, Gilles assumes the administration of all his property; he uses it from then on for his pleasure without consulting Jean de Craon, who still has the administration of his estate "on lease."[5]

**1425**

Yolande d'Aragon, whose daughter, Marie d'Anjou, is the wife of Charles VII, wants the defeat of England. She attempts to reconcile France with Brittany. She convinces her son-in-law to make Arthur de Richemont (the brother of Jean V of Brittany) — now the chief of his army — the Constable of France. She has confidence in the energy, though a bit sluggish, of Arthur de Richemont. She had not counted on Georges de La Trémoille. La Trémoille wins Charles VII over to his side rather quickly, and reduces the new constable to powerlessness. He alienates Charles from Richemont, whose presence draws umbrage over his own. Richemont will not come into power until eight years later, when the opposing party, in turn, will alienate the scheming La Trémoille. Not until after 1433 will Richemont be in a position to consolidate Joan of Arc's victories. Only then can France, once and for all, free itself of the English.

October 7

Yolande d'Aragon takes the initiative: an interview takes place between Charles VII and Jean V of Brittany. Jean de Craon, some of whose domains depend on the duchy of Brittany but who is Angevin principally, works in accord with Yolande d'Aragon for the reconciliation of

---

[4] A. BOURDEAUT, *op. cit.*, p. 56, note 1.

[5] Dom H. MORICE, "Mémoire des héritiers de Gilles de Rais pour prouver sa prodigalité," in *Mémoires* . . . , vol. II, col. 1337.

France and Brittany. Yolande d'Aragon asks him to negotiate the marriage of Isabelle de Bretagne, Jean V's oldest daughter, to her own son, Louis d'Anjou III. Gilles de Rais attends the interview at Saumur, which ends October 7th in an accord between the parties. It is his first known encounter with the young King.

**1426**

March 6

Arthur de Richemont, the brother of the Duke of Brittany and recently Constable of France, is beaten by the English at Saint-James-de-Beuvron. The Chancellor of Brittany, anglophile Jean de Malestroit, is possibly at the origin of this defeat. Salomon Reinach[6] thought that the hostility of Jean de Malestroit toward Gilles dated from Saint-James. One knows that Malestroit, in 1440, was to have Gilles hanged. Nothing proves that the hostility between the two men dates back this far. Nothing proves that Gilles even fought at Saint-James. But after this defeat, Jean V reconciles with the English and recognizes for a second time the Treaty of Troyes, which made Henry V heir to the crown of France. With the support of his brother gone, Arthur de Richemont loses his influence to the advantage of Georges de La Trémoille. La Trémoille's influence at this moment decides the military career of Gilles de Rais, his cousin. It is a known fact: this influence was disastrous. La Trémoille will fight against Joan of Arc's zeal. He will even hinder her work outside Paris. It is up to him, then, to destroy a prestige that the taking of Paris would have made decisive.

**1427**

June 19
Campaign in Maine
against the English

Yolande d'Aragon appoints Jean de Craon her lieutenant general. Evidently with good reason Abbot Bourdeaut[7] connects this dignity with the rise of La Trémoille, who had yet to become Yolande d'Aragon's declared enemy. In fact, it is through the Craons that La Trémoille is a cousin of Gilles; from now on, Gilles himself will occupy an important place in France's struggle against the English. He is rich, and he generously pays numerous spies. The first role in a pitched battle then belongs, on the French side, to an able captain of low birth, Ambroise de Loré; but judging from the look of things, the entrance of Gilles de Rais on the scene, at the head of Jean de Craon's troops, provides a new burst of activity. To Gilles' mad riches are added, moreover, undeniable bravery, resolution, and military valor. The castles of Rainefort and Saint-Laurent-des-Mortiers in Mayenne, and those of Lude and Malicorne in Sarthe, are seized by the English. We have several reasons

[6] S. REINACH, *Gilles de Rais*, p. 270.

[7] A. BOURDEAUT, *op. cit.*, p. 64.

**(1427)**        to associate this favorable French campaign with the intervention of La Trémoille.

Around 1427      Étienne Corrillaut, originally from Pouzauges, then about the age of ten, enters Gilles de Rais' service as a page; later he will become his valet; then he will act as a procurer; he will help kill the children and, on September 16, 1440, will be executed with his master.

**1428**

October      The English prepare the Siege of Orléans. After having hesitated between Orléans and Angers, they will employ all the resources at their disposal in France against Orléans.

**1429**

March 6
Chinon and the arrival
of Joan of Arc

Gilles de Rais is at court in Chinon when Joan of Arc, direct from Vaucouleurs, meets the King there. She wants to chase the English from French soil. She wants to first liberate Orléans, then lead Charles VII to Reims. Charles VII must be coronated at Reims in order to possess the sacred character that designates a king.

April 8
Pact between Gilles and
Georges de La Trémoille

Gilles is engaged by Georges, Lord de La Trémoille, to do everything in his power to serve him, "to death if need be, in spite of everything and against every lord and man, with no exception . . . , in the good graces and love of the King." The letter is dated from Chinon, signed in Gilles' hand and carrying his seal. Gilles' mission answers to this letter; it is Gilles de Rais who will lead the troops entrusted to Joan of Arc by the King. He will not be alone, but he will have this privileged mission. He will have it because of his pact with the man who plays the role of prime minister. This person justly wants to keep the situation in hand; he must control the course of events. He must, above all, maintain his interest. No other can come between the favorite and the King. No one must extract from the events an excessive prestige, dangerous to La Trémoille's reputation.

April 28
Departure of Gilles and
Joan of Arc for Orléans

An important convoy of provisions has been prepared at Blois, where Joan of Arc arrives in the company of Lord de Gaucourt. Gilles de Rais and his personal army, as well as the Duke of Alençon and Ambroise de Loré, join the convoy. They leave with an escort of ten to twelve thousand men for Orléans. Joan of Arc begins the march with the song *Veni Creator*. But, on the advice of Gilles de Rais, the cavalcade passes over the Blois bridge and along the Sologne so that, arriving in front of the besieged city, it will be separated by the Loire. Joan of Arc's protests were unable to prevent this compromising solution. Joan had wanted to approach Orléans along the right bank, to enter the city without boating across the Loire.

The royal army is on the left bank facing Chécy. Joan of Arc sends two hundred men and provisions in several boats under the command of the Bastard of Orléans, who arrived in the city before her. Gilles de Rais and the bulk of the escort return to Blois.

April 29

After some equivocation, the royal army departs from Blois again, this time along the right bank. It will arrive at the city on the side where the assailants are best entrenched, and it will arrive there without detour. Hoisting her banner, Joan of Arc, accompanied among others by Florent d'Illiers and La Hire, will march before the army. The Maid, the companies from within Orléans, and the army from Blois enter the city in good formation past the English forts to the west. Then Joan shows up, on the east, before the fort of Saint-Loup, which she takes after a fierce battle. It is the first battle in which Gilles de Rais is required to participate close to Joan of Arc. On the following day, Ascension Day, the army rests.

May 4
Battles before Orléans

The captains hesitate. But the army attacks the English on the right bank, where Joan of Arc determines the success of the assault from the fort of the Augustins. The captains think they have done enough now: the city is full of provisions; they advise guarding it while waiting for the King's aid. Gilles de Rais is doubtless of the same opinion.

May 6

Joan refuses to be inactive. First she persuades the Bastard of Orléans and La Hire; but quickly Gilles de Rais and others follow her before the fort of the Tourelles, the bridgehead on the right bank. At one o'clock in the afternoon, Joan of Arc, having erected a ladder, is shot through the shoulder with a quarrel from a crossbow. The captains surround her and express their regret at seeing her hurt; they think that they should resume the assault tomorrow. But Joan is resolute; she demands her horse and the struggle continues. By the end of the day the Tourelles fall. The battered English experience many deaths; their chief, Glasdale, among others, is thrown into the Loire. In this battle that determines the future of a country, Gilles de Rais fights boldly. The Battle of the Tourelles is one of those where he acquires the reputation, which survived his infamous condemnation, "of being a very valiant knight of arms."

May 7
Gilles in the decisive
Battle of the Tourelles

# (1429)

| | |
|---|---|
| **May 8**<br>Liberation of Orléans | The English lift the Siege of Orléans. The entire city and army celebrate its liberation with an immense procession that, from then on and up to the present, is reenacted May 8th of each year. |
| **June 12**<br>Taking of Jargeau | Joan of Arc, with the army placed under the command of the Duke of Alençon, takes Jargeau, on the Loire, twenty kilometers upstream of Orléans. Nothing indicates that Gilles de Rais had any part in the seizure of Jargeau. |
| **June 17**<br>Taking of Beaugency | With Gilles de Rais present, the royal army takes Beaugency, twenty-five kilometers downstream of Orléans on the Loire. |
| **June 18**<br>Victory at Patay | Defeat of the English at Patay, north of Beaugency. Gilles de Rais fights alongside Joan of Arc. |
| **June 19** | The victorious army is at Orléans. |
| **June 24** | The army sets off again. It arrives at Gien that same day, but the departure for Reims gives way to equivocation. |
| **June 29**<br>Departure for Reims | Charles VII, Joan of Arc and, among other captains, Gilles de Rais, leave for Reims. |
| **July 10** | After several days, the town of Troyes surrenders to the royal army marching to Reims. |
| **July 17**<br>Consecration of<br>Charles VII at Reims<br>Gilles de Rais<br>Marshal of France | Charles VII is solemnly consecrated at the Reims cathedral in the presence of Joan of Arc. Gilles de Rais is charged with transporting from the Saint-Rémy abbey, which he enters on horseback, the phial containing the Holy Chrism which serves in the royal unction. On this day he is made Marshal of France. He is not yet twenty-five years old. After the coronation, Joan embraces the King's knees while crying. Charles VII himself and those around him are in tears. At this moment Gilles de Rais, who later laughs with his accomplices about the children whose throats they will have cut, probably cries with the heroine. |
| **August 10** | Charles VII and the royal army enter Compiègne. Beauvais, Creil, and Chatilly surrender. |
| **August 23** | Joan and the Duke of Alençon leave Compiègne in the direction of |

78

Paris. At the same time, Constable de Richemont invades Normandy. The regent Bedford, preoccupied with Normandy, has left a very feeble garrison in Paris.

Joan of Arc is at Saint-Denis.

August 26

Charles VII and the Burgundians, allied with the English, conclude a truce.

August 29

Charles VII himself arrives at Saint-Denis. The Bastard of Orléans, Marshals de Boussac and de Rais, La Hire, and Xaintrailles accompany him.

September 7

After having gathered around her those in agreement with her,[8] Joan of Arc leads the assault on the walls of Paris in the company of Marshal de Rais and Lord de Gaucourt. Together they take the boulevard protecting the Saint-Honoré gate (close to the Théâtre Français square). It seems from within Paris that the city is about to fall. But near evening, Joan is shot through the thigh by a crossbow. The quarrel remains lodged; thinking she is close to death, she asks for Lord de Rais by her side, which indicates, at any rate, that she appreciates his military valor. According to Quicherat, Perceval de Cagny is the best informed and most reliable of all the chroniclers.

September 8
Gilles de Rais under the walls of Paris
Joan of Arc is wounded

The Duke of Alençon and Joan of Arc, in spite of her injury, prepare for battle early. But the command returns to the King at Saint-Denis. Logically, La Trémoille is restless. The extraordinary prestige that the taking of Paris, which then seemed probable, would have accorded the Maid, would also have brought offense to the favorite. At the same time, he was probably fearing the Duke of Alençon's glory. Without a doubt, La Trémoille is responsible for abandoning the Siege of Paris. A weary Charles VII has to approve. Whatever happened, the decision that same day to destroy a bridge that, thrown over the Seine, ought to have facilitated the attack is often attributed to the King himself. Gilles de Rais must, should the occasion arise, serve La Trémoille's interests. On the 8th he fights, but on the 9th he follows orders.

September 9

Charles VII leaves Saint-Denis. He withdraws toward the Loire. This retreat compromises the liberation. The towns that surrendered to

September 13

[8] PERCEVAL DE CAGNY, in QUICHERAT, *Procès . . . de Jeanne d'Arc*, vol. IV, p. 26.

**(1429)**

Charles VII now lie abandoned, and their situation is dangerous. The decline of Joan of Arc, followed by prison and torment by fire, begins with the order to retreat from Paris.

September

Near the end of September, letters patent from Charles VII bestow on Marshal de Rais an "orle" of "gold lilies on an azure field," supplementing his armorial bearings. These letters consider his "lofty and recommendable services" and the "great perils and dangers" to which the Marshal was exposed, "as in the taking of Lude and many other handsome deeds, the lifting of the siege that the English recently laid before the town of Orléans . . . and also on the day of the Battle of Patay when, the said siege raised, our said enemies were crestfallen; and, since then, the cavalcade made recently, as well in Reims, for our coronation and consecration, as elsewhere, beyond the Seine, for the repossession of many of our regions . . ." The fact that these letters are dated from Sully-sur-Loire, that is, from a castle belonging to Georges de La Trémoille, succeeds in underlining the accord between Gilles de Rais and Charles VII's favorite. In any event, Joan of Arc is not mentioned. Some have spoken of Gilles' affection for Joan, or Joan's for Gilles. It is nothing but supposition, with no other foundation than the naïveté of certain authors, recent enough, who in speaking of Gilles de Rais wanted to contrast a seductive aspect to his odiousness. Some have said that he corrected his ways when fighting in Joan's company: it is not likely; it is only likely that he showed some interest in the memory of Joan of Arc during his long stay at Orléans (1434 and 1435); the Maid was then enjoying a marvelous popularity among the people of Orléans, and Gilles benefited by recalling that he had fought at her side. But in September 1429, Charles VII's offices could even insist, in the face of everything, on designating to the general sympathy this Marshal of lofty birth, who was not even twenty-five years old (but whose celebrity today is based on his unheard-of crimes). Joan of Arc was not immediately abandoned, but the leaders no longer wanted to allow her to have the primary role.

By the end of the year
Birth of Marie,
Gilles' daughter

The birth, evidently at Champtocé, of Gille's daughter, Marie.

Out of the blue
First sale of the domain

We know that at the age of twenty-five (he was born in 1404), with the sale of the patrimonial estate of Blaison, Gilles starts liquidating his immense fortune. From 1434 on, this liquidation should accelerate and rapidly lead him to ruin.

At the beginning of 1430 (or the end of 1429), Gilles de Rais is captain of Sablé, in Sarthe. Yolande D'Aragon, regent of the duchy of Anjou, is now at war with La Trémoille; Gilles' occupation of Sablé is one of the episodes of the quarrel. Leaving Sablé, Gilles attempts to take Château-l'Hermitage, occupied by Jean de Bueil, a renowned captain, great lord, and author of a book which is both chronicle and fiction. This book, *Jouvencel*, without mentioning names, reports the events of this war in detail. Gilles cannot take Château-l'Hermitage. Jean de Bueil sounds the alarm in time; but, while sounding it, he falls into the hands of Gilles' men. The prisoner is led to Sablé. Gilles has him imprisoned "all alone in a great tower, in which he had the happy leisure to reflect, think, and imagine." He prepares his revenge astutely. He pays his ransom and, free, carries out the taking of Sablé that he had meditated on in prison. Later on, Gilles de Rais retakes the town: the date is difficult to specify, but Abbot Bourdeaut reasonably estimates it to have been prior to the conspiracy against La Trémoille in July of 1433 that ends the career of his favorite and his quarrel with Yolande d'Aragon. Yolande d'Aragon's man, Jean de Bueil, participates, incidentally, in this conspiracy.

*Around 1430*

It is necessary, moreover, to situate before July 1433, probably before February 1431 even, the armed attack to which Yolande falls victim, which Gilles de Rais or Craon — or the both of them — prepared: the Queen of Sicily riding peacefully in her own domain, in Anjou, entering the city of Ancenis on the Loire (at least forty kilometers upstream of Nantes); men from the Champtocé garrison (situated twenty kilometers farther upstream) arrest and imprison part of her escort and steal their horses and baggage. The great lords, in this epoch, are subject to banditry as well.

*The Ancenis' plot against Yolande d'Aragon*

Gilles de Rais dates from Louviers an I.O.U. of two hundred and sixty gold crowns to one Rolland Mauvoisin, captain of Princé (in the land of Rais). These two hundred and sixty crowns are destined for the purchase of a horse for another of Gilles' captains, Michel Machefer. Gilles' presence in Louviers, at the moment when Joan of Arc is held prisoner at Rouen, appeared to be in preparation of an armed attack to spring her. The hypothesis appears badly founded. First of all, Charles VII did nothing in his power to gain the freedom of the woman to whom he owed his kingdom. Above all Gilles de Rais is bound to La Trémoille, Yolande d'Aragon's enemy; but Yolande is, if necessary, the only one in the King's entourage who shows an interest in Joan; Gilles, by all

*December 26
Gilles de Rais in Louviers*

**(1430)**

appearances, shares the general indifference of all those gravitating around Charles VII.

**1431**

February 22 to 24

Gilles de Rais and Jean de Craon mediate on La Trémoille's behalf complex deals with Jean V of Brittany and Yolande d'Aragon; they also mediate between Yolande and Jean V. The castle of Champtocé serves as a meeting place. As early as 1430, Constable Arthur de Richemont, Jean V's brother, accompanied by another brother of the Duke (Richard, Count d'Étampes), meets Yolande herself, or her envoys, there; this has to do with preparations for an alliance between the houses of Anjou and Brittany.[9] In any case, during a conference that lasts from February 22nd to the 24th, Georges de La Trémoille meets Jean V. They exchange letters — completely theoretical — of eternal friendship. But the marriage of François de Bretagne, Jean's son, to Yolande d'Aragon is then agreed upon (it takes place August 20th of the same year in Nantes); it will end a tension threatening to provoke war between Anjou and Brittany. We are not exactly sure of the role of Gilles de Rais and his grandfather in these arduous affairs. But their devious spirit was able to delight in them, in keeping with the spirit of La Trémoille.

May 30

Joan of Arc is burned at Rouen.

December 16

Young Henry VI of England is crowned King of France at Notre-Dame in Paris. In spite of Joan of Arc's execution, and however solemn the demonstration at Notre-Dame, England is in a bind. Only the pernicious influence of La Trémoille permits her to maintain her positions several years hence.

**1432**

August 10
Battle of Lagny

The possession of Lagny assures French control over the lower Marne region, not far from Paris. The regent Bedford himself came to reinforce the siege of the city. Gilles de Rais, with the Bastard of Orléans, Lords de Gaucourt, Xaintrailles, and others, battle the English. The victorious royal army forces the English regent to lift the siege. Lagny and the Tourelles are the two great feats of arms that confirm the Marshal's valiant reputation.

November 15
Death of the grandfather

Jean de Craon dies, apparently alarmed at having understood what his oldest grandchild is capable of. Not only was he terrified by Gilles' extravagance, but he must have foreseen where his vices and cruelty would lead.

[9] E. COSNEAU, *Arthur de Richemont*, p. 180.

In Craon's bitterness — it was to the younger grandson, to René, that he left his sword and cuirass! With the approach of death, he is profoundly troubled in other respects. He is bound to reexamine his pride and his freebooter brutality; he asks, therefore, for a humble funeral.

Gilles makes good the damage done to the chaplaincy of Louroux-Bottereau by his grandfather's embezzlement of funds, which were allocated on behalf of this charitable foundation by his great-grandmother, Catherine de Machecoul, at the end of the 14th century.

November 26

Poitou, up until then Gilles de Rais' page, becomes his "child valet," but apparently he does not enter his master's secrets before 1437.

Around 1432

**1432-1433**

The first child murders

Here is what we draw from his confessions (p. 193) on the day Gilles' crimes began: "Interrogated as to where he perpetrated the said crimes, and when he began . . . , he stated and responded: in the first place, at the Champtocé castle, in the year when Lord de La Suze, his grandfather, died." We have just seen how this lord, Jean de Craon, died November 15, 1432; we should not forget that in the Middle Ages the new year began in spring.

The confession adds: "At which place he killed children and had them killed in large numbers — how many he is uncertain; and he committed with them the . . . sodomitic and unnatural sin; and at this time Gilles de Sillé alone knew . . ." (p. 197).

In his confession before the secular court, Poitou, who was clearly in Gilles de Rais' service since 1427 at the age of the ten, affirms that Gilles committed murders in his room at Champtocé during the life of Jean de Craon. Poitou had heard him say this (p. 274), but it is not necessarily convincing. Poitou claims, in the bill of indictment, that Gilles had been killing since 1426. We ought to hold, it seems, to the date given by Gilles himself: he began killing in the year his grandfather died. However, he does not say *after his death*. He could have tranquilly killed in his room from the moment the old man was feeble enough that he was as good as dead. Keeping in mind that before this death Gilles could have killed elsewhere, the fact remains that on, or on the approach of, this death, a feeling of solitude, strength, and freedom managed to intoxicate him. Clearly his grandfather, the predatory old man, had an influence over him. He had initiated him into the life. He had assisted him, counseled him in the profession of arms, which rested on violence and disregard for human life. He had taught him how to act like a gangster. True, by 1424 Gilles refuses the administration of his finances. But, when in 1427 he begins to fight, it is as Jean de Craon's lieutenant general, which puts him on a par with experienced captains in Anjou. He commands Craon's troops in Maine; it is through Craon that he clings to his cousin Georges de La Trémoille. Georges de La Trémoille comes from Craon's family. Apparently Gilles' living example was his grandfather. The grandson was at ease with this unstoppable man. He was at home and fascinated! But the thought of sex crimes haunted him; and sex crime would have scandalized the old man. On the other hand, Craon would have been anxious to avoid those mad expenditures that gave Gilles a sort of vertigo that he could not resist. With the grandfather dead, the grandson found himself at the helm of an increased fortune; there was no longer anything to bridle the rage that tormented him. Only crime, that negation of every bridle, was to give him the unlimited sovereignty that the old man had possessed in Gilles' adolescent eyes. Gilles was the rival of the man who raised him, whom he followed — and admired — and who was now dead, who had surpassed him in life. He was going to surpass him in turn. He would surpass him in crime. Even if he does not think in this fashion, the emancipation is no less intoxicating, no less liberating to unspeakable debaucheries.

As to the date of his crimes, Gilles' confession is contrary to the bill of indictment: the latter states "fourteen years earlier." This document, in advance of the confessions, has the first murders dating back to 1426, but without proof, and of a simply conjectural nature. Had he agreed with the indictment on this point, Gilles would not have aggravated his position when he confessed. Elsewhere there is a concordance between the date given in the confession and that of the first testimonies on the disappearances of children.

These testimonies, it is true, do not concern Champtocé, which comes under the duchy of Anjou: the judges in Nantes were inquiring within the limits of their jurisdiction, in the duchy of Brittany alone.

The five following testimonies relate to Machecoul, but the approximate date to which they refer is 1432-1433, that is to say, in the old style, in the year when "Lord de La Suze died":

1. Around 1432, a child of Jean Jeudon, of Machecoul, aged twelve, was apprenticed to Guillaume Hilairet, a furrier, himself living at Machecoul. Guillaume Hilairet, who testifies along with his wife, Jeanne, declares that he gave the child to Gilles de Sillé under the pretext of the child carrying a message to the castle. Much later that same day, Guillaume Hilairet asks Gilles de Sillé and Roger de Briqueville what has happened to his apprentice. They do not know a thing, they say, unless he left for Tiffauges; "a place," relates the said Sillé, "where

he thought that thieves had taken his said valet for a page."

Jean Jeudon, subpoenaed as a witness, confirms Hilairet's statements. These first witnesses' affirmations are confirmed by André Barbe, a shoemaker; by Jeannot Roussin and Jeanne (Aimery Édelin's widow); and, finally, by Macé Sorin and his wife, all of them from Machecoul. It will be seen how this last couple, just around the same period, had themselves complained of the disappearance of a child. Hilairet's deposition dates from September 28, 1440 (or one or two days after); he sets the date of the disappearance of Jean Jeudon's son at seven or eight years earlier. Hilairet's memory, therefore, would agree with the years 1432 or 1433. Further on one will see other disappearances which shall follow quickly after, assigning an appreciable probability to this date of 1432-1433 (pp. 258-261).

2. A child of Jeannot Roussin, aged nine, disappears while watching the animals in the countryside near Machecoul ("*es villages*" of Machecoul). He disappears, the witness remembers, precisely the day after the lamentations motivated by the disappearance of Jean Jeudon's son. Actually, it is impossible not to associate the disappearances which, following one after another, clearly lend a feeling of terror. Gilles de Sillé is as closely connected to the disappearance of Jeannot Roussin's child as to that of Jean Jeudon's son. The child knew Lord de Rais' accomplice well; someone had seen Gilles de Sillé speaking with him, wearing a long mantle and a veil over his face.

As for the date, the testimony of Jeannot Roussin declares that it happened "about nine years ago." We therefore ought to attribute this disappearance, and that of the first four known victims, to 1431 because the second is subsequent to the first and, as we shall see, the third and fourth follow closely after the second. But these extremely belated estimations are necessarily pretty vague; in addition, with Roussin's son having vanished at the age of nine, the figure nine could have passed from the age of the child to the number of years since his disappearance. Finally, the number eight (and even seven once) is used for the date in other cases of missing children that testimonies define with relative precision as contemporaneous (pp. 259-261).

3. Aimery Édelin's widow, Jeanne, formerly Jean Bonneau's wife, complains of the loss of her son, who was living with the plaintiff's mother opposite the castle of Machecoul. He was an eight-year-old schoolboy who "was very beautiful, very fair, and clever."

His disappearance happened unexpectedly, some eight years earlier, fifteen days before that of Macé Sorin's child, and after those of the children of Jean Jeudon and Jeannot Roussin. Macé Sorin and his wife are witnesses to the fact that this child was never seen again (pp. 260 and 261).

4. The disappearance of Macé Sorin's child is not attested to by the father himself; he does, however, in concert with his wife, depose to the disappearances of children belonging to Aimery Édelin's widow, Jeannot Roussin, Jean Jeudon (given then, apparently by mistake, as Guillaume Jeudon), and Alexandre Chastelier. Apparently, this is nothing but a gap in the documents handed down to us incomplete, since Jeanne (Aimery Édelin's widow) herself specifies that, fifteen days after the disappearance of Macé Sorin's child, Jeanne's disappeared in turn; this is the most precise fact. We must, however, point out an oddity. Macé Sorin and his wife suggest that the child of Jeanne (Édelin's widow) was not "of the said Sorin." Whatever the case, there must be a gap here which could explain this anomaly (pp. 258, 260, 261).

5. The disappearance of Alexandre Chastelier's son (pp. 257 and 259) is attested to by André Barbe, Guillaume Hilairet and his wife, and Macé Sorin and his wife. We are told that this disappearance took place "about that time" that the child of Édelin's widow vanished, fifteen days before the loss of Macé Sorin's son.

These first five testimonies indicate the considerable emotion generated by this series of abductions; such emotion that, eight years later, seven people remember what happened with sufficient precision. On the other hand, a short while after the abductions, people at Machecoul made very little effort to speak out for fear, said the shoemaker André Barbe (p. 257), of the men in Lord de Rais' chapel or others in his hire; the inhabitants feared imprisonment or abuse if their complaints became known. All of a sudden there is a great clamor in the region. In response, Gilles de Sillé invents a story: the children were led away to ransom his brother Michel, a prisoner of the English; the English had demanded a certain number of young boys to make pages (p. 261). But, the lie revealed, fear swiftly commands silence. The tongues loosen only at the trial. And at the trial eight years later, all the testimonies agree. The role bestowed upon Gilles de Sillé is the same in the parents' testimony as in Lord de Rais' confession. This Gilles de Sillé, a cousin of Gilles de Rais, belongs to the same family as Anne de Sillé, who belatedly married Jean de Craon. Gilles de Sillé is the companion of the monster of Machecoul, at the very latest from 1432 up until 1440, when the trial occurs, whereupon he successfully slips away in time. He leads the children to Gilles de Rais, and often kills them before his eyes. This latter never seems to experience difficulty turning his companions — later, his servants — into accomplices. Gilles de Sillé is the first. Then comes Roger de Briqueville, whom Lord de Rais cites immediately in his confession and whom the testimony of Guillaume Hilairet already mentions, bearing witness to the first attested abduction.

**1433**

Around July 10
La Trémoille's disgrace and the end of Gilles de Rais' career

By order of Charles d'Anjou, the son of Queen Yolande d'Aragon, and the nephew of Charles VII through marriage, Jean de Beuil (a captain in Yolande's service), Pierre de Brézé, and Prégent de Cöetivy (an important lord who will marry Gilles de Rais' daughter after 1440) abduct Georges de La Trémoille during the night and from a castle full of people. They kidnap him despite the presence of Charles VII in the castle; La Trémoille was his favorite. "In great danger of death," he is put up for ransom; he must swear never to return to court. Yolande d'Aragon and Constable de Richemont's party take the upper hand. Charles VII has an almost physical aversion to La Trémoille's adversary, the Constable; by contrast, he evinces the tenderest sentiments for Charles d'Anjou, then twenty years old. From then on, Yolande d'Aragon virtually rules. Charles VII allows his mother-in-law to act, whose son steps forward. Under these conditions, the energetic Arthur de Richemont, the true enemy of La Trémoille, is ready to effectively support the burden of war against the English.

Joan of Arc secured victory for the French, but only Richemont knows how to organize the situation. He alone can repair a situation compromised by La Trémoille's intrigues and personal politics. In any event, *his removal marks the end of Gilles de Rais' career.*

**1434**

March
The Sillé-le-Guillaume affair

After La Trémoille's disgrace, Marshal de Rais appears yet again in the royal army, in the Sillé-le-Guillaume affair where the French and English are content to size one another up without fighting. Constable de Richemont commands the royal army this time. He leads "Marshals de Rais and de Rieux, Lord de Rostrenen, and several knights and squires from Brittany and Poitou." Queen Yolande had sent her son, Charles d'Anjou, with men from the King's retinue who wanted to follow. Lords de Bueil, de Brézé, de Cöetivy, de Chaumont, and Viscount Thouars responded to the call.[10] The Duke of Alençon, Lord de Lohéac, and still others are there. Very few of the captains present, save Gilles de Rais, are not enemies of La Trémoille. This day is merely a demonstration of power on both sides, a parade. Immobile, the enemies observe one another without attempting to attack. Finally, the English retire to a neighboring village where they fortify themselves. They yield by mutual

[10] E. Cosneau, *op. cit.*, p. 208.

**(1434)**

agreement and return to Sablé whence they came. However, they attack the relatively unimportant city of Sillé a little later. Within three days the city capitulates. Richemont returns to court the day after.

For Gilles de Rais, the Sillé affair is a personal matter: on the one hand, Sillé is the fief of his stepmother, his grandfather's widow; and, on the other hand, the most faithful of his companions and accomplices in debauchery — we have spoken of him already (p. 86) — is Gilles de Sillé, Anne's cousin.

Gilles de Rais was seemingly determined to come out ahead in this affair.[11] The Angevins, en route from Maine, could admire his men. From now on he has — perhaps he has enriched the pomp after the death of his grandfather — a military company of excessive splendor. The decline of his career and the consciousness of his crimes doubtlessly invite him to appear with all the more luster, whereas in reality, without his possibly doubting it, his star is on the wane; distress must play a role in his growing magnificence and extravagance.

Spring . . .
The Burgundy expedition

However, La Trémoille, in disgrace, has retained numerous supports in spite of everything. His influence is now negligible, but it is still of the utmost importance in Gilles de Rais' life. The town of Grancey in Burgundy belongs to the Duke of Bourbon, who remains on good terms with La Trémoille. This town is being besieged by the Duke of Burgundy's troops, and La Trémoille has two companies of armed men in the town and region. He wants Marshal de Rais to raise the Siege of Grancey. Gilles needs money. La Trémoille lends him 10,000 royals, with the assurance that Charles VII will compensate him. Gilles collects a sufficient company of men in Brittany, and at Tours obtains from the King the mission to liberate Grancey. Charles VII has ceased calling his old favorite to meetings of council; all the same, he lends him support in this secondary enterprise. But Gilles at least feels he is finished; he knows he can expect nothing anymore from that quarter. He is confined to keeping up a false front. He places the troops under the direction of his young brother, René de La Suze, then twenty years old. From Tours he does not return to Orléans, as some have said, but to Poitiers.

August 15
Gilles, canon of Saint-
Hilaire of Poitiers

The town of Grancey surrenders on August 15th to Philippe le Bon's army.

The same day, Gilles — who Charles VII has put in charge of liberating the town of its besiegers — prepares to be received as canon of the

[11] A. BOURDEAUT, *op. cit.*, p. 76.

church of Saint-Hilaire of Poitiers. The abandonment of Grancey and the ceremony of Saint-Hilaire signify the final orientation taken in the life of this singular Marshal of France. Obviously, something in the violence of battle attracts Gilles. Certainly he excels at it. But soon he places the greatest interest in his taste for parades, where his magnificence shines. In the Sillé-le-Guillaume affair, he is noted for the beauty of his company of men-at-arms. From the moment he is Marshal of France, he maintains a splendid military family. He is rich, especially since the death of his grandfather in 1432. He is decidedly lost from the time of his grandfather's departure. His escort is that of a prince. The triumphant extravagance of great religious ceremonies intoxicates this criminal pederast even more. As on wine and strong drink, he gets drunk on *church hymns*. Liturgical offices have then, despite the ruins of war, an astonishing allure. They still have a fascinating quality diminished today by other spectacles. Jean de Bourdigné interrupts his recital of historic events to demonstrate the excellence of religious services in the cathedral of Angers that, during a stay in the city, Charles VII hears daily: "In France," says the chronicler, "there is no other church where the Lord's service could be celebrated more reverently, or the hymns, anthems, or other things one sings in church more deeply pitched and accentuated, or the ecclesiastical ceremonies performed with greater triumph . . ."[12] Assuredly, Gilles de Rais, who stayed frequently in the city, was familiar with these ceremonies in Angers; he must have observed and been fascinated by them, as he later must have been enraptured passing before the costumes of the canons of Lyon.

In any event, the visit to Poitiers sheds light on essential aspects of Gilles de Rais' life. The formation of his ecclesiastical entourage and office greatly preoccupies him. Now he travels in the company of men from his chapel, who follow on horseback. This must be the case, particularly on the day he is awarded an ecclesiastical dignity previously only awarded, among the laity, to the dukes of Aquitaine. Moreover, at Poitiers he keeps company with two young men whose voices he finds enchanting, whom he leads into his debauchery: André Buchet of Vannes, who at least twice procures for him two young victims; and Jean Rossignol of La Rochelle. Dressed as a canon, Gilles institutes on that day in the Saint-Hilaire church two stipends for these young men.

From Poitiers the Marshal-Canon returns to Orléans where, publicly, his extravagance runs away with him. He is in Orléans as early as

September 27
Stay at Orléans

---

[12] Jean de BOURDIGNÉ, *Histoire agrégative des annales et chroniques d'Anjou . . .* , fol. 137 verso.

**(1434)**

September 27th, when we know that certain of his servants stand guard for him. At this point, the impossibility of regulating his enormous expenditures has become banal.

Documents preserved in the notarial archives of Orléans, until the fires of 1940, provided precise information on these expenditures, with which Abbot Bossard's work[13] in part familiarizes us.

During his stay (or stays) at Orléans, Gilles de Rais is accompanied by his ecclesiastical entourage and his men-at-arms. He himself resides at the "Croix d'Or" Hotel which, rather than being a resting place for guests en route, must be put at his disposal as a private home. According to the bill of indictment of 1440, he and his cronies tried invoking evil spirits in this house (p. 174). His brother, René de La Suze, is lodged at the "Petit Saumon." His "college," which includes the ecclesiastic dignitaries of his chapel, is at the "Écu de Saint Georges," Guillaume Antes' place; his "cantor" at the "Enseigne de l'Épée," Jean Fournier's place; his men-at-arms and, among them, his herald, whom he has called Rais-le-Héraut, at the "Tête Noire," Agnès Grosvillain's place; his captain of the guard, Louis l'Angevin, called Louynot, at the "Grand Saumon," Guyot Denis' place; as well as other companions, among them the frightful Gilles de Sillé; his knights, Monsignors de Martigné and Foulques Blasmes, Jean de Rains, and Bauléis at the "Image de Sainte Marie-Madeleine"; Jean de Montecler at Colin le Godelier's place; his gunsmith, Hector Broisset, at the "Coupe," Macé Dubois' place; his and René's horses at the "Roche-Boulet" Hotel, run by Marguerite, Thévenon Hué's widow; his college's horses, the vicar of his chapel, Ollinet, a man named Petit-Jean, Father Le Blond, and his barber, at the "Enseigne du Fourbisseur," run by Jean Couturier, called Jeudi; Lord Jean de Vieille, his provost Boisoulier, a trumpeter named Georges, at Jeannette la Pionne's; Thomas, his "illuminator," at "Dieu d'Amour," Marguerite's place; still other servants are divided among the "Cheval Blanc," Charles de Halot's place, the "Homme Sauvage," Sébille la Trasilonne's place, and the "Écu d'Orléans," Foulques d'Estrapon's place.[14]

October

Scandalized by a life of dissipation, to which he attributes the capitulation of Grancey, La Trémoille fetches Gilles at Orléans. He wants them to go together to the aid of the Duke of Bourbon. The old favorite apparently has influence over the Marshal; together they reach Issoudun. From there they head toward the Bourbons, where the war continues

[13] E. BOSSARD, *Gilles de Rais, Maréchal de France,* pp. 70-77.

[14] *Op cit.,* p. 70.

between Charles VII's supporters and the Burgundians.

The Orléans documents utilized by Abbot Bossard[15] inform us of Gilles' passage to Montluçon in October. We know that he stays there until December, at the "Écu de France." There he signs a note for eight hundred and ten gold royals, of which he can only pay four hundred and ninety-five when leaving. He continues to travel with his troops, not to mention a considerable body of retainers. His expenditures have become such that he is in constant difficulty. Georges de La Trémoille continues to travel with him.

On this date, Gilles returns to Orléans for an indefinite length of stay. He signs a deed on December 28th. He was at Montluçon in October and stays in the region for a while with La Trémoille. He was able to return to Orléans as of November, where he remains until January.

December 28<br>Roger de Briqueville's<br>procuration

The deed he has drawn up on December 28th is strange, to say the least. He receives a very young cousin whose Norman family, loyal to Charles VII, was ruined by the English; the testimonies of Machecoul concerning 1432 or 1433 already mention this Roger de Briqueville. From 1432 onwards he gets his livelihood from Lord de Rais; with Gilles de Sillé, he becomes Gilles de Rais' counselor and companion in debauchery. According to the Marshal's own confession, it is not long after Gilles de Sillé that Briqueville is initiated into his secrets. On December 28, 1434, Gilles gives him an outrageous power of attorney. From then on Briqueville can act in his name; according to as he sees fit, he can sell his master's castles and lands in Brittany; what is more, he is fully empowered to negotiate and conclude the marriage of his master's daughter! Marie is then about four years old. According to Abbot Bourdeaut, it would be necessary to assume a night of debauchery and drunkenness in order to explain this scandalous power of attorney. At the least, the child's birthday at the end of 1429 coincides with the subsequent absence of a father who seems to no longer have relations with his wife . . .

**1435**

Gilles de Rais strives one last time, at least apparently, to keep his position in the game he began playing with La Trémoille. Traveling together, the cousins arrive at Forez just when peace is signed between Charles VII and Philippe of Burgundy.

Beginning of<br>February<br>Expedition against<br>Jean de Luxembourg

This peace, long desired by the King, puts an end to that war between the French that the assassination of Jean sans Peur on Montereau bridge

---

[15] E. BOSSARD, *op cit.*, pp. 77-78.

**(1435)**

had decidedly aggravated. Duke Philippe decided after seventeen years to forgive his father's murder, in which Charles VII must have been an accomplice. It was only a great lord's desire for personal vengeance that had mattered; the sufferings of the people did not. The peace treaty is finally signed at Nevers, February 5 and 6, 1435.

We have already said that La Trémoille and Gilles are in Forez. They decide to go together to Langres, then to Laon, where the fighting continues; Jean de Luxembourg, Phillip le Bon's ally, refuses peace. He persists in menacing Laon. Evidently La Trémoille hopes that by attacking him, and possibly liberating Laon, he can recover a little of the influence lost vis-à-vis Charles VII.

The two cronies' troops could have occupied themselves in the area, but money is short. Gilles, evidently in order to rid himself of La Trémoille, accepts going to Lyon and using his influence there to borrow money from bankers to pay the soldiers' back pay. Gilles returns to Langres with some resources, but as soon as it is a question of marching on Laon he comes up against the captains' refusal; the distributed money does not suffice. Gilles did not actually know how to handle money matters; he was swindled regularly. It would have been "clear in the eyes of many" that La Trémoille took advantage of his cousin's credulity and mad extravagance. La Trémoille is reproached for it, but he only laughs; "it is good," he said, "to encourage him to be bad . . ."

"A cynical phrase that shows in what degree of esteem Marshal de Rais was held by Charles VII's former minister and many others."[16] The fact remains that at Langres, Gilles once again abandons the affair in progress, leaving his brother the responsibility of leading the troops, if possible, to Laon. He leaves for Orléans under the pretext of seeking the wanted money. He even signs a declaration at Langres in which Champtocé will go to Georges de La Trémoille should he and his brother die heirless.[17] It is impossible to conclude from this, as Abbot Bourdeaut has done, that Gilles' intention was to bind himself more closely to Georges de La Trémoille. The clause is purely conventional. At the same time, Gilles decidedly abandons the path on which La Trémoille had started him.

February 26
Second stay at Orléans

At Orléans Gilles sells, or pawns, a silver head of Saint-Honoré.[18]

[16] A. BOURDEAUT, *op cit.,* p. 78.

[17] *Op. cit.,* p. 79.

[18] E. BOSSARD, *op cit.,* p. 78.

This transaction appears connected to the pretext given to La Trémoille, but in fact it inaugurates a series of transactions having no other explanation than a life of unbridled dissipation, which from here on out alone interests the Marshal.

Paradoxically, it is a pious endowment for the chapel at Machecoul that we ought to cite first in this dissipated life. Gilles has two Orléans notaries, Jean Caseau and Jean de Réconin, draw up a deed confirming the endowment of this chapel that, by the splendor of its ceremonies and the wealth of its clergy, rivaled a collegiate church and even a cathedral. The minute of this deed existed prior to 1940 in Orléans. Abbot Bossard reproduced a portion of it that we think we ought to cite here.

The text sheds light on one of the most curious aspects — the most disconcerting — in the life of the child killer: "Whereas noble lord, Monsignor Gilles, Lord de Rais, Count of Brienne, Lord of Champtocé and Pouzauges, Marshal of France, had recently, for the benefit and salvation of his soul, and in order that, before Our Lord Jesus Christ, it serve as a memorial to him and his deceased father, mother, relatives, friends, and benefactors, made an endowment to the memory of the Holy Innocents at Machecoul-en-Rais, in the duchy of Brittany; and whereas he had established and ordained a vicar, a dean, an archdeacon, a treasurer, several canons, a chapter, and a college in this endowment; and also whereas he had ordained and granted a lease for annuities, revenues, and possessions for their life and needs, in order that the divine service might be augmented and, from then on, performed and celebrated in the said place of Machecoul; and for this that the said Lord had and still has the good intention and firm purpose of maintaining the said endowment, which he has certainly demonstrated and demonstrates each day effectively, desiring with all his heart that the said vicar, dean, and chapter be after his death peacefully maintained and guarded in good possession and seizure, thus provided for and assigned to them by him as has been said, and the former preserved and defended against every oppression, this Lord has given to the King of Sicily and the Duke of Anjou, from whom he holds them in fief in respect of the duchy of Anjou, the castle and castlery of Champtocé, exclusive of the payment or toll house of the place where the said endowment is located, and he has given to the Duke of Brittany half of all the manor, barony, and land of Rais lest Madame Catherine de Thouars, the wife of the said Monsignor de Rais, or Mademoiselle Marie de Rais, his daughter, or other relatives, friends, heirs, and trustees, who in the name of the said young lady Marie or otherwise, with some claim or in some manner or for some

**(1435)**

reason whatsoever it might be, gainsay or obstruct the said endowment; in order that the said Lords King of Sicily and Duke of Anjou and Duke of Brittany might bear, support and defend them . . ."[19]

Certainly such clauses have very little meaning. In particular, the gift of Champtocé to La Trémoille (if Gilles should happen to die without an heir) is irreconcilable with that conditional bequest to King René. In both cases they are empty assertions. These words, however, show Gilles' attachment to the endowment that ruins him.

We have seen how the inhabitants of Machecoul, the parents of the innocent victims of its founder, were frightened by the thought that their complaints might reach the ears of the "men in Lord de Rais' chapel"! A chapel of the *Holy Innocents*, the haunt of a killer of children! This Jean Rossignol, this André Buchet, who participate in Gilles' butcheries, divinely singing in memory of the Holy Innocents!

A contemporary document, not included in the text of March 26, 1435, gives us precise information on so bloody a sanctuary. A record by which the heirs of Lord de Rais intend, after his death, to prove their kinsman's extravagance goes as follows: "Gilles kept a chapel of singers in his retinue wherever he went, in which he had twenty-five to thirty people, children, chaplains, young clerks, and others; he brought them with him on his travels so that his retinue comprised, on account of this chapel, including their servants, more than fifty people at his expense, and as many horses. Similarly, in this chapel he had a quantity of gold and silk cloth vestments, candlesticks, censers, crosses, plates, etc., of great sumptuousness, which cost three times their value, with several pairs of organs, one of which required six men to carry. And likewise the chapel included a dean, cantors, archdeacons, vicars, a schoolmaster, etc., as in the cathedrals, and one of them was called a bishop; to some he paid four crowns, to others three hundred, and he covered their expenses; he dressed them in trailing, scarlet robes with fine fur, etc., they wore fine, gray hats, lined with thin vair, etc., and there was nothing but vanity in their devotionless, orderless service. And when he was seized with a desire to prefer one of them, he gave him legacies, in addition to his wages, to that person's relatives even, as he had done to one Rossignol of La Rochelle, and a choirboy from Poitiers, to whom he gave the land of La Rivière, close to Machecoul, worth two hundred pounds in annuity; moreover, he gave his father and mother more than two hundred crowns."[20]

These mad expenditures have Gilles entering upon a path where he *ˌ*

[19] E. BOSSARD, *op. cit.*, pp. 61-62.

[20] Dom H. MORICE, *op. cit.*, vol. II, col. 1357-1358.

will founder. He cannot control these expenditures. Thus in Orléans he pawns personal property and real estate for hard cash. We have already seen him sell (or pawn) a silver reliquary on February 26th.

On April 16, 1435, he pawns "a cope, a vermilion baldachin, figured in green, inweaved with little gold birds, garnished with a hood and orphreyed in Paris with a chasuble and a dalmatic for a deacon."

He pawns "two hoods for church copes, the one embroidered with the Trinity, the other with Our Lady's coronation, a crimson, violet, velvet cope, with gold cloth, worked in images two by two, a figured black satin dalmatic with a silk cloth; a baldachin measuring thirteen ells, with little gold birds, from Cyprus."

April 30

We are unable to extract from the documents a specific fact touching on Gilles' participation in the 1435 festival in honor of Joan of Arc, but we have good reason to believe it was of paradoxical importance. Doubtless it accounts for that unheard quantity of gold crowns that vanished in a matter of months.

May 8
Gilles de Rais
The festival of Joan of Arc and the scandalous expenditures

In the first place, we know from the *Mémoire des héritiers* already cited (p. 94) that the theater played a very large role in his expenditures. He produced several sorts of pieces: "mysteries," "plays," "farces," "moresques," "impersonations," "moralities." The Marshal demanded sumptuous spectacles. "Each time he had them play, he had them dress in new outfits, depending on the piece." One could speak of the theater at this time as beautiful compositions in the style of tapestries. Here, as elsewhere, Gilles' desire for magnificence goes out of bounds. His need to dazzle was so great that under the scaffolds carrying the scene and decorations, which were necessary to build for each performance, he had wine and hippocras distributed, not to mention delicacies destined for the spectator.

We also know that at each anniversary following 1429 the liberation of Orléans was celebrated with a great festival; in any case, by a procession. For the year of 1435, we read in the city's accounts:

"To Guillaume Le Charron, to Michelet Filleul, as a donation made to them in order to help cover the cost of their scaffolds and other expenses incurred the eighteenth day of May 1435, when they put on certain mysteries on the boulevard of the bridge during the procession."

It evidently had to do with the *Mystère du Siège d'Orléans*.[21] This enormous theatrical machine, comprising more than twenty thousand

[21] *Le Mystère du Siège d'Orléans*. Published after the Vatican manuscript . . . This very long theatrical piece, which dates from the years following the siege, represents its various episodes.

**(1435)**

lines of verse and requiring close to five hundred actors, has fallen into oblivion. But it has been pieced together after a 15th-century French manuscript preserved in the Vatican library, where it evidently ran aground after the pillage in 1562 of the abbey of Saint-Benoît-sur-Loire, neighboring on Orléans. This mystery was composed not long after the events, by an Orléanais, and it was written to be performed, because scene directions are given with constant precision. But it could only be performed at Orléans, for the people of Orléans. Now another passage from the records shows us that, in fact, the episodes of the siege were performed in the city at just about the same time. This passage figures in the 1439 accounts:

"To Jehan Hilaire, for the purchase of a standard and a banner that belonged to Monsignor de Rais, to show in what manner the Tourelles were assaulted and taken from the English, the eighteenth day of May, VII Tournois pounds . . ."

It is difficult to imagine that the mystery that was played on the boulevard of the bridge in 1435 had nothing to do with the *Mystère du Siège d'Orléans*, if we are assured that during the same period the assault on the Tourelles was represented in Orléans. The fort of the Tourelles was the bridgehead. Therefore it is in the neighborhood of the bridge in both cases; yet the assault on the Tourelles is only the decisive episode of the siege and, by consequence, of the *Mystère du Siège d'Orléans*. That is not to say that the mystery was performed in its entirety, but at least one episode was played during the procession on May 8th.

Gilles de Rais' character plays an important part in the *Mystère du Siège d'Orléans*. His standard and banner are, in effect, necessary if one represents the assault of the Tourelles, where he distinguished himself. The city buys them in 1439. We cannot be sure who sold them to Jehan Hilaire; we know only "that they belonged to Monsignor de Rais," and that they belonged to him originally.

It is somehow certain that Gilles de Rais took part personally in the spectacles performed at the festivals honoring Joan of Arc in 1435 at Orléans. Under what conditions and the extent to which he took part are unknown to us. But the *Mémoire des héritiers*[22] informs us that during his stay at Orléans (which in two or more visits extends from September 1434 to August 1435) Gilles spends 80,000 to 100,000 gold crowns (hundreds of millions, maybe a billion, of our own money).

Moreover, our overall feeling is that his fortune was affected after the stay in Orléans. We know of his passion for magnificent spectacles and

[22] Dom H. MORICE, *op. cit.*, col. 1338.

96

how it ruins him. Therefore it is logical to suppose that he participated in the costs of spectacles given in May 1435. These last are exceptional; they never seem to have been repeated.

His expenditures, and the massive sales of domains that alone permitted him to meet them that year, are enough to rouse his family. In the tone that the Marshal has set, his brother and his cousin, André de Laval-Lohéac, obtain letters of interdict from Charles VII, dated from Amboise July 2, 1435. Gilles forfeits the right to sell his property and nobody is allowed to contract with him thereafter. This interdict is loudly proclaimed in every region where Rais is accustomed to staying: Orléans, Tours, Angers, Champtocé, Pouzauges, Tiffauges . . .

Already before this, at least during the Orléans period, the sales of important domains succeeded one another so rapidly that when the interdict did come — not that it was possible to "establish a balance sheet of the unfortunate baron's sales" — one can safely say that he had nothing left in Poitou except his wife's property, which custom withheld from his touch; nothing in Maine; nothing in Anjou, except Ingrandes and Champtocé. Only his property in Brittany remained for the most part intact.[23]

As he liquidates his domains, Gilles is reduced to every expedient. Thus he pawns gold candlesticks at Orléans on July 7th. They probably belonged to the Machecoul chapel.

He pawns to Charles de Halot, the innkeeper at the "Cheval Blanc," a certain number of extremely valuable objects for the sum of two hundred and sixty gold royals: a manuscript by Valerius Maximus; the *City of God*, in Latin, by Saint Augustine; a second copy of the *City of God*, this time in French; and two ecclesiastical copes, one of them damask, and a black satin chasuble.

Around the same time he pawns, this time to Jean Boileau, a fourth manuscript, Ovid's *Metamorphoses*; we understand that it was of parchment "bound in red leather, decorated with copper keys and a gilded silver clasp." This last manuscript, it is true, was recovered two years later.

Once more during his stay at Orléans he pawns his horses, even his own prized horse, Cassenoix; he pawns his wagons and harnesses.

---

[23] A. BOURDEAUT, *op. cit.*, pp. 86–87.

**(1435)**

August-September | Gilles leaves Orléans and retires to his lands, apparently in the region of Rais. Because of his excessive expenditures and the interdiction, he is creditless. He is, if not disgraced, at least profoundly impaired. Only those of his companions who live like parasites, greedy for his blind extravagance, remain about him.

Gilles de Rais'
military councils
Guillaume de La Jumelière
conclusively abandons him

A knight such as Guillaume de La Jumelière, who had followed him from the start, who had been with him at Orléans, where we know that he was at his service (Gilles installs him at the "Image de Sainte Marie-Madeleine"; he is cited in the documents under the name of Monsignor de Martigné), conclusively abandons him. This abandonment signifies the feeling of inconsistency and deviation that he now exudes.[24]

It could also be that Guillaume de La Jumelière, over and above the sales and scandalous squanderings, caught wind of the Marshal's criminal atrocities. The scandal evidently did not come to light in one day. The public rumor spreads only slowly. The poor folk do not speak without trembling; the lords keep quiet for another reason. Occasionally they act like the clergy, induced to throw a veil over the faults of one of their own: they condemn their faults, but they keep them quiet.

Year's end

The following testimony can, if necessary, be connected to his return from Orléans. But first it must be said that it cannot be taken too seriously. The notary public at the trial retained it, but its little sense can only serve to weaken the case for the accusation. If we mention it, like others of equal value, our purpose is to be thorough, and to take the opportunity to emphasize that the accusation rests *in toto* on those testimonies that are precise, whose number is in every way considerable.

At the trial in 1440, an inhabitant of Machecoul, Guillaume Hilairet, a witness of the first alleged disappearance (p. 258), claims to have "previously heard one of Rais' women, whose name he did not know, complaining at Machecoul of the loss of a child of hers." These words follow the statement of an event that the witness says dates back "about five years," that is theoretically to 1435. But this encounter with a stranger proves nothing and could have taken place on another occasion anyway (p. 259). Whatever the case, that vague recollection of a mother's lamentation gives a good indication of the atmosphere that must have developed in the region of Rais since the return of the man who dominated it under the protection of high walls.

[24] A. Bourdeaut, *op. cit.*, pp. 91, 92, and 93.

Gilles has entered into a violent quarrel with Michel de Fontenay, one of the two teachers to whom his father, drafting his will on his deathbed September 28, 1415, had been anxious to entrust him. Michel de Fontenay, an Angevin priest, out of friendship had seen to the publication in Champtocé, near the University of that city, of the royal letters interdicting Gilles. While passing through Angers, Lord de Rais abducts him. It was an act of violence whereby he publicly claimed authority he did not have. This abuse of authority was all the more crazed as Michel de Fontenay was an ecclesiastic and a notable. Gilles has him imprisoned at Champtocé, then at Machecoul; he probably would have come to the same end in these prisons as the unfortunate Gilles Meschin did in 1423 (p. 73). But because of protests from the Bishop, officers, and the University, Lord de Rais frees the man who had been in charge of his education since his childhood.[25]

*May*
*Assault on*
*Michel de Fontenay*

The family — primarily Gilles' brother, René de La Suze, and a cousin, André de Laval-Lohéac — is obviously resolved to oppose any deal that Jean V, the Duke of Brittany who openly refuses to abide by the letters of interdict, pursues with Gilles. Intending to respond in advance to the intentions of the two lords, who are bound to him by ties of vassalage, Jean V exacts an oath of fidelity from them.

*August 24 and 25*

Fearing the intrigues and, evidently, the preparation for attack on the part of these two lords, Jean V shows up in person at Machecoul. There he receives an oath of fidelity from the captains occupying garrisons belonging to Gilles in Brittany, which had not yet been sold: Michel de Sillé, Gilles de Sillé's brother, and his lieutenant, Jean de Dresneuc, of Machecoul; Conan de Vieilchatel of Saint-Étienne-de-Mermorte; Yvon de Kersaliou of Pornic; Valentin de Mortemer of Le Louroux-Bottereau. Captains like these might have been more faithful to his family than to Gilles himself.

*September 5*

Yolande d'Aragon's youngest son, Charles, governs Anjou in the name of his brother René, the King of Sicily, "the good King René," then prisoner of Philippe de Bourgogne; at the same time Charles is in fact, since 1433, Charles VII's prime minister. Charles d'Anjou, Count of Maine, holds an interview on September 13th with Jean V of Brittany and Constable de Richemont on the banks of the Loire at Ancenis.

*September 13*

[25]A. BOURDEAUT, *op. cit.*, pp. 95, 96.

**(1436)** Gilles de Rais is still able to sell his lands within the limits of the duchy of Brittany where, as we have seen, an important portion of his fortune remains. But above all he still possesses, in Anjou, the beautiful fortresses of Ingrandes and Champtocé that Jean V would like to acquire at any cost; Champtocé, on the Loire, is in a sense the key to Brittany. Champtocé is disputed at Ancenis in the presence of Gilles' brother, René, now a lieutenant of Constable de Richemont, and André de Lohéac, his cousin, who helps him defend the family's interests. Dunois and Jean de Bueil also are present at this conference. The question of Champtocé, posed by Gilles' financial distress, is of first-order importance. Apparently Jean V only wants to buy time. We do not know what he does to appease them, but he agrees to exchange letters of alliance with Yolande d'Aragon's son. He does not intend to observe them! Alliance, fidelity are sworn to on both sides, but nobody intends to keep his word!

**1437**
Near the beginning of the year Gilles de Rais' valets Poitou and Henriet

Étienne Corrillaut, called Poitou, originally from Pouzauges, becomes Gilles de Rais' valet. He is not yet twenty years old. According to Poitou's deposition at the ecclesiastical trial (p. 228), Gilles has intercourse with him from the moment he enters his service; after which Gilles wants to kill him and had picked up a dagger to do so, but Gilles de Sillé prevented him, explaining how beautiful a lad he was and that he must keep him. But in his confession at the civil trial (p. 279), it is said that ten years after having entered Gilles' service (he entered his service then sometime around 1427), he saw two dead children in his master's room; Gilles wanted to kill him, but Briqueville and Sillé prevented him. Gilles then had sexual intercourse with him and made him take an oath never to reveal what he had seen or would see (pp. 228 and 279). He will observe Gilles' secret, that he often cut the throats of his victims, and he will become his procurer; he will be hanged at the same time as his master (p. 138).

The other valet, the Parisian Henriet Griart, is at this time in Lord de Rais' service as of three years, but he has not been introduced to his master's secrets. A little later Poitou will be trusted with doing so.

Murder of Catherine Thierry's brother

Shortly into 1437, Catherine, the wife of a painter named Thierry, living in Nantes, entrusts her brother to Henriet with the intention that he be admitted to the master's chapel at Machecoul. He is the first child whom Henriet, according to his confession, had led to Machecoul into the room where he is killed. Henriet does not seem to have understood at first what is going on. In the first place, his master asks him to take an oath: he must not repeat what he is about to learn. Thereupon he is surprised, according to his confession, at the disappearance of Catherine Thierry's brother. It is then that Henriet suspects: Gilles himself killed the child.

Poitou and Henriet's testimonies agree but, according to Henriet, this murder happened three years before the trial. Poitou speaks of four. These differing versions alone permit us to deduce the approximate dates on which Poitou, then Henriet, became their master's accomplices (pp. 227, 235, 276).

René d'Anjou, a prisoner of Philippe de Bourgogne, is freed January 28th. He returns at once to Anjou. On his return, René de La Suze and André de Lohéac ask him to affirm his opposition to the possible sale of Ingrandes or Champtocé, citing Gilles de Rais' acts of violence and banditry: was his mother not robbed by his men? René d'Anjou declares Champtocé confiscated to his profit; then he obtains a signed and sealed promise from Jean V not to buy the land. Jean V will even swear "over our Lord's dead body during the singing at Mass."[26]

Jean V does not stop, for all that, to discuss the terms of sale with Lord de Rais!

> February or March

By Breton custom, Jean V had no right to buy his vassals' lands. It is in the name of his son Pierre, therefore, that he buys the manor of La Bénate for ten thousand crowns. He gives sixty pounds to Prince, Gilles' herald of arms, who has served his interests in this affair. But he runs into the opposition of Anne de Sillé; during his lifetime, Jean de Craon, whose widow she now is, had in fact assigned this land which belonged to him as a dowry to his wife.

> May 26

Having learned of Jean V and Gilles de Rais' deals but resolved to decide the issue, René de La Suze and André de Laval-Loeheac take Champtocé. Gilles takes fright and, fearing an attack on Machecoul, requests Gilles de Sillé and Robin Romulart to remove "from a tower near the lower hall" of the fortress the "bones of forty children or thereabouts" and burn them. Later, according to Poitou, Gilles de Sillé said to him and Henriet: "Wasn't Milord Roger de Briqueville a traitor to have asked Robin Romulart and me to watch Lady Jarville and Thomin d'Araguin through a slit when we removed the said bones?" (p. 238). Evidently Briqueville's noble friends were attracted by an unhealthy curiosity. The story need not be invented; it responds to the sensation

> October
> Gilles' family takes control of Champtocé
>
> Gilles has the children's bones burned at Machecoul

[26] A. BOURDEAUT, *op. cit.*, p. 98.

**(1437)**

that Lord de Rais' crimes provoked in the seigneurial world: rather vague indignation, outright scandal, occasionally an unspeakable disturbance. The number of accomplices that Gilles easily finds at his service alone illustrates to him that his crimes were then not so monstrous; all in all, it had to do with a great lord and miserable children. Justice reacted on the occasion of another affair; under certain political circumstances, justice might have closed its eyes.

*November*
*Gilles' family takes*
*Machecoul and discovers*
*the skeletons of two*
*children*

The bones are burned fifteen days or three weeks before Lords de La Suze and de Lohéac arrive at the castle of Machecoul (p. 229). Gilles' brother and cousin take Machecoul in November. In spite of Gilles de Sillé's and Robin Romulart's cleaning efforts, one could still find the skeletons of two children in that lower part of the tower from which forty victims' bones were removed. The captain of one of the companies who took the garrison asks Poitou and Henriet if they knew about this. In their deposition, the valets say that they responded no: Gilles "had not revealed his secrets" to them yet. Obviously they are lying. If they had not been privy to his secrets until after the taking of Machecoul, that is, logically, since the transfer from Champtocé (p. 275), they would have been initiated together. But as we have seen, Poitou initiated Henriet (p. 100).

Evidently the discovery of skeletons played a role in the rumors that started growing from that moment. This time, those in the know apparently are lords; and not just Gilles' relatives, but his enemies.

*November 2*

Jean V, alarmed, feared seeing Anjou enter into war with Brittany. Jean de Bueil could invade his territory from Sable. That is why the Duke calls for a reunion in Vannes of all the vassals in the duchy, among them Lords de Rohan, de Châteaubriant, de Malestroit, and de Rais. Jean V exchanges letters of brotherhood in arms with Gilles. He removes the lieutenant generalship of Brittany from André de Laval-Lohéac, his brother-in-law, giving it to the man whom he has just made a brother in arms under the pretext of services rendered. There is, he thinks, a plot by Laval against him . . .

Even though Arthur de Richemont is occupied with war against the English, his brother asks for his help against Laval-Lohéac. He definitely intends to get his hands on Champtocé.

*December 25*

Gilles stays at Vannes, where Jean V holds court. He is now reduced to the very self-serving, sole protection of this grasping feudal lord. Henceforth he is burned on all sides, and Jean V's pretended friendship

102

will not prevent the latter in the near future from handing Gilles over to the judges at Nantes. But at this moment Gilles is at Vannes with his chapel; they sing the Divine Office before the Duke on Christmas.

Gilles signs a pact with Jean V; he hands over Champtocé in exchange for one hundred thousand gold crowns. His fortune is on the brink and this is the last chance he has to turn it around. But, to begin with, Gilles must recapture the castle that his brother now occupies. To that end he enters into tortuous transactions with the latter. In coordination with René d'Anjou, the royal power tries to substitute René de La Suze. But the brothers slyly succeed in coming to terms; René will cede the fortress, pretending to defend it, while Gilles will give him seven thousand gold crowns and the possession of La Mothe-Achard in exchange.

**1438**

February-March
Murder of Guillaume Delit

Guibelet Delit's son, Guillaume, frequented the Hotel de La Suze, where he helped Gilles' chef, named Cherpy, roast meat. According to his mother, named Jeanne, a certain Master Jean Briand, who was staying at the hotel in Gilles' service, told Cherpy that it was not a good idea to let the child help in this manner. Afterwards she never saw the child again, nor had any news of him.

That happened in February or March of 1438, as related at the trial of 1440 ("a year ago last Easter"). Three or four months later (around May), she complains to Jean Briand's wife. "They say," she affirms, "that Lord de Rais has small children caught to be killed." No sooner said, Gilles' men appear, the names of whom she does not know. Jean Briand's wife speaks to them: according to Jeanne Delit, Lord de Rais had the children killed; she adds that Jeanne is wrong to speak like this, something bad could happen to her.

With that, the miserable Jeanne apologizes before Gilles' men (p. 269).

Around June
Gilles de Rais' recovery
of the Champtocé garrison
and transportation to
Machecoul of three
coffers filled with children's
skeletons

At a date difficult to specify, René de La Suze abandons, as agreed, the Champtocé garrison to his wife, whom he had instructed accordingly. Twenty of Gilles' armed men under Yves de Kersaliou, the captain of Pornic, put on an act of defending the garrison. Jean de Malestroit, the Bishop of Nantes and Chancellor of Brittany, who later indicts Gilles, will take possession of it in Jean V's name. But before this can happen, Gilles has requested five of his manservants — Gilles de Sillé, Hicquet de Brémont, Robin Romulart, and the two valets Henriet and Poitou — to proceed to the tower of the fortress and remove the skeletons of some forty children. They place them in three coffers which they take "as secretly as possible" to Machecoul, partly by water. At Machecoul two singers in Gilles' chapel, Jean Rossignol and André Buchet, whom we have mentioned above (p. 89), replace Hicquet de Brémont and Robin Romulart. It is at Machecoul where the bones are burned; they cannot be burned at Champtocé, the fortress about to be handed over without delay to the Duke. Henriet and Poitou's testimonies inform us that "the bones were already desiccated . . . because of the length of time" they had spent in the tower. We do not know exactly when the children had been killed. We should only think they were made to leave as of autumn of 1432, after the death of Jean de Craon (pp. 82-83).

Evidently Gilles was then supposed to return to Vannes under the pretext of receiving from the Duke what was his due, which, we can be sure, came to nothing; as a matter of fact he held on to his Breton domains, which he had previously pawned for money. Apparently the advances he received on these domains were equivalent to the value of Champtocé. But it is perhaps on this occasion that André Buchet, who, as we have seen, belonged to Lord de Rais' chapel, sent a child, nearly nine, dressed as a page from Vannes to Machecoul through a certain Raoulet. In principle, the settlement of accounts should have followed upon the recovery of Champtocé (pp. 228, 236, 277). We know from Henriet's testimony that André Buchet sent the child when Gilles received money from the Duke for Champtocé; but Gilles could have pretended to receive it.

Around June 16
Murder of Jean
Jenvret's son

Jean Jenvret and his wife complain of the disappearance of their son, a schoolboy of nine, who occasionally frequented the house of La Suze. Lord de Rais was at Nantes, in that house, at the moment of this disappearance "two years ago, eight days before Saint John the Baptist's Day," (around June 16, 1438). Jean Jenvret was staying with Monsieur d'Étampes, that is to say that he was a domestic for Richard, Count d'Étampes, the brother of the Duke of Brittany.

Before dying in the prison at Nantes, Perrine Martin, the most famous of Gilles' procuresses, confesses to having led the child to the castle at Machecoul. Poitou himself affirms that he could have killed him in the house of La Suze. Perrine Martin perhaps only took the cadaver to Machecoul. Four witnesses of the Sainte-Croix parish of Nantes knew this child; they heard his parents lamenting his disappearance and, since then, they have never seen him again (pp. 267, 268, and 281).

On or about June 24
Murder of Jean, Jeanne
Degrepie's son

A twelve-year-old schoolboy, Jean, the son of Jeanne Degrepie, Regnaud Donete's widow, of the parish of Notre-Dame-de-Nantes, disappeared on or about Saint John's Day (June 24, 1438); Gilles de Rais was then staying at Hotel de La Suze, where the child sometimes came. Perrine Martin is supposed to have led him to Gilles' room; Gilles is supposed to have ordered her to lead him to the doorman at Machecoul, which she is supposed to have done. The mother and six people from the same parish testified to that disappearance (pp. 155, 161, 266, 269-270, and 273-274).

According to the testimonies, Jean and Nicole Hubert's son, named Jean like his father, was killed by Gilles de Rais at Hotel de La Suze. Of all the presumed victims of Gilles de Rais, this Jean Hubert, age fourteen, is without a doubt the one which the depositions allow us to know the fate of the most precisely. In the spring of 1438 he still lives with his parents, Jean and Nicole, in the Saint-Léonard parish of Nantes. Later they move to the Saint-Vincent parish. The child continues going to school, at least until his parents entrust him to a certain Mainguy, with whom he lodges. But this Mainguy dies and Jean returns to his parents. We are approaching Saint John's Day (June 24, 1438).

Around June 26
Murder of Jean Hubert

A man named Pierre Jacquet (or Jucquet), better known as Prince, is staying in Nantes at this time; he is the herald of arms in Gilles' retinue.

He could have acquired the nickname Prince on account of his family's origin: Prince, or Prinçay, was a village not far from Chémeré, where Lord de Rais had a castle and stayed occasionally.

Sometime around June 17th, this Prince "employs" the young and "very beautiful" Jean Hubert. He makes him fine promises; he will be his page, and not only the child but his parents will benefit greatly by this.

The child recounts to his parents how Prince, his master, is frightened of his own horse; he does not dare to mount it for fear of being killed . . .

The "employment" lasts eight days, until Saint John's Day. But already the parents have reason to be disappointed. The child should have been better lodged, and the promises are not kept. Prince stops speaking of retaining him; the parents would like him to return to school. In fact, Prince hands the child over to Gilles' valet Henriet Griart, who leads him to the Hotel de La Suze where he meets a gentleman, evidently a Scotsman, in Gilles' military retinue. Little Jean speaks of him as a "proper gentleman," and the parents' testimony calls him Spadine (which probably corresponds to Spalding).

Little Jean expects to benefit from "Spadine" also; this "proper gentleman" is expected to leave with him for a distant land. We are forced to anticipate his approaching disappearance . . . Spadine is apparently charged with seducing the child who seems, to the master's handymen, to agree with his tastes. Henriet, on the other hand, speaks of making the child into one of Gilles' valets, in the place of Poitou, who was going to retire and go home. Promises cost nothing to smooth talkers; they knew his death was imminent . . .

Whatever the case, the parents accept everything, having been reassured by Spadine. (In fact, in the capacity of both accomplice and killer, Spadine figures in the bill of indictment; but, apparently by escape, he seems to have avoided arrest).

Little Jean could have run into Spadine at La Suze as of June 18th. On the 17th he is still with Princé, whom he leaves the same day, provided with Spadine's assurances. He spends the night with his parents, who give their consent; from then on he will take up quarters at Hotel de La Suze, where he lodges until his death eight days later, when he is violently slain with the Marshal's *braquemard*.

Moreover, during these last seven days the parents see him continually . . . This is when Gilles "was absent for four or five days," leaving some of his men and the child at the Hotel de La Suze. Having returned, the great lord admits the valet into his room to clean and shows him kindness, gives him some white wine to drink, has Spadine provide him again . . . with a round loaf of bread especially baked for him. Again the child gives his mother the loaf, telling her that Spadine wants him to stay with him, to ride with him in the company of Lord de Rais, and the mother says that it is all right. The child said goodbye to his mother several times that day and, in fact, "left . . . the very next day," and she never saw him again nor knew what became of him. This final separation would have taken place June 26th, 1438, the Thursday following Saint John's Day.

If we can trust the parents' testimony of what happened after June 26th, Lord de Rais stayed fifteen days at Nantes in his hotel. Then Spadine sends for the father, asking him what happened to the child. Stupefied, the father demands his child back from the "proper gentleman." He entrusted little Jean to Spadine. Now the father, taken for a fool, is accused of having lost the child himself. The parents complain several times to Lord de Rais' men. They are told that a Scotsman, who was very fond of him, led him away. Spadine gone, these men pretend to think that he had taken the child away! Desperate now, the father returns to Princé; Princé was to blame, he "had committed a mortal sin for not having really tended and governed the child." Princé responds that it is not his problem and that "he was undoubtedly with a proper gentleman, who would do him much good."

People from Nantes who know Hubert and his wife well come to testify; they say that before Saint John's Day in 1438 they saw the child at home, but that after this date his parents were lamenting his loss, and that no one has seen him again.

Gilles de Rais himself, in his confession, acknowledged killing or causing to be killed two pages, one of them belonging to Pierre Jacquet, commonly called Princé, about eighteen months earlier (theoretically, in the spring of 1440).

The two valets' testimonies corroborate their master's. Poitou declares that he delivered him "to be a valet" in his place. Henriet specifies that Gilles abused the child "sexually and shamefully, in his unnatural lust," until he finally killed him by his own hand (pp. 155, 161, 200, 227, 236, 267, 269, 272 and 273).

Jean Fougère's son, from the Saint-Donatien parish near Nantes, is very beautiful; he is twelve years old; he is lost in the month of August 1438, and nobody knows what happened to him. True, nothing proves that Gilles de Rais was responsible for his disappearance. We do not even know whether he was at Nantes then (p. 269). *August*

Returning from Vannes, apparently on his way to Machecoul, Lord de Rais stops at Roche-Bernard, where he stays with a certain Jean Colin. Poitou obtains consent from Peronne Loessart to entrust her ten-year-old son to him. A schoolboy, he is one of the most beautiful children in the region. Poitou promises Peronne that he will continue sending the child to school, where he learns so well. Poitou was to provide the unfortunate child "with many advantages." He adds that the child "would be the source of numerous benefits" for Poitou himself. Moreover, Poitou promises Peronne one hundred sous for a dress. But a little later, Poitou gives her four pounds. Peronne responds that one pound is missing, one hundred sous making five pounds. Poitou denies this; he never promised five pounds. Thereupon the valet escorts the young Loessart to Jean Colin's house. He is charged with escorting him to Machecoul where, as Poitou himself testifies, he will have his throat cut. *September / Murder of Peronne / Loessart's son*

The day after the child is delivered, Peronne sees her son and Lord de Rais leaving the house of Jean Colin together. Speaking to the great lord, the mother attempts to get her child back. But Gilles does not deign to respond. He turns to Poitou, who is there: "the child," he says, was "well chosen" because he is "as beautiful as an angel." "Not long after this," he accompanies the murderer "on a pony that the said Poitou had bought from Jean Colin."

**(1438)**

This last fellow and his wife Olive testify at the trial; they confirm that in the month of September 1438 Gilles de Rais, coming from Vannes, lodged with them, and that Poitou obtained consent from Peronne Loessart to entrust her son to him. Two or three months later, Colin comes across the pony ridden by another. To the women complaining of no news of the child, some of Lord de Rais' men respond that he is at Tiffauges while others say that he is dead. He died, they say, crossing over the bridges of Nantes: "the wind had blown him into the river." They pretend, finally, that Poitou left the region, that he went in the direction of Redon (pp. 253, 254).

Around September

The son of Jean Bernard, of Port-Launay, on the right bank of the estuary near Coueron, is about twelve years old; he leaves for Machecoul around September 1438 to ask for alms. The four witnesses from Port-Launay who remember him cite "the charity that was customary there" In fact Port-Launey is fifteen kilometers from Nantes, where one must cross the Loire; from there, Machecoul is another forty kilometers. That implies, in any case, the notoriety of alms-giving by the prodigal of Machecoul. Jean Bernard's child does not reappear; another child, with whom he went begging, waits for him in vain more than three hours, even though they were supposed to meet at an appointed spot in the Machecoul borough. Nobody had any more news of him and the witnesses heard the mother, who could not come to the tribunal because of the grape harvest, "complaining bitterly" (p. 256).

October
Murder of Perrot Dagaye

Perrot Dagaye, aged about ten, the son of Éonnet Dagaye and the nephew of Éonnet Le Charpentier, a butcher in the parish of Saint-Clément-hors-les-murs of Nantes, disappears in October 1438. Two witnesses from the parish of Saint-Clément attest to the mother's laments and to the fact that the child was never seen again after this. Tiphaine, Éonnet Le Charpentier's wife, declares that her nephew Perrot "was lost about two years ago and that since this time, she has had no news of him until Perrine Martin, also known as La Pellissonne, admitted, as has been said, that she had delivered him over to Lord de Rais' men" (p. 270).

**1437-1438**

Jeanne, Aimery Édelin's widow, of Machecoul, who had previously lost her own son (p. 260), reports that "about two or three years before, she saw at Machecoul a man named Oran, who lived in the direction of Saint-Mesme, lamenting piteously and crying over the loss of a child; he was asking about him in the said place of Machecoul but so far as the said Jeanne knows, had no news of him" (p. 260).

Contrary to the promise made when his brother René let him retake **Around year's end**
Champtocé, Gilles refused to release La Mothe-Achard to him. More-
over, he seizes the Saint-Étienne-de-Mermorte castle, which he had given
him in 1434.

**1439**

An amiable settlement is concluded at Nantes between the two broth-   **January 15**
ers who, after the Saint-Étienne-de-Mermorte affair in 1438, have gone
to court. Gilles definitively transfers La Mothe-Achard to his brother
while keeping Saint-Étienne for himself.

The eight-year-old son of Micheau and Guillemette Bouer, of Saint-   **April 12**
Cyr-en-Rais, a village adjoining Bourgneuf-en-Rais, goes begging at
Machecoul on Low Sunday (April 12) of 1439. He does not return and
from then on his mother will have no more news of him, even though
the child's father "had made inquiries after him in various places." There
is no implicit connection to an event that Guillemette Bouer reports
later, namely: "on the following day, the day they distributed alms at
Machecoul for the deceased Mahé Le Breton, as she was watching the
animals, a large man dressed in black, whom she did not know, came to
her and asked, among other things, where her children were, why they
were not watching the animals. To which she responded that they had
gone begging at Machecoul. Whereupon he left her and vanished." The
story reconstructs, however, the fairy-tale atmosphere in which the disappearances occurred, one which does not always permit calling Lord de
Rais into question with certainty.

Ysabeau, Guillaume Hamelin's wife, of Fresnay, who herself loses two
children at the end of the year (p. 263), learns of the above disappearance on December 16, 1439. There is a good case, therefore, for Low
Sunday of 1439 and not 1440 (p. 263).

Gilles de Rais is living at Tiffauges during this period, so his connection with the disappearance is at best doubtful.

Prelati and Blanchet arrive together at Saint-Florent-le-Vieil, on the   **End of April**
right bank of the Loire. They spend several days there. Gilles, informed   **François Prelati's arrival**
by Blanchet of their arrival, dispatches two squires, accompanied by   **in France**
Henriet and Poitou, in order to lead them to Tiffauges (pp. 210 and
210).

## (1439)

<table>
<tr>
<td style="vertical-align:top; text-align:right; width:20%">

May 14
Prelati at Tiffauges

</td>
<td>

Later, on Ascension Day (May 14, 1439), François Prelati arrives at Tiffauges, accompanied by Blanchet and others. Gilles de Rais exuberantly rejoices at what Blanchet tells him.

Prelati and Blanchet are installed in the castle, in the same room with an alchemist (a goldsmith from Paris named Jean Petit) and an old woman named Perrote. They are supposed to lodge in the castle together. In fact, a little later there is a problem with a cold wind that, coming from a neighboring hall (the lower hall of the fortress), passes through "the said castle" (p. 217).

</td>
</tr>
<tr>
<td style="vertical-align:top; text-align:right">

Around May

</td>
<td>

Guillaume Sergent and his wife Alyette, of La Boucardière, a hamlet neighboring on Machecoul, connected to the Saint-Croix parish of Machecoul, who around Pentecost (May 24) of 1439 went digging in a field in order to plant hemp, did not find their eight-year-old son again, whom they had left at home to watch over their infant daughter of eighteen months. They had no more news of him in spite of their inquiries in the Machecoul parish and other parishes (p. 258). Gilles de Rais is presently installed at Tiffauges; this testimony therefore is of little interest.

</td>
</tr>
<tr>
<td style="vertical-align:top; text-align:right">

June 29

</td>
<td>

Olivier Darel, the son of Jean and Jeanne Darel, of the Saint-Saturnin parish of Nantes, aged seven to eight, disappears on Saint Peter's Day. He disappears into the crowd, on Rue du Marché or in front of Saint-Saturnin church, while he is with his maternal grandmother. The father, ill that day, declares that he inquired about him in several regions; his wife and her mother testify with him. Éonnette, Jean Bremant's wife, living in the marketplace of Nantes, knew the child well and declares that, since the time when his parents were complaining of his disappearance, he never returned home (p. 272).

Gilles de Rais being, so far as it seems, at Tiffauges, this testimony is no more important than the previous one.

</td>
</tr>
<tr>
<td style="vertical-align:top; text-align:right">

Around June
The phony Joan of Arc in Gilles de Rais' service

</td>
<td>

On a date difficult to specify, but evidently before the spring of 1439, Gilles receives a phony Joan of Arc, a double, who since 1436 is seeking to make people believe that, having escaped the executioner's flames in Rouen, she is truly "The Maid."[27] This phony Joan of Arc is, like the original, able to ride a horse and command armies; Gilles entrusted her

</td>
</tr>
</table>

----

[27] J. QUICHERAT, Procès . . . de Jeanne d'Arc, vol. V, pp. 319 and ff.

110

with a part of his men-at-arms, with a view towards an enterprise in the direction of Mans. But in the course of 1439 it seems this phony Maid is unmasked by Charles VII, who wanted to meet her. The King quizzes her about the secret they had between them. Thereupon the impostor, who meanwhile has married and after her marriage goes by the name of Lady des Armoises, kneels before Charles VII and confesses her deceit.[28] Gilles, having no doubt found out, sends one of his men, the Gascon captain Jean de Siqueville, to take her place, instructing him to operate in the expectation of his arrival and, if he can, seize the Mans garrison. It is probable that the Marshal does not even try to join him. Mans remains in the hands of the English until 1448.

Gilles de Rais and François Prelati, aided by Gilles de Sillé, Eustache Blanchet, Henriet and Poitou, prepare the large lower hall of the castle at Tiffauges for an invocation of the demon. After dinner, before midnight, they trace several circles with the tip of a sword on the ground where they inscribe crosses, characters, and signs "in the manner of armories." Then Eustache Blanchet and Henriet carry in incense, myrrh and aloes, a lodestone, earthen pots containing a great quantity of coal, which they light, torches, candles, and candlesticks. They also carry in a book in which one can find the names of many demons, and formulas of conjuration and invocation. Gilles and François arrange these various objects; François adds certain signs, then has the four windows of the hall opened.

Around June-July
The great invocation in the lower hall of the castle at Tiffauges

Thereupon Eustache Blanchet, Henriet, and Poitou are asked to retire to Lord de Rais' room. From then on Gilles and François, left alone, remain — sometimes standing, sometimes sitting, and sometimes kneeling — while adoring the demon and reading from the book that they have brought. However the demon does not appear, and two hours after having been left alone, Gilles and François rejoin the others in the room where they wait. It is about one o'clock in the morning (pp. 173, 217, 219, 230, 238, 239, 278 and 280).

It is apparently at this invocation that Gilles holds in his hand a note that he has signed, ready to give it to the devil should he appear. Since the latter does not appear, the note is not delivered (p. 198). We do not have the text of that note, but it is doubtless the same as what, on the following evening, Prelati prepares to offer to Barron if he appears. (We are familiar with the second note's text, several lines of which we will cite later.) The note is still undelivered the following day, but since Gilles in

[28] J. QUICHERAT,, *op. cit.,* vol. V, p. 281.

**(1439)**

his confession acknowledges having had one delivered to the devil (p. 194), we are forced to conclude that Prelati pretended to deliver it during one of the ten or twelve invocations that he did for Gilles, and where Barron, according to him, appeared (p. 213).

*Nocturnal invocation in a field under adverse weather*

Rather late the following evening, by Gilles' order, François Prelati and Poitou make their way to a field not far from an uninhabited old house, about a kilometer from Tiffauges in the direction of Montaigu. They carry incense, a lodestone, and a book. They make a circle and signs out of the book with the aid of a knife. They themselves enter the circle that they evidently have traced in the soil. In spite of François' interdiction, Poitou secretly crosses himself. Oral invocations having begun, the valet hears Prelati pronounce the name of "Barron" several times in a loud voice. They stay about half an hour, but nothing appears.

From the start, the moment they enter the circle it rains profusely; a violent wind then starts up, and so great a darkness falls that they have difficulty returning once finished (pp. 198, 212 and 231).

What is more, we know from Prelati's testimony (p. 213) that before this invocation, Gilles had given him this letter (or note) for the devil written in French in his own hand, of which this is the text: "Come at my bidding, and I will give you whatever you want, except my soul and the curtailment of my life." The devil did not come, and François, that same day, returns the note to Gilles.

Gilles and François want to try another invocation by other means, but they give up the attempt for lack of a particular stone (p. 211). They content themselves with repeating the attempts which Gilles no longer attends. Here we should emphasize that in Gilles' absence the devil does not fail to appear, according to Prelati's confession. In renewing these invocations, arranged in the same way as the ones at the beginning in the lower hall of Tiffauges, "the devil named Barron" is said to have appeared "as many as ten or twelve times, in the form of a handsome young man about twenty-five years old" (p. 301).

*May to November Prelati beaten by the devil*

Moreover, it is right around the same time that we place another of Prelati's invocations, where the charlatanism that Gilles apparently never perceived is clearly revealed. In any event, this invocation takes place during the period when, in 1439, Blanchet is staying at the castle of Tiffauges: between Ascension Day (May 14) and All Saints' Day (November 1). The ecclesiastic, having left that same day, is summoned by his master. He runs to Gilles and finds him in shock. Lord de Rais is convinced: Prelati is dead! In fact, there was a loud noise in Prelati's room

112

and they heard a great many groans and blows, "as if someone were beating a featherbed." His horror of the devil is then so great that Gilles is terrified. He does not dare enter the room and weakly asks Blanchet to do it in his stead. The latter trembles no less than his master. Blanchet at last has the courage to look through a kind of interior window rather high up, from which one can peer into the room. Prelati does not respond to the calls; he is content with multiplying his groans. When he finally exits the room, the pitiful man, he recounts how the devil *beat him horribly*. He is wounded; he will remain ill for a week. Gilles himself nurses him, not letting anyone enter his room. He has him confessed. Prelati thinks that the punishment he has received is due to the anger of the spirits indignant with him for having, in his conversations, held them for demons of little consequence and little power. Doubtless it is for this reason that he attempts a kind of reparation; he had heard it said, so he says anyway, that the said spirits were "begotten from material nobler than the Blessed Virgin Mary" (p. 223).

This comedy gives a fair idea of Gilles' credulity. It is also necessary to say that sympathy and affection then motivated this credulity. Prelati is twenty-two years old, eleven years younger than his master, who is apparently charmed by Italy and her culture, and fascinated by the Devil and those who can invoke him. In addition, the young Prelati must have had a personal charm, the charm of a rake. In his confession, Gilles will declare that he was clever; he spoke Latin eloquently, was agreeable, and worked zealously at the tasks that his master asked of him (p. 200).

In addition, the two characters understood each other all the better for having the same absence of scruples and the same brutality. Particularly in his violence with Perrine Rondeau (p. 121), Prelati is nothing but a young hooligan; an elegant hooligan, perhaps charming, but a hooligan. At the time of Gilles' trial, he was able to avoid death. He was only condemned to life in prison, and René d'Anjou obtained his freedom; he still must to die by hanging though (p. 144). Only the farewells that Gilles made to him in the presence of the judges have in their bizarreness something human, something moving or at least paradoxical.

François Prelati's testimony mentions the year when Gilles was away, when he was at Bourges.

*July-August
Journey to Bourges*

Obviously Gilles could not have stayed a full year at Bourges, between Prelati's arrival at Tiffauges in May 1439, and arrest on September 13, 1440. But these two dates fix the limits of his stay there. To begin with, it seems important to consider that the Estates General convened in that city on February 15, 1440, the sole event that we know could have moti-

**(1439)**

vated this journey. The Estates General were called but could not be held; Charles VII was unable to show on account of that princely revolt wherein his son (the Dauphin and future Louis XI) and the Duke of Bourbon played the principal role, and which we know by the name of the Praguerie. A certain number of notables did show at the convocation. But, on the one hand, there is no reason to think that Gilles in disgrace would have been invited to the Estates General in 1440; on the other hand, it is from Tiffauges that he left for Bourges, and to Tiffauges that he returned. In 1439, from Ascension Day to the end of the year, he effectively stays in the castle at Tiffauges; but it is then at Machecoul that he will install himself. In fact, on December 25, 1439, Prelati is at Machecoul and clearly ought to remain there with his master who, from then until his arrest, no longer changes his principal residence; so it is at Machecoul, not Tiffauges, that he resides in February 1440. The stay at Bourges is therefore in 1439. But there is obviously some time between Gilles' departure for Bourges and Prelati's arrival at Machecoul. Apparently the stay at Bourges takes place before a relatively brief stay at Bourgneuf, therefore in July or at the beginning of August. It could as well be placed in October or November, but this is when the religious offering of children's members is supposed to occur. A rapid succession that is not inconceivable; it is, however, improbable (pp. 214-215).

August
A serpent's apparition

Whatever the case, Gilles de Rais, staying at Bourges, left Prelati at Tiffauges, entrusting him with continuing the invocations in his absence. Prelati keeps him current; he writes him cryptic notes. With Gilles at Bourges, Barron is supposed to have appeared to Prelati and given him a "black powder, on a piece of slate," in order that it be conveyed to his master. This gift from the infernal spirit is supposed to have been actually transmitted to Bourges; Gilles is supposed to have worn it several days from his neck in a silver box, but he got rid of it, "discovering that it was not doing him any good" (pp. 199 and 214-215). Gilles having returned from Bourges to Tiffauges, Prelati performs an invocation in which the devil, or Barron, is supposed to have appeared to him in a human form. Prelati asks him for riches on Gilles' behalf. Whereupon he is supposed to have seen "a large quantity of gold" in a room. At first he is forbidden to touch them, but Gilles wants to see this mass of gold. The two of them approach the room. François is once again at the entrance when "a huge, winged, and vigorous snake, as big as a dog" appears to him. He cries to Gilles not to enter; he just saw a serpent! Gilles runs for cover . . . he returns. He has fortified himself with a crucifix containing a splinter of the Holy Rood. Thus armed, he presents himself at the room's entrance.

114

François tells him that it is not a good idea introducing the "blessed cross" into this business. François strives to prevent his entering with the cross; it goes on like this until finally Gilles approaches a fake ingot; all he finds there, he says, is a "sort of foil," a worthless sheet of brass, which he does not touch (pp. 199 and 215).

The invocation thus concluded is one of three invocations by Prelati that the Marshal personally attended. The first is the solemn invocation attempted in June or July in the large lower hall of Tiffauges. This is the *great invocation of Tiffauges.* The second is the *invocation of the serpent,* which we have just given an account of, whose location Gilles forgot. The third is the *invocation of Bourgneuf,* which evidently occurred toward the end of August (pp. 198-199 and 212-213).

Guillaume Avril's son, the nephew of Denis de Lemion, a weaver of the parish of Notre-Dame-de-Nantes, disappeared "one morning in August 1439, or thereabouts." He is "of small build and pale complexion," having a mark on the ear "similar to a small ear." Colin's aunt, Agathe, Denis de Lemion's wife, had been asked by one of Lord de Rais' men to loan him the child in order to show him "the house of the Archdeacon of Merles"; it was understood that the child would receive a round loaf of bread. Agathe accompanies the child on the first day, but on the following day Colin returns to the Hotel de La Suze, where, moreover, he is used to going once in a while under the pretext of returning with a round loaf. He does not return, and nobody has any news of him since. Agathe affirms that Lord de Rais was residing at the Hotel de La Suze then. In his confession, Henriet remembers delivering to his master at the Hotel de La Suze a child named Lemion, with whom Gilles "had intercourse" and who was "killed and burned" (pp. 155, 160-161, 266-267, 268-269).

> Around August
> Murder of Guillaume Avril's son

At Bourgneuf-en-Rais Gilles has come to see the Duke, who is passing through and whose assistance he certainly needs. He wants Jean V to take him into his good graces. No doubt he has understood that the Duke, no longer expecting anything from him, is tired of him. He is unable to ignore his partner's natural duplicity and indifference. He knows the rumors which he is the object of; he knows he is penniless, vulnerable. He had expected gold in abundance from the demon; he is reduced to begging him for the favor of a few coins. It is with this humiliating intention that he asks Prelati to invoke this Barron in his presence, who had never deigned to appear to him. Therefore he tries a second time to confront the entity who makes him tremble. Once again, he will

> August
> Meeting of Jean V and Gilles de Rais at Bourgneuf

**(1439)**

be abandoned to his fear; the evil one scorns him (pp. 174, 214 and 277).

Around August 25
Murder of
Bernard Le Camus

Deceived by the Devil, Gilles returns to his criminal debauchery. Perhaps he had an inconclusive interview with Jean V . . . His men escort a young, "very beautiful and smart" boy, fifteen years old, into his room in the convent where he is staying at Bourgneuf. The boy, originally from Brest, lives with Guillaume Rodigo, originally from Guérande. A Breton from Brittany, Bernard Le Camus is in Bourgneauf to learn French. The testimonies taken as a whole incriminate Poitou, and that of Rodigo himself accuses Blanchet as well. The child speaks with Poitou and leaves. He leaves Rodigo's house for Gilles de Rais' room on the evening of August 25th (St. Bartholomew's Eve), about six o'clock; he has forewarned the chambermaid, Marguerite Sorin. Poitou had spoken in a low voice to the child in front of the chambermaid. The chambermaid wanted Bernard to tell her what Poitou had told him. Poitou, the boy said, had not told him anything. He leaves without saying where he was going, leaving his robe, his shoes, and his hood behind. We are assured by the confessions of Gilles, Henriet, and Poitou that the child died. Gilles says he killed him with Henriet. Henriet claims to have not assisted in the death. All three criminals agree in reporting that the body was burned at Machecoul (pp. 175-176, 200, 228, 235-237, 277 and 281-282).

In any event, Gilles founders; the pleasure which he has attained is sinister. He is more than ever susceptible to remorse. He speaks of his intention to change his life. Eustache Blanchet testifies how "some time ago" he repeatedly heard him saying, as much at Machecoul as at Bourgneuf-en-Rais, "that he intended to amend his wicked life and make a pilgrimage to the Holy Sepulcher, in Jerusalem, in order to ask forgiveness of his sins."

He does not reform himself, but lets remorse overcome him now and then (pp. 124, 177, 202, 215-216 and 222).

August 28

Jean Toutblanc of Saint-Étienne-de-Montluc, having left at home on August 28, 1439 a thirteen-year-old boy, whom he was the tutor of, no longer finds him on his return. Since then, "a year ago last Saint Julian's Day," he has had no more news of him (p. 269).

Of all the testimonies concerning the murders, this is the most negligible, Saint-Étienne-de-Montluc being too far away from Tiffauges.

Autumn

Two sons of Robin Pavot, of Chanteloup near Rennes, both of them approximately nine years old, used to frequent the fairs in the region of Rais, carrying their bales of notions; Pierre Badieu, a haberdasher in the

116

same village, no longer saw them there after October 1439 — or there-abouts — where he usually used to see them, he testifies before the judges of Nantes. For their part, their father and mother, not seeing them return, try vainly to make inquiries. One of their brothers even travels to "various regions in the hope of obtaining some news," but learns nothing (pp. 271-272).

The connection of this double disappearance to Gilles de Rais is no less doubtful.

Prelati alleged that the devil Barron had stipulated during one of his appearances that Gilles "would provide a meal to three people on three solemn feasts." Gilles does it once only, on the feast of All Saints of 1439. According to Prelati, "this was why the same Barron refused to appear in the said Gilles' presence" (pp. 175-176 and 215-216).

November 1

All Saints' Day of 1439 is the day on which Eustache Blanchet leaves Tiffauges after an argument with Gilles' companion and accomplice, Robin Romulart; the diabolical invocations are supposed to have generated the disagreement. Blanchet goes to stay at Mortagne with an innkeeper named Bouchard-Menard. He will stay there seven weeks (pp. 217-218).

King Charles VII issues the great ordinance of 1439 following a meeting of the Estates General of Orléans, held in October. This essential text points to the continual progress, in spite of overwhelming disorder, of administration and law over arbitrariness and violence. Its purpose is to put an end to "the tremendous excesses and pillages" that are desolating the realm. It seeks above all to substitute a regular army based on discipline and military hierarchy for the bands of brigands commanded by lords or captains who are themselves brigand chiefs. This ordinance, dictated by reason, marks the birth of a modern world, a bourgeois world, where the unrestrained violence of a Gilles de Rais will find no place.[29]

November 2

What is our Gilles de Rais at this time?

His title of Marshal, in 1439, is not justified by any legal act. Nobody asks anything of him, nobody thinks of him. He is useless; the permanent army, created by the ordinance of 1439, is the antithesis of this naïve brigand, inebriated on wine or blood, who never stopped believing himself above the law. The little we know of his military role in this

Gilles de Rais in 1439

---

[29] G. du Fresne de BEAUCOURT, *Histoire de Charles VII*, vol. III, p. 402.

**(1439)**

period bears evidence of sporadic activity, wherein he leads companies of men analogous to all the companies of mercenaries and extortioners infesting the country, some fighting for the King, some against him. He is nothing else in 1439 than a brigand chief, in many respects analogous to those whose ferocity made them notorious. He is not the least ferocious; he is ferocious in another manner; he does not possess that sly realism of famous brigand chiefs, and they do not possess his shame. But he does belong to the same horrible world.

We know in particular that Jean de Siquenville is one of these men. It is with him that sometime around June Gilles replaces the false Maid, whom he had charged with fighting on his behalf. But Jean de Siquenville is without a doubt one of these brigand chiefs; there is no difference in this era between the captain of a warring company, in the service of whoever needs him, and a brigand chief. This Jean de Siquenville and his men lived on *spoils*: they pillaged villages, violating, burning, and, if necessary, torturing and killing. Before the end of the year, the Dauphin finds him at Tiffauges. Having him arrested, he has him imprisoned in the castle at Montaigu. Siquenville, on the verge of being hanged, escapes.[30]

The life of a Siquenville evokes the world where Gilles, during his last years, led the battle against his neighbor, the castellan of Montaigu, Jean de Harpedenne,[31] or against the captain of Palluau (pp. 200 and 215). But we know practically nothing of the circumstances or episodes of those feudal battles at a time when, little by little, their anachronism is becoming flagrant.

*Around the beginning of December*
*The public rumor*

Jean Mercier, castellan of La Roche-sur-Yon, traveling to Mortagne, stays at the hotel of Blanchet's landlord; this latter asks him for news in the regions of Nantes and Clisson. Here is what Blanchet reports: according to Mercier, public rumor in these regions accuses Gilles de Rais of killing, and causing to be killed, a large number of children . . . he was writing a book in his own hand with their blood. This book finished, he expects to seize all the fortresses he wants . . . From then on nobody will be able to harm him (p. 218).

Lord de Rais' emissary, the goldsmith Jean Petit, then working at Tiffauges with Prelati, arrives at Mortagne on the following day. He is charged with leading Eustache Blanchet back, but Blanchet refuses. Blanchet is supposed to have told Petit that Gilles and the Italian should

[30] J. QUICHERAT, *op. cit.*, vol. V, p. 334.

[31] A. BOURDEAUT, *op. cit.*, p. 108.

stop: it was not good to commit these crimes, and public rumor was growing against them. According to Blanchet, Gilles threw the goldsmith into the prison of Saint-Étienne-de-Mermorte on his return. He is supposed to have stayed there a long time . . . (p. 218).

It is without a doubt around this period that Gilles, caught in Prelati's grasp, contemplates the worst. Why couldn't the gift of dead children's members have appeased this devil, whose silence and hostility overwhelm him? In his incoherence, the shady, fearful, and versatile Eustache Blanchet himself suggested to Henriet and Poitou that their master could not accomplish what he had begun without offering the feet, hands, or other members of the slaughtered children to the Devil (pp. 229 and 237). *Around the end of the year*

Each day Gilles is a little more impatient to see the Devil and Prelati, who will vouch for it later, tells him that if he wanted the Devil to appear and speak to him, he ought to offer a cock, hen, dove, or pigeon . . . , and if he really wanted what he was asking for, then it would be necessary to offer a child's member (p. 212).

Blanchet could be repeating Prelati's words. Gilles' testimony indicates that Prelati himself had affirmed that the Devil required the gift of a certain number of dead children.

In fact, Prelati reports having seen in the large hall at Tiffauges, where the invocations occurred (and not in Lord de Rais' room), a dead, outstretched child. He saw him in the presence of Gilles de Sillé, who Prelati thinks had just killed him (p. 212).

This dead child would have been seen by him a year before his deposition, consequently around October 16, 1439. But he does not tell us that he was offered to the Devil. Gilles would not have yielded so quickly; it is possible that, corrupt as he was, he was not of such a temperament as to be able to sacrifice children to the Devil without trembling. We can surmise that by mentioning members, particularly the hand, heart, or eyes, Prelati wanted to scare him. He was not ignorant of Gilles' anguish. It was possible for him to gain time by this trick.

In the end — but in what a state of terror — this killer, trembling before the Devil, makes his promise!

One day in his room, in Poitou's presence, he puts a child's hand (Poitou does not know whether it was the right or the left) and heart in a glass that he covers with a piece of fine linen. Then he inserts the glass into his sleeve (sleeves were long and large then), forming a large enough pocket. He goes like this into Prelati's room. Perhaps the glass also con- *Offering of a child's hand and heart to the devil*

**(1439)**

tains the child's eyes and blood. It seems that there was only one offering: various versions differ, but no important contradiction in detail exists among them. François Prelati presents the horrible offering to the invoked demon, but the demon does not appear; a little while later he himself buries these human remains in sacred soil, close to the castle's chapel (pp. 176, 198, 212, 239-240, and 280).

December

The Viennese Dauphin, Charles VII's son, the future Louis XI, is sent into Poitou "to put an end to the pillages, and expel the warring men who were in that region." Accomplishing his mission, he is led to visit two of the fortresses where Gilles de Rais garrisons his troops, Pouzauges and Tiffauges. A brigand chief like Marshal de Rais was expressly targeted on this visit and, as we have already said (p. 118), one of the captains under the castellan of Tiffauges, Jean de Siquenville, is arrested; this Jean de Siquenville is thrown into the prisons of the castle at Montaigu, where the Dauphin had fixed his residence. Sensing the imminent hanging, Gilles' captain escapes from that prison; this is why he must consequently procure letters of pardon, which we possess and in which the incident is related to us.[32]

The Dauphin's passage through Tiffauges has other consequences. First of all, Gilles hastens to have the alchemical ovens that he had installed in the fortress demolished (pp. 182-183). But, the Dauphin gone, Gilles is still afraid and decides to leave the royal domain and stay in Brittany, where the deceptive friendship of Duke Jean reassures him. He is at Machecoul at least toward the end of December. He cannot do without Prelati; if the conjuror's presence is noted in the vicinity of the castle (p. 122), it is because the master is staying there.

Around December 10

About fifteen days before Christmas, Jeannette, Eustache Drouet's wife, of Saint-Léger, sends two of her sons, aged seven and ten, to ask for alms at Machecoul, "because she had heard that Lord de Rais had them distributed there, and that, moreover, the men in that village willingly gave charity." Several people told her of seeing her children in the following days, but when she went there she could not find them, nor learn what became of them, even after she herself and her husband made several inquiries. Maybe Gilles had actually returned to Machecoul. But it is not certain (p. 266).

Around December 20

Gilles — disquieted by the knowledge that Eustache Blanchet is out

---

[32] J. QUICHERAT, *op. cit.*, vol. V, pp. 332-334.

of his control, whose hostility, not to mention his wicked tongue, he is now familiar with — sends a certain number of his servants, including Gilles de Sillé, Poitou and Henriet, to Mortagne with the order to bring Blanchet back forcibly or voluntarily. They bring him to Roche-Serviére by the road leading from Mortagne to Machecoul. They are principally charged with imprisoning him in the castle of Saint-Étienne-de-Mermorte, where, in his terror, he thinks Lord de Rais will leave him to die. Apparently it is only to frighten him; in any case, he makes so many vows that they lead him to Machecoul, where he lives freely until his arrest on September 13, 1440 (p. 218).

At any rate, the solution of Machecoul explains itself by the fact that, for the moment, Lord de Rais is living there again.

Ysabeau, Guillaume Hamelin's wife, living in Fresnay, sends two of her children, aged fifteen and seven, to buy bread. They do not return;. since then, she is unable to find out what became of them. However, François Prelati and the Marquis de Ceva, both of whom she says she knows well and she knows stay with Gilles de Rais, visit her the following day. The Marquis poses strange questions and interrogates her on the subject of a son and daughter she has at home; he asks her whether they are hers, and finally whether she does not have others; she answers that she does have others, but dares not tell him that they have disappeared. When they leave, she hears the Marquis say to François that two children left that house.

Eight witnesses from Fresney confirm the disappearance of two children.

Eight days before that disappearance, Ysabeau heard talk of the disappearance of Micheau Bouer's son (pp. 263-264), who left for Machecoul as well but eight months earlier, this time to ask for alms and coming from Saint-Cyr-en-Rais (p. 263).

Clément Rondeau of Machecoul is dying and receives extreme unction. His wife Perrine, in tears and lamentations, is installed toward evening in the highest room of the castle, where both Prelati and the Marquis de Ceva sleep. Having returned for supper, these latter, furious to see her there, take her by the shoulders and feet to throw her down the stairs. Prelati finishes by kicking her in the lower back, but at the last moment Perrine's nurse catches hold of her robe, saving her (p. 261).

In the period when Eustache Blanchet resides at Machecoul, the Marquis de Ceva procures for Prelati to serve him as page "a young, very

Around December 25
Murder of two children

End of December
Prelati's brutality

**1440**

January-February

**(1440)** beautiful child, saying that he was from the Dieppe region and that he was of a good family." This page ought to have been fifteen or sixteen then. He remains two weeks with Prelati, then vanishes. The hostess of the place asks him what happened to the child. Prelati responds that the child cheated him; he left, he insists, with his two crowns.

Henriet tells us that he had the child's throat cut; according to his first confession, he had him "struck down at Machecoul"; in his second, he does not know who cut his throat, he was not there, but he knows Gilles abused him just like the others (pp. 218-219, 227, 235-236, 259, 276-277 and 281-282).

The page of a certain Daussy is about the same age as Prelati. Like the last one, he is put to death at Machecoul in the period when Blanchet, who reports it, lived there at the beginning of 1440, or maybe a little later (pp. 200 and 219). Gilles de Rais, who speaks of him as a "little" page, mentions him at the same time as Prelati's page or the young Jean Hubert (pp. 105-107), but this latter was killed close to June 26, 1438.

Jean de Lanté, the prior of Chéméré, a priory within the order of Saint-Benoît, entrusts his nephew to a fellow named Tabard, intending to have him learn to read and write. As with the pages of Prelati and Daussy, he is fourteen or fifteen years old, and like them he is put to death at Machecoul in the period when Blanchet lives there (pp. 218-219 and 275).

February The convocation as witness of Jean de Lanté will be required at the ecclesiastical trial at the same time as that of the Marquis de Ceva, Bertrand Poulein, Jean Rousseau, and Master Gilles Heaume (p. 186). André Barbe, a cobbler living at Machecoul, says that "he heard a man complaining in the church of the Trinité at Machecoul, whom he did not know, who was asking whether anyone had seen his child, whom he claimed was seven years old; and this about eight months earlier": basically, it is a question of February 1440 (p. 257). This testimony is, in principle, dubious.

March A poor man from Touvois named Mathelin Thouars laments and anguishes, around March 1440, over the disappearance of his twelve-year-old child; he is clueless as to what may have happened to him. Four witnesses from Touvois profess to have heard his complaining. Testimony like this obviously adds nothing to that which merits our attention (p. 259).

February The Dauphin, the Count d'Alençon, and Dunois meet at Niort; the

122

Duke of Bourbon, the Count de Vendôme, and La Tremoillé meet at Blois; they each enter into rebellion against the King; the Duke of Brittany, Jean V, supports the rebels, but the Constable de Richemont subdues the movement; by July 17th the affair is completely terminated.

Nobody asked for Gilles de Rais' help. Nobody henceforth pays the slightest attention to him.

One morning before Easter (March 27th) at Machecoul, Blanchet is said to have seen Poitou arriving at the castle, accompanied by the son of the pastry-cook, Georget Le Barbier. This child, Guillaume, ought to have been approximately sixteen then. Georget Le Barbier lives in front of the entrance to the castle. Her son is placed with a certain Jean Péletier, the tailor of Lady de Rais, as well as several of the men in Lord de Rais' household. The child and his master, the tailor, regularly come to eat at the castle. According to Blanchet, who basically knows what to expect, the lad's entrance into the castle was answered with his death.

*Before March 27*
*Murder of Guillaume Le Barbier*

According to the father's testimony, the child supposedly did not disappear until Saint Barnabas' Day (June 11). But we know that the father was managing badly. And two of our testimonies speak of sometime around Easter (pp. 220, 257, 258 and 281-282).

On Easter Sunday (March 27th), in the Sainte-Trinité church of Machecoul, Eustache Blanchet sees a priest, Monsignor Olivier des Ferrières, hearing Gilles de Rais' confession. Soon after, the Marshal receives the Eucharist together with people of little means. The latter want to move aside for him, but Gilles orders them to remain where they are and partake in Communion as usual (p. 219).

*March 27*
*The confession and humble communion of Gilles de Rais*

Between Easter and Ascension Day of 1440, the widow of Yvon Kerguen, a mason from Sainte-Croix, of Nantes, entrusts her nearly fifteen-year-old son, whom she will never see again (pp. 155 and 200), into the service of one of Lord de Rais' men, named Poitou, who had asked her for him. Thomas Aisé and his wife, poor people who were still living in Port-Saint-Père around May 15, 1440, send one of their sons, who is about ten years old, to beg at the castle of Machecoul at a time when Lord de Rais is staying there. A little girl is supposed to have told her mother that alms were first given to the girls, and then she heard someone in the castle say to the young Aisé that if he has not received any meat, he will get some: the child is then made to enter. Since that day the mother no longer had any news of her son (pp. 260 and 265-266).

*March 27 to May 15 (between Easter and the Pentecost)*

## (1440)

May 15
The Saint-Étienne-de-
Mermorte scandal

A company of about sixty men-at-arms lies in wait in the woods out-side the church of Saint-Étienne-de-Mermorte. They are armed, and Gilles de Rais is at the head. The moment they have been waiting for comes, the High Mass is finished; he brandishes a double-sided axe (ter-minating in a kind of pike, which one calls a "gisarme"), and rushes into the church. Inside the church he insults Jean Le Ferron, the brother of Geoffroy Le Ferron; Geoffroy is the treasurer of Brittany and the man to whom Gilles has sold the estate of Saint-Étienne-de-Mermorte. "Ha, ribald," he shouts. "You beat my men, and extorted from them; come outside the church or I'll kill you on the spot!" Poor Jean Le Ferron, a tonsured cleric trusted by his brother to watch over the fortress, is called upon to return it to Gilles; he is imprisoned in this same fortress which Gilles' men have invaded (pp. 240-244). Gilles has violated ecclesiastical privilege and encroached on the rights of the Duke of Brittany, his own sovereign.

In a short while, the reaction of the Duke and that of his chancellor, Jean de Malestroit (who possesses, insofar as he is the Bishop of Nantes, the ecclesiastical jurisdiction of the diocese to which the Saint-Étienne church belongs), will lead Gilles to the gallows. The outrage against Jean Le Ferron corresponds to the puerile excessiveness wherein Gilles founders. From here on out Gilles is a tragic energumen; he has lost his senses and nobody is around to support him. Remorse wracks him. The Holy Land haunts him; he would like to change his evil life and implore forgiveness of his sins.

He has already confided this intention the year before (p. 116). He repeats it at least once, evidently prior to the outrage of Saint-Étienne (more than four months prior to the deposition on October 16th).

A hope of faraway travel and devotion uplifts his spirits (pp. 177, 202-203, 216 and 222). But everything suggests that it is too late. Like a dog, he returns to his vomit. In any case, he struggles with himself in vain.

June

Gilles tries to escape from the Duke of Brittany, who has slapped him with a fine of 50,000 gold crowns (a considerable amount of money, rep-resenting half the value of his fortresses at Ingrandes and Champtocé). He transfers his prisoner Jean Le Ferron to Tiffauges, with Poitou, in the royal domain.

After June 24

Seven witnesses from Saint-Étienne-de-Montluc, including a clergy-man, had known the orphaned son of a certain Guillaume Brice, a poor man in their parish, for about three years. This Guillaume died around February 1439. Since Saint John's Day of 1440 (June 24th), the witnesses have not seen this boy again; he responded to the name of Jamet, was quite beautiful, and approximately eight or nine years old (pp. 255-256). No doubt it is difficult to see the reason for seriously accusing Gilles of the disappearance of a child in Saint-Étienne-de-Montluc, north of the Loire estuary. But he will resume the course of his wanderings, at least after July.

One apparent means of escape remains: why doesn't Gilles go looking for Jean V? Insofar as his interests dictated, Jean V had showed him kindness. Provided that Gilles was not totally ruined, the Duke could thereby hope to profit.

Gilles is in effect blind enough not to see that, in exchange for a favor which he needs more than anyone else, he has nothing left to offer Jean V.

He ought to know: he is ruined. There is nothing he could expect from the King. Escape? He refuses. His whole nature balks at the idea; anyway, what cover exists for such a visible person?

He confronts the storm decisively. He will join the Duke at Josselin; he will explain himself there. But he measures the risk. It is impossible to know, before setting out, whether he will return from this trip. That is why, before setting out from Machecoul, he orders Prelati to interrogate the devil Barron; he wants to know whether he can meet the Duke safely; he wants to know whether he will return . . .

The devil says yes!

They leave Machecoul, and on the way Gilles asks the conjuror to pose the question again; it makes him restless. He has it posed again at Nantes and, upon arriving at Josselin, Prelati is requested to pursue the invocations. He has him pursue them in a field. Gilles does not attend. According to François, Barron appears this time clad in a mantle of violet silk. Once again he guarantees their return; Gilles de Rais will take the road to Machecoul (p. 215).

We know nothing of the interview between Gilles and Jean V. We also know nothing of the hospitality that the Duke must have shown the Marshal. Prelati must seek the devil in a field. It is also in a field that Henriet says he led three children, whom he kills. Poitou, who is ill, is absent. This is all we know.

Gilles tells his servants that he has come to see the Duke about the money he owes him. But they know the score; their master is from then on reduced to feigning.

# (1440)

Murder at Vannes

Presumably the stay at Josselin was painful for him, and for this reason Gilles wanted to leave as soon as possible for Vannes to find André Buchet, the choirboy he had introduced, at the latest in 1434, into his chapel. He knew what to expect. At Vannes, Gilles is lodged outside the walls of the city, near the episcopal manor in a place called La Mothe, in the house of a man named Lemoine. Evidently André Buchet belongs as of this period to the chapel of the Duke, which often resides at Vannes (at any rate he belonged to it some weeks later, at the time of the trial). Buchet leads Gilles to the son, nearly ten, of a neighborhood resident, Jean Lavary by name. But there is no place secret enough to kill a child at Lemoine's. The child is led to a house relatively nearby, run by a man named Boetden. The head of the child is severed — then burned — in Gilles' room. The body, tied with a belt, is carried to the latrines of this Boetden's house and Poitou, apparently recovered from his illness, is supposed to descend into the pit; it is necessary to shove down and cover the corpse so that it will not be found. Henriet and Buchet are then supposed to help Poitou up out of the pit.

Poitou insists that Buchet, who belonged to the ducal chapel at the time of the trial, knew everything. Gilles himself states that Buchet was not ignorant of any of the children's murders (pp. 231-232).

July 29
Results of the secret inquest
by the Bishop of Nantes

The Bishop of Nantes and Chancellor of Brittany, Jean de Malestroit, publishes in the form of letters patent the results of the secret inquest that seems to have immediately followed the outrage of Saint-Étienne-de-Mermorte. It establishes that Gilles de Rais, subject and justiciable of the Bishop, abused numerous children, whom he killed; moreover, he invoked demons and signed a pact with them; public rumor accuses him of all these crimes.

Around August 15
Last murder

Raoulet de Launay, a tailor in Nantes, makes a doublet for Éonnet de Villeblanche's child. This child does not live with his parents then, but with Poitou. It is Poitou who pays Raoulet twenty sous for the doublet. Poitou, in his deposition, acknowledges that the child's mother, who goes by the name of Macée, gave him the child as a page and that he had to clothe him himself. According to Poitou the child was killed and burned, and Raoulet de Launay, in his testimony, testifies that he never saw him again. This is the last alleged murder; it occurs after the letters patent issued on July 29th (p. 270).

126

Although all that Jean V has ever done is hide when faced with Gilles de Rais, he now decides to be done with him. His chancellor, Jean de Malestroit, must have convinced him easily enough: public rumor is too strong; on the day of the Saint-Étienne affair, Gilles exceeded the limits; there are no opposing interests from here on out.

August 24
Collapse: Constable de Richemont seizes Tiffauges

But the Duke is anxious at this moment to reconcile, at least tacitly, with the King. Jean V knows that Charles VII is no longer interested in the Marshal; however, it is not useful to give him the pretext for an intervention possibly motivated by the memory of the Duke's hostile attitude at the time of the Praguerie. That is why he thinks of involving one of the crown's principal officers, his brother Arthur de Richemont, the Constable of France.

Arthur is disposed to lend his brother the requested support. He has the greatest horror of sorcerers and undoubtedly never liked the Marshal, a creature of his worst enemy, La Trémoille. In exchange Arthur will receive two lands, completing the appanage of which the Duke, his brother, has not yet fulfilled. He will receive in particular Bourgneuf-en-Rais, a fief that Gilles still has in Brittany. Gilles is not dead, but the cards have been dealt — the Duke is already distributing the spoils.[33]

On August 24th, the Duke confers with his brother at Vannes. Only his brother, the King's officer, can take Tiffauges (and Poitou), where Gilles hoped to keep his prisoner from Saint-Étienne-de-Mermorte, Jean Le Ferron, safe from a ducal action. Everything hastens when Arthur accepts the responsibility of seizing Tiffauges; Jean Le Ferron is freed. Gilles no longer has a hostage. He ought to know by now what awaits him. Nothing can save him. On hearing the news of the Constable's entrance into Tiffauges, Gilles de Sillé and Roger de Briqueville decide to hit the road. They must have amassed a sufficient fortune in anticipation of this event . . . Only those who have no recourse to escape remain: the foreigner Prelati, the priest Blanchet, and the two valets-factotum, Henriet and Poitou. Gilles himself could have fled perhaps, if it were not for a constant, absurd hope. With enduring naïveté, he cannot believe that anyone would come to take him.

Emissaries of the secular court have in turn entered the region. They have led an inquest of their own. They have heard almost the same complaints as the ecclesiastical court (p. 249). They are the ones who have decided on Gilles' arrest and have done whatever was necessary to effect it.

Prior to September 15

---

[33] E. Cosneau, *op. cit.*, p. 309.

## (1440)

September 13
Gilles is indicted for
the murder of children and
invoking demons

Gilles is cited before the ecclesiastical tribunal of Nantes; he is indicted for the murder of children and sodomy, the invocations of demons, the offending of Divine Majesty, and heresy.

September 15
Arrest

The Duke of Brittany's men appear at the portal of Machecoul with captain of arms Jean Labbé in the lead, assisted by notary public Robin Guillaument, in the name of the Chancellor and Bishop Jean de Malestroit.

Marshal de Rais is arrested.

François Prelati, Eustache Blanchet, Henriet and Poitou are arrested at the same time.

On the road to Nantes prison, Henriet, who is terrified, thinks of cutting his own throat (p. 276).

After September 15

Appearing before the secular court of Nantes, Gilles de Rais is supposed to answer for two chief counts: the murders of children and the Saint-Étienne-de-Mermorte affair (the outrage against Jean Le Ferron and his detention; the occupation of the castle of Saint-Étienne, which he had transferred to Geoffroy Le Ferron, the treasurer-general of Brittany). All we have of the hearing is a semi-official report, which gives us only Gilles' response to the second count. Absolutely no response to the murders. Had the accusation of the prosecuting attorney carried on that item, given Gilles' attitude before the ecclesiastical judges on October 8th, he evidently would not have been so conciliatory about the Saint-Étienne affair. Apparently the civil judges maintained the same prudence that the ecclesiastical judges did, and from the beginning kept quiet on the very serious aspect of the affair. The author of the report could have seen it as an oversight, but he did not take it upon himself to introduce Gilles' response concerning the children into his notes.

September 18
Lamentations of the
victims' parents

Pierre de L'Hôpital, the President of Brittany,[34] has the upper hand on the secular proceedings in the action brought against Lord de Rais. A cleric, Jean de Touscheronde, charged with the inquest, begins by hearing testimonies concerning the murders of Peronne Loessart's son, of La Roche-Bernard, and Jamet Brice, of Port-Launay (pp. 253-256).

---

[34] The "President of Brittany" or "Universal Judge of Brittany" sits on the secular court of Nantes and, above that, on judicial sessions in the general parliament of the duchy. Along with the Chancellor of Brittany, Jean de Malestroit, and the treasurer-general, Geoffroy Le Ferron (the brother of Jean Le Ferron, Gilles' victim), he is one of the most important officers of the Duke of Brittany. "In the Breton judicial organization, he occupies the foremost position," affirms DURTELLE DE SAINT-SAUVEUR in his *Histoire de Bretagne des origines à nos jours*, 4th ed., vol. I, p. 331.

# The Historical Facts in Chronological Order

September 19

Trial proceedings against Gilles de Rais open at Nantes in the great upper hall of the castle of La Tour Neuve (p. 159). Gilles de Rais, the accused, appears before Jean de Malestroit, Bishop of Nantes. He hears the charges read by the "prosecutor" (charged with petitioning against him), Guillaume Chapeillon. He accuses him of having admitted to "doctrinal heresy." For this reason he is ordered to appear, at the same time as before the Bishop, before the Vicar of the Inquisitor, Jean Blouyn, who is charged with the Inquisition in the city and diocese of Nantes. He will appear September 28th before these two judges, whose jurisdiction he at first acknowledges. It then seems to him perhaps relatively easy to respond to the sole accusation of heresy.

September 27

Jean de Touscheronde prosecutes the civil inquest; he hears witnesses on the subject of the disappearance of Jean Bernard, of Port-Launay (p. 256).

September 28

The Bishop, Jean de Malestroit, and the Vicar of the Inquisitor, Jean Blouyn, a Dominican, are present in the chapel of the episcopal manor for the appearance of ten plaintiffs accusing Lord de Rais of having shamefully abused and massacred either their son or their nephew (pp. 159-163). They complain "grievously and tearfully." However, Gilles de Rais, whose presence was anticipated, does not show this day.

September 28, 29, and 30

Jean de Touscheronde prosecutes his inquest; he hears witnesses concerning the disappearance of: the children of Georget Le Barbier, Jean (or Guillaume) Jeudon, Jeannot Roussin, Alexandre Chastelier, Guillaume Sergent, Mathelin Thouars, Jeanne Édelin, Macé Sorin, one named Oran, Thomas Aisé, Guillaume Hamelin and Micheau Bouer; Bernard Le Camus; and the child of Jeannette Drouet. Furthermore, he listens to the personal complaint made by Perrine, Clément Rondeau's wife, on the subject of Prelati (pp. 257-262).

October 2

Continuation of Jean de Touscheronde's inquest; in question are the disappearances of: a child of Regnaud Donete; Jean Hubert; a son of Jean Jenvret; a son of Colin Avril; a child of Guibelet Delit; a pupil of Jean Toutblanc; a son of Jean Fougère; and a son of Éonnet de Ville-blanche (pp. 269-270).

October 6

Continuation of the same inquest concerning the disappearance of Perrot Dagaye (p. 270).

**(1440)**

October 8   Continuation of the same inquest; concerning the disappearance of: the two sons of Robin Pavot; Olivier Darel; Jean Hubert; the son of Regnaud and L. Donete (pp. 270-274).

In the lower hall of the castle of La Tour Neuve, the ten plaintiffs of the earlier hearing return for the accusation brought "clamorously, grievously, and tearfully" before the Bishop and the Vicar of the Inquisitor (pp. 162-163). Besides murder and sodomy, it is a question of the "invocation of evil spirits" and "many other crimes concerning ecclesiastical jurisdiction."

The same day, but this time "in a great upper hall" of the castle of La Tour Neuve, Gilles de Rais and the "prosecutor" appear together before the Bishop and the Vicar of the Inquisitor. On that day the prosecutor's accusation, delivered verbally, cites the totality of crimes and offenses brought against the criminal, such as they are found in the forty-nine articles of the "bill of indictment" presented later. Gilles reacts immediately and appeals to his judges, but his appeal is rejected at once as frivolous. He thereupon objects to his judges with a savage denial. In spite of four demands and the threat of lawful excommunication, he refuses to take an oath.

That day then is the true beginning of the trial; the entire accusation on this day is announced. Pierre de L'Hôpital, in charge of the secular court's action, is for the first time admitted to the ecclesiastical court proceedings (pp. 162-165). From then on, he (as well as the Bishop of Saint-Brieuc, Jean Prégent, who will participate with him in the examination of the "out-of-court" confession of October 21st) is present at all the proceedings, except on October 20th, when the application of torture is decided upon, and the morning of the 21st, when it is supposed to be applied. It is remarkable how, on October 15th, Gilles de Rais addresses him as if he understands his indignation and, on October 20th, asks to be heard by him (and Jean Prégent) in the absence of the ecclesiastical judges.

October 11   The Bishop and the Vicar of the Inquisitor adjourn the session slated for the prosecutor and the accused until the following day. They are satisfied with hearing for a third time, in the lower hall, the complaints and tears of the unfortunate people imploring them to attend to the "necessary justice" (pp. 164-165).

# The Historical Facts in Chronological Order

At nine o'clock in the morning, in the great upper hall of La Tour Neuve castle, before the Bishop and the Vice-Inquisitor, and before numerous Nantes officials, the prosecutor formulates the charge as it is written in the forty-nine articles of the bill of indictment; it is then read aloud to the judges.

October 13
The bill of indictment
in 49 articles

The first fourteen articles (the entire bill of indictment is provided on pp. 169-179) are nothing but preliminary: they are meant to demonstrate, in these circumstances, the Bishop's, the Vice-Inquisitor's, and the ecclesiastical court of Nantes' qualifications. But Articles 15 through 49 finally explain the various crimes of which Gilles de Rais is accused. The statement is disordered and confused, but it is complete enough. Indeed it agrees — on the whole at least — with other facts provided elsewhere in the documents. (Nevertheless, the year of 1426 as given for the beginning of the child murders is contradicted by the accused's confession; we should add that generally the *dates* given in the bill of indictment are hardly convincing: thus the Saint-Étienne-de-Mermorte affair, whose date, May 15, 1440 is established with as convincing a precision as can be, is attributed to 1438.) This bill of indictment considers three principal points actually: first, the crimes against children; second, heresy, or essentially the invocation of demons, combined with the practice of the magical arts and more or less dogmatic statements by the conjurors and other practitioners; third, the violation of ecclesiastical immunity.

The indictment affirms that for about fourteen years (that is, since 1426) one hundred and forty children, girls and boys, had been the victims of Gilles de Rais and his accomplices. They had been led away, either by his principal accomplices assisting in his murders, or by procurers or procuresses. Various services to be rendered to Gilles de Rais served as pretexts, and the benefits that the children themselves — or their parents — derived from these services were emphasized. In fact, the children had their throats cut, were killed, and "shamefully tortured." What is more, the accused practiced the sin of sodomy on them while they were alive, when they were dead, or when they were dying. Gilles de Rais disdained the "natural vessel" of the girls. In the end, the victims were dismembered and burned.

The indictment fails to precisely designate all but two victims, a child who was living in Bourgneuf-en-Rais with a fellow named Rodigo, and the son of a certain Jean Lavary of Vannes.

It takes into account the conveyance of forty-five skeletons from Champtocé to Machecoul, where they were burned.

The use of fine wines, hippocras, and claret, not to mention gluttony,

131

are linked to the sin of sodomy insofar as they served the accused as stimulants with a view to practicing that sin "with greater abundance, ease, and pleasure."

The indictment records fleeting periods of remorse and whims of conversion by the criminal who wanted to change his life and make a pilgrimage to the Holy Sepulcher, but did not know how to carry out his resolution and returned to his criminal deviations, as "a dog returns to its vomit."

It names the places of the crimes: the Champtocé castle; the house of La Suze at Nantes; the Machecoul and Tiffauges castles; the house of the Frères Mineurs at Bourgneuf-en-Rais; a certain Lemoine's house at Vannes.

Moreover, the indictment dates Gilles de Rais' condemnable heretical activity from 1426, for which he is answerable to the Inquisition. He is accused of associating with the heretics who indoctrinated him; moreover, he is supposed to have read and studied heretical books. In particular, he is accused of having made for himself a dogma of the conclusions and mistakes of diviners and conjurors. He is equally supposed to have practiced and held as dogma the magical, prohibited arts of geomancy and necromancy. Finally, he did not forget to affirm his criminal principles publicly, principles considered as so much dogma.

But the bill of indictment enumerates much more than thoughts or words; it lists condemnable acts. Essentially, the invocation of demons. In various places Gilles de Rais invoked, and caused to be invoked, various demons: at Orléans (under the sign of the Croix d'Or); at the Machecoul and Tiffauges castles; at the Frères Mineurs house in Bourgneuf-en-Rais; and at Josselin, close by the Duke of Brittany's castle. Gilles de Rais is equally reproached for the child sacrifices at Tiffauges, offering the hands, heart, and eyes of a child in a glass. The accused hoped to bind himself to the Devil by a pact, to which end he prepared a note or letter of commitment binding himself, but with the exception of his soul and the curtailment of his life. As well the indictment mentions certain rites celebrated for five years, on All Saints' Day in particular; in the course of which alms were distributed to the poor.

Violation of the Church's immunity is the third grievance justifying his appearance before the ecclesiastical tribunal. This is connected to the Saint-Étienne-de-Mermorte affair. The indictment specifies how Gilles de Rais entered the church "furiously and recklessly" waving his offensive arms, threatening the cleric Jean Le Ferron with death; the latter he subsequently keeps bound hand and foot in irons, holding him hostage first in the castle of Saint-Étienne-de-Mermorte, then in that of

Tiffauges. This is how the accused "gravely and shamefully violated the jurisdiction of said Reverend Father, Lord Bishop of Nantes."

In the conclusion of these forty-nine articles, the prosecutor asks that the accused be recognized by the Bishop and the Vicar of the Inquisitor as guilty of the various crimes reported in the indictment; thus he must incur "excommunication and other lawful punishments"; thus he must be "punished and salubriously corrected, as the law and canonical sanctions demand."

At the prosecutor's request, Gilles is interrogated by the Bishop and the Vicar of the Inquisitor on the topic of the forty-nine articles of the bill of indictment (pp. 165-166); he denies their authority and refuses to recognize them as judges, then he treats them like so many "simoniacs" and "ribalds": "he would much prefer," he says, "to be hanged by a rope around his neck than respond to such ecclesiastics and judges." After several demands, his excommunication is pronounced. Gilles appeals, but his appeal is immediately denied in view of "the nature of the case and the cases of this order, and also on account of the monstrous and enormous crimes" brought against him.

*Interrogated, Gilles refuses to respond, and insults his judges*

Thereupon a reading is given of the letters of authority accorded in 1426 by Guillaume Mérici, the Inquisitor of Heresy in the French realm, to his Vice-Inquisitor, Jean Blouyn.

With the same faces reunited in the same hall, there is a decisive turn of events (pp. 180-181): Gilles de Rais recognizes the Bishop and the Vicar of the Inquisitor as competent judges, he owns up to having "maliciously committed and perpetrated" the crimes charged, and "solicited humbly, devoutly, and tearfully" his judges to pardon him for the "insults" and "offensive things" addressed to them. For the love of God, the judges immediately acquiesce. The accused acknowledges the content of Articles 1 through 4 and 8 through 14 (Articles 5 through 7 excepted, they concern Jean Blouyn; but Article 8, which is acknowledged, accepts his authority).

*October 15 Beginning of the confessions*

Gilles de Rais, on the same day, continues to deny one of the chief points of the accusation, the invocation of demons; he only confesses to insignificant facts, for which he even volunteers to undergo a "test of fire."

The prosecutor and the accused swear on the Holy Gospels, whereupon the prosecutor produces, by way of witnesses in view of their examinations, the valets Henriet and Poitou, the alchemist Prelati, the priest Blanchet, a certain Tiphaine (Robin Branchu's widow), and the

**(1440)**

procuress Perrine Martin, all of whom are admitted to take oaths. (The testimonies of Henriet, Poitou, and Prelati, heard on the following days, were preserved; not so those of Tiphaine and Perrine Martin, which are missing in the documents handed down to us (p. 183).)

October 16
The testimony of Prelati

Hearing of the testimony of François Prelati, an Italian alchemist and conjuror in the service of Gilles de Rais from May 1439 to September 15, 1440 (p. 209). The place where this testimony was heard is not indicated.

October 17
The testimonies of
Blanchet, Henriet
and Poitou

Hearing of the testimonies of the priest Eustache Blanchet and the two valets, Henriet Griart and Étienne Corillaut (called Poitou), all three of them in the service of Gilles de Rais for several years until their arrest (pp. 216, 223 and 233).

It is possible that the hearing of these three witnesses took place in the morning, seeing that the prosecutor and Gilles de Rais were present — the court sits in the afternoon, at the hour of Vespers — in the great upper hall for the presentation and swearing in of fifty witnesses, soon to be heard, in particular, on the subject of the violation of ecclesiastical immunity: Lenano (the Marquis de Ceva), Bertrand Poulein, Jean Rousseau, Gilles Heaume, and Friar Jean de Lanté (pp. 186, 240-241).

October 19

At nine o'clock in the morning the court sits, with Gilles de Rais and the prosecutor in attendance, in the great upper hall of the castle, for the presentation and swearing in of fifteen additional witnesses (pp. 187 and 238).

October 20
The judges consider torture

Still in the great upper hall at nine o'clock in the morning, the prosecutor and Gilles de Rais appear before the Bishop and the Vicar of the Inquisitor (p. 189); these latter, at the prosecutor's request, want to know what Gilles has to say or object to in the indictment, but the accused responds that he has nothing to say and, upon request, he agrees to the immediate publication of the testimonies that have just been collected. The prosecutor, "in order to shed light on and more thoroughly scrutinize the truth," nonetheless asks the judges to apply torture; consequently the judges confer with the "experts," who assist them in deciding that Gilles ought to be submitted to "interrogation and tortures."

October 21

Sitting on the bench at nine o'clock in the morning in the lower hall of La Tour Neuve, the judges send for the accused to have him tortured (p. 190). Gilles, brought forward, humbly begs them to defer the session until the following day: he will force himself to speak without the necessity of "interrogation." He proposes speaking outside the room where the torture has been prepared to the Bishop of Saint-Brieuc, Jean Prégent, the representative of the ecclesiastical court, and to the President of Brittany, Pierre de L'Hôpital, the representative of the secular court. The judges consent to this proposition and accord the necessary delay.

At two o'clock in the afternoon, the Bishop and the Vicar of the Inquisitor appear in the same lower hall (pp. 191-192); they send the Bishop Jean Prégent and Pierre de L'Hôpital to Gilles de Rais. They send them to the castle's "high room" where the accused Marshal, who retained the privilege of decent quarters, resides.

The interrogation takes place with the attendance of Jean Petit, notary of the ecclesiastical court; Jean Labbé, the captain in the Duke of Brittany's service who proceeded with the Machecoul arrests; his squire, Yvon de Rocerf, who was also at Machecoul; and finally the cleric Jean de Touscheronde, who leads the secular inquest.

First confession "Out of court"

These are the circumstances in which Gilles first confessed, that is to say "out of court" (pp. 191-195), independent of the ecclesiastical as well as the secular proceedings. It was noted to have been given "voluntarily, freely, and grievously."

It is in this first confession that the accused mentions how his first crimes began in the year "his grandfather, Lord de La Suze, died"; in other words, in 1432. He then testifies that, despite Pierre de L'Hôpital's insistent questioning on this point, he committed his crimes "according to his imagination and idea, without anyone's counsel and following his own feelings, solely for his pleasure and carnal delight, and not with any other intention or to any other end."

The two commissioners then send for François Prelati. Gilles and this latter together give a detailed account of the invocations that followed on the arrival of the Italian alchemist, notably the offering of the hand, eyes, and heart of a child, which was prepared but not carried out. Gilles' farewells to his accomplice follow.

After this interrogation, the two commissioners return to the lower hall of the castle, where they present the confession that they have obtained (p. 192), which must satisfy the judges since there is no more talk of torture after this.

At the hour of Vespers, Gilles de Rais and the prosecutor appear again before the Bishop and the Vicar of the Inquisitor (p. 195) (no doubt in the upper hall of the castle).

October 22
The great or "in-court confession"

**(1440)**

The judges ask the accused whether he wants to say anything else or object to what has already been said. He says no, but then spontaneously confesses before the judges what he already confessed "out of court." The records represent him as speaking "with great contrition of heart and great grief, according as it appeared at first sight, and with a great effusion of tears." Without straying from the first confession, he attempts to complete it, to remedy its faults or insufficiencies. He initially and significantly insists upon the first disorders of his youth, and asks that his confessions be published in French for those present, "the better part of whom did not know Latin." He urges the strictness of fathers, mothers, and the friends of all children . . . He specifies the various tortures that he and his accomplices inflicted on their victims. He speaks of choosing the most beautiful heads of the dead children, and goes so far as to say that while watching them die he laughed with his accomplices.

He adds to that which concerns the murders some details on the invocations and his relations with Prelati. He recalls some of the murders in particular: the one at Bourgneuf, those of Jean Hubert and another page. Finally the murder at Vannes, where the body of the decapitated child was dropped into a cesspool.

He supplies some details on the attempts at invocation prior to Prelati's arrival in 1438, and speaks of the intention he sometimes had of renouncing his wicked life and making a pilgrimage to Jerusalem.

He finally exhorts "the people," and above all the numerous "ecclesiastics" attending his trial, to venerate our Holy Mother Church. He urges fathers of families to watch over their children, who ought not to be "too finely dressed," or live in "laziness." He expressly incriminates the excesses of eating and drinking, declaring that "laziness, an insatiable desire for delicacies, and the frequent consumption of mulled wine, more than anything else, kept him in a state of excitement that led to the perpetration of so many sins and crimes."

He implores God's pardon, then that of the parents and friends of the children whom he "so cruelly massacred . . . ," asking all Christ's faithful and worshipers for the assistance of their devoted prayers.

After this long confession, the text of which is the only conclusive one we have, the prosecutor asks that a day be fixed for "definitive sentences." Among others, Jean Prégent and Pierre de L'Hôpital attend that hearing.

October 23

The secular court, after having heard their confessions — which sometimes followed almost literally, but at other times were complementary to, their depositions as witnesses before the ecclesiastical court (pp. 275 to 276) — condemns to death Gilles de Rais' two valets, Henriet and

Poitou, who are executed on the same day as their master, immediately after him.

The Bishop, Jean de Malestroit, and Friar Jean Blouyn, the Vicar of the Inquisitor, are sitting on the bench in La Tour Neuve castle's great upper hall at nine o'clock in the morning when the prosecutor asks them for a conclusion of the trial and the promulgation of definitive sentences, with Gilles de Rais "hearing, understanding, and not contradicting" (p. 204). By a double sentence of the ecclesiastical court, the accused is declared, in the first place, "guilty of perfidious apostasy as well as of the dreadful invocation of demons"; in the second place, "guilty of committing and maliciously perpetrating the crime and unnatural vice of sodomy on children of both sexes" (pp. 207-208). He is excommunicated and subject to other lawful punishment. This condemnation of the secular court proceeds from that of the ecclesiastical court, following without delay the same day.

October 25
The condemnation by the ecclesiastical court

This promulgation once made, the judges immediately propose to reincorporate Gilles de Rais into the Church; Gilles de Rais thereupon begs them "devoutly, on his knees," "with sighs and moans." Reincorporated, he asks to be confessed, and immediately the judges instruct a religious of the Carmelite Order, Jean Jouvenel, to hear his private confession.

The religious trial is concluded.

Gilles de Rais is then transferred, very close by, to the castle at Bouffay, before the secular court, reunited under the presiding office of Pierre de L'Hôpital, President of Brittany. Now he confesses to the Saint-Étienne-de-Mermorte affair. Pierre de L'Hôpital, having asked the advice of several assistants, declares that, in this affair, the accused has incurred the previously pronounced fine (50,000 gold crowns), to be appropriated in property and paid to the Duke of Brittany; and that for his other crimes he shall be hanged and burned, the sentence to be carried out on the following day at eleven o'clock (pp. 281-284).

The secular condemnation

Gilles de Rais then asks that his servants Henriet and Poitou, also condemned to death, not be executed until after him, who had been the cause of their crimes; he fears that, if not, they might think that he, the principal guilty party, had gone unpunished. Pierre de L'Hôpital accords him this favor and, moreover, decides that the body of the condemned, rescued in time from the flames, shall be buried in a church of his choice. Gilles de Rais finally asks his judge to ask the Bishop to arrange, for the following morning, "a general procession in order to ask God to maintain in him and his said servants the firm hope of salvation." Pierre de L'Hôpital agrees.

October 26
Death

After the procession, followed by an immense crowd, Gilles de Rais is hanged, then delivered to the flames, but soon pulled from the flames. He is then buried "beside four or five ladies or young women of noble lineage."[35]

Henriet and Poitou are executed in turn and reduced to ashes, but Gilles' remains are carried inside the church of Notre-Dame-du-Carmel of Nantes. His service is celebrated there, and he is placed in a tomb. He lies buried like this alongside other imposing persons of distinction. But the Revolution wreaked a macabre havoc on this church, which no longer exists.

[35] Jean CHARTIER, *Chronique de Charles VII* . . . , recent ed. . . . by VOLLET DE VIRIVILLE . . . , vol. II, pp. 5-6.

# Various Problems and Historical Facts

## NUMBER, AGE, AND SEX OF THE VICTIMS

The question of the number of Gilles de Rais' victims is unsolvable.

The civil trial is perhaps being reasonable when it says (p. 250): "the said Lord took many young children, and had them taken, not merely ten, nor twenty, but thirty, forty, fifty, sixty, one hundred, two hundred and more, such that the exact number can not be certified."

The number provided in Article 27 of the ecclesiastical trial's bill of indictment is a little more precise: Gilles had killed, or caused to be killed, "one hundred and forty, or more, children, boys and girls" (pp. 174-175).

Other figures provided by the trial are no more precise: Poitou and Henriet, by themselves, are said to have taken sixty and up. Elsewhere that figure is reduced to forty. These numbers are troublesome . . . On the other hand, Henriet is said to have killed twelve by his own hand. He would have killed eleven or twelve in the house of La Suze . . .

Henriet's deposition before the ecclesiastical judges (p. 237) perhaps makes more sense. According to Henriet, Gilles "delighted in looking at their severed heads and showed them to him, the witness, and Étienne Corrillaut . . . , asking them which of the said heads was the most beautiful of those he was showing them, the head severed *at that very moment, or that from the day before, or another from the day before that* . . ."[1] It is not impossible to imagine that embellishment has perfected that horrible text; but in principle we are faced with a scene wherein, on one day alone, three children's heads could be lying together. This inclines us to propose, at least vaguely, the hypothesis of a very large number.

No exact count of the number of victims can emerge any longer from the apparently serious, precise testimonies. Still, a logically drawn total could pass

---

[1] Our emphasis.

for the minimum. It is then possible to say that thirty-five victims represent that minimum; a figure, in any event, well below probability . . .

As for age, I noted precise indications of two children seven years old, four eight, three nine, two ten, two twelve, one fourteen, two fifteen, one eighteen, and one twenty.

One knows that the children's sex varied. Without a doubt Gilles preferred boys, but in their absence resorted to girls. Let us only say that among the victims cited in the testimonies, not one was a girl. However, it is possible to think that if Lord de Rais did kill girls it was by exception, when the procurers or procuresses were unable to find young boys.

Henriet's confession before the secular court describes with a certain precision his master's relations with girls (pp. 278-279): ". . . occasionally the said Lord chose little girls, whom he had sex with on their bellies in the same way as he did with the male children, saying that he took greater pleasure in doing so, and had less pain, than if he had enjoyed them in their nature; thereafter these girls were put to death like the said male children."

## THE HEIRS AND LEGACY OF GILLES DE RAIS

### 1. Catherine de Thouars, Gilles de Rais' wife.

Abbot Bourdeaut states clearly that we know nothing, absolutely nothing, about Gilles de Rais' wife. This is what he says about this woman, Catherine de Thouars, and Marie de Rais, the child she had — or is recorded to have had — by Lord de Rais: "They pass and repass before us, effaced shadows, with not so much as a gesture or a feature that might permit us to fix their moral physiognomy."[2] We know that Catherine de Thouars must not have opposed the abduction whereby Gilles de Rais married her and acquired her legacy. But it is clear that her husband quickly stopped bothering with her; she was a negligible quantity for his whole life. However that might be, it is difficult to imagine that she didn't know about the crimes that the trial of 1440 succeeded in revealing.[3]

When Gilles de Rais was gone, she married as soon as possible Jean de Vendôme (also his second marriage), the *vidame* of Chartres, who in 1441 became the Duke of Brittany's chamberlain.

Catherine de Thouars retained Pouzauges, Tiffauges, and generally all the possessions she had brought into her previous marriage. She also had the tute-

---

[2] A. BOURDEAUT, *Chantocé, Gilles de Rays et les Ducs de Bretagne*, p. 148.

[3] That is Abbot Bourdeaut's opinion (*op. cit.*, p. 148).

lage of Marie in 1440. But this latter's possessions were so important that she quickly escaped the control of Catherine, herself a minor personage, whose husband was content to personally take charge over Jean V of Brittany's interests.

## 2. Marie de Rais, Gilles de Rais' daughter; fiancée, then bride, to Admiral Prégent de Cöetivy (1442-1450).

Gilles de Rais' daughter was about ten years old when he died. She inherited all those properties of his that did not come from his wife. Her interests conflicted with the rapacity of Jean V, who urgently pronounced a confiscation. But in principle such a confiscation was then incapable of suppressing the rights of innocent inheritors. Gilles' family and the court — always ready to frustrate the Breton Duke — considered entrusting those rights and important residences to Admiral Prégent de Cöetivy, a high-ranking personage, one of the most brilliant and able men then gravitating around Charles VII. The King will later declare that he himself married Marie de Rais to the Admiral.[4] If anything, a marriage of convenience. Prégent de Cöetivy was a farsighted shark of Breton origin. An enemy of La Trémoille (he participated in the 1434 plot), he must have also been an enemy of Gilles de Rais. The marriage was arranged, but not celebrated, in the spring of 1442.

From then on the Admiral acted as a businessman, ready to draw the greatest advantage from his position. He was unscrupulous and relatively inattentive to honor (obviously he was chosen because of these traits; it was a question of marrying the daughter of a man condemned to death).

As early as 1443 he renounces an attempted lawsuit to clear the name of his father-in-law, who in a prepared but later abandoned text was declared to have been convicted erroneously. He renounces it and obtains the right not to bear Rais' arms, as he had originally agreed. Apparently he believed at first in the possibility of clearing his name, maybe even in Lord de Rais' innocence, which the French court would have been interested in maintaining; he did well to profit by whatever could discredit the Duke of Brittany. But it is certain that after 1443 nobody expected anything of this kind. It seemed a foregone conclusion that by then the evidence was apparent everywhere.

The important part of the game, in fact, concerns the Champtocé and Ingrandes fortresses. On March 25, 1443, Cöetivy obtains from René d'Anjou the titles to these two essential manors. Then he has Charles VII pronounce their confiscation. The two places belonged to Jean V's son, Gilles, known by the name of Gilles de Bretagne, who was in league with the English. A proof of treason justified an act that, additionally, at the same time as he pronounced

<hr/>

[4] A. BOURDEAUT, *op. cit.*, p. 114, note 2.

the confiscation, conferred their possession on Admiral Cöetivy.[5]

One year later he married young Marie; she was then fourteen years old.

In this way, the protégé of Charles VII played a game in France's, but above all in his own, best interests; he won it with the help of a trump card in his greedy hands, the daughter of a child murderer. At any rate the sequel to Gilles de Rais' life, though less tragic than his murders, is no less sordid.

But the legacy of the criminal Marshal was unlucky for the Admiral. The very day he could boast to his friends of finally being Lord of Champtocé, he was fighting in the Siege of Cherbourg (a garrison the English still held July 20, 1450), and a harquebus-shot to the head killed him.


### 3. Marie de Rais, wife, by a second marriage, to her cousin André de Laval-Lohéac (1451-1457).

For whoever would have the chance to marry her, the widow Marie de Rais remained the major trump she had been for Cöetivy. She was taken by her cousin André de Laval-Lohéac, who had fought on the side of René de Rais, or La Suze, for the rights of the Laval family in the face of Gilles de Rais' extravagance (p. 97 and *passim*). The marriage took place at Vitré in February 1451. Abbot Bourdeaut underlines the fact that this marriage occurred on the same day André's brother Guy de Laval XIV married Françoise de Dinan, the widow of Gilles de Bretagne, whom her brother (Duke François II) had left dying at the bottom of a deep pit half-full of water. "The two women," we read,[6] "made their solemn entry together into the town of Laval."

Marie de Rais spent all of her second marriage in a lawsuit over Champtocé, which the Cöetivy family persisted in claiming as their own by reason of her marriage contract with the Admiral.

Marie de Rais died at thirty-seven, without children, on November 1, 1457. "She was buried in the choir of Notre-Dame at Vitré, where mothers still show their children the tomb of Bluebeard's daughter."[7]


### 4. René, Gilles de Rais' brother (1457-1473).

With the death of Marie, her father's legacy passed to his brother, René de La Suze, now Baron de Rais.

[5] A. BOURDEAUT, *op. cit.*, p. 121.

[6] *Op. cit.*, p. 135.

[7] *Op. cit.*, p. 137.

In order to justify his claims on Champtocé, which he seized immediately, René de Rais was induced to demonstrate his brother's extravagance; and it is on account of his efforts that the *Mémoire des héritiers* was published.

René maneuvered among different powers but failed, dying in 1473 and leaving a daughter, Jeanne, married to François de Chauvigny. This Jeanne, who died in 1481, had a son and daughter, but these latter had no children.

Champtocé was a continued object of litigation while René de Rais was alive; the Cöetivy family sought funds for indemnification. The fortress' destiny was determined during the course of Louis XI's reign. In the war against Brittany he had it partially razed, then had it seized after contending with René d'Anjou.

However, the seizure was lifted in 1483; whereupon the Duke of Brittany gave one of his bastards the castle from which Gilles de Rais had left in 1429 for Chinon, from there to the Siege of Orléans, and where, in 1432, he is supposed to have cut the throat of the first of his victims.

## ROGER DE BRIQUEVILLE AFTER GILLES DE RAIS' DEATH

When Gilles de Rais' arrest seemed near and inevitable, his trusted men (and occasionally his accomplices), Gilles de Sillé and Roger de Briqueville, fled. We do not know what became of Sillé, but Briqueville entered into the service of Prégent de Cöetivy, who could apparently familiarize himself with many of the details of his father-in-law's affairs through him.

Briqueville, whose rich and noble father had been chased out of Normandy by the English, was related to Gilles and consequently to Marie de Rais. It was in this capacity that the Admiral hired and protected him. Marie de Rais even watched over his children. But Briqueville feared trouble for having participated in the father-in-law's crimes. Cöetivy must have needed the services — no doubt base services — that such a miserable man might provide; he obtained for him letters of pardon. These letters have a definite interest for us. They constitute the only official document, independent of the justice of Jean de Malestroit and Jean V, that mentions the murder of children, of which Briqueville was an accomplice. They are letters of pardon, but they record the crimes Gilles' noble servant was guilty of: he was "nourished" by his master, and "he was then a young squire of little understanding"; however, that master had the children "killed and put to death," and Briqueville says he was forced to send them to him. It appears in the trial documents that he participated in the murders themselves, but what he acknowledges in the letters of pardon is limited. First of all, he knew nothing about the homicides; later, as soon as he began to suspect them, "he left the company and service of that Lord de Rais, who, five years after the fact, was taken and punished with his accomplices." We have seen (p. 91) that this Briqueville was, in the most deplorable sense, a man for hire. This is no place to linger on his denials, but rather on his admissions, which give the thesis of Gilles' culpability much more support than Admiral Cöetivy originally could have believed possible, as we have mentioned, in proving the innocence and clearing the name of his father-in-law. Did he not agree to bear the family arms? But he quickly assumes the right to renege. His ultimate attitude is expressed, in black and white, in the letters he obtained from the King, which are dated from Sazilly, near Chinon, in the month of May 1446.

## FRANÇOIS PRELATI AFTER GILLES' DEATH (1440-1445)

Salomon Reinach drew the argument for his thesis (see below) from the fact that the magician Prelati was not condemned. But this argument is based on error. The Inquisitor slapped him with a sentence of life in prison.[8] It was, according to Abbot Bourdeaut, the "only punishment that could have been inflicted on him, as he had not been immersed in the homicides committed by Baron de Rays." When imprisoned, Prelati's skills at sleight of hand and his gift of gab without a doubt facilitated his escape. They even permitted him to gain the favor of René d'Anjou, who believed, like Gilles, that the Italian could make gold. Moreover, the "good King René" made him captain of La-Roche-sur-Yon, where we also find our old friend the priest, Étienne Blanchet, and, according to Bourdeaut, "a swarm of ancient servitors of Baron de Rais." But Prelati, who recalled having been arrested September 15, 1440, has Geoffroy Le Ferron arrested in turn, as he was passing through La Roche. However, on his release, Le Ferron soon proves to be the stronger; he has the Italian hanged.

Up to the end he thus pursued the career of an impostor and adventurer: he was in every respect undeserving of the scene on October 21st (pp. 193-194). He helped himself to some blank checks that Geoffroy Le Ferron had on his person to forge others that compromised noble persons.[9] This is what did him in.

---

[8] It is through Abbot Bourdeaut, by means of the archival documents, that we know of Prelati's adventures after his master's death (*op. cit.*, pp. 128-130).

[9] A. BOURDEAUT, *op. cit.*, p. 130.

SALOMON REINACH'S THESIS OF GILLES DE RAIS' INNOCENCE

Every now and again somebody doubts Gilles de Rais' culpability. A sentence by Voltaire[10] indicates a certain bias: "In Brittany they killed Marshal de Rais, accused of magic and having cut the throats of children to do so-called magic spells with their blood." Other authors in the same period follow the same line, but it was not until the 20th century that someone proposed the thesis of innocence based on a perhaps superficial but nevertheless genuine study of the documents. In 1902, Salomon Reinach undertook the case of Gilles de Rais . . .

To tell the truth, his thesis[11] — at least on the whole[12] — has fallen by the wayside. Practically nobody picks it up anymore. Similarly, nobody today returns to the ideas on totemism by the same Salomon Reinach . . . I do not speak of Saïtapharnès' all-too-famous tiara, or Glozel's[13] excavations, which certainly did not add to his credit . . .

At any rate, it is easy to demonstrate how this indisputable though naïve scholar came to think that Marshal de Rais' trial had been fabricated.

In 1902, on the occasion of the Dreyfus affair, it was natural to suspect the authenticity of a trial. This was, moreover, a trial under the Inquisition barely ten years after that of Joan of Arc, who was condemned like Gilles de Rais and had been her companion-in-arms.

Unfortunately, the theoretician of totemism elaborated his thesis before attaining a sufficient understanding of the trial against which he had inscribed himself. He advanced his arguments before having read the civil trial, contenting himself with the ecclesiastical trial, just published in 1902. Consequently

---

[10] In *Essai sur les Mœurs*, ch. LXXX.

[11] Salomon REINACH, "Gilles de Rais," in *Cultes, Mythes et Religions*, vol. IV, (Paris: 1912), in 8vo, pp. 267-299.

[12] We cite as an exception the work of Dr. Lodovico FERNANDEZ, the pseudonym of Fernand FLEURET: *Le Procès inquisitorial de Gilles de Rais* (Paris: 1922), in 8vo. The author, in a preface that is an essay for rehabilitation and that precedes a very defective translation from Latin, restricts himself to reproducing Salomon Reinach's arguments. On the other hand, scholars like Emile Gabory (*La Vie et la Mort de Gilles de Rais* . . . Paris, 1930) and Abbot Bourdeaut (*Chantocé, Gilles de Rays et le Duc de Bretagne*, Rennes, 1924) have no doubt about the guilt that emerges from the totality of documents. In particular, Abbot Bourdeaut has an extraordinary familiarity with the details. It is he who pointed out that the sum due Jean Labbé for the Marshal's arrest was not paid until 1467, which, if he had been an accomplice in the plot, would not have been conceivable.

[13] Falsehoods that he believed himself capable of authenticating by his own authority, as unduly as he believed himself capable of styling the falsification of Gilles de Rais' trial.

he had to contest Noël Valois' argument, which was based on the precise testimonies received by the secular court. He should have been able to see his mistake when his principal arguments fell apart, but honesty is sometimes difficult, and evidently he became sincerely entangled. Let us recognize, on the other hand, that the hesitation of an authorized historian[14] could have encouraged him. But he did not have the experience that familiarity with the documents would have given him. It seems pointless to me to enter into too-detailed of an argument here. It is difficult while reading the testimonies and confessions below not to be seized by emotions that a hoax could hardly provide. That emotion is compounded by a multitude of lively, striking, overwhelming details . . . Of course, it is not immediately conclusive; it is always possible to imagine a fabrication. But the reader, who can henceforth even here refer to the documents, will be the judge; if the testimonies provided in this publication are fabricated, the author or authors of the fraud merit admiration. In a nutshell, Salomon Reinach's argument does not hold up in the light. It implies a sketchy familiarity, an ignorance, or a lack of prolonged contact. The texts and detailed analyses of the present publication were considered beforehand in such a manner that the opinion of the guarantor of Saïtapharnès' tiara can finally — decisively — be forgotten.

I will only insist on one argument, in view of illuminating one surprising aspect of the documents provided here. We read on pages 277-278 of Salomon Reinach's study: "The two most damaging depositions for the prosecution, those by Henriet and Poitou, Gilles' servants, bear on facts already several years removed from very complex crimes; but they agree in the minutest details; there is not a single important contradiction among them; there is not, not in the one nor the other, any of the omissions which one would naturally expect."

Let us add that Reinach could not have produced evidence at the moment he was writing these lines (when he had formed his opinion he was not aware, as we have said, of the civil trial documents): at least one of the confessions by these same Henriet and Poitou that the civil court received — Poitou's — comes close, if not literally then just short of that, to the deposition before the ecclesiastical court. That this is bizarre, shocking even, goes without saying. But without going further, is it sensible to draw from such facts the proof of falsification? Would it be impossible to imagine that the interrogation of the two witnesses, known in advance to have witnessed the same scenes together, being conducted by the same judges — these judges proceeding in a patently censurable manner by framing the question according to the preceding deposition — theoretically in order to confirm? Likewise, to speed things up, the secular interrogation of Poitou must have proceeded with responses he had

---

[14] Charles-Victor Langlois, former director of the French Archives.

made earlier to the ecclesiastical judges. Salomon Reinach insists on one point in particular. Not only in Poitou and Henriet's depositions before the ecclesiastical judges (dated October 17th: pp. 232 and 234), but in Gilles' own confession (dated October 22nd: p. 196), it is told how Gilles, sitting on the bellies of the victims while they were dying, delighted in watching them die. The trouble taken by the same judge to repeat the question on such a point after the first response does not seem so strange to me. And that he would have reproduced the phrases he had before his eyes is explainable: could he have not helped himself to the phrases already put down, being satisfied with the respondent's consistency in answering, and neglecting to find any new or different expression? The fact that the Latin phrases of the documents indirectly translate the responses made personally and directly in French suffices to account for Salomon Reinach's surprise to the point of his writing: ". . . suspicion becomes (under these conditions) the certitude of fraud . . . !"

Such frivolity is, above all things, surprising. Let us add that the first statement on which his argument is based is not of a nature to give it much weight. According to Salomon Reinach, these depositions "bear on facts already several years removed." It is enough to look at the documents: the crimes in which Henriet and Poitou are both recorded to have assisted multiplied from 1435 to 1440, and up to the day of the criminal's arrest!

It would be easy to show how, in other areas, Salomon Reinach's thesis involves mistakes and moot judgments.

I think it is pointless to insist.

I believe only that it is necessary to finish by stating the decisive reason I have for believing in the authenticity of the documents.

I have already said to what point these documents' fabrication was, effectively, unthinkable. Unthinkable because of their coherence. The coherence only suffers secondary imperfections. Who could imagine a similar voluminous document where the logic never suffered? But it only suffers quite rarely, and essentially it is strikingly rigorous. Who in the 15th century, before Sade, before Freud, could have correctly depicted, without a false note, these horrible butcheries, *which would not be realistic in the absence of modern knowledge?*

Salomon Reinach, in effect, lacked this knowledge; faced with these insane murders, he imagined them to simply be a classic case of Medieval indictments, artificially brought against those one wanted to ruin: Templars, Jews, heretics. He had no idea of the cesspool above which monstrous desires multiply. Gilles de Rais' atrocities possessed no reality in his mind. He considered this trial an invention in the same way that he considered psychoanalytic hypotheses as ignominious. He was the opposite of a generation that sees with both eyes open, and that is today no longer surprised to learn that a female Gilles de Rais existed . . . ,[15] that knows, above all, that child murders heightened by sexual desire are unfortunately frequent.

## TWO BRETON LEGENDS: GILLES DE RAIS-BLUEBEARD

For a long time I have been anxious to cite (pp. 19-21) Abbot Bossard's original inquiry into the local traditions relating the legend of Bluebeard to the story of Gilles de Rais. In tracing it, the author reproduces two texts[16] borrowed from the *Grand Dictionnaire Universel du XIX<sup>e</sup> siècle*, by Pierre Larousse.[17] I feel obliged to reproduce them here in turn. Above all, it is the first of them that succeeds in giving an indication that nothing is exactly situated, but is no less moving, in the formation of a legend based on frightening crimes. The following text is a Breton lament, obviously drawn up in old Breton, and given in translation in an anthology by Count Amezeuil.[18]

OLD MAN. — "Lasses of Pléur, why so silent then? Why go you not to feasts and gatherings?"

LASSES. — "Ask us why the nightingale keeps silent in the wood, and who causes the orioles and bullfinches to stop singing their sweetest songs."

OLD MAN. — "Pardon, lasses, but I am a stranger; I come from afar, from beyond the land of Tréguier and Léon, and I know not wherefore the sadness o'ershadowing your faces."

LASSES. — "We cry for Gwennola, the most beautiful and beloved amongst us."

OLD MAN. — "And what has happened to Gwennola? . . . You keep yourselves silent, lasses! . . . What has happened here then?"

LASSES. — "Las! alas! the villain Bluebeard has done the gentle Gwennola in, as he did his wives in!"

OLD MAN, *with terror.* — "Does Bluebeard live near here? Ah! escape, escape quickly, children! The wolf who ravishes be ne'er more terrible

[15] That consequently these crimes are not as inexplicable as they seemed to him. This is a question, in fact, of a great Hungarian lady, Erszebeth Bathory, of the royal family, whom Valentine Penrose (*Mercure de France* publications) made the object of a study. In truth, Erszebeth Bathory did not kill children: she tortured and put to death young girls, but in her castle her victims were, like the Marshal's, innumerable. Behind the high walls of feudal lords and ladies many horrors were possible: arresting persons of princely rank did not catch on quickly. At least in times as backward as, for France, the first part of the 15th and, for Hungary, the end of the 16th century.

[16] E. BOSSARD, *Gilles de Rais* . . . , 1st ed. (1885), pp. 393-397.

[17] Vol. II (Paris, 1867), in 4vo, pp. 214-215.

[18] *Légendes bretonnes* (Paris, 1863), in 18mo.

than the ferocious baron; the bear be gentler than the damned Baron de Rais."

LASSES. — "We cannot escape: we are serfs of the barony of Rais, and body and soul we belong to Lord Bluebeard."

OLD MAN. — "I will deliver you, I, for I am Jean de Malestroit, Bishop of Nantes, and I have sworn to protect my flock."

LASSES. — "Gilles de Laval does not believe in God!"

OLD MAN. — "He shall die a terrible death! I swear by the living God! . . ."

Here is the end of that plaint:

Today the lasses of Pléeur sing with open hearts and go dancing to feasts and pilgrimages. The nightingale's sweet accents echo in the wood; the orioles and bullfinches resound their gentlest songs; all of nature has once again put on its festive attire: Gilles de Laval is no more! Bluebeard is dead!

You can see how this version of the legend tries to reconcile the story of the seven wives with the true story of Gilles de Rais, who, not being a murderer of his wives any more than of girls, killed young boys. However, he also did kill girls; and it is Jean de Malestroit, Bishop of Nantes, who in fact has him condemned.

The great Larousse dictionary fails to give the source of the second legend known to him, which Bossard also reproduces, and which I shall cite now:

Weary of fighting against the English, Milord Gilles de Laval retired to his castle in Rais, between Elven and Questembert. He spent all his time "at celebrations, banquets and merry-making." One evening there passed by the castle, on his way to Morlaix, a knight, Count Odon de Tréméac, Lord of Krevent and other places; beside him was riding a beautiful young lady, Blanche de L'Herminière, his fiancée. Gilles de Rais invited them to rest awhile and emptied a glass of hippocras with them. But Gilles de Rais became so pressing, and above all so friendly, that evening came before anyone had thought of leaving. Suddenly, with a signal by the lord, archers seized Count Odon de Tréméac, whom they threw into a deep prison; then Gilles broached marriage to the young girl. Blanche shed abundant tears, while the chapel lighted up with a thousand candles, and the clock tolled joyously, and everyone prepared for the nuptials. Blanche was led to the foot of the altar; she was pale like a beautiful lily and trembling all over. Monsignor de Laval, superbly dressed, and whose beard was a most beautiful red, came and stood beside her: — "Come, Milord Chaplain, marry us." — "I will not take

Monsignor for my husband!" cried Blanche de L'Herminière. — "And I, I want us to be married." — "Do nothing of the kind, Milord Priest," responded the young girl sobbing. — "Obey, I order you." Then, as Blanche was attempting to escape, Gilles de Rais grabbed her in his arms. — "I will give you," he says, "the most beautiful finery." — "Let go!" — "To you my castles, my woods, my fields, my meadows!" — "Let go!" — "To you my body and my soul! . . ." — "I accept! I accept! do you hear me, Gilles de Rais? I accept; and from now on you belong to me." Just then Blanche changed into an azure-blue devil, taking her place beside the baron. — "Curses" cried the latter. — "Gilles de Laval," says the demon with a sudden, sinister laugh, "God has abandoned you for your crimes; you belong to Hell now and from this day forward you shall wear its livery." At the same time he makes a sign and Gilles de Laval's beard, from the red that it was, turned the darkest hue. And that is not all; the demon says again: "You shall no longer be Gilles de Laval in the future; you shall be Bluebeard, the most terrifying man, a bogeyman for young children. Your name shall be cursed for all eternity and after your death your ashes shall be scattered to the wind, while your villainous soul shall drop to Hell." Gilles shrieked that he was repenting. The devil told him of his numerous victims, of his seven wives whose cadavers lay buried in vaults within the castle. He added: "Lord Odon de Tréméac, whom I accompanied in the disguise of Blanche de L'Herminière, rides at this very moment on the road from Elven in the company of all the gentlemen of Redon." — "And what do they want?" — "To avenge the deaths of all those you've killed." — "Then I'm done for?" — "Not yet, because your hour hasn't struck yet." — "Who'll stop them then?" — "I, who have need of your help and aid, my good knight." — "Would you do that?" — "Yes, I will; for, alive, you're worth a thousand times more than dead. And as for now, see you later, Gilles de Rais, and remember, you belong to me body and soul." He kept his word in stopping the gentlemen riders of Redon; but from then on, Gilles was always known by the name of the man with a blue beard.

Even though the writer of this version of the legend did not know that Rais' body was not reduced to ashes after his execution, he did have a relatively precise knowledge of events. It appears he must have known that at some point the demonic Marshal, who had proposed a pact with the devil, would have been careful to refrain from promising his body and soul ("his life and his soul" to be exact), which the devil took possession of by way of a ruse.

# The
# Trial Documents
## of
# Gilles de Rais

# PART ONE

# Verdict
# of the
# Ecclesiastical
# Court

# I

## PRELIMINARY RECORDS

**July 29, 1440. Letters from the Bishop of Nantes. Information on the secret ecclesiastical inquiry and disclosure of Gilles de Rais' infamy.**

To those who may see the present letters, we, Jean, by divine permission and the grace of the Holy Apostolic See, Bishop of Nantes, give Our Lord's blessing, and ask that they lend credence to the present letters.

Let it be known by these letters that, on visiting the parish of Saint-Marie, in Nantes, where Gilles de Rais, designated below, often resides in the house commonly called La Suze, and is a parishioner of the said church, and on visiting other church parishes designated below, frequent and public rumor first reached us, then complaints and declarations by good and discreet people: Agathe, the wife of Denis de Lemion; the widow of the deceased Regnaud Donete, of the said parish of Notre-Dame; Jeanne, the widow of Guibelet Delit, of Saint-Denis; Jean Hubert and his wife, of Saint-Vincent; Marthe, the widow of the deceased Éonnet Kerguen, of Saint-Croix-de-Nantes; Jeanne, the wife of Jean Darel, of Saint-Similien, near Nantes; and Tiphaine, the wife of Éonnet Le Charpentier, of Saint-Clément-hors-les-murs, of Nantes; all parishioners of the aforesaid churches, supported by synodic witnesses of the said churches and other prudent, discreet, and trusted persons.

We, visiting these same churches according to our office, have had them diligently examined and by their depositions have learned, among other things of which we have become convinced, that the nobleman, Milord Gilles de Rais, knight, lord, and baron of the said place, our subject and under our jurisdiction, with certain accomplices, did cut the throats of, kill, and heinously massacre many young and innocent boys, that he did practice with these children unnatural lust and the vice of sodomy, often calls up or causes others to practice the dreadful invocation of demons, did sacrifice to and make pacts with the latter, and did perpetrate other enormous crimes within the limits of our jurisdiction; and we have learned by the investigations of our commissioners and procurators that the said Gilles had committed and perpetrated the abovementioned crimes and other debaucheries in our diocese as well as in several other outlying locations.

On the subject of which offenses, the said Gilles de Rais was and is still defamed among serious and honorable persons. In order to dispel any doubts in the matter, we have prescribed the present letters and put our seal upon them.

Given in Nantes, July 29, 1440.

By mandate of the said Lord Bishop of Nantes,
[Signed:] *J. Petit.*

**September 13, 1440. Letters from the Bishop of Nantes. Summons of Gilles de Rais before the ecclesiastic tribunal.**

We, Jean, Bishop of Nantes, by the grace of God and the Holy Apostolic See, to each and every one of the rectors and their vicars of church parishes, chaplains, curates and non-curates, clerics, notaries and notaries public, constituents of our city and diocese of Nantes, and to each of them in particular, send Our Lord's blessing and request their firm obedience to our mandates.

You should know that recently in our city and diocese of Nantes, and principally in the church parishes of Notre-Dame, Saint-Denis, Saint-Nicolas, Saint-Vincent and Saint-Croix of Nantes, Saint-Similien near Nantes, Saint-Clément-hors-les-murs of Nantes, and Saint-Cyr-en-Rais, in our said diocese, in the course of our visit to which we are bound by our pastoral office, we listened repeatedly to the shocking complaints made by as many good and discreet synodic witnesses of the said churches as by several other credible people of probity, at the same time as by many parishioners of these same churches, whose depositions we have directed our notaries public and scribes to draw up and publish in the registers of the said pastoral visits, and as well by the oft-repeated public rumor as by the preceding denunciations, we discovered that the nobleman, Milord Gilles de Rais, baron of the said lands in our diocese, had killed, cut the throats of, and massacred many innocent children in an inhuman fashion, and with them committed, against nature, the abominable and execrable sin of sodomy, in various fashions and with unheard-of perversions that cannot presently be expounded upon by reason of their horror, but that will be disclosed in Latin at the appropriate time and place; that he had often and repeatedly practiced the dreadful invocation of demons and took care that it be practiced; that he sacrificed and made offerings to these same demons, contracted with them; and wickedly perpetrated other crimes and offenses, professing doctrinal heresy in offense against Divine Majesty, in the subversion and distortion of our faith, offering a pernicious example unto many.

We, not intending that like crimes and a like heretical malady, which "spreads like a canker" if not immediately extirpated, should go unremarked because of dissimulation or heedlessness; moreover, desiring to apply suitable remedies swiftly, by the terms of the present letters, require and demand of you, each and every one, barring one's relying on another, or exculpating himself through another, that you peremptorily summon, by a single peremptory edict, to appear before Us or our official in Nantes, on the Monday following the feast of the Triumph of the Holy Cross, namely September 19th, the noble Lord Gilles de Rais, knight, our subject and justiciable in this case, whom We summon accordingly by the terms of the present letters before Us as well as before the case prosecutor of our court in Nantes, charged with proceeding in the affair, in order to answer for its protection in the name of faith, as well as law; and for this, it is Our wish that our present letters be duly executed by you or by another among you.

Given the previous Tuesday,[1] September 13th, in the year of the Lord 1440.

> Signed as such: by mandate of the said Lord Bishop,
> *Jean Guiolé*
> who transcribed it.

**Legal notice for the letters of September 13, 1440.**

I, Robin Guillaumet, cleric, notary public in the diocese of Nantes, was careful to render executory as intended these letters promulgated against the said Gilles, knight, baron of Rais, named as principal in this same writ, and executed by me in my own right this September 14th, in the aforesaid year, according to the form and manner mandated by the same letters.

---

[1] Apparently this concerns the transcript, drafted the next day, as reported in the legal notice that follows.

# II

## RECORDS OF THE HEARINGS

**Monday, September 19, 1440.**

The Monday following the feast of the Triumph of the Holy Cross, in trial before the Reverend Father, Lord Bishop of Nantes, sitting on the bench to administer the law in the great hall of La Tour Neuve in Nantes, personally appeared the honorable Master Guillaume Chapeillon, case prosecutor of the said court, reproducing in fact the said summons inserted above, with the published execution, on the one side, and the said Milord Gilles, knight and baron, the accused, on the other.

*Gilles de Rais' first appearance.*

Which Milord Gilles, knight and baron, after numerous accusations on the part of said prosecutor against the said Milord Gilles, to ascertain whether he would admit to doctrinal heresy, insofar as the said prosecutor affirmed, expressed a desire to appear personally before the said Reverend Father, Lord Bishop of Nantes, and before any other ecclesiastical judges, as well as before whatsoever examiner of heresy, to clear himself of the same accusations. Whereupon the said Reverend Father Bishop fixed and assigned to Milord Gilles, aforesaid knight and baron, and consenting thereto, the 28th of the said month, to appear also before the male religious, Friar Jean Blouyn, Vice-Inquisitor into Heresy in the aforesaid realm, to answer for the crimes and offenses brought against him by the said prosecutor, in order to proceed, with the aforesaid Reverend Father Bishop, Vice-Inquisitor, and prosecutor, in the name of faith as well as law and as it ought to be, and was assigned to the said prosecutor.

In the said place in the presence of discreet men, Master Olivier Solidé, of Bouveron, Milord Jean Durand, of Blain, church parish rectors in the Nantes diocese, witnesses specially called and requested.

[Signed in the margin:] *J. Delaunay, notary, J. Petit and G. Lesné.*

# Document I — Verdict of the Ecclesiastical Court

## Wednesday, September 28, 1440.

Hearing of complaints in Gilles de Rais' absence, whose second appearance is adjourned to October 8.

In the name of the Lord, amen.

Wednesday, September 28, 1440, the tenth year of the pontificate of the Most Holy Father in God, Monsignor Eugène, by Divine Providence Pope, the fourth of that name, and during the general council of Basel, before the Reverend Father of God, Lord Jean de Malestroit, by the grace of God and the Holy Apostolic See, Bishop of Nantes, and before the male religious, Friar Jean Blouyn, of the Dominican Order, bachelor of Holy Writ, and Vicar of the male religious, Friar Guillaume Mérici, of the aforesaid Dominican Order, professor of theology, Inquisitor into Heresy in the realm of France, delegated by apostolic authority and by this same Friar Guillaume, specially appointed to the office of inquisitor in the city and diocese of Nantes, presently in the chapel of the episcopal manor of Nantes and in the presence of us: Jean Delaunay,[1] Jean Petit, Nicolas Géraud, and Guillaume Lesné, notaries public and scribes before the same in the case and the cases of this order, expected to write faithfully before these same Lords Bishop and Vice-Inquisitor aforesaid on each and every one of the things that occur in the said cases, and, finally, deputized and entrusted to draw this up in a public form, according as they deputized all and every one of us; and in the presence of the witnesses inscribed below, personally appeared the persons named below who exposed to the said Lords Bishop and the aforesaid Vice-Inquisitor, while complaining tearfully and grievously, the loss of their sons, nephews, and others, assuring that the said sons, nephews, and others had been treacherously seized and then inhumanly butchered and massacred by the said Gilles de Rais and certain of his accomplices, abettors, followers, and familiars; that the same had abused them shamefully and unnaturally and that they had wickedly committed the sin of sodomy on them; that they had many times both summoned evil spirits and rendered them homage; that they had perpetrated many other enormous and unusual crimes and offenses as far as ecclesiastical jurisdiction is concerned; which plaintiffs humbly supplicated the said Reverend Lords Bishop of Nantes and Friar Jean Blouyn, Vicar of the aforesaid Inquisitor, to deign to apply a swift, just, and timely remedy to the above appeal.

Agathe, the wife of Denis de Lemion, a parishioner of Notre-Dame-de-Nantes, complained that Colin, her nephew, the son of Guillaume Avril, aged about twenty, who was of small build and pale complexion, so she says, having a particular mark on one of his ears similar to a small

---

[1] In Latin: *de Alnetis.*

ear, left one morning in August 1439, or thereabouts, for the house called La Suze, in Nantes, relatively near the church of Notre-Dame. Which house then belonged to Lord de Rais. And afterwards she never saw the said Colin again and had no more news, until the day when a certain Perrine Martin, known as La Meffraye, was arrested and imprisoned by the secular court of Nantes. After whose arrest, she heard it said by many, and this was the public rumor, that a number of children and young men had been taken and killed by the said Lord de Rais. She does not know for what end.

Item, the widow of the late Regnaud Donete, a parishioner of Notre-Dame-de-Nantes, also complained that Jean, her son, frequented the said house of La Suze and, since Saint John the Baptist's Day in 1438, she had heard no more news of him, until Perrine Martin, known as La Meffraye, arrested and imprisoned as noted above, confessed that her son had been handed over to the same Lord de Rais and his men.

Jeanne, the wife of Guibelet Delit, a parishioner of Saint-Denis-de-Nantes, complained similarly that Guillaume, her son, frequented the same house of La Suze and that he had gone there during the first week of last Easter. And she heard Master Jean Briand say that he had seen Guillaume in the same house seven or eight days consecutively, and that then he no longer saw her son; moreover, he suspected that her son had disappeared in the same house.

Jean Hubert and his wife, parishioners of Saint-Vincent, of Nantes, complained that one of their boys, named Jean, aged about fourteen, two years ago last Saint John the Baptist's Day, entered the house of La Suze and returned to his parents' house; and he told his mother that he had cleaned the said Lord's room in the house of La Suze, for which he was given a loaf of bread that he carried home and gave her; he told her also that he was in the good graces of the said Lord, who had made him drink some white wine. Once he returned to the house of La Suze, his parents never saw him again.

Jeanne, the wife of Jean Darel, a parishioner of Saint-Similien, near Nantes, complained that on the previous solemnity of Saints Peter and Paul, she was returning home around eventide from Notre-Dame-de-Nantes, followed by her son, aged seven or eight, and in the proximity of Saint-Saturnin, of Nantes, she turned about, thinking that he had been following her all that way and was continuously in her company, but she did not see him any more and never has seen him again since.

The widow of Yvon Kerguen, stonecutter, a parishioner of Sainte-Croix, of Nantes, complained that she gave her son to a man named Poitou, a servant of the said Lord de Rais, who had asked her between

(Hearing of complaints in Gilles de Rais' absence, whose second appearance is adjourned to October 8).

Easter and last Ascension Day for him to be admitted into the latter's service, as the same Poitou confirmed, which son was about fifteen years old; and she has never seen him again since.

Tiphaine, the wife of Éonnet Le Charpentier, butcher, a parishioner of Saint-Clément, near Nantes, complained that her nephew Pierre, the son of Éonnet Dagaie, aged ten, was lost about two years ago and that since this time, she has had no news of him until Perrine Martin, also known as La Pellissonne, admitted, as has been said, that she had delivered him over to Lord de Rais' men.

The wife of Pierre Couperie equally complained that she had lost two of her sons, one eight years old, the other nine.

Jean Magnet complained that he had lost one of his sons. The same plaintiffs suspected and said that they suspected the same Lord de Rais and his accomplices of having been, and being, knowingly guilty of the loss and murder of the same children.

Which complaints having been brought to the knowledge of the said Lords Jean, Reverend Father in God, Bishop of Nantes, and Friar Jean Blouyn, said Vice-Inquisitor, the same Lords Bishop and Vicar having been informed, insisting that these misdeeds should not go unpunished, peremptorily decreed and mandated all clerics to summon the same Lord Gilles de Rais, Saturday, October 8th, to respond as by law to the said Lord Bishop of Nantes and said Friar Jean Blouyn, Vicar of the aforesaid Inquisitor, and for whatever he might have to object to by way of defense in the name of the faith; as well as the prosecutor by them appointed in the case and in the cases of this order.

Done September 28th, in the year of the same said pontificate and said council.

In the presence of the venerable and circumspect persons, Jacques de Pencoëtdic, doctor in both civil and ecclesiastical law, official of Nantes, and Jean Blanchet, bachelor of law, cleric in the Nantes diocese, as well as of many other witnesses called to this and expressly requested.

[Signed:] *Jean Delaunay, Jean Petit, G. Lesné.*

## Saturday, October 8, 1440.

Second appearance by Gilles de Rais. Record of the "*litis contestatio*."

Thereafter, October 8th, in the year of the aforesaid pontificate and council, the said plaintiffs again appeared in person before the said Lords Bishop and Vicar of the Inquisitor in the lower hall of La Tour Neuve in Nantes, and complained anew to the said Lords Bishop of Nantes and the aforesaid Vice-Inquisitor, clamorously, grievously, and tearfully, of the loss of their children, asserting, as above, that these had been taken by the said Lord de Rais and his accomplices and adherents, who had maliciously abused them sodomitically and practiced on them the sin of sodomy; and they had called up evil spirits, rendered them homage, and committed many other crimes concerning ecclesiastical jurisdiction; which plaintiffs humbly supplicated the said Reverend Father in God, Bishop of Nantes, and said Friar Jean Blouyn, aforesaid Vicar, to be willing in this to provide a timely and lawful remedy.

In the year of and during the aforesaid pontificate and general council of Basel, Saturday, October 8th, in trial before the Reverend Father in God, Lord Jean de Malestroit, Bishop of Nantes, and Friar Jean Blouyn, bachelor of Holy Writ, the aforesaid Vicar, sitting on the bench to administer the law, in the morning, at the hour of Terce, in the great upper hall of the castle of La Tour Neuve in Nantes, specially destined to the expedition and decision of the cases of this order, and in the presence of us, Jean Delaunay, Jean Petit, Nicolas Géraud, and Guillaume Lesné, notaries public and scribes for the case and the cases of this order, before the same, and in the presence of the aforesaid scribes and witnesses, the honorable Master Guillaume Chapeillon, case prosecutor of the ecclesiastical court of the place, specially called to the case and the cases of the faith by the same Lords Bishop and Vicar of the Inquisitor, plaintiff, on the one side, and Milord Gilles de Rais, knight, baron and lord of this same region, accused or defendant, on the other, personally appeared, by mandate of the said Reverend Father and Vicar of the Inquisitor this Saturday, October 8th, peremptorily summoned to appear before them by the discreet fellow Robin Guillaumet, cleric, who to the said Lord Bishop and Vice-Inquisitor and to us, aforesaid notaries public, reported verbally to have peremptorily summoned the same Lord Gilles, the accused, personally apprehended, before these same Lords Bishop and Vicar of the Inquisitor, and the said prosecutor because of faith, and faith's moving us thereunto, in the abovesaid form and manner; and yet the said prosecutor reproduced the aforesaid summons in the name of the said Reverend Father Bishop and said Vice-Inquisitor, with its duly performed execution.

Against which Gilles de Rais the said prosecutor verbally pronounced the articles of the bill of indictment, reserving providing them in writing until a more favorable time and place. And the said prosecutor proposed, pronounced, and affirmed in fact verbally against the same Gilles, the accused, all and every particular of the things contained in the circumstances and articles provided below. Which Gilles, the accused, then said, verbally and not in writing, that he was appealing to the Lords

(Second appearance by Gilles de Rais. Record of the *"litis contestatio"*).

Bishop and Vicar of the Inquisitor as well as to the prosecutor. He was immediately told by the said Lords Bishop and Vicar of the Inquisitor that this kind of appeal, because it was frivolous and not presented in writing, taking into account the nature of the case and the cases of this order, could not be complied with by law; that is why the same Lords Bishop and Vicar of the Inquisitor did not comply in the least, attesting to the said Gilles that they had not overruled and did not intend to overrule him malevolently; nevertheless they declared that proceedings would subsequently be brought against the said Gilles by themselves and by the said prosecutor, by reason of faith and faith's moving them thereunto. Instantly the said Gilles, the accused, denied the truth of the said articles, contesting that there was anything to proceed with, unless it were that he confessed to having received the sacrament of baptism and to having renounced the devil and his ceremonies, making assurances of his having been and being a true Christian; upon which positions and articles thus denied, in the case and the cases of this order, the prosecutor swore that he himself was telling the truth, and not calumniating; and at the prosecutor's insistence the said Gilles, the accused, was asked to take the same oath, which the said Gilles, the accused, having been requested to do by all entreaties, warned and called upon one, two, three, and four times by the same Lords Bishop and Vicar, and threatened with lawful excommunication, declined and refused.

Notwithstanding which, at the insistence and request of the said prosecutor, the said Lords Bishop and Vicar of the Inquisitor fixed and assigned the following Tuesday for the same prosecutor and Gilles de Rais, present, hearing, and understanding, to state and enumerate and to see stated and enumerated in the case and the cases of this order, and to summon the said Gilles, the accused, to respond, and to proceed subsequently as by law.

Of which the said prosecutor requires us, the aforesaid notaries public and scribes, to draft one and several public instruments.

In this place in the presence of the Reverend Father in God, Milord Jean Prégent, Bishop of Saint-Brieuc, honorable and discreet gentlemen Master Pierre de L'Hôpital, President of Britanny, licensed in law, Robert de La Rivière, licensed in both courts of law, Hervé Lévy, of the Léon diocese, seneschal of Quimper, Jean Chauvin, burgher of Nantes, Geoffroy Piperier, treasurer[2] of Notre-Dame-de-Nantes, Gatien Ruytz

[2] Translator's note: *Chefcier*, or *chevecier*, has more complexity than "treasurer." According to E. Littré (Paris: Librairie Hachette et Cie, 1876), a *chevecier* was a "dignitary who attended to the chevet of the church, that is to say, the apse of the church . . . the same as the treasurer in other churches, because he guarded the treasure of the church; he also attended to the lighting of the church; and his rare knowledge, as simple churchwarden, raised him by degrees to the rank of chevecier."

and Guillaume Groygnet, both licensed in law, Olivier Solidé and Jean de Châteaugiron, both ecclesiastical canons of Nantes, Robert Piperier, seneschal, Jean Guiolé, allocated to Nantes, and Jean de La Grangiére, allocated to the court of Nantes, and many other witnesses assembled there in large numbers, called and requested in particular.

[Signed:] *Jean Delaunay, J. Petit, G. Lesné.*

## Tuesday, October 11, 1440.

On Tuesday, October 11th, which had been assigned for the prosecutor and Gilles de Rais, the accused, by the aforesaid Bishop of Nantes and Friar Jean Blouyn, the Vicar of the Inquisitor, the said Lords Bishop and Vicar of the Inquisitor, being certain of the cases stated, did not sit on the bench to administer the law; rather they adjourned the session scheduled for this Tuesday to the following Thursday and assigned that day for the same prosecutor and Gilles, the accused, so as subsequently to proceed in the case and the cases of this order, as by law.

*Gilles de Rais' appearance adjourned to the following Thursday.*

On which October 11th, the aforesaid men and women complained grievously and tearfully anew to the said Bishop of Nantes and Vice-Inquisitor of the loss of their children, as has been set forth in detail above, in the lower hall of the castle of La Tour Neuve, supplicating them in this to render the requisite justice swiftly.

## Thursday, October 13, 1440.

On the Thursday already indicated, October 13th, before the said Lords Bishop of Nantes and Friar Jean Blouyn, Vicar of the said Inquisitor, sitting on the bench to administer the law, in the great upper hall and at the anticipated hour, namely at the hour of Terce, personally appeared in arraignment the said Master Guillaume Chapeillon, prosecutor and plaintiff, on the one side, and the aforesaid Gilles, the accused, on the other, in order to fulfill the writ of the term of this order, being instructed by the said Friar Jean Blouyn of the authority and jurisdiction belonging to him as noted immediately hereafter.

*The accusation put forward, the bill of indictment having been read by the authority of the justices, the accused, having refused to respond and having insulted his judges, is held in contempt of court and excommunicated; his request for appeal is denied.*

The said prosecutor gave, produced, and developed against the said accused certain articles and certain positions, put down in writing, concluding in the tenor written below; on the subject of which the prosecutor requested for the said Gilles, the accused, that each of the articles be read judicially to Gilles, the accused, by the venerable and

[The accusation put forward, the bill of indictment having been read by the authority of the justices, the accused, having refused to respond and having insulted his judges, is held in contempt of court and excommunicated; his request for appeal is denied.]

circumspect person, Milord Jacques de Pencoëtdic, official of Nantes and doctor in both courts of law, by mandate of the said Lords Bishop and Vicar of the aforesaid Inquisitor, in order for Gilles to respond distinctly, in French, and under oath, to each point contained in the positions and articles, for as many positions and articles as there were, and finally, if he intended to speak or raise objections against them, a certain peremptory term being fixed and assigned as convenient by the said Lords Bishop and Vicar of the Inquisitor to the same Gilles, the accused, to speak or raise objections to any of the same articles, this same Gilles, the accused, expecting to be interrogated himself by the same Lords Bishop and Vicar of the Inquisitor, to know whether the content of the said articles were true.

Thereupon the same Lords Bishop and Vicar of the Inquisitor interrogated the said Gilles, the accused, at the said prosecutor's request, to know whether he himself intended to respond to these same positions and articles or contradict them, or discuss the issue. To which Gilles said and responded proudly and haughtily that he did not intend to respond to these same positions and articles, stating clearly that the said Lords Bishop and Vicar of the Inquisitor had never been nor were his judges, and that he would appeal. Moreover, now speaking irreverently and rudely, the said Gilles, the accused, declared that the said Lords Bishop of Nantes and Friar Jean Blouyn, Vicar of the Inquisitor, and all the other ecclesiastics, were simoniacs and ribalds; that he would much prefer to be hanged by a rope around his neck than respond to such ecclesiastics and judges, and that he could not tolerate appearing before them. And when the said official of Nantes, prudent Master Geoffroy Piperier, treasurer[3] of Notre-Dame-de-Nantes, in the name and place of the said prosecutor, deputized by the aforesaid Lord Bishop of Nantes and Vicar of the aforesaid Inquisitor, explained in French for the said Gilles, the accused, certain passages of the content of the said articles and said depositions, the said Gilles, the accused, irreverently contradicted the said official and treasurer and, turning toward the said Lord Bishop, delivered these words in French: "I will do nothing for you as Bishop of Nantes."[4]

Then, at the said prosecutor's insistence, the said Lords Bishop of Nantes and Friar Jean Blouyn, Vicar of the aforesaid Inquisitor, interrogated the said Gilles de Rais, the accused, to know whether he intended

[3] Translator's note: see p.158, note 2.

[4] In Old French in the original Latin text: "Je ne feroye rien pour vous comme evesque de Nantes."

166

to speak or object against the said articles and positions, verbally or in writing, adding that another suitable term would be assigned to speak against the same positions and articles. Then the same Gilles de Rais, the accused, said and responded that he did not intend to say anything against the said positions and articles.

Upon which, at the insistence and request of the prosecutor, the said Lords Bishop and Vicar of the Inquisitor summoned, requested, and called upon the said Gilles, the accused, and also exhorted him one, two, three, and four times, upon threat of excommunication, to respond to the said positions and articles exposed, read, and recited to him, as reported, in French. Which Gilles, the accused, refused to respond to them, attesting that he was as familiar with the Catholic faith as they were who had given and proposed the said articles against him, and that he was as good a Christian and true a Catholic as they themselves, avowing and saying that if he had committed the charges given and proposed against him, as declared and designated in the said articles, he himself would have committed a crime directly against the Catholic faith, and would have deviated from it, and that he would not pretend ignorance in this matter. And he said that he did not want to enjoy any ecclesiastical privilege and that he was shocked that the said Master Pierre de L'Hôpital, President of Brittany, would allow the said ecclesiastical lords knowledge of such crimes thus proposed against him and, moreover, that they could accuse him of such abominable acts.

And at the request of the prosecutor, the aforesaid Reverend Father, Lord Bishop of Nantes, and the aforesaid Vice-Inquisitor declared that the said Gilles, the accused — canonically exhorted, but refusing to respond to the same propositions and articles — be held in manifest contempt of court; next they excommunicated him by writing, then pronounced and published the excommunication, decreeing nonetheless, at the said prosecutor's entreaty, that Gilles de Rais be duly proceeded against in the case and the cases of this order.

From which decree and from the said Lords Bishop of Nantes and Friar Jean Blouyn, Vicar of the aforesaid Inquisitor, the said Gilles, the accused, simply, orally, and without writing, appealed. With which appeal, pointless as it was, on account of the nature of the case and the cases of this order, and also on account of the monstrous and enormous crimes brought against the same Gilles, the accused, which crimes being, so they said, incapable of appeal, the Lords Bishops and Vicar of the aforesaid Inquisitor did not intend to comply, affirming that they ought not, nor were constrained to do so by law; and so that the said Gilles would be allowed by the said Lords Bishop and Vicar of the Inquisitor to

[The accusation put forward, the bill of indictment having been read by the authority of the justices, the accused, having refused to respond and having insulted his judges, is held in contempt of court and excommunicated; his request for appeal is denied.]

examine the said articles and said positions; so that the said prosecutor would be allowed to produce his witnesses, should he desire, in the case and the cases of this order; and so that the said Gilles, the accused, would be allowed to see them produced, received, and sworn in, but that in return he would be allowed to speak orally or in writing against the said articles and positions; so that he could finally be proceeded against afterwards, as by law, they fixed and assigned to the said Gilles, the accused, and the said prosecutor a term of the following Saturday.

Then the said Friar Jean Blouyn, said Vicar of the Inquisitor, exhibited and produced by authority of justice certain licensed letters belonging to the aforesaid male religious, Friar Guillaume Mérici, of the Dominican Order, professor of theology, Inquisitor into Heresy in the realm of France, deputed by apostolic authority; which letters were affixed with his own seal of red wax on a pendant label of the parchment; which letters in the presence of the said Gilles were read publicly by the said Lords Bishop and Vicar. Then, after the production and exhibition of the said letters, the Reverend Father, Bishop of Nantes, and Friar Jean Blouyn, Vicar of the aforesaid Inquisitor, interrogated the aforesaid Gilles de Rais to know whether he had anything to say or object against these same letters, orally or in writing; which Gilles said and responded haughtily that he intended to say nothing against them. The writing, the signature, the seal, and the subscription having been attested by faithful witnesses in the presence of the said Gilles, the accused, these letters were declared sufficient by the said Lords Bishop and Vicar of the Inquisitor.

Of which the said prosecutor requires that we, notaries public and scribes, make one and several public instruments.

In the presence of the Reverend Father in God, Lord Jean Prégent, Bishop of Saint-Brieuc, Master Pierre de L'Hôpital, President of Brittany, Robert de La Rivière, as well as the said nobleman Guillaume de Grantbois, squire, Jean Chauvin, licensed attorney, cleric in the Rennes diocese, Guillaume de Montigné, lawyer of the secular court of Nantes, and many other witnesses particularly requested and required.

[Signed:] *Jean Delaunay, Jean Petit, Guillaume Lesné.*

**Documents read on October 13, 1440.**

*The transcript provides the following text as a heading for the articles:* "The content of the said articles and positions, and of the letters of authority of the said Friar Jean Blouyn, Vicar of the said Inquisitor, in the case and the cases of this order, exhibited and produced as mentioned above, are as follows":

Positions and articles that before you, Reverend Father in God, Lord   1. Bill of Indictment.
Jean de Malestroit, Bishop of Nantes, and male religious, Friar Jean
Blouyn, bachelor of Holy Writ, of the Dominican Order and convent of
Nantes, Vicar to the male religious, illustrious and excellent Friar
Guillaume Mérici of the same order, professor of theology, Inquisitor
into Heresy in the French realm, deputed by apostolic authority, and this
same Vicar by the same Friar Inquisitor Guillaume, specially deputed,
instituted, and ordained to the city and diocese of Nantes, honorable
Master Guillaume Chapeillon, priest, and rector of the church parish of
Saint-Nicolas-de-Nantes, prosecutor in the case and the cases of this
order, specially deputed by you, puts on, gives and exhibits in trial, as
plaintiff, against Lord Gilles de Rais, knight, lord, and baron of the said
region of Rais, your subject and justiciable in this case and in your jurisdiction, delinquent and accused. And to the content of these same
articles and depositions, also provided in a narrative style, in order, alto-
gether or separately, or as you wish, the same prosecutor requests that
the said Gilles, the accused and defendant, respond article by article, in a
satisfactory manner, under oath; and if these same articles be denied, he
asks your permission to make their proof; which he offers to do lawfully,
with the exception of superfluous proofs against which he expressly
protests.

I. In the first place, the said prosecutor affirms and, if necessary, intends to
prove that ten, twenty, thirty, forty, fifty, sixty, seventy, eighty, ninety and one
hundred years ago, more or less, and for so long even that there is no record to
contradict it, in the province of Tours and in the city of Nantes, there was and is
still a certain solemn and notable church cathedral, commonly called the church
cathedral of Nantes, having at its head a bishop, and for members a dean and several prebendal canons who form a chapter, and several attributes compose a
church cathedral and designate it as such publicly and famously; that it must be
thus, and that this is true.

II. Item, that for and during this time, the said bishopric of Nantes had and
has still precise boundaries and limits with other bishoprics of the said province of
Tours, distinguishing and separating them one from the other, as with those of
other neighboring provinces; and that there were from one end to the other of
the said diocese many church parishes and a people spiritually entrusted, subject
to it, and under its jurisdiction; thus it transpired, and that this is a public and
notorious truth.

III. Item, that for the last twenty years, if not more, the aforesaid Reverend
Father was and is Bishop of Nantes, having and exercising for the spiritual cure of

souls the government and administration of the said bishopric inasmuch as he is its titular, and that, by every evidence, he is regarded and held as Bishop of Nantes, commonly, publicly, and famously; thus it transpired, and this is a true rendering.

IV. Item, that for and during the aforesaid early period the correction, punishment, and reformation, regarding criminal offenses as well as sin, of each and every one of the offenders in the said city and diocese of Nantes, as well as their instruction and the decision of punishable and criminal cases, belonged to the then-existing Bishop of Nantes as it belongs lawfully to the aforesaid Reverend Father, present Bishop of Nantes; that the same existing Lord Bishop of Nantes, or aforesaid Reverend Father, present Bishop of Nantes, was and is regularly qualified to punish, correct, or reform every subject guilty of villainous and shameful acts, as with every criminal, whencesoever they came and whatsoever their place of origin, provided that they committed an offense in the said city or said diocese of Nantes, and the right being reserved to him in the aforesaid cases to bring and promulgate against them sentences, censures, and excommunications, inflict other penalties on them, condemn them and enjoin them to salutary penances, and deliver them over to the secular arm according to the urgency of the cases and the enormity of the excesses, offenses, and crimes; thus it transpired, and this is a public, notorious, and manifest truth.

V. Item, that recently the said Friar Guillaume Mérici, Inquisitor of the faith and of heresy in the realm of France and in the province of Tours, was deputed by apostolic authority, constituted, and ordained the power of substituting in his place another friar or other friars of the same order, with this qualification or these qualifications; thus it transpired, and this is a true rendering.

VI. Item, that the aforesaid Guillaume Mérici, before the said apostolic letters were dated, was and is still forty years old, a professor of Holy Writ, of the aforesaid order, and commonly reputed capable of exercising an office of this kind; so be it, and this is a true rendering.

VII. Item, that as much by law as by custom, usage, mores, and observance in the city and diocese of Nantes, lawfully prescribed since the aforesaid times and strictly observed up to the present, the instruction, decision, and punishment of heresy, sorcery, apostasy, idolatry, divination, and superstition, and principally the heresy, apostasy, and idolatry perpetrated by learned persons in the city and diocese of Nantes, every time that the case occurs, belonged according to this custom and continues to belong to the Reverend Father, Lord Bishop of Nantes, and to the Inquisitor into Heresy delegated to the said city and diocese of Nantes, as much separately as conjointly; thus it transpired, and this is a true rendering.

VIII. Item, that as much by law as by usage, mores, observance, and custom in the said French realm, and principally in the said city and diocese of Nantes, practiced since the aforesaid period and commonly observed up to the present time by virtue of the privilege conceded by the aforesaid apostolic authority to the said Order of Dominicans, the aforesaid Friar Guillaume Mérici, Inquisitor into Heresy, was empowered to substitute in his place and to depute and ordain to this office another friar or other friars of the same order; thus it transpired, and this is a true rendering.

IX. Item, that the said Gilles de Rais, the accused, was and is a parishioner of the parish of Sainte-Trinité, of Machecoul, in the said diocese of Nantes, and that he is held and reputed commonly, publicly, and famously as such.

X. Item, that the aforesaid Gilles de Rais, the accused, has been since the period of his youth and adolescence, and is still, subject and justiciable of the said Lord Bishop of Nantes and the Inquisitor, but above all of the Lord Bishop, for the aforesaid crimes; thus it transpired, and this is a true rendering.

XI. Item, that, since the aforesaid time and presently, within the limits of the said diocese of Nantes were regularly and are still found the castle or fortress of the said place as well as the church parishes of Saint-Trinité, of Machecoul, and Saint-Étienne-de-Mermorte; and that the parishioners of these same church parishes are subjects and justiciables of the same Lord Bishop regarding things of the spirit, as they are also of the aforesaid Inquisitor for the crimes mentioned above and below; that they are publicly and notoriously; thus it transpired, and this is a true rendering.

XII. Item, that the said Friar Guillaume Mérici, already Inquisitor, in Nantes, July 26, 1426, instituted in his place, deputed and ordained as his vicar, capable of exercising his office in the aforesaid city and diocese of Nantes, Friar Jean Blouyn, of the aforesaid convent and order, by letters destined to that effect, to the content of which the same prosecutor refers, which he will produce when it is exposed more fully later following the articles and depositions; thus it transpired, and this is a true rendering.

XIII. Item, that the said Friar Jean Blouyn, forty years old, before the granting of the said letters establishing him in that office was and did belong to the aforesaid Dominican Order and monastery in Nantes, that he is a priest, belongs to the fellowship of the faithful, and is otherwise capable of exercising the office of the said vicariate; and that he is held and reputed commonly, publicly, and famously as such; and that this is a true rendering.

XIV. Item, that all the abovenoted has long been common knowledge.

XV. Item, considering what was reported at first by public rumor, then by the secret inquiry led by the said Reverend Father, Lord Bishop of Nantes, in his city and diocese, at the same time as by his commissioners, deputed by apostolic authority, in the course of their pastoral visit, as well as by that led by the aforesaid prosecutor of the ecclesiastical court of Nantes, by the authority of the said father, on the cases expounded below, crimes and offenses concerning ecclesiastical jurisdiction; and considering also the preceding denunciations reiterated grievously and tearfully, with lamentations, by many persons of both sexes as much in the aforesaid city as in the aforesaid diocese of Nantes, bemoaning the loss and murder of their children, boys and girls, stating positively that these same boys and girls were taken by the said Gilles de Rais, the accused, Gilles de Sillé, Roger de Briqueville, Henriet Griart, Étienne Corrillaut, also known as Poitou, André Buchet, Jean Rossignol, Robin Romulart, a man by the name of Spadine, and Hicquet de Brémont, familiars and frequent guests of the same Gilles de Rais, the accused, and that by them these children had had their throats cut inhumanly, had been killed and finally dismembered and burned, and in other respects shamefully tormented; that the same Gilles de Rais, the accused, had sacrificed the bodies of these children to demons in a damnable fashion; that according to many other reports the said Gilles de Rais had evoked demons and evil spirits and sacrificed to them, and that with the said children, as many boys as girls, sometimes while they were alive, sometimes after they were dead, sometimes as they were dying, Gilles had horribly and ignobly committed the sin of sodomy and exercised his lust on the one and the other, disdaining the girls' natural vessel: the aforesaid prosecutor declares and intends to prove, if necessary, that by all evidence, for the past forty years, every year, every month, every day, every night and every hour of these forty years, under the governments of Lords Martin, Pope, the fifth of that name, of blessed memory, and Eugène, by divine Providence, Pope, the fourth of that name, and of Most Reverend Father in God, Lord Philippe, Archbishop of Tours, and of Reverend Father in God, Lord Jean, aforesaid Bishop of Nantes, as well as of the very illustrious Prince and Lord Jean, Duke of Brittany, and whatever the offices and titles of those who reigned respectively and successively then, the aforesaid Gilles de Rais, imbued with evil spirit and forgetting his salvation, took, killed, cut the throats of many children, boys and girls; that these were taken, killed, butchered, as much by him as by the aforesaid Gilles de Sillé, Henriet Griart, and Étienne Corrillaut, also known as Poitou, and that he caused and ordered the bodies of these children to burned, reduced or converted to ashes, and their ashes thrown into secret and out-of-the-way places; that on these same children he committed the said unnatural sin of sodomy and abused them ignominiously; and that he committed and perpetrated in many and various places, and in the residences designated below, all that is set forth above and following.

XVI. Item, that in order to shed light on the disclosures of the preceding article, the same prosecutor declares and intends to prove that it is permitted to Christ's worshipers who desire to be united with the angelic society neither to delight in lust, consecrated as they are to God once and for all by baptism and by the engagement and profession of the Catholic faith, nor to turn their eyes or their minds toward this world's vanities and follies, but that it is, rather, more suitable for them to place their hope in Our Lord God and in contemplating His features, with all their heart and mind, and to impregnate their sight, as the prophet David witnesses, saying: "Blessed is the man who puts his hope in the Lord and does not loiter in the vanities and the follies of the world!" and once again the same David shouting and exhorting: "Sons of men, up to what point will the hardness of your heart go, cherishing vanity and searching after falsehood?"; but the aforesaid Gilles de Rais, who had received the sacraments of baptism and confirmation as a true Christian, and who, in receiving them, had renounced the devil, his ceremonies, and his work, relapsed into that which he had renounced. And more or less five years ago in a lower hall of the castle at Tiffauges, belonging to his wife, in the diocese of Maillezais, he had several signs, figures, and characters traced by certain masters like François Prelati, of Italian descent, self-styled expert in the forbidden art of geomancy; and in a wood close by the castle at Tiffauges he had these same signs traced in the earth by Jean de La Rivière, and Antoine de Palerne, a Lombard, as well as by a man named Louis, and other magicians and conjurors of demons, and had them conjure and divine, and he invoked and had them invoke evil spirits answering to the names of Barron, Oriens, Beelzebub and Belial, by means of fire, incense, myrrh, aloes and other aromatics, the windows and openings of the said lower hall being fully opened, while they genuflected to obtain responses from these same evil spirits, ready to offer and sacrifice to them and to adore them; the said Gilles, the accused, wanted to conclude a pact with them in order to obtain and recover knowledge, power, and riches with the assistance of these evil spirits; thus it transpired, and this is a true rendering.

XVII. Item, that the said Gilles de Rais, the accused, made a pact with the aforesaid evil spirits, by virtue of which he would do their will; and that by this pact the said accused secured that the same evil spirits would provide him with knowledge, riches and power; thus it transpired, and this is a true rendering.

XVIII. Item, that once, around the same period, the aforesaid François[5] — whom a certain Milord Eustache Blanchet, a priest from the diocese of Saint-Malo, had sent for from Italy and introduced to Gilles, the accused, in order to initiate this latter into the art of conjuring evil spirits — in a field one quarter of a league outside the castle of Tiffauges, using fire and having traced a circle in the same place, summoned certain evil spirits in the company of the said Étienne Corrillaut, also known as Poitou, specially charged by the said Gilles de Rais to assist the said François; and that previously the same accused had delivered unto these same François and Étienne[6] a note written in his own hand, destined for the evil spirit called Barron in the event that the latter responded to the said invocation and said conjuration, and to be exhibited and offered in the said Gilles' name, which note said that the same Gilles, the accused, would give Barron everything he asked for with the exception of his soul and the curtailment of his life, provided he procured knowledge, power, and riches for Gilles; thus it transpired, and this is a true rendering.

XIX. Item, that on another occasion around the same time, the aforesaid Gilles de Rais and François Prelati, in a certain field near the castle and town of Josselin, that side of the suburbs adjoining the said castle and said town, summoned evil spirits and performed other superstitions there also; thus it transpired, and this is a true rendering.

XX. Item, that again around the same time, namely one year ago more or less, when he went to see the aforesaid Duke of Brittany for the last time, the said Gilles, the accused, finding himself in Bourgneuf, in the diocese of Nantes, in the

[5] François Prelati.

[6] Étienne Corrillaut, called Poitou.

(1. Bill of Indictment.) house of the Frères Mineurs, in the company of the said François, had this latter invoke and conjure evil spirits several times, and summoned them himself in the hope of and intending for the same Lord Duke to take the said Gilles into his good graces; thus it transpired, and this is a true account.

XXI. Item, that at approximately the same time the aforesaid André Buchet, of Vannes, led the son of Jean Lavary, a young boy of about ten, from the market-place in Vannes to where the said Gilles de Rais was staying, at the house of a man named Jean Lemoine, close to the episcopal palace of Vannes, outside and close to the walls of the city; which said young boy the said accused sodomized sinfully before putting him to death and while watching him die, abused him shamefully and disreputably, then cruelly killed him in the house of a neighbor named Boetden, and after having severed and retained the head, he had the body of this young boy thus massacred thrown into the latrines belonging to the said Boetden's house; thus it transpired, and this is a true rendering.

XXII. Item, that the said Gilles, the accused, wrote notes in his own hand, concluding a well-established pact with the aforenamed evil spirit Barron and proposing such things as are mentioned above; thus it transpired, and this is a true rendering.

XXIII. Item, that each and every one of these things is common knowledge.

XXIV. Item, that during the said forty years or thereabouts, the said Gilles de Rais, the accused, sent the aforesaid Gilles de Sillé, then his director, accomplice, abettor, instigator, and support, into many and various parts of the world and into various regions and various places, to seek after and see if he could locate and bring back to Gilles male or female diviners, invokers, and conjurors, who could secure him money, reveal to him and discover hidden treasures, initiate him into other magical arts, procure for him great honors, and permit him to take and hold castles and cities; thus it transpired, and this is a true rendering.

XXV. Item, that in the same period the said Gilles, the accused, sent also the aforenamed Eustache Blanchet into Italy and Florence to locate invokers, con-jurors, and diviners, which Eustache, having then found the aforesaid François Prelati in Florence, brought him to the same Gilles; thus it transpired, and this is a true rendering.

XXVI. Item, that the said Gilles, the accused, more or less around the same time, as much in the city of Nantes in his house of La Suze as in Orléans in the house and under the sign of the Croix d'Or, where he was staying, and in the said castles of Machecoul and Tiffauges, made many and various invocations and con-jurations of evil spirits; thus it transpired, and this is a true rendering.

XXVII. Item, that during the said forty years approximately, Gilles de Rais, the accused, as much in the castles at Champtocé, in the Angevin diocese, and Machecoul and Tiffauges, as in the house of the said Lemoine, at Vannes, in the upper chamber of the same house where he was staying at that time, and in the said house called La Suze, situated in the Notre-Dame parish of Nantes; that is, in a certain upper chamber where from time to time and often he would retire and pass the night, killed treacherously, cruelly, and inhumanly one hundred and forty, or more, children, boys and girls, or had them killed by the said Gilles de Sillé, Roger de Briqueville, Henriet, Étienne,[7] André[8] and aforementioned others, respectively and successively; showing himself horribly and inhumanly guilty, since, according to what Hermogène says: "Each time a man usurps the office of the Creator by abolishing His creatures, the celestial Virtues will not cease crying before the divine Judge, until vengeance be exacted on the murderer who shall burn in eternal flames" — more especially as the said Gilles de Rais immolated the members of the said innocents as sacrifices to evil spirits; with which innocents, before and after their death and also during, he committed the abominable sin of sodomy, which defiles heaven, and which he abused contrary to nature in order to satisfy his carnal, illicit, and damnable concupiscence; and then burned and had the said Gilles de Sillé, Henriet Griart, and Étienne Corrillaut, also known as Poitou, burn in these same places respectively the bodies of these boy and girl innocents, and had them throw the ashes into the pits as well as into the *moats*[9] of the said castles and into the sinks of the house of La Suze, so named of old after Lord Jean de Craon, his grandfather, the said Gilles de Rais' mother's father, who was during his lifetime Lord of the domain of La Suze and of the house where he lived and died. Into the hiding places of this same house of La Suze were thrown fifteen out of about one hundred and forty of the said innocents killed by order of the said Gilles, the accused, as much by himself as by the said Gilles de Sillé, Henriet, and Étienne, successively and respectively, in the same way as was done in other secret, out-of-the-way places in the aforesaid cities and castles; thus it transpired, and this is a true rendering.

XXVIII. Item, during the period of these said forty years or thereabouts, the said Gilles de Rais, the accused, and, in his name and by his order, the said Gilles de Sillé, Roger de Briqueville, Henriet, Étienne, and André Buchet, requested procurers, procuresses and old female go-betweens whom they charged — under the pretext of certain services that the said children might render the said Gilles, who himself would prove of service to these same children, their parents, and their friends — with procuring children, as many boys as girls, to nab them and bring them to him, so that Gilles de Rais, the accused, could perform the sin of sodomy on them, cut their throats and kill them, or have their throats cut and have them killed; which procurers and female go-betweens damnably procured the said innocents for Gilles de Rais and for his aforesaid accomplices; thus it transpired, and this is a true rendering.

XXIX. Item, that less than a year ago, by order of the said Gilles de Rais, the accused, then staying in the said place of Bourgneuf, in the house of the Frères Mineurs, the aforesaid Henriet and Étienne procured for and delivered to him a boy fifteen years old or thereabouts, so that the accused could commit on him the oft-mentioned sin of sodomy; the said Henriet and Étienne took this adolescent,

---

[7] Étienne Corrillaut, called Poitou.

[8] André Buchet.

[9] Translator's note: italicized in the French {*douves*}.

(1. Bill of Indictment.) originally from Lower Brittany, who was living in the house of a man named Rodigo, an inhabitant of Bourgneuf, and brought him to the said Gilles de Rais, the accused, in a room of the said convent, where the same Gilles de Rais, the accused, was lodged and regularly stayed, and he exercised the oft-mentioned detestable vice of sodomy on him, in the same way as on the aforesaid others, in damnable fashion, and then he killed him on the spot and had his body carried to the castle at Machecoul to be burned; this was done by the said Gilles de Rais, the accused, and by the said Henriet and Étienne; thus it transpired, and this is a true rendering, notorious and public.

XXX. Item, that the said Gilles de Rais, the accused, ate delicacies and drank fine wines, hippocras, claret, and other sorts of alcoholic drinks for the purpose of working himself up to the said sin of sodomy and practicing it unnaturally on the said boys and girls with greater abundance, ease, and pleasure, often and often again, in an excessive and unusual manner; and that he abused his eating and drinking habits daily; thus it transpired, and this is a true rendering.

XXXI. Item, that in his room in the castle at Tiffauges, the said Gilles, the accused, placed the hand, eyes, heart, and blood of one of the said children in a glass to offer it in homage and as tribute to the aforesaid demon Barron, and that he had this oblation offered in his name by the said François Prelati; the same François being designated for this and knowing how to conjure evil spirits, as abovenoted; thus it transpired, and this is a true rendering.

XXXII. Item, that for about five years, more or less, the said Gilles de Rais had celebrated, on many solemn feasts and in particular on last All Saints' Day, a certain very conspicuous solemnity to honor the evil spirits, and in keeping with the pact concluded between him and the said evil spirits, as has been reported above; during which feasts, by virtue of the abovesaid pact, in the name of these same evil spirits and for their exaltation, he offered and caused to be offered alms to the poor; thus it transpired, and this is a true rendering.

XXXIII. Item, that the said Gilles de Rais, the accused, set his purposes, his hopes, and his belief in the invocation of evil spirits, divination, the murder of the said innocent children, the sin of sodomy, and unnatural lust; thus it transpired, and this is a true rendering.

XXXIV. Item, that more or less during the aforesaid forty years the said Gilles, the accused, conversed with diviners and heretics; that he repeatedly solicited their assistance for what he intended to perpetrate; that he communicated and collaborated with them, that he accepted their dogmas and studied and read their books touching on the interdicted arts; that he brought all his attention, hope, and mind to and fixed on these detestable dogmas to discover the ways and means proper to summoning evil spirits; and that he made a dogma of the conclusions and errors of diviners and conjurors; thus it transpired, and this is a true rendering.

XXXV. Item, that the said Gilles de Rais, the accused, more or less during these forty years frequented the invokers and conjurors of evil spirits, diviners and sorcerers, and that he received, favored, and protected them; that he believed them; that he learned, practiced, and held as dogma the magic arts of geomancy and necromancy forbidden by divine, canonical, and civil law; thus it transpired, and this is a true rendering.

XXXVI. Item, that five years ago, more or less, when the aforesaid Lord Duke of Brittany attacked the castle of Champtocé, and before the siege of the said castle, which the aforesaid Gilles de Rais, the accused, then possessed, the said Gilles de Rais, the accused — for fear that the Lord Duke, his men, his officers, and other persons might discover them — had the said Gilles de Sillé, Henriet, and Étienne Corrillaut, also known as Poitou, remove and place in coffers, to be transported by them to the castle at Machecoul in order to be burned, forty-five heads, with the bones of innocents inhumanly killed by the said Gilles, the accused,[10] on which children he had detestably committed the sin of sodomy and other crimes against nature; and at the said castle of Machecoul these heads and bones were burned by the aforesaid Henri Griart, Gilles de Sillé and Étienne Corrillaut, also known as Poitou, by order of the said Gilles, the accused; thus it transpired, and this is a true rendering.

XXXVII. Item, that Gilles de Rais, the accused, Henriet Griart, Étienne Corrillaut, Gilles de Sillé, Jean Rossignol, Spadine, Roger de Briqueville, André Buchet, and aforesaid others, as for each and every one of the crimes, offenses, and villainies, lent mutual assistance, counsel, and support, and were consenting agents and accomplices, each one among them respectively; thus it transpired, and this is a true rendering, public, notorious, and manifest.

XXXVIII. Item, that the said Gilles de Rais, the accused, two years ago, more or less, examining in himself the great number of villainies, to wit, perfidious apostasy of the faith, offenses, and accursed crimes and sins designated above and others that he had detestably perpetrated which his conscience was oppressing him with, swore, vowed, and promised by God and by His saints that never again from there on out would he perpetrate or commit similar horrors and abominations, that he would abstain immediately and absolutely, and that for this purpose he would go on a pilgrimage to Jerusalem where he would visit the Holy Sepulcher of the Lord; thus it transpired, and this is a true rendering.

XXXIX. Item, that notwithstanding these aforesaid oaths, vows, and promises, the said Gilles de Rais, the accused, since then, as a dog returns to its vomit, inhumanly killed children and caused them to be killed, and cut their throats and caused their throats to be cut, both boys and girls, in the aforesaid places; and that he committed the said sin of sodomy, in which he wallowed, and that he continued, as abovesaid, in his accursed, unnatural lust; but it is because of the said unnatural sin of lust, according to the disposition of justice, that tremors, famines and pestilences occur here on earth; and that he invoked and conjured evil spirits and caused others to do so, and that for these reasons the said Gilles, the accused, relapsed into and persisted in the aforesaid crimes; thus it transpired, and this is a true rendering, public, notorious, and manifest.

XL. Item, that regarding each and every one of these crimes, there were and

[10] These facts are inexactly related: see p. 97.

are public rumblings and clamor.

XLI. Item, that for the aforesaid reasons the abovenamed Gilles de Rais, the accused, should be taxed with infamy; that he has committed the sin of sodomy, and that he has lapsed and relapsed into heresy, idolatry, and apostasy of the faith; thus it transpired, and this is a true rendering.

XLII. Item, that two years ago the said Gilles de Rais, acting in a sacrilegious manner notwithstanding a fear of God, with several of his fellow accomplices furiously and recklessly dared to enter the said parochial church of Saint-Étienne-de-Mermorte, in the diocese of Nantes, with offensive arms; and that in a foolish display of violence he laid and caused others to lay hands on a certain Jean Le Ferron, cleric, originally of Nantes; and he had Le Ferron violently and forcibly chased and expelled from the said church by a certain Lenano, Marquis de Ceva,[11] a Lombard, and by his other associates; then he had him imprisoned for days and months as much in the said castle at Saint-Étienne-de-Mermorte as in the aforesaid castle at Tiffauges, where he was detained, irons on his feet and hands; and that the said Gilles, the accused, violating the immunity of the Church, inasmuch as he violated it himself and also caused others to violate it, has incurred the sentence of excommunication, in accordance as much with the law as with the authority of the Council of Tours and the synodal statutes of the Church of Nantes; thus it transpired, and this is a true rendering, public, notorious, and manifest.

XLIII. Item, that the said Gilles de Rais, the accused, in many and various places and before many honorable persons said, divulged, and publicized the aforesaid crimes done and perpetrated by himself; and that he considered them as so much dogma; and that he had practiced and practiced often the said magic arts, the said invocations and divinations, and other superstitions, with the purpose of increasing his honor, knowledge, and power; thus it transpired, and this is a true rendering, notorious and public.

XLIV. Item, that the said Gilles de Rais, the accused, committed and perpetrated the sin of sodomy unnaturally, and the other aforesaid crimes, sins, and villainies, in each of the aforesaid places and their vicinities, as abovesaid; and thus it transpired, and this is a true rendering.

XLV. Item, that the common opinion of men, the belief and assertion of the people, the true report, the common memory, the public voice and rumor, as much in the aforesaid parishes of Saint-Trinité, Machecoul, Saint-Étienne-de-Mermorte, Saint-Cyr-en-Rais, in the Nantes diocese, as in the greatest portion of the Breton duchy and in other adjoining regions, in which the said Gilles de Rais, the accused, was and is known, is that he was and is a heretic, a relapsed heretic, a magician, a sodomite, a conjuror of evil spirits, a seer, a cutter of the throats of innocents, an apostate, an idolater, having deviated from the faith and being hostile to it, a diviner, and a sorcerer. Thus it transpired, and this is a true rendering, commonly said, held, believed, presumed, seen, heard, reputed, public, notorious, and manifest.

[11] Spelled *Sceva* or *Seva* in the Latin text.

178

XLVI. Item, that the said Gilles de Rais, the accused, had and has the habit of committing and perpetrating the said crimes and offenses for which he is publicly and notoriously defamed by honest and serious people and of which he is vehemently accused in each and every one of the aforesaid places; thus it transpired, and this is a true rendering.

XLVII. Item, that the aforesaid things in general and in particular are clearly detrimental to our Catholic faith and our Holy Mother Church as well as to the public as a whole, inasmuch as they are a pernicious example unto many, and as they contribute to the peril of the said Gilles' soul; thus it transpired, and this is a true rendering.

XLVIII. Item, that each of these things and all of them were and are notorious and manifest in the said places to the extent that they could not be hidden by subterfuge or denied by retraction; on the subject of which there are public rumblings and rumors. And all these aforesaid things the said Gilles, the accused, acknowledges, and acknowledges as true.[12]

XLIX. Item, that considering the aforesaid crimes, excesses, and misdemeanors committed and wickedly perpetrated, the said Gilles de Rais incurred the aforesaid authorities' sentence of excommunication and other punishments expected to be promulgated against like presumptuous people as are diviners, sorcerers, conjurors and summoners of evil spirits, abettors, adepts, believers in and partisans of evil spirits, magicians, and all those who have recourse to the illicit and forbidden arts; that, moreover, he lapsed and relapsed into and continues in heresy, that he offended Divine majesty, that he committed the crime of Divine high treason, against the Ten Commandments, against the rites and observances of our Holy Mother Church, that he damnably sowed the most flagrant of errors, which are noxious to Christian believers, and that on the other hand, he gravely and shamefully violated the jurisdiction of said Reverend Father, Lord Bishop of Nantes; thus it transpired, and this is a true rendering, notorious, and public.

*Conclusion.* This is why the said prosecutor requests that you, Reverend Father, Lord Bishop of Nantes, and you, Friar Jean Blouyn, aforesaid Vice-Inquisitor into Heresy — or whomever of you it so pleases — by your definitive sentence, decree and declare that the said Gilles de Rais, the accused, is a heretic and perfidious apostate; declare that he committed and maliciously perpetrated the dreadful invocation of demons; that he has incurred by this the sentence of excommunication and other lawful punishments; and as a heretic, an apostate, and a conjuror of demons, that he ought to be punished and corrected as the law demands and canonical sanctions stipulate. Moreover, that you, Reverend Father, Lord Bishop of Nantes, and by your definitive sentence, decree and declare that the said Gilles de Rais, the accused, committed the crime and practiced the unnatural vice of sodomy on the aforesaid boys and children; that he maliciously perpetrated sacrilege, namely the violation of ecclesiastical immunity, and has incurred for this the

---

[12] Evidently this last sentence was tacked on after a formal reading of the bill of indictment, which occurred October 13, 1440. Gilles de Rais' first confessions date from October 15th.

(1. Bill of Indictment.) sentence of excommunication and other lawful punishments; and that he ought to be punished and salubriously corrected, as the law and canonical sanctions demand; the said prosecutor humbly implores your gracious office to duly see to the swift fulfillment of justice in all of the aforesaid and every one of them.

And the said prosecutor gives, speaks, and establishes the proof of each and every one of the aforesaid things by the best means possible and proper, and he requests your permission to establish that proof, which he offers to do, with the exception of all superfluous proofs, as noted, which he expressly affirms; and with the exception of the right to correct, add, change, diminish, interpret, ameliorate, reiterate, and prove, if necessary, at a reasonable time and place.

[Signed:] *J. Delaunay, J. Petit, G. Lesné.*

2. Letters, dated July 26, 1426, from the Inquisitor into Heresy in the French realm; Friar Jean Blouyn commissioned as Vicar of the Inquisitor.

Friar Guillaume Mérici, of the Dominican Order, professor of theology, Inquisitor into Heresy in the French realm, delegated by apostolic authority, to our beloved brother in Christ, Jean Blouyn, of the convent of the same order in Nantes, greetings in the author of the faith, Our Lord Jesus Christ.

Since according to the Apostle the evil of heresy spreads like a canker and insidiously destroys simple souls if not extirpated in time by the diligent hoe of the Inquisition, it is appropriate to proceed advantageously with all the solicitude and circumspection of the office of the Inquisition against heretics and their defenders, and also against those accused or suspected of heresy and against hinderers and disturbers of the faith. Also, putting complete trust in the Lord as to your ability and your aptitude for exercising the work of the Lord in this domain, by virtue of the counsel provided us by several discreet friars of the same order, we have made, instituted, and created by the terms of the present letters, and make, institute, create, and ordain you, the best we could do in every manner and form of law, our vicar in the city and diocese of Nantes, giving and conceding to you the power to inquire of, cite, accuse, pursue, seize, detain, and proceed against, by all available opportune and judicial means, to a definitive sentence inclusively, all and every one of whatsoever heretics and aforesaid others there may be, but also to do all other things relevant, as much customarily as lawfully, to the said office of the Inquisition; to which charges in our place as much as possible we commit you by the present letters, as much by virtue of the common law as by that of the aforesaid Inquisition's special privileges. In witness whereof we have affixed our seal to the present letters.

Given in Nantes, July 26, 1426.

Thus signed: *G. Mérici.*

**Saturday, October 15, 1440.**

On Saturday, October 15th, arraigned before the said Reverend Father in God, Lord Bishop of Nantes, and Friar Jean Blouyn, aforesaid Vice-Inquisitor, sitting on the bench to administer the law in the great upper hall of La Tour Neuve, in the morning at the hour of Terce, the said Milord Guillaume Chapellion, prosecutor and plaintiff, on the one hand, and Gilles de Rais, knight and baron, the aforesaid accused, on the other, personally appeared.

At the said prosecutor's request, the aforesaid Lords Bishop of Nantes and Friar Jean Blouyn, Vice-Inquisitor, told the said Gilles de Rais, the accused, that even though elsewhere he chose not to speak or object against anything in the said articles and positions, nonetheless they would permit him, to the extent that they permitted him earlier, to speak or object to anything. Which Gilles responded that he did not intend to speak or object against anything in the said articles, and at the said prosecutor's request, the said Lords Bishop of Nantes and Friar Jean Blouyn, Vice-Inquisitor, interrogated the said Gilles, the accused, to see whether he intended to say or propose anything and contest that Lords Bishop of Nantes and Friar Jean Blouyn, Vicar, were his judges in the case and the cases of this order. Which accused then said no; moreover, he intended and intends to concede that the said Reverend Father in God, Lord Bishop of Nantes, and Friar Jean Blouyn, Vicar, had been and were his competent judges in the case and the cases; furthermore he intended and intends to acknowledge that the said Reverend Father in God, Lord Bishop of Nantes, and Friar Jean Blouyn, Vicar of the aforesaid Inquisitor, Guillaume Mérici, had been and were in the case and the cases of this order his competent judges, confirming and approving their jurisdiction, as he asserted; and he consented to recognize them and whatever judge among them that they wanted; and he voluntarily averred that he had maliciously committed and perpetrated the expressed crimes and offenses within their jurisdiction; and he solicited humbly, devoutly, and tearfully the said Lords Bishop of Nantes and Friar Jean Blouyn, Vicar, and all other ecclesiastics about whom he had spoken badly and indiscreetly, to pardon him for the insults and offensive things that he had addressed to them, and he admitted his shame for having pronounced them. Which Lords Bishop of Nantes and Vicar of the Inquisitor pardoned this same Gilles, the accused, for the said insults, and did so for the love of God.

Then, in the presence of the said Gilles de Rais, the accused, hearing and understanding and expressly consenting to this, the said prosecutor

Gilles de Rais' submission and first confessions. Swearing-in of the accused and production of the first witnesses.

181

(Gilles de Rais' submission and first confessions. Swearing-in of the accused and production of the first witnesses.)

and plaintiff earnestly solicited the aforesaid Lords Bishop of Nantes and Vicar of the Inquisitor for permission to establish the proof of the aforesaid articles; which Lords Bishop and Vicar, at the said prosecutor's request, declared the said articles and positions admissible to this effect. Consequently the aforesaid prosecutor requested the said Gilles, the accused, to respond to the aforesaid articles and positions. Which Gilles, under oath, acknowledged spontaneously and declared to be true the First, Second, Third, Fourth, Eighth, Ninth, Tenth, Eleventh, and Fourteenth Articles set forth in order and in French by the Reverend Father, Lord Jean Prégent, Bishop of Saint-Brieuc, by mandate of said Lords Bishop of Nantes and Vicar of the aforesaid Inquisitor; and acknowledged and declared more particularly that there had existed and existed still a church cathedral in Nantes, and that according to the content of the Thirteenth Article, the said Reverend Father, Lord Jean de Malestroit, was the true bishop of that same church; that so far as concerns the spirit he himself was that same Lord Bishop's subject and justiciable; in addition, that the Machecoul and Saint-Étienne-de-Mermorte castles stood within the limits of the said diocese of Nantes. Item, he avowed voluntarily that he had received the sacrament of baptism and renounced the Devil and his ceremonies, but that he had never invoked, nor caused others to summon evil spirits, or offered or caused to be offered anything whatsoever in sacrifice to these spirits; that he had received from a certain Angevin knight, now imprisoned for heresy, a certain book on the art of alchemy and on the invocation of demons, which he read, and caused to be read several times publicly in a certain room at Angers before several listeners; that he had spoken with the said knight now in prison about practicing the said art of alchemy and the invocation of demons; which book he claimed to have returned to the said knight and not to have held for very long. Moreover, the said Gilles de Rais, the accused, confessed to having practiced the said art of alchemy for a certain period of time and to having had it practiced by certain Lombards named Antoine[13] and François,[14] and by a certain Parisian goldsmith,[15] that in practicing this kind of art and experimenting in it he had frozen mercury and had it frozen, which he affirms to be quicksilver; and that he would have carried out many other experiments in this art, which he had believed and believes led to results in the said art, if it had

[13] Antoine de Palerne.

[14] François Prelati.

[15] Jean Petit, the alchemist, not to be confused with Jean Petit, notary public of Nantes.

not been for the Lord Viennese Dauphin's arrival at Tiffauges castle, where he had constructed and prepared furnaces for practicing the said art, which furnaces were demolished upon the Lord Viennese Dauphin's arrival. As for other deeds contained and narrated in the said promulgated articles, the aforesaid Gilles de Rais, the accused, denied their veracity; he denied also the invocations of evil spirits mentioned in the published articles, claiming and attesting that in the event that it were proved by witnesses whom the said prosecutor would produce against him in the cases, and in the depositions wherein he wanted to believe and maintain as above or elsewhere that the accused had invoked demons; or had them invoked, or entered into contracts with them; or sacrificed to them or caused others to sacrifice to them, or made oblations to them; then in that event, he would voluntarily undergo the test of fire. Moreover, the said Gilles de Rais, the accused, voluntarily requested that the said prosecutor produce against him in the case or the cases of this order witnesses to the deeds expressed in the articles by the prosecutor; that there was a broader declaration of the things contained in the prescribed articles and other things not expressed in those articles; and that their depositions had value; which the same Gilles also consented to believe. Whereupon the said prosecutor requested of the Reverend Father in God, Lord Bishop of Nantes, and Vicar of the said Inquisitor, in the presence of the aforesaid Gilles de Rais, the accused, hearing and understanding, that they be allowed to swear not to resort to calumny. Thereupon the said Lords Bishop and Vicar, judging that the said prosecutor and Gilles, the accused, ought to be allowed to take the said oath seeing as both of them asked for it, allowed them to do so. And immediately, at the request of the said Lords Bishop and Vicar, touching the Holy Writ, and upon the Holy Gospels which were in the hands of these same lords, they took according to usage, each of them successively, an oath to abstain from calumny and to tell the truth by all and every one of the clauses in the oath, as much regarding the promulgated articles as all the case and the cases of this order. Which oath thus taken, the said prosecutor, fulfilling the assignment of the term, and in the presence of the said Gilles de Rais, who consented to this, produced in the capacity of witnesses Henriet Griart,[16] Étienne Corrillaut,[17] also known as Poitou, François Prelati[18] of Monte-Catini, Milord Eustache Blanchet,

[16] His deposition, of October 17, 1440, is given below (p. 226).

[17] His deposition, of the same day, is given below (p. 217).

[18] His deposition, of October 16, 1440, is given below (p. 203).

priest,[19] Tiphaine, the widow of the deceased Robin Branchu, and Perrine Martin,[20] peremptorily summoned by the said Robin Guillaumet, cleric, by mandate of the said Lords Bishop and the aforesaid Vice-Inquisitor, according as the same Robin reported verbally to have summoned them in the capacity of witnesses in this same trial, before the said Lords Bishop of Nantes and Vicar and before us, aforesaid notaries public and scribes, immediately to bear witness to the truth in the case and the cases.

Which witnesses thus produced, the aforesaid Lords Bishop of Nantes and Vicar of the aforesaid Inquisitor, in the presence of Gilles de Rais, the accused, judged that they should be admitted and allowed them to take an oath, and consented to absolve them under surety since they had to depose in the case and the cases of this order. All of which witnesses thus admitted, in the presence of the said Gilles de Rais, the accused, swore on the Holy Gospels to tell, and depose, and attest to, the truth, the whole truth, and nothing but the truth, insofar as they knew it, on the subject of the articles put forward and expressed by the said prosecutor in the case and the cases of this order, and also on the subject of the things in general and in specific not expressed in the articles, on which they were soon to be examined and interrogated: to which the said Gilles, the accused, then consented; entreaty, love, fear, favor, rancor, hatred, mercy, friendship, or enmity being set aside and ceasing totally among the parties. The said Gilles, the accused, for his own part, consented to believe in the depositions of the said witnesses and also in those of no matter what other witnesses the said prosecutor would have to produce; he also agreed to adhere to things not covered in the articles, and declared that he did not intend to speak, object to, or allege anything against the allegations or characters of the witnesses. Of which witnesses and of any others that the prosecutor would have to produce for his part in the case and the cases of this order, the said Lords Bishop of Nantes and Vicar of the Inquisitor charged us, aforesaid notaries public and scribes, to proceed faithfully with the examination.

This being done, the said Lords Bishop of Nantes and Vicar of the aforesaid Inquisitor, at the said prosecutor's request, asked the said Gilles de Rais, the accused, whether he himself intended to interrogate the witnesses as to what they would present that merited examination and questioning, in expectation of which case they fixed and assigned for

[19] His deposition, of October 17, 1440, is given below (p. 210).

[20] These two witnesses' depositions are not included in the documents that have come down to us. We know that Perrine Martin died in prison, apparently some time after October 15th. And a certain Stephanie, or Tiphaine, appears below as detained at the same time as La Meffraye (p. 265 and note 22).

Gilles, the accused, the same day and all the following day to do so. Which Gilles responded then to the Lord Bishop and Friar Jean Blouyn, aforesaid Vice-Inquisitor, that he did not intend to interrogate anyone in the case and the cases, relying on the said witnesses' conscience for that. And things being arranged in the aforesaid manner, the aforesaid Gilles de Rais, the accused, falling to his knees and expressing contrition by great sighs, grievously and tearfully, begged humbly to be absolved in writing of the sentence of excommunication brought against him, as has been recorded above, by the said Lords Bishop of Nantes and the aforesaid Vice-Inquisitor on account of the fact that the same Gilles, the accused, although requested and exhorted canonically, had refused to respond to the said depositions and said articles. To which accused the said Lord Bishop of Nantes, in his name, the Vicar of the Inquisitor consenting to this, absolved the same accused in writing and restored him to participation in the sacraments and to the unity of the faithful in Christ and our Holy Mother Church, in due form of law and according to the customs of the Church, a salutary penance corresponding to the fault being ordained by the aforesaid Lord Bishop of Nantes for the same Gilles, the accused; whereupon he had the absolution everywhere publicly announced.

Then, at the said prosecutor's request, the aforesaid Lords Bishop of Nantes and Vicar of the aforesaid Inquisitor assigned and fixed to the prosecutor and said Gilles de Rais, the accused, in order to proceed immediately in these same cases as by law, the following Monday, so that the said Gilles could see the other witnesses produced on the part of the prosecutor in the case and the cases of this order.

Of which the said prosecutor requested us, aforesaid notaries public and scribes, to make one and several public instruments,

In the aforesaid place, in the presence of the Reverend Father in God, Milord Jean Prégent, Bishop of Saint-Brieuc, the honorable and discreet Master Pierre de L'Hôpital, President of Brittany, Regnaud Godelin, licensed in law, the aforesaid Guillaume de Grantbois, Jean Chauvin, Guillaume de Montigné, Robert de La Rivière, licensed in both courts of law, and many other witnesses assembled in large numbers, specially called and requested.

[Signed:] *Delaunay, J. Petit, G. Lesné.*

## Monday, October 17, 1440.

Monday, October 17th, arraigned before the aforesaid Bishop of Nantes and Friar Jean Blouyn, aforesaid Vice-Inquisitor, sitting on the

Production of various witnesses.

185

(Production of various
witnesses.)

bench to administer the law in the great upper hall of the said Tour Neuve, at the hour of Vespers, the said prosecutor and plaintiff, on the one side, and Gilles de Rais, the accused, on the other, appeared in person.

Which prosecutor, satisfying the term, produced in the capacity of witnesses the men named Lenano, Marquis de Ceva,[21] Bertrand Poulein,[22] Jean Rousseau,[23] Master Gilles Heaume, licensed in law,[24] and Friar Jean de Lanté, Benedictine prior of Chéméré, in the said diocese of Nantes, peremptorily summoned by the aforesaid Robin Guillaumet, cleric, by mandate of the said Lords Bishop of Nantes and Friar Jean Blouyn, Vicar of the aforesaid Inquisitor, as the said Robin reported verbally to have summoned them before the said Lords Bishop of Nantes and Friar Jean Blouyn, Vicar, and us, aforesaid notaries public and scribes in the same court, in order to bear immediate witness to the truth in the case and the cases of this order; which witnesses the said Lords Bishop of Nantes and Friar Jean Blouyn, Vicar of the said Inquisitor, in the presence of the said Gilles de Rais, the accused, judged that they should be admitted and allowed them to take an oath, and they required to excuse them from bail since they would have to depose in the case and the cases of this order. All and every one of which witnesses thus admitted, in the presence of the said Gilles, the accused, swore to tell and attest to the truth, the whole truth, and nothing but the truth, as they knew it, on the subject of the articles put forward by the said prosecutor in the case and the cases of this order, and also on all and every one of the things on which they would be interrogated; entreaty, favor, love, fear, rancor, mercy, friendship, and enmity being set aside and ceasing totally among the parties. This being done, at the said prosecutor's request the said Lords Bishop of Nantes and Friar Jean Blouyn, Vicar of the aforesaid Inquisitor, asked the said Gilles, the accused, whether he himself intended to interrogate the witnesses as to their merit in examination and interrogation, in expectation of which the said Lords Bishop and Vicar assigned to the accused the same day and all the following day to do so. Which Gilles, the accused, then responded to the said Lords Bishop of Nantes and Friar Jean Blouyn, Vicar of the Inquisitor, that he

[21] His deposition is given below (p. 236).

[22] His deposition is given below (p. 237).

[23] His deposition is given below (p. 234).

[24] Gilles Heaume's and Jean de Lanté's depositions cannot be found in the documents handed down to us.

did not intend to interrogate any witnesses. Of which witnesses the said Lords Bishop of Nantes and Friar Jean Blouyn, Vicar of the aforesaid Inquisitor, charged us, aforesaid notaries public and scribes, to proceed faithfully with the examination. Moreover, at the said prosecutor's request, the aforesaid Lords Bishop of Nantes and Friar Jean Blouyn, Vicar of the Inquisitor, fixed and assigned to the prosecutor and Gilles, the accused, the following Wednesday, so that the aforesaid Gilles, the accused, could see certain other witnesses by the said prosecutor produced, received, and admitted to take an oath in the case and the cases of this order.

Of which things the said prosecutor requested us, aforesaid notaries public and scribes, to make one and several instruments.

In the said place in the presence of the Reverend Father in God, Lord Jean Prégent, Bishop of Saint-Brieuc, Masters Pierre de L'Hôpital, President of Brittany, Robert de La Rivière, Regnaud Godelin, Jean Chauvin, Hervé Lévy, Guillaume de Montigné, and the aforesaid Milord Guillaume Després, rector of the church parish of Bourg-Barré, in the Rennes diocese, and Master Olivier Solidé, canon of Nantes, with many other witnesses assembled in the same place in large numbers, specifically called and requested.

[Signed:] *Delaunay, J. Petit, G. Lesné.*

## Wednesday, October 19, 1440.

Wednesday, October 19th, the aforesaid Master Guillaume Chapeillon, prosecutor and defender, on the one hand, and the said Gilles de Rais, the accused, on the other, appeared personally in arraignment before the Reverend Father in God, Lord Jean de Malestroit, Bishop of Nantes, and Friar Jean Blouyn, Vicar of the aforesaid Inquisitor, sitting on the bench to administer the law in the aforesaid place, at the hour of Terce, in the morning.

Continuation of the production of witnesses.

Which prosecutor, satisfying the writs of the term, produced in the case and the cases of this kind in the capacity of witnesses the venerable Milord Jacques de Pencoëtdic, a professor in both courts of law, Jean Audilaurech, André Seguin, Pierre Vilmain, Master Jean Lorient, Jean Briand, Jean Le Veill, Jean Picard, Guillaume Michel, Pierre Drouet, Eutrope Chardavoine, Robin Guillemet, surgeon, Robin Riou, Jacques Tinnecy, and Jean Letournours, whom the aforesaid Robin Guillemet, cleric, by mandate of the said Lords Bishop of Nantes and Friar Jean Blouyn, Vicar of the aforesaid Inquisitor, had peremptorily summoned,

(Continuation of the production of witnesses.)

and whom the same Robin reported verbally to the aforesaid Lords Bishop of Nantes and Friar Jean Blouyn, aforesaid Vicar, and us, notaries public and scribes, to have summoned before them in this same trial to bear immediate witness to the truth, in the presence of the said Gilles, the accused. Whom the Lords Bishop of Nantes and Friar Jean Blouyn, aforesaid Vicar, received as witnesses and consented to excuse them under surety since they had to depose in the case and the cases. Who thus received as witnesses, in the presence of Gilles, the accused, swore upon the Holy Gospels to tell, and attest to, the truth, the whole truth, and nothing but the truth, as they knew it, of the things upon which they would be examined and interrogated; entreaty, esteem, love, fear, favor, hate, rancor, mercy, kindness, friendship, and enmity ceasing and being equally set aside. And on this account the said Lords Bishop and Friar Jean Blouyn, the aforesaid Vice-Inquisitor, asked Gilles de Rais, the accused, whether he intended to interrogate the witnesses, in which case they assigned for him, the accused, the same day and all of the following; which Gilles responded that he intended to interrogate no one. Of which witnesses the aforesaid Lords Bishop of Nantes and Vicar of the Inquisitor charged us, the aforesaid notaries public and scribes, to make a faithful examination. That done, the said Lords Bishop and Vicar of the Inquisitor, at the said prosecutor's request, assigned to the same prosecutor and the said Gilles, the accused, the following day, so that the defending party could see produced any and every claim, by which they intended to strengthen the case and the cases of this order, and in order to proceed immediately. Then the said Gilles de Rais, the accused, at the said prosecutor's request, was interrogated by the said Lords Bishop of Nantes and Friar Jean Blouyn, Vicar of the aforesaid Inquisitor, to know whether he intended to give, say, propose, allege, or produce on his behalf or in his justification some important motive for the crimes, offenses, or deeds brought against him and declared in the articles promulgated. Which accused responded immediately that he did not know what to say other than what he had already said.

Of which things the said prosecutor requested us, aforesaid notaries public and scribes, to make one and several public instruments,

In the aforesaid place in the presence of the aforesaid Reverend Father in Christ, Jean Prégent, Bishop of Saint-Brieuc, Master Pierre de L'Hôpital, President of Brittany, nobleman Milord Robert d'Épinay, knight, Master Gilles Lebel, Robert de La Rivière; Raoul de La Moussaye, provost of the church of Guérande, in the Nantes diocese, Regnaud Godelin, licensed in law, and Jean Guiolé, provost allocated to Nantes, with many other witnesses specifically called and requested.

[Signed:] *Delaunay, J. Petit, G. Lesné.*

# Records of the Hearings

## Thursday, October 20, 1440.

On Thursday, October 20th, arraigned before the aforesaid Lords Bishop of Nantes and Friar Jean Blouyn, Vicar of the aforesaid Inquisitor, sitting on the bench to administer the law in the said great upper hall of La Tour Neuve, in the morning at the hour of Terce, the said Master Guillaume Chapeillon, prosecutor and defender, on the one side, and the aforesaid Gilles de Rais, the accused, on the other, appeared in person.

*The judges decide to torture Gilles.*

And fulfilling the appointed term, the aforesaid prosecutor, asking and soliciting the said Lords Bishop of Nantes and Friar Jean Blouyn, Vicar of the aforesaid Inquisitor, to fix and assign a convenient term for the said Gilles de Rais to speak or object to anything he wanted, orally or in writing, against the said things produced, the said Lords Bishop and Vicar of the aforesaid Inquisitor fixed and assigned to the same Gilles, the accused, on which to speak thus, the following Saturday, as well as to the prosecutor himself, on which to proceed immediately in the case as by law.

Then, however, at the said prosecutor's request the said Lords Bishop of Nantes and Friar Jean Blouyn, the aforesaid Vice-Inquisitor, interrogated anew the said Gilles, the accused, to know whether he intended to give or propose something of importance on his behalf or in his justification, on the subject of the offenses and crimes raised and proposed against him, specified and declared in the aforesaid articles, and to say whatsoever it might be against the things thus produced. Which accused responded no, but that he was abiding by what he had already said at another time.

After which the said prosecutor in the presence of the said Gilles, the accused, hearing and understanding, requested Lords Bishop and Friar Jean Blouyn, Vicar of the Inquisitor, to fix and assign as well a term to the same Gilles, the accused, during which to see published the statements and depositions of the aforenamed witnesses. Which Gilles, the accused, said that that was not necessary, considering what he had already confessed and intended to confess again. Notwithstanding which, at the said prosecutor's entreaty the said lords asked the accused whether they ought to publicize the witnesses' statements and depositions. Which accused responded yes. Which statements and which depositions the aforesaid Reverend Father, Lord Bishop of Nantes, and Vicar of the Inquisitor published at once with the consent of the said Gilles, the accused; and once again, at the said prosecutor's insistence, the Reverend Father, Lord Bishop of Nantes, and Vicar of the aforesaid

(The judges decide to torture Gilles.)

Inquisitor asked the said Gilles, the accused, whether he intended to say or allege, orally or in writing, anything of importance against the said witnesses' characters or against their depositions. Which accused voluntarily responded no.

In response, the said prosecutor declared that considering the confession of the said Gilles, the accused, considering the production of witnesses, their statements, and their depositions that sufficiently established the intent of the accused in the case, he entreated no less earnestly of the same Lords Bishop of Nantes and Friar Jean Blouyn, his judges, that in order to shed light on and more thoroughly scrutinize the truth, torture or the rack ought to be applied to the said Gilles, the accused.

Which Lords Bishop and Vicar of the said Inquisitor, having discussed everything with their experts, and having considered everything that had gone before, ordered the rack or torture for the said Gilles de Rais, and decided that the said Gilles should suffer torture and be submitted to interrogation and tortures.

Of which things the aforesaid prosecutor requested us, the aforesaid notaries public and scribes, to prepare him one and several public instruments. Present, in the aforesaid place, Reverend Father in God, Milord Jean Prégent, Bishop of Saint-Brieuc, nobleman Milord Robert d'Épinay, knight, the aforesaid Masters Hervé Lévy and Robert de La Rivière, Milord Durand, rector of the church parish of Blain, in the said Nantes diocese, and Milord Michel Mauléon, rector of the church parish of Ancenis, in the said Nantes diocese, as well as many other people present and witnesses assembled there in large numbers, specially called and requested.

[Signed:] *Delaunay, J. Petit, G. Lesné.*

## Friday, October 21, 1440.

1. Gilles humbly begs his judges to postpone the application of torture to the following day: they delegate the Bishop of Saint-Brieuc and the "President of Brittany" to hear the confessions of the accused.

Friday, October 21st, the said Lords Bishop of Nantes and Friar Jean Blouyn, Vicar of the Inquisitor, presented themselves again in the morning, at the hour of Terce or thereabouts, in the lower hall of La Tour Neuve, stating and asserting that on the preceding day, namely Thursday, October 20th, they had decided to torture the said Gilles or submit him to canonical interrogation according, as it is written, to a judicial instrument of the said Thursday read before them in the presence of the said prosecutor and Gilles de Rais, the accused, and that, even though they themselves had fixed and assigned Saturday to Gilles, the accused, to say or object, orally or in writing, anything he wanted against what had been produced in the case or the cases of this kind, as well as to the said lord prosecutor, in order to proceed in the case and the cases of this kind; afterwards, since it would not be illegal, however, they intended to proceed with the torture ordered by them, as has been said, and to ensure its application; and at the request of the said prosecutor, appearing in person in the same location, they mandated that the said Gilles, the accused, be made to submit to the said torture.

The latter, by order of the said Lords Bishop of Nantes and Vicar of the Inquisitor, came and appeared personally before them in the said lower hall to submit to the said torture. And as the said Lords Bishop of Nantes and Vicar of the Inquisitor intended, in fact, to proceed with the application of the said torture or said interrogation of the said Gilles, the said Gilles begged them humbly to be willing to postpone the said application until the following day, which had been assigned as noted; saying that in the meantime he would deliberate somehow on the subject of the crimes and offenses brought against him, he would satisfy them to the extent that it would not be necessary to question him thereon; supplicating and requesting that the said Lord Bishop of Saint-Brieuc, in the interest of the ecclesiastical court, namely in the interest of the said Lords Bishop of Nantes and Vicar of the Inquisitor, and that the said Lord President, in the interest of the secular court, hear outside the place where the aforesaid torture had been ordered what the said Gilles de Rais, the accused, himself intended to confess on the subject of the articles proposed against him, and that the Lords Bishop of Nantes and Vicar of the Inquisitor yield their place to the said Lord Bishop of Saint-Brieuc; the said Lords Bishop of Nantes and Vicar of the Inquisitor consenting to the said accused's supplication, yielded their place on this score to the said Bishop of Saint-Brieuc, then present and accepting the charge graciously; and in favor of the accused, they postponed the application of the said torture to the second hour of the afternoon of the present day, in the following manner: that if by chance the said Gilles, the accused, confessed the crimes with which he was reproached, or anything similar, then, at that hour even or later, the former would postpone the said application of torture to the following day.

On the subject of each and every one of which things the said prosecutor asked us, aforesaid notaries public and scribes, to make one and several public instruments.

In the presence of noblemen Milord Robert d'Épinay, knight, Yvon de Rocerf, Master Robert de La Rivière, Pierre Juete, Jean de Vennes, and a large number of other witnesses specifically called and requested.

At this second hour of the afternoon on the said Friday, the said

# DOCUMENT I — VERDICT OF THE ECCLESIASTICAL COURT

(1. Gilles humbly begs his judges to postpone the application of torture to the following day: they delegate the Bishop of Saint-Brieuc and the "President of Brittany" to hear the confessions of the accused.)

Lords Bishop and Vicar of the Inquisitor presented themselves person-ally in the said lower hall and, at the request of the said prosecutor, himself appearing personally in the same place, the said Lords Bishop and Vicar, by virtue of the aforesaid commission, sent to the said Gilles, the accused, in a certain upper chamber in the said castle of La Tour Neuve in Nantes, which he was given to inhabit and then supposed to remain in, the aforesaid Lords Bishop of Saint-Brieuc and President of Brittany, along with Jean Petit, one of the four aforesaid notaries public and scribes, in order to hear and report on whatever the accused might say on the subject of what was proposed to him, as it has been said. Which lords commissioners visited the said Gilles and, on the same day, having returned to the said lower hall, said and reported to the said Lords Bishop of Nantes and the Vicar that they had spoken to the said accused, who made a long confession in their presence, the content of which is provided below, which they then exhibited.

[Signed:] *J. Delaunay, G. Lesné.*

2. Gilles de Rais' "out-of-court confession."

What follows is the oft-mentioned out-of-court confession of Gilles de Rais, the accused, made in the presence of the said Lords Bishop of Saint-Brieuc, appointed by the said Lords Bishop and Vicar, so far as concerns ecclesiastical jurisdiction, and Master Pierre de L'Hôpital, President, Jean Labbé, Yvon de Rocerf, squire, Jean de Touscheronde, cleric, and me, Jean Petit, aforesaid scribe and notary public, specially convoked for this in the convenient room given in La Tour Neuve castle in Nantes to the said Gilles, in which to stay, repose, and sleep during the trial. As said above, the said confession was made voluntarily, freely, and under no constraint, on the afternoon of Friday, October 21st, in the aforesaid year.

And first, on the subject of the abduction and death of many children; the libidinous, sodomitic, and unnatural vice; the cruel and horrible manner of killing; at the same time, the invocations of demons, obla-tions, immolations or sacrifices; the promises made or the obligations contracted with them by him or other things mentioned in the first or subsequent articles; the said Gilles de Rais, interrogated by the said Lord Bishop of Saint-Brieuc and the said President, in their presence and in the presence also of several other people, voluntarily, freely, and grievously said and confessed that he had committed and maliciously perpetrated on numerous children the crimes, sins, and offenses of homicide and sodomy; he confessed also that he had committed the invocations of demons, oblations, and immolations, and made promises and obligations to demons, and done other things that he had confessed recently in the presence of the said Lord President and other people.

Interrogated by the said Reverend Father and President as to the place where and time when he began perpetrating the crime of sodomy, he responded: in the Champtocé castle; he professed not to know when or in what year, but to have begun doing it the year his grandfather, Lord de La Suze, died.

Item, interrogated by the said Lord President as to who had persuaded him to the aforesaid crimes and taught him how to commit them, he responded that he did and perpetrated them according to his imagination and idea, without anyone's counsel and following his own feelings, solely for his pleasure and carnal delight, and not with any other intention or to any other end.

And the said Lord President being surprised, as he said, that the said accused would have accomplished the said crimes and offenses of his own accord and without anyone's instigation, summoned the said accused again to tell from what motives, with what intent, and to what ends he had the said children killed and committed on them the said sins and had their cadavers burned, and why he gave himself up to other aforesaid crimes and aforesaid sins, adjuring him to be willing to declare these things thoroughly, in order to disburden his conscience, which most likely was accusing him, and to secure more easily the favor of the most clement Redeemer; whereupon the said accused, indignant at being solicited and interrogated in this manner, spoke in French to the said Lord President: "Alas! Monsignor, you torment yourself and me along with you."[25] Which Lord President responded to him in French: "I don't torment myself in the least, but I'm very surprised at what you've told me and simply cannot be satisfied with it. I desire and would like to know the absolute truth from you for the reasons I've already told you often."[26] To which Lord President the said accused responded: "Truly, there was no other cause, no other end nor intention, if not what I've told you: I've told you greater things than this and enough to kill ten thousand men."[27] With this, the said President ceased interrogating the said accused and ordered that François Prelati be brought into the said

[25] In Old French in the original Latin text: "Hélas! monseigneur, vous vous tourmentez et moy avecques."

[26] In Old French: "Je ne me tourmente point, mais je suis moult émerveillé de ce que vous me dictes and ne m'en puis bonnement contenter. Ainçois, je désire et vouldroye par vous en savoir la pure vérité pour les causes que je vous ay ja souvent dictes."

[27] In Old French in the original Latin text: "Vrayement il n'y avoit autre cause, fin ne intencion que ce que je vous ay dit: je vous ay dit de plus grans choses que n'est cest cy et assez pour faire mourir dix mille hommes."

(2. Gilles de Rais'
"out-of-court confession.")

room. And François was brought forth in person before the said Gilles, the accused, and other people present, and he and the said Gilles, the accused, were interrogated together by the said Lord Bishop of Saint-Brieuc, on the invocation of demons and the oblation of the blood and members of the said small children — which the said Bishop said that the said Gilles and François had just confessed — and the places where they performed the said invocations and oblations already confessed by them.

Which Gilles, the accused, and François responded that the said François performed several invocations of demons, and of one named Barron specifically, by order of the said accused, as much in his absence as in his presence; and moreover, the said accused said that he was present at two or three invocations, especially at the said places of Tiffauges and Bourgneuf-en-Rais, but that he was never able to see or hear any demon, even though the said accused, as they both said, had conveyed an obligatory note written and signed in his own hand to the same Barron by way of the said François, by which the said Gilles submitted to the said Barron and to his mandate, and promised to obey his orders, while retaining his soul, however, and his life; and that the said accused promised the said Barron the hand, eyes, and heart of a child, which François was supposed to offer him, as he said, but the aforesaid François did not do it, of which the aforesaid accused and François said that they had given a full statement in their recent confession; insofar as it was concerned, the said François agreeing with the said confessions.

Which Lord President then ordered the said François to return to his room or wherever he was being guarded. Whereupon the said accused, turning to the said François, spoke in tears and gasps to him in French: "Goodbye, François, my friend! never again shall we see each other in this world; I pray that God gives you plenty of patience and understanding, and be sure, provided you have plenty of patience and trust in God, we will meet again in the great joy of paradise! Pray to God for me, and I will pray for you!"[28] upon which saying, he embraced the same François, who was taken away immediately.

[Signed:] *Jean Petit.*

**Saturday, October 22, 1440.**

Gilles de Rais' "in-court
confession."

Saturday, October 22nd, arraigned before the said Lord Bishop of

[28] In Old French in the original Latin text: "Adieu Francoys, mon amy! jamais plus ne nous entreverrons en cest monde; je pri Dieu qu'il vous doint bonne pacience et esperance en Dieu que nous nous entreverrons en la grant joye de paradis! Priez Dieu pour moy et je prieray pour vous."

Nantes and Friar Jean Blouyn, Vicar of the Inquisitor, sitting on the bench to administer the law in the place designated above, at the hour of Vespers, the said Master Guillaume Chapeillon, prosecutor and plaintiff, on the one hand, and the said Gilles de Rais, the accused, on the other, appeared in person.

In conformity with the appointed term, the prosecutor asking that the said Lords Bishop of Nantes and Friar Jean Blouyn, Vicar of the Inquisitor, interrogate the said accused to know whether he intended to say anything else against or object to what had been said in the case, the accused said and responded that he did not intend to say anything, but voluntarily and freely, with great contrition of heart and great grief, according as it appeared at first sight, and with a great effusion of tears, confessed what he had confessed out of court in his room in the presence of the Reverend Father, Lord Bishop of Saint-Brieuc, Master Pierre de L'Hôpital, President of Brittany, Jean de Touscheronde, and Jean Petit. And he acknowledged that each and every one of the things contained and published in the said articles were and are true. And the accused himself adding to his other out-of-court confession without straying, wanted to repeat and recite it here, and to remedy its faults in the event that he had omitted anything, and to make more thorough declarations of the points developed summarily in the aforesaid articles; he voluntarily confessed and declared that he had committed and perpetrated iniquitously other high and enormous crimes, since the beginning of his youth, against God and His commandments, and that he had offended our Savior on account of the bad management he had received in his childhood when, unbridled, he applied himself to whatever pleased him, and pleased himself with every illicit act, and he urged those present who had children to instruct them in good doctrines and instill in them the habit of virtue during their youth and childhood.

After this confession made in arraignment by the said Gilles de Rais, the accused, as has been recorded, on the subject of the content of the aforesaid articles, and once the out-of-court confession had been repeated and recited — seeing as he affirmed that, among the crimes and offenses, there figured enormous crimes, *e.g.*, the sin against nature not as fully stated in the articles, already voluntarily acknowledged as true by him and whose secret confession he had made before the Reverend Father in God, Lord Jean Prégent, Bishop of Saint-Brieuc, and noblemen Pierre de L'Hôpital, President of Brittany, and Jean Labbé, squire, and me, Jean Petit, notary public, general examiner of witnesses for the ecclesiastical court of Nantes, and Jean de Touscheronde, scribe also to the secular court of the same place — so that the said secret confession would be committed the best way possible to the memory of men, it pleased the same Gilles, the accused, not to diminish but rather to fortify and reinforce it; and he asked that the aforesaid confession be published in the vernacular language for any and all of the people present, the better part of whom did not know Latin, and that the publication and confession of perpetrated offenses be set forth for his shame, in order for him to attain more easily the forgiveness of his sins and God's grace in absolving them; he said that in his youth he had always been of a delicate nature and for his pleasure and according to his will had done whatever evil he could, and that he had put his hope and intention in the illicit and dishonest acts and things that he did; he most tenderly besought and exhorted the fathers, mothers, friends, and neighbors of every young boy and every child to raise them with good manners, by good examples and doctrines; and to instruct them in these things and chastise them lest they fall in the trap wherein he himself had fallen. By which secret confession that in the said Gilles' presence was read in trial and published, and approved by him, the said Gilles de Rais, the accused, voluntarily and publicly, before everyone, confessed that, because of his passion and sensual delight, he took and had others take so many children that he could not determine with certitude the number whom he'd killed and caused to be killed, with whom he committed the vice and sin of sodomy; and he said and confessed that he had ejaculated spermatic seed in the most culpable fashion on the bellies of the said children, as much after their deaths as during it; on which children sometimes he and sometimes some of his accomplices, notably the aforesaid Gilles de Sillé, Milord Roger de Briqueville, knight, Henriet and Poitou, Rossignol and Petit Robin, inflicted various types and manners of torment; sometimes they severed the head from the body with dirks, daggers, and knives, sometimes they struck them violently on the head with a cudgel or other blunt instruments, sometimes they suspended them with cords from a peg or small hook in his room and strangled them; and when they were languishing, he committed the sodomitic vice on them in the aforesaid manner. Which children dead, he embraced them, and he gave way to contemplating those who had the most beautiful heads and members, and he had their bodies cruelly opened up and delighted at the sight of their internal organs; and very often, when the said children were dying, he sat on their bellies and delighted in watching them die thus, and with the aforesaid Corrillaut and Henriet he laughed at them, after which he had the children burned and their cadavers turned to ashes by the said Corrillaut and Henriet.

Interrogated as to where he perpetrated the said crimes, and when he began, and the number of deaths, he stated and responded: in the first place, at the Champtocé castle, in the year when Lord de La Suze, his grandfather, died, at which place he killed children and had them killed in large numbers — how many he is uncertain; and he committed with them the said sodomitic and unnatural sin; and at this time Gilles de Sillé alone knew, but then Roger de Briqueville, then Henriet, Étienne Corrillaut, also known as Poitou, Rossignol, and Robin successively became his accomplices; and he said that he had the bones of the children killed at Champtocé removed, heads as well as bodies, which had been thrown into the base of the tower; and he had them put in a coffer and transported to the castle of Machecoul, where they were burned and reduced to ashes; and that in the said place of Machecoul he had taken and killed other children, and caused them to be taken and killed — a large number of them, how many he did not know — and in the house named La Suze, in Nantes, which he possessed at that time, he killed, caused to be killed, burned, and turned to ashes many children, whose number he could not remember, whom he abused and defiled, committing with them the unnatural vice of sodomy, as above. Which crimes and offenses he committed solely for his evil pleasure and evil delight, to no other end or with no other intention, without anyone's counsel and only in accordance with his imagination.

Moreover, the said Gilles said and confessed that a year and a half ago the said Milord Eustache Blanchet brought to the said Gilles, the accused, from Florence,[29] in Lombardy, the said Master François Prelati, with the intention of practicing the invocation of demons; and that the said François told him that in the country he came from he had found the means by which to conjure a spirit who promised this same François that he himself could conjure a certain demon who called himself Barron as many times as the same François wanted.

Item, the said Gilles said and confessed that the said François performed many invocations by his order, as much in his absence as in his presence, and that he, the accused, had assisted François at three invocations performed by the latter: once at Tiffauges castle; again at Bourgneuf-en-Rais; he does not remember where the third one took place; he adds that the said Eustache Blanchet knew well that the said François was performing the aforesaid invocations, but that he was not present at them, because neither he, the accused, nor François would have tolerated it, seeing as the said Eustache was a vicious gossip, fertile with idle remarks.

---

[29] This concerns Florence, in Tuscany. Lombardy then signified Italy.

# DOCUMENT I — VERDICT OF THE ECCLESIASTICAL COURT

(Gilles de Rais' "in-court confession.")

Item, the said Gilles, the accused, stated and confessed that in order to perform the said invocations they traced signs in the form of a circle or of a cross, and of characters in the earth; and that the said François possessed a book that he had brought from Italy, so he said, in which there were the names of many demons and words to conjure and invoke them by, which names and which words he does not remember; which book the said François held and read for nearly two hours during the said conjurations and invocations; and that he, the accused, during none of these invocations saw or perceived any devil to speak to, which greatly irritated and disappointed him.

Item, the said accused stated and confessed that he was told on his return that at one invocation of the said François' in his absence, François had seen the demon named Barron and spoken with him, who said that he would not approach the accused because of his having fallen short of his promise and because he didn't fulfill it; and he, the accused, upon learning this, charged the said François to ask that same devil what he wanted of him and to assure him that whatever the devil wanted he would give, with the exception of his life and soul, provided that in this way, the devil conceded and gave to him what he asked for; the said accused adding that he intended to ask for knowledge, power, and riches, in order to recover the original state of his lordship and power; and that not long after this, the said François said that he had spoken with this same devil who, among other things, demanded that Gilles de Rais give him some members of a child; whereupon the said Gilles gave the said François the hand, heart, and eyes of a young boy to offer to the devil on behalf of Gilles, the accused.

Item, the said Gilles, the accused, said and confessed that before going to one of three invocations that he attended, he wrote a note in his own hand, which he signed with his own name in French: "Gilles"; but he does not remember the content of the said note, which he wrote intending to give it to the devil should he appear at the invocation performed by the said François; which he had done on the advice of the said François, who had told him that it was important to deliver the said note to the devil as soon as he appeared; and during the invocation he held the note constantly in his hand, awaiting the pacts or promises that the said François and the devil would formulate and their agreement as to what the said Gilles, the accused, would promise to accomplish for the devil; but the devil did not appear and did not speak with them.

Item, the accused stated and confessed that one night he sent the said Étienne Corrillaut, also known as Poitou, with the said François to perform an invocation; both of whom returned completely drenched and

198

soaked, telling him that nothing had come of the aforesaid invocation.

Item, the said accused stated and confessed that he wanted to be present at an invocation that the same François was to perform, but that the latter did not want his presence; and that on his return from the said invocation, he assured the said Gilles that if he had been present at that invocation, he would have been in great danger, because a serpent appeared that François was greatly afraid of; on hearing this, the said Gilles took hold of a splinter of the Holy Rood, which he possessed, and thought of going to the said place of invocation where the said François said he had seen the snake; which he did not do, because the same François dissuaded him.

Item, the same Gilles de Rais, the accused, stated and confessed that at one of the three invocations he attended, the said François related to the said accused how he himself had seen the demon named Barron, who had shown him a large quantity of gold, and among other things a gold ingot; but the said accused declared that he did not see the devil or the ingot but only a sort of foil in the form of a sheet or sheets of gold, which he did not touch.

Item, the accused stated and confessed that the last time he was at Josselin, in the Saint-Malo diocese, close to the Illustrious Prince and Lord Duke of Brittany, the same accused had several children killed who had been procured for him by the aforesaid Henriet; and that he committed and exercised on them the vice and sin of sodomy in the aforesaid manner.

Item, the same accused stated and confessed that the said François, by his order and in his absence, performed many invocations of the devil at Josselin, which nothing came of or appeared at.

Item, he said that before leaving for Bourges he sent the said François to Tiffauges, entreating him to conjure in his absence and to notify him of what he did and knew, and to write to him *in guarded terms*[30] that his work was going well; which François wrote to him and sent a sort of unguent in a silver tube, placed in a purse and a box made of silver also, writing to him that this here was a precious thing and that he ought to guard it carefully; and he, trusting the said François' affirmation, hung the said purse about his neck for several days; but shortly thereafter he threw it away, discovering that it was not doing him any good.

Item, the same accused stated and confessed that the said François once told him that the said Barron had ordered him to give a dinner to three poor people in his name on three important feasts of the year;

[30] The original says in Latin, "per verba seu vocabula cooperta," and glosses the expression in Old French as "par paroles couvertes."

which he, the accused, did only once, on All Saints' Day.

Interrogated as to the motive that made him keep the said François close to him and among his family, he responded that the said François was exceptionally gifted and agreeable to converse with, speaking Latin eloquently and learnedly, and that he applied himself zealously to the affairs of the said Gilles, the accused.

Item, the same accused stated and confessed that after last Saint John the Baptist's Day a beautiful young man who was living with a certain Rodigo, at Bourgneuf-en-Rais, where the accused himself was then staying, was brought to him one certain evening by the said Henriet and Corrillaut, and during the night he practiced the said unnatural and sodomitic vice with him in the aforesaid manner, then killed him and had him transported to Machecoul to be burned.

Item, he stated and confessed that having been alerted that the men of the castle at Palluau were planning to lay hands on the captain of the castle at Saint-Étienne-de-Mermorte, and for this reason indignant with them, one morning, what day he cannot remember, he left on horseback with his men-at-arms intending to surprise the men of the castle at Palluau, make them prisoners, and punish them; and at the outset of the expedition, the said François, being among his company, told him that he would not find them; and in fact, the said accused did not find them and his project was frustrated.

Item, the said Gilles de Rais, the accused, stated and confessed that he had killed two young pages, one of Guillaume Daussy's, and another of Pierre Jacquet's, called Princé, on whom he committed and exercised the said unnatural lust.

Item, the same accused stated and confessed that when he last went to Vannes, last July, André Buchet delivered a young boy to him, at his lodgings in the house of a man named Lemoine, with whom he committed the unnatural vice, as abovenoted. And having killed him, Gilles had him thrown by the said Poitou into the latrines of an inn owned by a man named Boetden, near the aforesaid Lemoine's house; the said friends of the accused lodging in Boetden's inn or house, near the marketplace of Vannes; which Poitou descended into the latrines, in order to sink the cadaver and cover it, so that no one might discover it.

Item, the aforesaid Gilles de Rais, the accused, stated and confessed likewise that before the said François' arrival, he had employed other conjurors, namely a trumpeter named Dumesnil, Master Jean de La Rivière, a man named Louis, Master Antoine de Palerne, and another whose name he does not remember. Which conjurors by his command performed many invocations, some of which he attended, as much as

Machecoul as at other places; and, in particular, to see drawn in the soil a circle or figure in the form of a circle, which is necessary in that sort of invocation where the intention is to see the devil and to speak and make a pact with him. But the said accused said that he was never able to see the devil or speak with him, although he did everything he could, to the point that it was not his fault if he could not see the devil or speak with him.

Item, the same Gilles de Rais, oft-named, stated and confessed that the aforesaid Dumesnil, conjuror, told him once that the devil, in order to do and accomplish what the said accused intended to solicit and obtain from this same devil, expected to see done and to receive from him a note signed in the hand of the accused himself with blood from his finger, by which the latter promised to give the said devil, when he appeared at his invocation, certain things which he did not remember; and for that reason and to that end he signed his name, *Gilles*, to the said note with blood from his little finger. As to what was written in the said note he did not remember, except that he promised the devil what was mentioned there, on condition that the devil give to him and procure knowledge, power, and riches. But he is absolutely certain that as he has affirmed, whatever he might have promised the devil he had always retained his soul and life, and he said that the aforesaid note was not delivered, the devil not appearing to him and not having responded to that same invocation.

Item, the said accused confessed that at an invocation by the aforesaid Master de La Rivière, in a wood not far from the garrison or the city of Pouzauges, the said La Rivière armed himself beforehand with weapons and gear, and then entered the aforesaid wood to perform the said invocation; and that he, the accused, with his servants and especially Eustache Blanchet, Henri, and Étienne Corrillaut, also known as Poitou, upon entering the wood, discovered the said La Rivière returning, who told him that he had seen the Devil in the guise of a leopard coming toward him, which passed by him without saying a word; and he, the accused, was frightened and terrified by what he said. And the accused added to his narration that the said La Rivière, to whom he had paid the sum of twenty gold royals, promised to return, which he did not do.

Item, the same accused stated and confessed that at another invocation of demons practiced by him and a conjuror whose name he does not remember, with Gilles de Sillé as well, in a room of the aforesaid Tiffauges castle, while he was in the said room, the said Sillé did not dare to enter the circle to perform the invocation, but retired to a window with the intention of throwing himself out of it if he perceived

(Gilles de Rais' "in-court confession.")

something fearful approaching, and he held in his arms an image of the Blessed Virgin Mary; the said accused himself was afraid in the circle, because the invoker had forbidden him to cross himself, because if he did, they would all be in great danger; but he remembered a prayer to Our Lady that begins with *Alma*, and at once the conjuror ordered him to leave the circle, which he immediately did while crossing himself; and he left the room promptly, leaving the invoker and locking the door behind him; then he discovered the said Gilles de Sillé, who told him that someone was beating and striking the invoker left alone in the room, which sounded as if someone were beating a featherbed; which he, the accused, did not hear, and he had the door of the room opened and at its entrance he saw the conjuror wounded in the face and in other parts of his body, and among other things, having a bump on his forehead so large he could barely stand up; and for fear that he might die in consequence of the said wounds, Gilles wanted him to be confessed and have the sacraments administered; but the conjuror did not die, and recovered from his wounds.

Item, the said Gilles de Rais, the accused, stated and confessed that he sent the said Gilles de Sillé into a region farther north, to find conjurors of demons or evil spirits. Which Gilles de Sillé, having returned, told him that he had found a woman who busied herself with like invocations: which woman had said to Sillé that if Gilles de Rais did not turn his soul away from the Church and his chapel, he would never accomplish what he desired; and that Sillé had met in the same region another woman who told him that if the said accused did not abandon a work begun by him or that he intended to pursue, or have it stopped, nothing good would ever come to him.

Item, that the said Gilles de Sillé had found in the same region an invoker whom he proposed sending to the said accused, which conjuror, who was preparing to join the said accused, drowned while crossing a river or stream.

Item, the said Gilles, the accused, stated and confessed that the said Sillé brought him another conjuror who also died immediately. And because of these unlucky deaths and the difficulties counterpoised to his guilty intentions in the aforesaid invocations or the like he said he believed that divine clemency and the intercession of the Church, from which his heart and his belief have never strayed, had mercifully arrived and prevented him from succumbing to so many tests and perils; and for this reason he intended to renounce his evil life, and make a pilgrimage to Jerusalem and the sepulcher of Our Lord and other places included in the Passion of his Redeemer and to do all that he could to obtain forgiveness for his sins, through the mercy of his Redeemer.

And then, after the said confession in arraignment, given freely and voluntarily, he exhorted the people there, and principally the ecclesiastics, there in considerably larger numbers, to always venerate our Holy Mother Church, and to honor her greatly and never to separate from her, adding expressly that if he himself, the accused, had not directed his heart and his affection toward that same Church, he never would have escaped the devil's malice and intention; moreover, he believed that had he not, because of the enormity of his villainies and crimes the devil would have long since destroyed his body and carried off his soul; exhorting, moreover, the fathers of families to watch that their children be not too finely dressed, and to tolerate no laziness, noting and asserting that many ills are born of laziness and of the excesses of eating and drinking, and declaring more expressly still that with him laziness, an insatiable desire for delicacies, and the frequent consumption of mulled wine, more than anything else, kept him in a state of excitement that led to the perpetration of so many sins and crimes.

On the subject of which crimes and offenses perpetrated by him, Gilles de Rais, the accused, humbly and tearfully implored the mercy and pardon of His Creator and most blessed Redeemer, as well as that of the parents and friends of the children so cruelly massacred, as well as that of everyone whom he could have injured in regard to whom he was effectively guilty, whether they were present there or elsewhere, and he asked all Christ's faithful and worshipers for the assistance of their devout prayers.

And this is why the aforesaid Master Guillaume Chapeillon, prosecutor, in the presence of the aforesaid Gilles de Rais, the accused, considering the voluntary confession of the said accused, and other proofs lawfully brought against him, requested instantly that a timely day and term be appointed to the accused in order to conclude — and at the same time, on the other hand, to see concluded — the sentence and definitive sentences by the said Reverend Father in God, Lord Bishop of Nantes, and Friar Jean Blouyn, Vicar of the said Inquisitor, and by each of them, or by those whom they would charge with this responsibility, sentences to be written and promulgated in the case and the cases of this order, unless the aforesaid Gilles de Rais, the accused, could give any valid reason this should not be done. Thereupon the said Lords Bishop of Nantes and Vicar of the Inquisitor assigned the following Tuesday to the prosecutor and Gilles de Rais, the accused, who did not object, in order to proceed as by law, as was necessary in the case and the cases of this order.

(Gilles de Rais' "in-court confession.")

Of which things the aforesaid prosecutor asked us, the undersigned notaries public and scribes, to make one and several public instruments.

In the aforesaid place in the presence of the Reverend Father in God, Milord Jean Prégent, Bishop of Saint-Brieuc, Masters Pierre de L'Hôpital, President of Britanny, Robert de La Rivière and Milord Robert d'Épinay, aforesaid knight, and nobleman Yvon de Rocerf, including the honorable Masters Yvon Coyer, dean, Jean Morelli, chorister, Gatien Ruytz, Guillaume Groyguet, licensed in both courts of law, Jean de Châteaugiron, Pierre Avril, Robert Viger, Geoffroy de Chevigny, licensed in law, the mayors of Nantes, Geoffroi Piperier, treasurer,[31] Pierre Hamon, Jean Guérin, Jean Vaedi and Jean Symon, canons from Notre-Dame-de-Nantes and Saint-Brieuc, Hervé Lévy, seneschal of Quimper, and Master Guillaume de La Lohérie, licensed in law, attorney to the secular court of Nantes, with many other witnesses assembled in the same place in large numbers, specifically called and requested.

[Signed:] *Delaunay, J. Petit, G. Lesné.*

**Tuesday, October 25, 1440.**

1. Official statement of the rendering of sentences.

The Tuesday following Saint Luke the Evangelist's Day, October 25, 1440, arraigned before the said Reverend Father in God, Lord Jean de Malestroit, Bishop of Nantes, and Reverend Friar Jean Blouyn, Vicar of the aforesaid Inquisitor, sitting on the bench to administer the law in the aforesaid great upper hall of La Tour Neuve, in the morning at the hour of Terce, the aforesaid Master Guillaume Chapeillon, prosecutor, for himself, on the one hand, and the aforesaid Gilles de Rais, the accused, also for himself, on the other, appeared in person.

Which prosecutor, fulfilling the appointed term in the case and the cases of this order, asked earnestly, in the presence of the said Gilles de Rais, the accused, hearing, understanding, and not contradicting, that this suit and the cases be concluded and held as concluded by the aforesaid Lords Bishop and Friar Jean Blouyn, Vicar of the aforesaid Inquisitor, and insofar as it depended on him, he had concluded in these same cases. And then the said Lords Bishop of Nantes and Friar Jean Blouyn, the said Vice-Inquisitor, in response to the prosecutor who had concluded and asked that it be concluded with him, in the presence of the said Gilles de Rais, the accused, not contradicting, but consenting to this, concluded and held it for conclusion and desired that it be held for

---

[31] Translator's note: see p. 158, note 2.

conclusion in these same cases.

Which conclusion accordingly made, the aforesaid prosecutor asked earnestly that the sentence and definitive sentences in the case and the cases of this order be immediately passed and promulgated in the presence of the aforesaid Gilles de Rais, hearing and understanding, in favor of the same prosecutor and against the said Gilles de Rais, the accused, by the same Lords Bishop of Nantes and Friar Jean Blouyn, Vicar of the aforesaid Inquisitor, following the conclusion and the conclusions of the published articles, and that these latter be passed and promulgated by these same Lords Bishop and Friar Jean Blouyn, Vicar of the aforesaid Inquisitor, or by whomever it pleased of the two, or by yet another delegated to that effect.

Thus the same Lord Bishop of Nantes and Friar Jean Blouyn, the same Vicar of the Inquisitor, sitting on the bench, as above, to administer the law, in the presence of the aforesaid Gilles de Rais, the accused, hearing, understanding, and not contradicting — considering, in the first place, all bills and speeches for the defense, all letters and documents, all developments and all confessions by the said Gilles, the accused, diligently examined by them; considering all depositions of witnesses and all other instruments and guarantees in the case and the cases of this order, held, exhibited, and produced, and each of these same things having been duly recorded with diligence and circumspection; considering the slow and careful deliberation on all these same things by the reverend fathers, lords bishops, doctors, jurists, theologians, illustrious practitioners and other honest men to whom the Lord Bishop of Nantes and Friar Jean Blouyn, aforesaid Vice-Inquisitor, presented a complete and faithful relation of the legal grounds of the case and the cases of this order; considering the counsel and agreement of these same lords bishops, doctors, jurists, theologians, practitioners and other honest men; therefore, the Lord Bishop of Nantes and Friar Jean Blouyn, Vicar of the aforesaid Inquisitor, proceeded and deemed it appropriate to proceed with their sentence and to all their definitive sentences which need be promulgated and passed in the case and the cases of this order, regarding the former and the latter, according to the things that by the bills, the speeches for the defense, the developments and the other instruments and guarantees, they examined and investigated, and that they now examine and understand; sentences that by means of the venerable and circumspect man, Milord Jacques de Pencoëtdic, practitioner in both courts of law and an official of Nantes, they passed and promulgated respectively and successively, the content of which is integrally contained below, conforming to certain memoranda that the aforesaid

(1. Official statement of the rendering of sentences.)

Pencoëtdic had delivered into his hands, which in the same place the Lords Bishop of Nantes and the Vice-Inquisitor had the aforesaid Milord Jacques, aforesaid doctor and official, read aloud in a clear voice. This promulgation of sentences being thus read, for his part and for that of the aforesaid Vicar of the aforesaid Inquisitor, the Lord Bishop of Nantes interrogated the aforesaid Gilles, the accused, to know whether he wanted to be reincorporated with the Church, our Mother, and to return to her, on account of the aforesaid errors, invocation of evil spirits, and other deviations from the Catholic faith. Which accused responded and said that he had never known what heresy was, that he did not know that he had lapsed into and committed it; however, ever since the Church judged that the acts he had committed smacked of heresy, as much by reason of his confession as by other proofs, in consequence of this judgment he devoutly supplicated to her on his knees — and did so while sighing and moaning — to be reincorporated by the said Lords Bishop of Nantes and Friar Jean Blouyn, Vicar of the aforesaid Inquisitor. To which reincorporation the aforesaid Lords Bishop of Nantes and Friar Jean Blouyn, Vicar of the said Inquisitor, received and admitted the aforesaid Gilles, the accused, who solicited it humbly; and they reincorporated him. Which Gilles, thus reincorporated, humbly and on his knees, with continued sighing and moaning, supplicated to be absolved of the sentences of excommunication brought against him in the aforesaid promulgation of definitive sentences and of all others that he could have incurred; as much for the aforesaid offenses by him committed and perpetrated in an iniquitous fashion as for the violation of immunity of the said parochial church of Saint-Étienne-de-Mermorte with that of all other churches, or for the detention and imprisonment of the said Jean Le Ferron, cleric, or for the insults proferred by him respecting the same Lords Bishop of Nantes, Vicar of the Inquisitor, and other ecclesiastics, and for the offenses to God and his Church; imploring them to grant him pardon. Which lords accorded it to him for the love of God, and thereupon the aforesaid Gilles de Rais, the accused, was absolved, in writing and in customary Church form, of the sentence of excommunication passed by the aforesaid Lord Bishop of Nantes, and restored to participation in the sacraments and to the unity of the faithful in Christ and his Church. Finally, at the earnest request of the said Gilles, the accused, the aforesaid Lords Bishop of Nantes and Friar Jean Blouyn, Vicar of the aforesaid Inquisitor, charged the male religious, Friar Jean Jouvenel, of the Carmelite Order of Ploermel, in the Saint-Malo diocese, to hear the secret confession of the accused, to absolve him of his sins previously confessed or needing to be confessed, and to impose and enjoin on him for all his sins a salutary penance in proportion to his faults, as much for those he had judicially confessed as for those he would confess at the tribunal of his conscience, and to absolve him of every other sentence of excommunication brought against him by the aforesaid judges in their lawful authority, conjointly as well as separately.

Of which things the said Master Guillaume Chapeillon, prosecutor, requested us, aforesaid notaries public and scribes, to make one and several public instruments.

In the aforesaid place in the presence of the Reverend Fathers, Milords Jean Prégent, Bishop of Saint-Brieuc, and Denis de La Lohérie, Bishop of Laodicée, and Guillaume de Malestroit, elect of the church of Mans, as well as the aforesaid honorable and noblemen Master Pierre de L'Hôpital, President of Brittany, Robert de La Rivière, and Milord Robert d'Épinay, knight, Yvon de Rocerf, and the aforesaid Masters Jean de Châteaugiron, Olivier Solidé, canon of Nantes, and Milord Robert Mercier, canon of the church of Saint-Brieuc, Guillaume Ausquier, rector of the church parish of Sainte-Croix-de-Machecoul, in the aforesaid Nantes diocese, Jean Guiolé, Guillaume de La Lohérie, licensed in law, Olivier and Guillaume Les Grimaux, attorneys for the secular court of Nantes, and many other witnesses assembled in the same place in large numbers, particularly called and requested.

[Signed:] *Delaunay, J. Petit, G. Lesné.*


## 2. Sentence brought against Gilles de Rais, guilty of heresy.

In the name of Christ,[32]

We, Jean, Bishop of Nantes, and Friar Jean Blouyn, bachelor of Holy Writ, of the Dominican Order in Nantes, Vicar of the said Inquisitor into Heresy for the city and diocese of Nantes, sitting on the bench and with our minds set on naught but God alone, considering the counsel and agreement of the reverend fathers, lords bishop, jurists, doctors, and masters of theology, by this true definitive sentence that we place in these instruments, considering the depositions of witnesses summoned by us and by our prosecutor, on this side delegated by us in a case of the faith, against you, Gilles de Rais, our subject and justiciable, on that side produced and diligently interrogated, and the faithfully drafted depositions of those same witnesses, considering your confession given voluntarily before us, and other items and matters considered on that

---

[32] The following text is preceded in the transcript by these words: "Content of the aforesaid memoranda of promulgation mentioned above, which follow and are such."

(1. Official statement of the rendering of sentences.) side that justly roused our souls, we decree and declare that you, the aforesaid Gilles de Rais, present before us in trial, are found guilty of perfidious apostasy as well as of the dreadful invocation of demons, which you maliciously perpetrated, and that for this you have incurred the sentence of excommunication and other lawful punishments, in order to punish and salutarily correct you and in order that you are punished and corrected as the law demands and canonical sanctions decree.

[Signed:] *Delaunay, J. Petit, G. Lesné.*

**3. Sentence brought against Gilles de Rais, "guilty of crime and unnatural vice with children."**

In the name of Christ,

We, Jean, Bishop of Nantes, sitting on the bench and with our minds set on naught but God alone, having examined and investigated the legal grounds and developments of the case of the faith brought before us on the part of our prosecutor, deputed by us to the case, and claimant against you, Gilles de Rais, our subject and justiciable, the accused party; considering the depositions of witnesses for their part and that of our prosecutor, in this case produced, sworn in, and diligently examined; considering the faithful account of their depositions; considering your confession, voluntarily given by you before us in trial, and publicly pronounced; and every other item and matter considered, which, from a canonical point of view, engrossed our minds; having taken counsel with the reverend fathers, the masters of theology, and the jurists, by the definitive sentence that we set down in these instruments, we decree and declare you, the aforesaid Gilles de Rais, appearing personally before us in court, guilty of committing and maliciously perpetrating the crime and unnatural vice of sodomy on children of both sexes; and for it with these instruments we excommunicate you and conclude that you have incurred other lawful punishments, in order to punish and salutarily correct you and in order that you be punished and corrected as the law and canonical sanctions demand.

[Signed:] *Delaunay, J. Petit, G. Lesné.*

# III

## DEPOSITIONS OF WITNESSES[1]

**I. Depositions regarding the children and the invocations.**

**1. François Prelati, cleric. October 16, 1440.**

And first:

FRANÇOIS PRELATI, examined and interrogated October 16, 1440, during the aforesaid pontificate and general council, on all things contained in the promulgated articles, successively and in order, deposed that he originally came from Monte-Catini in Val di Nievole, near Pistoia, in the diocese of Lucca, in Italy; a cleric, as he affirms, having received the clerical tonsure from the Bishop of Arezzo; having studied poetry, geomancy, and other sciences and arts, in particular alchemy; aged twenty-three or thereabouts, to the best of his belief.

Item, he stated and deposed that about two years ago, while he was staying at Florence with the Bishop of Mondovi, a certain Milord Eustache Blanchet, a priest, came to him, who made his acquaintance through the mediation of a certain master from Monte-Pulciano, and that then the same Eustache and he saw each other frequently for a time, eating and drinking together, and doing other things; finally the aforesaid Eustache asked him, among other things, whether he knew how to practice the art of alchemy and the invocation of demons; to which the aforesaid François responded yes; and then the same Eustache asked whether he wanted to come to France. To which the aforesaid

---

[1] "Affidavits of witnesses produced on the part of the aforesaid Master Guillaume Chapeillon, the prosecutor, before the aforesaid Reverend Father in God, Milord Jean, Bishop of Nantes, and Friar Jean Blouyn, Inquisitor into Heresy, by order and mandate of the aforesaid lords judges, faithfully and diligently examined, insofar as possible, on the abovecited articles of the aforesaid prosecutor, by us, Jean Delaunay, Jean Petit, Nicolas Géraud and Guillaume Lesné, aforesaid notaries public and commissioners, scribes deputed in the case and the cases of this order, by the aforesaid lords judges."

François responded that a relative of his acquaintance, named Martellis, lived in Nantes in Brittany, and that he would be glad to see Martellis. Then the aforesaid Eustache told the same François that in France there lived a great personage, namely Lord de Rais, who much desired to have about him a man learned and skilled in the said arts, and that, if the aforesaid François were skilled in that department and wanted to accompany him to the aforesaid Lord, he could receive generous accommodations. Whereupon, on account of the aforesaid things, the aforesaid François consented to accompany the same Eustache to the aforesaid Lord de Rais, and with that they took to the road to France; and the same witness carried with him, from Florence, a book dealing with invocations and the art of alchemy. And they arrived at Saint-Florent-le-Vieil, a city that belongs to no diocese, situated in the ecclesiastical province of Tours, and they stayed there for several days. And from this same place the aforesaid Eustache wrote to the aforesaid Lord de Rais in order to announce their arrival; upon learning which, the said Lord immediately sent the men named Henriet and Poitou, namely Étienne Corrillaut, his familiars, with two others, to travel towards the said witness and said Eustache, who arrived at Tiffauges, in the diocese of Maillezais. After their arrival, having received the aforesaid François and Eustache, and having been informed by the latter that this François was skilled and learned in the aforesaid arts, Lord de Rais rejoiced immensely; with which Lord the aforesaid witness stayed continuously for a period of about sixteen months thereafter.

Item, he said that after staying a while at Tiffauges he made the acquaintance of a certain Breton from Brittany who, at the same place, at Tiffauges, in the diocese of Maillezais, was lodging at the house of Geoffroy Leconte, the captain of the castle of the same place, and was caring for his wife, who was suffering from an eye malady; among this Breton's things the witness found a book bound in black leather, part paper, part parchment, having letters, titles and rubrics all in red. Now, this book contained invocations of demons and several other questions concerning medicine, astrology and more; which books[2] the witness showed a little later to the aforesaid Gilles. After having looked at and glanced through them, the same Gilles decided that together they would try out and test the contents of these books, particularly those parts regarding the aforesaid invocations. Thus, one night after dinner, in the large lower hall of the castle at Tiffauges, the aforesaid Gilles and witness, having taken candles and other things, with the book in question that the witness had brought, as he said, drew, using the tip of a sword in the soil, several circles comprising characters and signs in the manner of armories, in the composition and drawing of which the aforesaid Gilles de Sillé, Henriet, and

[2] Breton's and the one Prelati himself had brought from Italy.

Poitou, also known as Étienne Corrillaut, as well as Milord Eustache Blanchet, participated. After the aforesaid circles and characters were drawn and the light was lit, all the aforesaid except Milord Gilles de Rais and the witness, by order of the aforesaid Milord Gilles, left the aforesaid room, while the same Gilles and witness placed themselves in the middle of the aforesaid circles, at a certain angle close to the wall, where the witness traced another character with burning coal from a earthen pot; upon which coals they poured some magnetic dust, commonly called *magnetite*,[3] incense, myrrh, aloes, whence a sweet-smelling smoke arose. And they remained in the same place for almost two hours, variously standing, sitting, and on their knees, in order to worship the demons and make sacrifices to them, invoking the demons and working hard to conjure them effectually, the aforesaid Gilles and witness reading by turns from the aforesaid book, waiting for the aforesaid invoked demon to appear, but, as the witness affirms, nothing appeared that time.

Item, the witness said that one could read in this book how demons had the power to reveal hidden treasures, teach philosophy, and guide those who acted. The words of invocation that they used then were conceived thus: "I conjure you, Barron, Satan, Belial, Beelzebub, by the Father, Son and Holy Ghost, by the Virgin Mary and all the saints, to appear here in person to speak with us and do our will." Interrogated to know whether, in the event the demon had appeared in the same place, they would have made some gift or offering, the witness said yes: a live cock, dove, pigeon, or turtledove to engage him not to harm them during his invocation, and so that he would more easily grant them what they solicited.

Item, he said that the same Gilles and he made plans on another occasion to summon in the aforesaid place by other means, namely, with the aid of a stone called diadochite, and a crested bird; but lacking the stone, they did not do so.

He said, moreover, that in the same place the aforesaid Gilles and he performed several such invocations in the aforesaid manners and forms.

Item, he said that one night, he and Poitou, namely Étienne Corrillaut, the aforesaid servant of the aforesaid Rais, the latter knowing and prescribing it, and in his name, left the aforesaid castle at Tiffauges, in the aforesaid diocese of Maillezais, bringing the aforesaid book with tapers, magnetic dust, and other aromatics with which to summon demons, and arrived at a field about the distance of an arrow's flight below the pond of the aforesaid place, close to Montaigu; and there they drew a circle and characters similar to the aforesaid others and then lit the fire as above, and made the aforesaid invocations. And the witness recommended that the aforesaid Poitou, namely Étienne Corrillaut, not cross himself while entering the circle, and while they remained

---

[3] Rendered in French {*d'aimant*} in the original Latin text.

there, lest it prevent the invoked demon from appearing; and they performed the said invocation as the witness and said Gilles had in the aforesaid room, and nothing appeared; and they remained there about half an hour; they made that invocation about an arrow's flight away from an old, uninhabited house. As they were returning from the place of the said circle it began to rain torrentially, and the wind blew violently, and it was pitch dark.

Item, he declared that he had heard it said by a certain Guillaume Daussy, a familiar and servant of the said Gilles, that the same Gilles killed young boys, and caused them to be killed, in his room at Tiffauges, and in his room at Machecoul and at the entrance to the same said place, and that he offered their blood and members to demons, performing the aforesaid evocation of these same demons.

Item, that he had heard the man named Guillaume say that the said Gilles committed sodomy on the said boys.

Item, he said that about one year before, he had seen a child six months old, in the said room at Tiffauges, killed and stretched out on the floor, in the presence of Gilles de Sillé; which child he believes was killed by the said Sillé.

Item, that, as the said Gilles and witness performed several invocations together, at which the conjured demon did not appear, the said Gilles asked the witness why it happened thus and for what reason the invoked demon had not appeared or spoken to them, and he told the witness himself to ask the same thing of the devil. To find out, the witness made an invocation, and obtained from the invoked demon the response to the aforesaid question, which was that the said Gilles promised to give the conjured demons many things, but did not keep his promises; and that, if the same Milord Gilles intended the demon to appear and speak to him, each time he appeared and spoke to him, Gilles would have to give a cock, hen, dove, or pigeon, provided that the same Gilles did not solicit from this invoked demon anything considerable, and that if by chance he solicited something of the sort, he was then obligated to provide the demon some member of a young boy; and this is what the witness reported to the aforesaid Gilles.

Item, he said that this being brought to the attention of the said Gilles, the same Gilles, on one occasion a little later, carried into the said François' room the hand, heart, eyes, and blood of a young boy, kept in a glass, and gave them to him so that, as soon as they performed an invocation, François could offer and give them to the demon should he respond to the said invocation; as to whether the said members were those of the child the witness said he had seen dead in the said hall at Tiffauges, or those of another, he does not know, as he affirms.

Item, that not long after the aforesaid, the witness and the said Gilles, in the aforesaid place, that is, in the hall at Tiffauges, performed an invocation with the aforesaid ceremonies, with the intention of offering and giving the hand, heart, eyes, and blood to the demon if he appeared; at which invocation the demon did not appear, which is why a little later the witness wrapped the aforesaid hand, heart, and eyes in a piece of linen and buried them close to Saint Vincent's chapel, within the enclosure of the said castle at Tiffauges, in sacred soil, to the best of his belief.

Item, he said that he practiced several invocations in the aforesaid hall, placing incense, myrrh, and aloes on the fire lit in the earthen pot set in the center of the circle. At which invocations the devil named Barron appeared to him often, and as many as ten or twelve times, in the form of a handsome young man about twenty-five years old.

Item, he said that he had practiced three invocations in the presence of the said Milord Gilles at which the devil did not appear, nor had he ever again appeared to Gilles in the presence of the witness, and the witness did not know whether he had ever appeared to Gilles again.

Interrogated to know with whom, or by whom, and where the witness learned the art of the aforesaid invocations, he responded that it was in Florence and with a certain Master Jean de Fontenelle, a doctor, three years before.

Interrogated as to the manner by which he learned, he stated that the said Master Jean led him into an upper chamber of his house where, one day, he sketched a circle like the one mentioned before, and that he then performed invocations in the aforesaid manner. Which having been done, up to twenty birds like ravens appeared. Which birds did not speak to them. And nothing else was done for the time being.

Item, that on another occasion, in the aforesaid place, in the presence of the witness, the same Fontenelle performed the said invocation, and that then the devil named Barron appeared in the form of a young man, as previously noted, whom the said Jean de Fontenelle introduced to the witness; and the witness, closing a deal with the devil, promised to give him a chicken, dove, turtledove, or pigeon, each time he appeared to the witness.

Item, he said that when, accompanied by Poitou, namely Étienne Corrillaut, he went into a field outside the village of Tiffauges, as was reported before, the said Milord Gilles gave him a letter, written in French in Gilles' own hand, to deliver to the devil if he appeared at the invocation that the witness and the said Poitou, namely Étienne Corrillaut, were about to perform, and that they did as stated before; which letter contained, in effect, the following: "Come at my bidding, and I will give you whatever you want, except my soul and the curtailment of my life." Which letter he later returned to Gilles, the devil not having appeared at the aforesaid invocation.

Interrogated to know who provided the said Gilles with the formula in which the said letter was cast, he responded that he did not know.

Item, he declares that he heard the same Gilles say that he had practiced the art of the said invocations for about fourteen years, but that he had never seen the devil nor spoken with him.

Item, he heard a certain *La Picarde*, now dead, who was living at the time in the borough of Saint-Martin-de-Machecoul, say that she herself had received into her house as a guest someone who professed to practice the art of invocations with the said Gilles, but he did not hear her mention the said guest by name.

Item, he said that he performed an invocation at Bourgneuf, which the aforesaid Milord Gilles attended, and another at Josselin in a field, in the absence of the said Lord, the witness then being alone; and the aforenamed devil Barron appeared to him in the aforesaid form of a young man, clad in a mantle of violet silk.

Item, he said that less than a year before, in the absence of the said Milord Gilles, who was then staying at Bourges, while he was performing an invocation in the aforesaid hall at Tiffauges, Barron appeared to him in the aforesaid form. Who carried and entrusted to the witness a black powder, on a piece of slate. And Barron then enjoined François, the witness, to pass the same powder on to the said Milord Gilles at Bourges, so that he could put it in a small silver vessel and carry it on his person, because he would see his affairs prosper by doing so. Which powder the witness gave to Gilles de Sillé who, by a certain Gascard de Pouzauges, had it passed on to the said Milord Gilles at Bourges.

Interrogated as to whether Gilles carried this powder on him, he responded that he did not know; but that on the return of the same Lord Gilles to Tiffauges, the aforesaid Poitou, namely Étienne Corrillaut, returned the powder to the witness, in a small silver vessel, enveloped in a piece of linen, commonly called *sandal*,[4] and that the witness received it in the aforesaid vessel; which vessel the witness carried for some time attached about his neck and that then he detached it to keep in a small coffer, or casket, which he had in his room in the house of a certain Master Pierre Rondel at Machecoul, and that up to the moment when he was arrested the small vessel was there, when he was not carrying it in his purse.

Item, on the return of the said Lord Gilles from Bourges, the witness performed an invocation in the aforesaid hall at Tiffauges, at which Barron appeared in human form; from whom the witness, in the name of the said Lord Gilles, asked for money. And not long after that, in fact, he saw a large quantity of gold ingots appear in the room; this gold remained there for sever-

---

[4] In French in the original Latin text.

al days. As soon as he saw it, the witness wanted to touch it, but the evil spirit's response was that he should refrain because it was not yet time. Which the witness reported to the said Milord Gilles; and the same Milord Gilles asked him whether he might see it, whether that were permitted; to which the witness responded yes; and the two of them headed for the said room and, as the witness opened the door, a huge, winged, and vigorous snake, as big as a dog, appeared to them on the ground; and then the witness told the said Gilles to take care not to enter the room, because he'd seen a snake there; frightened, the said Gilles started to run for cover and the witness followed. After this the said Milord Gilles took a cross that contained splinters of the Holy Rood in order to enter the room more safely; but the witness told him it was not good to use a holy cross in such an affair. A little while later the witness entered the said room and, when he touched the said apparition of gold, he perceived that it was nothing but fawn-colored dust, and he knew by this the duplicity of the evil spirit.

Item, he said that the last time the aforesaid Milord Gilles intended to approach the Lord Duke, and this was in the month of July, the witness, by order of the said Gilles, interrogated the said Barron to see whether the said Gilles could go to the Lord Duke and return in safety; Barron responded yes; the witness repeated the same interrogation, and Barron responded to him as often at Machecoul as in Nantes, and not long afterwards at Josselin.

Item, the witness said that to the questions he posed to him on behalf of the said Gilles de Rais, the accused, he never obtained a truthful response from the devil named Barron, except perhaps on two occasions: namely, when the said Gilles intended to go to the aid of the captain of Saint-Étienne-de-Mermorte, whom the men or the garrison of Palluau or Essars planned to surprise, Milord Gilles, on horseback, intending an ambush of that garrison, asked what course to take; whereupon the said François declared that Barron had responded that he would not find any troops of the said garrison, and so it happened. And the same François had again obtained another response from the said Barron when Gilles wanted to cross the sea; which Barron forbade him to do because, if François had to do it, he would perish; and it was before arriving in this country that Barron gave him the last response.

Item, he said that having, by Gilles' order, concluded a pact with the aforesaid Barron in the name of this same Gilles, by virtue of which every year the said Milord Gilles would provide a meal to three people on three solemn feasts, the same Milord Gilles offered a meal to three people on the last feast of All Saints; and as he had stopped doing so, the said François and Gilles supposed that this was why the same Barron refused to appear in the said Gilles' presence.

And these are the things that the said François testified, being diligently subjected to investigation, and interrogated, and he knew no more but what public rumor was spreading, which he said accorded with the facts deposed by him.

Item, the witness declared that on different occasions the aforesaid Gilles de Rais, the accused, affirmed to him a desire to amend thoroughly the wicked life he had led up to that point, and to undertake a pilgrimage to the Holy Land and Jerusalem, where he proposed bringing the witness too, in order to implore Our Redeemer to pardon their sins; this being four months ago, as often at Machecoul as on the island of Bouin, and also at Bourgneuf, in the parish of Saint-Cyr-en-Rais.

And the witness was enjoined in the usual form not to reveal anything of his deposition to anyone whomsoever, etc.

### 2. Eustache Blanchet, priest. October 17, 1440.

Milord Eustache Blanchet, priest, originally from Montauban, in the parish of Saint-Éloi, in the diocese of Saint-Malo, aged about forty to the best of his belief, a witness, as abovenoted, produced, admitted to take an oath to bear witness to the truth in this affair, and excused upon surety to depose in the case, examined this October 17th, in the year of the aforesaid pontificate and general council, interrogated on the promulgated articles and on the whole affair, said and attested that last Ascension Day he went to stay with the said Gilles de Rais, the accused, by his invitation and request; and that two years ago, he, the witness, being at Florence, saw François,[5] the preceding witness, who was frequently in the company of Nicolas de Médicis, a Florentine, and a certain François, in the diocese of Castellane, both of whom practiced the art of alchemy, as he attested; and, having begun to get acquainted with the said François, the preceding witness, this latter, knowing that he was originally from France, told him that he would gladly go to France and Brittany, namely to Nantes, where he had a cousin named Martellis, and that he would gladly go to Nantes to see his cousin; and he, the present witness, proposed that as he wanted to go they could go together; which preceding witness told him that if there were anyone in France who wanted to be initiated into the art of alchemy, within three months he could teach him. And the present witness responded that he would find men in France who would receive him for this. Having deliberated upon this, the said François and the present witness started on their way and traveled from Florence all the way to Saint-Florent-le-Vieil, a city which belongs to no diocese, situated in the ecclesiastical province of

[5] François Prelati.

Tours. Knowing from the beginning of his acquaintance with the said Gilles, the accused, that he was passionately fond of alchemy, the witness wrote to him from there, saying that the said François was coming from Florence and knew how to practice the art of alchemy, which he, the witness, had previously heard it said that the said Gilles practiced.

Its having come to the said Gilles' knowledge, he sent Étienne Corrillaut, also known as Poitou, Henriet Griart, and two others in order to lead them both to where Gilles was staying then at Tiffauges, in the diocese of Maillezais; and he, the witness, stayed there, that is, in the castle of the said place, last year, from Ascension Day to the following All Saints' Day. Which François, a certain Jean,[6] a goldsmith from Paris, and an old woman named Perrote, who now lives near the Saint-Nicholas church at Tiffauges, lodged together in one room. At that period, the said François and Gilles de Rais, the accused, worked daily with the said goldsmith at the art of alchemy. And the witness never saw him make the experiment but once.

Item, he attested that during this period the said Gilles arrived in the said room sometimes at night, sometimes in the day, sometimes at cock's crow. And, after the said Gilles' arrival, he, the witness, and Perrote left the said room, leaving the said François and Gilles alone; and the accused himself revealed to the said witness and said Perrote what they were in the process of doing: he said in effect that on another day, the said Gilles arriving, he, the witness, saw the said Gilles and François enter a low hall located behind the room where he, the witness, and the aforementioned others spent the night; in which hall the said Gilles, the accused, and François remained for a while. And suddenly the witness heard the said François speak these words, among other words spoken softly: "Come, Satan"; or "Come!" The witness believes that the same François added: "to our aid," and he knows nothing else. And the said François spoke several words that the witness was unable to hear clearly and that he is unable to recall; Gilles and François remained there approximately a half hour, in candlelight. And not long after the said words were pronounced, a cold wind blew violently through the said castle. The witness was frightened by this and heard nothing else, as he warranted. Reflecting on the above, he surmised that the said Gilles and François were invoking demons. By reason of which, as he attested, he held a discussion with a certain Robin, another familiar of the said Gilles. And he left the house of the said Gilles and went to stay with Bouchard-Ménard, an innkeeper residing at Mortagne, in Poitou, where he stayed seven weeks or thereabouts. During this time the said Gilles, the accused, wrote him several times to come see him, saying that if he did, he would find himself in good standing with the said Gilles and François. The

---

[6] Jean Petit.

said witness refused to go near the said Gilles. And in the interim Jean Mercier, the castellan of La Roche-sur-Yon, in the diocese of Luçon, came to lodge with the said Bouchard, whom the witness asked for news about the regions of Nantes and Clisson. The said Mercier responded that, according to the public rumor spread in the aforesaid region and elsewhere, the said Gilles de Rais was killing a large number of children, and having them killed, and that he was writing a book in his own hand with their blood. And that, with this particular book, the said Gilles, the accused, would take all the fortresses he wanted; and that with this said book, thus written, nobody could harm him. But on the following day the goldsmith, namely Jean Petit, came to tell him that the said Gilles and François were extremely desirous of seeing him and requested that he come; to whom he, the witness, responded that in no event would he go to meet them, because of the aforesaid rumor. And he requested that the said goldsmith tell the said Gilles and François to stop the aforesaid things, if they were true, and that it was wrong to perpetrate such crimes; and that public gossip thereupon was strongly against them. Which is what the said goldsmith told them, to the best of the witness' belief; wherefore the said Gilles became very indignant with the said goldsmith, for he had him imprisoned in the castle of Saint-Étienne-de-Mermorte, where the same goldsmith stayed a long time. Then the said Gilles sent Étienne Corrillaut, also known as Poitou, Gilles de Sillé, Jean Lebreton, and Henriet Griart, his manservants, to Mortagne, where the witness was then residing, in order to seize him; which they did, and they conducted him as far as Roche-Serviére, with the intention of conveying him to the said castle of Mermorte to imprison him; whereupon he, the witness, having been informed of it, refused to go; and he raised such a fuss about it that the aforementioned four led him to Machecoul; to which witness the said Poitou, namely Étienne Corrillaut, declared that if he had been taken to the castle at Mermorte, the said Gilles would have had him killed for the gossip he had related to the goldsmith about Gilles. And he lodged at Machecoul with Étienne Ferron, furrier, remaining there two months, whereupon he went to lodge at the house of the late Guillaume Richard. During the time he was lodging with the said Ferron, one morning before last Easter, what day he cannot remember, he saw the said Poitou arriving at the castle of the said place, accompanied by the son of Georget Le Barbier, pastry-cook, who lived in the said castle; and the next day he heard it said that Georget's son, aged fifteen or sixteen, was lost, and that after his entry into the said castle, he was never seen again by anyone in the city of Machecoul.

Item, he stated that while he was living at Machecoul, he heard it said that the young pages of a certain Daussy and of François, the preceding witness, and the nephew of the prior of Chéméré, had been lost, all from fifteen to sixteen years old, and the witness believes that they were killed in the said castle of Machecoul, on account of their credulity, as with Georget's[7] son, who, because his father was managing badly, wanted that part which reverted to him from his mother's estate, for which he had a silver mark, or a part equivalent to the value of this mark, which he carried in a jewel box to the said castle so that someone would keep it for him; which said jewel box a man named Jean, pastry-cook of Rais' wife, returned later with other possessions to the father, so he had heard it said; wherefore the witness presumes and believes that Georget's child was killed in the same place.

Item, he said that the common rumor was that several old women detained in the prisons of the Lord Duke of Brittany, in Nantes, whose names he did not know, led children to Machecoul and delivered them to the aforesaid Étienne Corrillaut, also known as Poitou, and Henriet Griart, who killed them.

Item, he attested to having several times heard it said by the said Gilles, the accused, that he did not believe it possible for a man to make the devil appear and that he knew a man who attempted it, but could not succeed. And the witness believed that the said Gilles, the accused, was speaking of himself, with reference to the abovenoted and attested.

Interrogated as to the people present at the time when the preceding words were spoken, he responded that he did not remember.

Interrogated as to the place where they were spoken and the reason behind, and the intention for, speaking them by the said Gilles, the accused, the witness responded as far as the place was concerned, that it was in the castle at Tiffauges, because the witness, coming and going through Bourgogne and Savoy, to and from the court of Rome, reported to the said Gilles that in these countries there were many heresies, which were growing rapidly. And he, the witness, saw and heard that many old women had been hanged there for the said heresies. And above all for summoning demons.

Item, he attested to having heard Alain de Mazères say many times that the latter had heard the said Gilles, the accused, say similar things.

Item, he said that recently, last Easter Sunday, as the aforesaid Gilles was leading the witness and Milord Gilles de Valois, priest, into his study or writing room in the castle at Machecoul, the said Gilles showed them a book that he was writing on the ceremonies of his school at Machecoul, and he, the witness, saw among the archives of the said Gilles, the accused, five or six leaves of paper with large borders, on which there were crosses, red signs, and red writing in the hand of the said Gilles, the accused; which writing he, the witness, presumed and suspected had been done with human blood, considering what he had heard previously: that the said Gilles, the accused, had children

---

[7] Georget Le Barbier.

killed for their blood, to write books with.

Item, he attested that last Easter Sunday he saw the said Gilles, the accused, and a certain Milord Olivier des Ferrières, priest, go together behind the altar of Our Lady in the Sainte-Trinité church at Machecoul, and he believes that the said Olivier heard the confession of the said accused. Because immediately after this the said accused received the Eucharist, at the same time as did the parishioners of little means, in the same place and in their company; which laymen of little means, seeing such a great lord approach, wanted to leave, but the said accused had no desire to let them leave and, moreover, commanded them to remain with him and partake in Communion as usual. And a certain Milord Simon Loisel, then officiating minister of the said church, dispensed the Eucharist.

Item, he attested that the children of Master Jean Briand, principally Perrinet, the youngest, and another one named Pierre, of the aforesaid Gilles' music school, constantly remained in the room of the said accused, and that the said Perrinet was his favorite.

Item, interrogated as to the ejaculation of sperm on the children by the said Gilles, the accused, he said that he had known nothing about it until he heard talk about it.

Item, the witness stated that he had heard it said by Mathieu Fouquet, speaking with him about the said children's deaths, and being shocked, as this was not new and as many people were speaking about it and had for a long time, and it had already been some time since they found the bones of the dead children in the castle at Champtocé.

Moreover, so far as concerns the invocations of demons and the murders of children, as to whether he assisted in them, he said that he was putting and puts his trust in the relation, confession, depositions and attestations of those accused: François,[8] the Marquis,[9] Poitou and Henriet; and that he wanted and wants to believe on that score, thereupon trusting their consciences, as he had already trusted them and would again.

Interrogated as to whether he went to Florence on his own initiative, to go about his own business, or was solicited by the said Gilles, the accused, to go there and seek conjurors of demons, he responded that he went there on his own business, which he explained to the said Gilles, who requested that in the said regions he seek a man skilled in the art of alchemy and learned in the invocation of demons, and that he send such a man, for which Gilles would compensate the witness. That is why he, the witness, upon arrival, remembered what the said Gilles had told him and sought very diligently for a man

[8] François Prelati.

[9] Lenano, Marquis de Ceva.

practicing the said arts; finally, through the agency of Master Guillaume de Montepulciano, he met François, the preceding witness; he associated with him and offered him abundant wine and food in order to do business with him, and to that end he explained many things to him, without concerning himself with what the other expounded to him, provided that he was able to bring the same François to the said Gilles, the accused; and thus, through his agency, as abovesaid, the same François arrived in this land at the castle of the said Gilles.

Item, interrogated as to whether, before bringing the said François, he knew that he was familiar with the highly criminal art of invoking demons and performing invocations, he responded yes, the said François having assured him of it in answer to his question.

Item, interrogated as to whether, by order of the said Gilles, the accused, he had sought other conjurors or had them sent to him, he responded yes, namely Master Jean de La Rivière, doctor, who knew how to perform the said invocations, as he asserted. He sent the said La Rivière, by order and at the request of the said Gilles, from Poitiers to Pouzauges, where subsequently he performed invocations on behalf of the said Gilles. One night, clad in white armor, with a sword and other weapons, he arrived in a wood situated near the said place of Pouzauges; and the said accused, the men named Étienne Corrillaut, Henriet, and himself, the witness, accompanied him as far as the wood; and the said La Rivière left the aforenamed behind at the entrance to the wood and entered it alone to work the said invocations, thus he himself asserted, and he, the witness, and the others waited; and to the best of his belief, he, the witness, heard the said La Rivière striking his sword against the said armor that he was wearing, or in some fashion striking it with terrible might, making noises as if he were in combat. Then the said La Rivière left the wood and came toward the place where he had left the said Gilles, the accused, and the others; and the said Gilles immediately asked him what he had seen, and whether it were of any consequence: and the said La Rivière, as if frightened and troubled, said he had seen a demon in the appearance of a leopard, which passed close by him while disdaining his presence and refusing to speak with him or tell him anything whatever: why, this same La Rivière did not indicate to Gilles, the accused.

Then the said Gilles, La Rivière, and the others went to Pouzauges, where they gave themselves over to merry-making and where they slept, and, on the following day, the said La Rivière claimed to need certain things necessary for the said invocations, and the said Gilles, the accused, gave him twenty gold crowns or royals, and told him to procure what was needed and return without delay, which he promised to do. And he left and never returned again to the said Gilles, insofar as the witness could tell or had heard.

Interrogated as to whether he, the witness, had been at any one of the invocations practiced by the said François or others, he responded no, but he did assist in making the circle and characters in the said hall of the castle at Tiffauges, and, likewise, in transporting coal, fire, and other things necessary for the invocations performed by the said François. All that, before the said François began the said invocations, by order of Gilles, the accused, immediately after having witnessed these preparations: he, Gilles de Sillé, Étienne Corrillaut, and Henriet betook themselves to the room of this latter where others were sleeping, and they slept; and the said accused men and François remained alone, performing the said invocations as they intended; and, as he warranted, he does not know if there were any apparitions.

Item, he stated that some time before he'd heard the said Gilles de Rais, the accused, say several times that he intended to amend his wicked life and make a pilgrimage to the Holy Sepulcher, in Jerusalem, in order to ask forgiveness for his sins; and that was as often at Machecoul as at Bourgneuf-en-Rais.

Item, he stated and deposed that once, the said Gilles de Rais, the accused, being at Angers, and lodging at the Lion d'Argent, he, the witness, by express mandate of the said Gilles, found and sent him a goldsmith who professed to be familiar with the art of alchemy, to have practiced it before, and to know how to practice it. To which goldsmith the said Gilles gave a silver mark to perform. Which the said goldsmith promised to do, but shut himself in a room where he got drunk and slept. Which Gilles found him asleep and, indignant, treated him like a drunkard, telling him that he no longer expected what he had looked for from him. Which goldsmith left with the said silver mark, which the accused had wasted.

And such was his deposition, and he knew no more, except the public uproar, which, according to him, agrees with what he has deposed.

Item, he stated and deposed that one day, exactly when he could not say, when he was in the city of Tiffauges, outside the castle of that place, but not when he was staying there — and as he attested, he often went to the castle to meet with clerics and on other business — the said Gilles sent for him to come immediately. And he, the witness, came as requested; and he found the said Gilles in a gallery of the castle, overcome with grief and sadness. Immediately upon his arrival, the said accused told him that he believed François was dead, that he had heard him shouting loudly in his room in the castle, and that he had heard the sound of blows, as if someone were beating a featherbed, but he did not dare to approach or enter the said room; and he begged the witness to go see what had happened. But the witness responded that he did not dare to go in either. However, to please the said Gilles, the witness approached the said room, which he did not enter, but, as the said room had an opening near the top, he called the said François through this aperture, who did not respond;

the witness, nonetheless, heard him groaning painfully like a man seriously injured; which he reported to the said Gilles, whom it greatly afflicted. Then the said François, extremely pale, came out, and went to the said Gilles' room; and he recounted how the devil had beaten him horribly in the said room; as a result of which beating, the said François contracted a fever and was ill for seven or eight days. And the said Gilles, the accused, devoted himself wholly to the said François during the said illness, permitting no one else to nurse him; and he had François confessed, and the said François recovered from his illness.

Item, interrogated as to whether he had known or had heard talk of the cause of that beating, he said that he had heard the said François say that it was because, having previously spoken with the present witness about the invocations of evil spirits that he himself was performing, the present witness had asserted that the said evil spirits were of a vulgar nature and powerless; which, indignant with the said François — and also because the said François was keeping his secrets from the present witness — they had beaten him, so he said. The present witness had heard François say that the said spirits were begotten from material nobler than the Blessed Virgin Mary.

And such was his deposition.

And he was ordered formally not to reveal his deposition to anyone.


### 3. Étienne Corrillaut, called Poitou. October 17, 1440.

ÉTIENNE CORRILLAUT, also known as Poitou, as he warrants, originally from Pouzauges, in the diocese of Luçon, aged about twenty-two to the best of his belief, a witness already produced in the case, admitted to swear to tell the truth, and excused upon surety, on the aforesaid day and in the year of the aforesaid pontificate and council, submitted to investigation and interrogated on everything contained in the promulgated articles, deposed by order and said that after René de Rais, Lord de La Suze, full brother of the said Gilles de Rais, the accused, had taken the castle at Champtocé, in the diocese of Angers, which formerly belonged to the said Gilles de Rais, the accused, the same René, Lord de La Suze, came to Machecoul, in the diocese of Nantes, and also took the castle of that place, two years ago.

Now after the taking of the said castle of Machecoul, the witness heard Milord Charles du Léon, knight, who was with the aforesaid Lord de La Suze in the same castle at Machecoul, say that they had discovered the bodies and bones of two children in the lower part of the tower of the said castle. And the said Milord Charles asked the witness whether he knew anything about this: which witness responded no, and really he did not know anything about it at that time, as he attested, because the said Gilles de Rais had not yet revealed any of his secrets to him, regarding the abduction, lecherous abuses, and murders of the said children, which he revealed to him later, in the manner noted below.

Item, he stated and deposed that, when the said Gilles de Rais had recovered the castle of Champtocé from the said Lord de La Suze, and he went there to hand it and its possession over to the Lord Duke of Brittany, to whom he had already transferred the lordship of the same place, then, for the first time, he had the witness swear not to reveal the secrets he intended to show him, and he commanded Gilles de Sillé, Henriet Griart, Hicquet de Brémont, Robin Romulart, and him, the witness, all of whom were servants of the said Gilles, the accused, to go to the tower of the castle at Champtocé, where the bodies and bones of many dead children were, to take them and put them in a coffer, and bring them to Machecoul, as secretly as possible; and in the said tower they found the bones of thirty-six or forty-six children, which bones were already desiccated, and he said he could not remember their number in any case, and the coffer where they were deposited was bound with cords lest it open and the scandal and iniquity of so egregious a crime should come out.

Interrogated as to the manner by which they determined the number of bodies, he responded that this would be by their head count; but he could not recall their true number, were it not that he knew for sure that there had been thirty-six, or forty-six, and he would have not otherwise recollected.

Item, he stated and deposed that the said bones were brought to Machecoul, into the room of said Gilles, the accused, and burned in the presence of the said Gilles, Gilles de Sillé, Jean Rossignol, André Buchet, Henriet Griart, and him, the witness.

Interrogated as to what was done with the ashes of the said burned bones, he responded that they were thrown into the pits or moats of the castle at Machecoul.

Interrogated as to by whom, he responded: by himself, the witness, and by the said Griart, Buchet, and Rossignol.

Interrogated as to why the bones were not burned at Champtocé, he responded that it could not be done, because after Gilles had recovered possession of the said place, he handed the castle over to the Lord Duke, or had it handed over to him in his name, or by his mandate.

Interrogated as to why the said bones were already desiccated, he responded: because of the length of time since they had been thrown into the said tower, before the taking of the castle, which after its capture Lord de La Suze held for as long as three years[10] or thereabouts.

Interrogated as to the person who killed the said children and deposited the

---

[10] This term is not probable. Perhaps it is a question of three months. See also p. 234.

bones in the tower, he responded that he did not know, but that before the capture of the castle Milord Roger de Briqueville, knight, and Gilles de Sillé called frequently on the said Gilles and knew his secrets, according to what he had heard, and he believed that they were well aware of it, but he does not know any more than that.

Moreover, the said witness stated and deposed that the said Sillé, Henriet, and he, the witness, found and led to the said Gilles de Rais, the accused, in his room, many boys and girls on whom to practice his lascivious debaucheries, as indicated below in greater detail, and they did so by order of the said Gilles, the accused.

Interrogated as to the number, he said very likely up to forty.

Interrogated as to the place or places to which the children were conveyed, he responded: sometimes to Nantes, sometimes to Machecoul, sometimes to Tiffauges, and elsewhere.

Interrogated as to the number of children that were given to the said Gilles, the accused, in each of the said places by him, the witness, and the said Sillé and Griart, he responded that in Nantes he saw fourteen or fifteen, and at Machecoul, the greater share of the said forty, otherwise he could not state the exact number.

Item, he stated and deposed that in order to practice his unnatural debaucheries and lascivious passions with the said children, boys and girls, the said Gilles de Rais first took his penis or virile member into one or the other of his hands, rubbed it, made it erect, or stretched it, then put it between the thighs or legs of the said boys and girls, bypassing the natural vessel of the said girls, rubbing his said penis or virile member on the bellies of the said boys and girls with great pleasure, passion, and lascivious concupiscence, until sperm was ejaculated on their bellies.

Item, he stated and deposed that before perpetrating his debaucheries on the said boys and girls, to prevent their cries, and so that they would not be heard, the said Gilles de Rais sometimes hung them by his own hand, sometimes had others suspend them by the neck, with ropes or cords, on a peg or small hook in his room; then he let them down or had them let down, cajoled them, assuring them that he did not want to hurt them or do them harm, that, on the contrary, it was to have fun with them, and to this end he prevented them from crying out.

Item, that when the said Gilles de Rais committed his horrible debaucheries and sins of lust on the said boys and girls, he killed them or had them killed thereafter.

Interrogated as to who killed them, he responded that occasionally the said Gilles, the accused, killed them by his own hand, occasionally he had them killed by the said Sillé or Henriet or him, the witness, or by anyone among them, together or separately. Interrogated as to the manner, he responded: sometimes beheading or decapitating them, sometimes cutting their throats, sometimes dismembering them, and sometimes breaking their necks with a cudgel; and that there was a sword dedicated to their execution, commonly called a *braquemard*.[11]

Interrogated as to whether the said Gilles de Rais perpetrated his lusts only once or more often on the said children, boys or girls, he answered only once, or twice at most, on each of them.

Item, moreover, he stated and deposed that the said Gilles de Rais sometimes practiced his lusts on the said boys and girls before injuring them, but rarely; other times, and often, after their suspension or before other injuries, sometimes after cutting into a vein in their neck or throat, the blood spurting, or having others make the cut, and other times after their deaths and when their throats had been cut, as long as the bodies were warm.

Item, he stated and deposed that the said Gilles de Rais practiced his lascivious debaucheries on the girls in the same way as he abused the boys, disdaining and bypassing their sex, and that he had heard several people say that he took infinitely greater pleasure in becoming debauched on the said girls thus, as abovesaid, than in using the appropriate vessel in a normal manner.

Interrogated as to what was done with the said boys and girls after their deaths, or with their cadavers, he responded that they were burned with their clothes.

Interrogated as to who made the fire, he responded that he, the witness, and Henriet often did.

Interrogated as to the manner, he responded that it was done on andirons in the room of the said Gilles, with thick pieces of wood, thereafter arranging faggots on the dead bodies, and kindling a large fire; they laid the clothes piece by piece on the fire, where they were consumed, so that they burned more slowly and no one would smell the nasty odor.

Interrogated as to the place where they threw the ashes or dust, he responded: sometimes in the sewers, other times in the pits or *moats*[12] or other hiding places, according to the various spots.

Interrogated as to the place of the murders, he responded as above: sometimes at Machecoul, for the largest share of them, and sometimes at Tiffauges and elsewhere.

Item, he stated and deposed that the largest part and number of the said boys and girls who had been lasciviously abused by the said Gilles de Rais and killed during the time when he, the witness, was in his service, were taken

---

[11] In French in the original Latin text. Editor's note: this is a cutlass, or short-sword.

[12] Translator's note: italicized in the French {*douves*}.

among the poor asking for alms, as much by the said Gilles as otherwise; that occasionally the said Gilles chose according to his pleasure, and occasionally he had the said Sillé, Henriet and him, the witness, choose, who then brought them secretly to the said Gilles in his room.

Item, he stated and deposed that Catherine, the wife of a painter named Thierry, then living in Nantes, entrusted the said Henriet with her brother, to bring him to the said Gilles de Rais and get him admitted among the children in his chapel, or at least with this hope, according to what the witness had heard this same Henriet claim; the said Henriet led the child to the said Gilles and delivered him to Machecoul. And not long afterwards, the said Gilles carnally and lasciviously soiled the said child and killed him by his own hand.

Interrogated as to how he knew this, he responded that he was there and saw Gilles do it.

Item, the present witness stated and deposed that, by order of the said Gilles, and thinking to merit his recognition thereby, he conducted a young and beautiful boy from La Roche-Bernard, in the diocese of Nantes, to Machecoul and handed him over to the said Gilles, who committed on him his abominable, lascivious crimes; until finally the young boy had his neck cut like the aforesaid others.

Item, he stated and deposed that the said Gilles took possession of a young boy who was the page of Master François Prelati, who was also very beautiful himself; and the said Gilles de Rais, after having abused him lasciviously, killed him or had him killed in the abovesaid manner.

Item, he stated and deposed that during Pentecost in 1439,[13] he, the witness, together with the said Henriet, took from Bourgneuf, in the parish of Saint-Cyr, in the diocese of Nantes, a very beautiful adolescent, approximately fifteen years old, who was staying with a man named Rodigo; and they led him to the said Gilles who was then lodging with the Cordeliers of the same place, where the said Gilles committed and exercised his lusts on the said child, in the aforesaid execrable manner, and the said witness and Henriet, by order of the said Gilles, killed the said child and brought him to the castle at Machecoul where they burned him in the room of the said Gilles, the accused.

Item, he stated and deposed that two and a half years before, as it seems to him,[14] a certain inhabitant of Nantes and native thereof, named Pierre Jacquet, commonly called Princé, who had a young, extremely suitable page of approximately fourteen living with him, gave this young boy to the said Gilles, the accused, to be his valet and his servant in place of him, the witness, who was then proposing to retire from service and had many times asked permission of

[13] In fact, Ascension Day, August 25, 1439.

[14] In fact, around June 26, 1439.

the said Gilles de Rais; who, after having made use of the said adolescent in his lascivious debaucheries, as he had done with the others, killed him by his own hand.

Item, he deposed and stated that a certain André Buchet, who was first in the chapel of the said Gilles de Rais and then in that of the Lord Duke, had led a child of approximately nine from the vicinity of Vannes all the way to Machecoul to the said Gilles, who received him, through one of his servants, named Raoulet; and the said child was dressed as a page, and to pay him back, the said Gilles gave the said Buchet a horse that Pierre Heaume had given him, which was valued at sixty gold royals; and the said Gilles practiced his lascivious debaucheries on the said child, who was then killed like the aforesaid others.

Item, the witness, present and hearing, stated and deposed that the said Gilles de Rais sometimes boasted of taking greater pleasure in killing and cutting the throats of the said boys and girls or having them killed, in seeing them languish and die, and in cutting off their heads and members and in seeing their blood, than in practicing his lust on them.

Item, he stated and deposed that when the said Gilles de Rais found or saw two boys or girls, brothers or sisters, or otherwise related, if one of them were not to his liking, and if he only wanted to practice his lust and become debauched on one but not the other, in order not to alert the displeasing one the other's having been taken, the said Gilles, the accused, took both of them, or had both taken, and practiced on him who was to his liking his carnal abominations in the manner expressed above, then cut both their throats or had them cut, one and the other.

Item, he said and deposed that the said Gilles, the accused, once performed the said carnal act on him, the witness, in the manner described above, as soon as he, the witness, came to stay with the said Gilles, and he said that he was afraid of being killed by him; and he thinks that he would have been, with a dagger, if the said Sillé had not prevented the said Gilles from doing so, saying that he was a pretty lad and that it was better that the said Gilles make him his page; and the said accused became enamored of him, the witness, and demanded that he take an oath not to reveal any of this or of his other secrets in any fashion.

Item, he stated and deposed that he heard it said by Master Eustache Blanchet, priest, who frequently saw the said Gilles de Rais, that he could not accomplish what he was intending to do and had undertaken, without giving or offering the devil a child's foot, hand, or other member.

Interrogated as to whether he saw or knew that some of the said members were given or offered to demons by the said Gilles, he responded no. But when in the company of others, he had once seen the said Gilles, after having taken the hand (he does not know whether it was the right or left) and heart of a child killed by his order in the castle at Tiffauges, put the said hand and heart in a glass chalice *on a cyma*[15] of the fireplace in his room, and cover them with a linen cloth, telling the witness and the said Henriet to close and lock the said room.

Interrogated as to what was done with the said members, he responded that he did not know, but he believed that the said Gilles, the accused, subsequently gave them to the said Master François Prelati to be offered to the Devil.

Item, he stated and deposed that the said Gilles de Sillé reported to him, the witness, and the said Henriet, that a fortnight or three weeks before Lords de La Suze and Lohéac arrived at the castle at Machecoul, the said Sillé, according to what he told him, the witness, and the said Henriet had removed and taken away from a tower near the lower hall of the said castle the bones of approximately forty children, and had them burned; and on that subject the same Sillé said that it happened in the nick of time for the said Gilles, the accused, Sillé himself, and all others who loved, and were loved by, the same Gilles, the accused. Thereupon, talking about these things to the witness and the said Henriet, the aforenamed Sillé told them, in French: "Wasn't Milord Roger de Briqueville a traitor to have asked Robin Romulart and me to watch Lady Jarville and Thomin d'Araguin through a slit when we removed the said bones? and his knowing full well everything that had been done?"[16]

Interrogated as to who killed the said children, and when, and who put them or their bones in the said tower, he responded that to the best of his belief, the said children were killed by the said Gilles de Rais, Gilles de Sillé, and Roger de Briqueville, before he, the witness, was living with the said Gilles; and he knew nothing else.

Item, he stated and deposed that when the said Gilles, the accused, was unable to find more children at his convenience, boys and girls on whom to practice his execrable debaucheries, he practiced them on the children in his chapel, in the manner set forth above; and principally, according to what he had heard, on the younger of two sons of Master Briand, resident of Nantes.

Interrogated as to whether Gilles de Rais killed any of the said children in his chapel after practicing his debaucheries on them, or had them killed, the witness responded no, because he esteemed them highly and because they themselves kept these acts secret.

Item, he stated and deposed that Milord Eustache Blanchet, a priest afore-

---

[15] In French {*sur une cimaise*} in the original Latin text. It doubtless concerns the mantelpiece above the fireplace. Editor's note: a "cyma" is a cornice molding.

[16] In Old French in the original Latin text: "N'estoit pas messire Rogier de Briqueville bien traistre, qui nous faisoit regarder, Robin Romulart et moy, à la dame de Jarville et Thomin d'Araguin, par une fante, quant nous oustions lesdits ossemens et savoit bien tout ce fait?"

named, by order and at the request of the said Gilles de Rais, went to Italy to bring back Master François Prelati and convey him to the said Gilles, the accused, at Tiffauges, to practice the art of alchemy and invoke demons. And he said that he heard Lord Eustache, speaking with the said Master François, say the following words in French: "He'll summon Master Aliboron,"[17] designating the devil by that name; and that the said Master François would summon the devil and cause him to appear for a jug of wine.

Item, he stated and deposed that the said Master François Prelati, in the presence of the said Gilles de Rais, Milord Eustache Blanchet, Henriet and himself, the witness, made and composed with the tip of a sword, in the large hall of the castle at Tiffauges, a certain large circle; and he drew crosses, signs, or characters, in the manner of armories, in the four parts of the said circle; and into the place where the said circle was made he, the witness, the said Milord Eustache, and Henriet carried a large quantity of coal, incense, a lodestone, in French *pierre d'aimant*,[18] an earthen pot, torches or candles, candlesticks, fire and other things that he does not remember, which the said Gilles, the accused, and François arranged in certain parts of the said circle; and a large fire was lit in the said pot which had a lot of coal. Then the said François made other signs or characters, always in the manner of armories, near or on the wall of the said hall, at an angle to the door; and he lit another fire near the last said signs. And immediately afterwards, the said François had the four windows of the said hall opened in the form or manner of a cross; and this done, the said Gilles de Rais ordered him, the witness, Milord Eustache, and Henriet to leave the hall and go into the room of the said Gilles, and wait for him there and guard it, forbidding them to approach in order to see or hear what the said Gilles de Rais and Master François were doing in the said hall, or to reveal to anyone what had happened. And the said witness, Milord Eustache and Henriet, by order of the said Gilles, went into the said room, the said Gilles, the accused, and Master François remaining alone in the said hall. As to what they did then, he stated that he did not know, but that later he heard the said Milord Eustache and Henriet say that they had heard Master François speaking in a loud voice, but could not understand what he was saying; then they also heard a noise as if a four-legged animal were walking on the roof of the house, intending to enter by a dormer window in the said castle near where the said Gilles, the accused, and François were, so they said; as he affirmed, he, the witness, heard none of this because, tired, he had fallen asleep upon entering the said room.

Interrogated as to the date and hour, he responded that it was in summer at

[17] In French {*il fera venir maitre Aliboron*} in the original Latin text.

[18] In French in the original Latin text.

night; he did not remember any more, except that it began around midnight and it was about an hour later when the said Gilles and François returned to the room of the said Gilles.

Item, he stated and deposed that on the following evening, at a relatively late hour, by order of the said Gilles and constrained by him, not daring to gainsay or refuse the performance of his order, and because the said Master François had promised and assured him that he would be running no risk, danger, or injury, he, the witness, left the said castle of Tiffauges with the said Master François, and together they went into a small field approximately a quarter of a league outside Tiffauges, in the direction of Montaigu, in the diocese of Luçon; actually, the said witness was afraid to go with the said Master François, knowing that he would probably summon the demon, and as much as he could he refused to go, and would not have gone if the said Gilles, the accused, had not ordered him to go and the said François had not reassured him, as above. And the said François and he, the witness, carried fire, coal, incense, a candle, a lodestone, and the book containing the invocations of demons that the said François brought along. And, having arrived at the said place, with the help of a knife the said Master François made a circle with crosses and characters, as he had done in the said hall. And, having lit the candle and coal, the said François forbade him, the witness, to cross himself and enjoined him to enter the said circle with him. And, both of them within the circle, the said Master François performed his invocations; and he, the witness, did not know which invocations, or what he said while doing so, because he did not understand a word, as he attested, except the name of "Barron," although Master François spoke in a loud voice; and he said and affirmed that, despite the said François' interdiction, he secretly crossed himself, which the said François did not see.

Interrogated as to whether something appeared at the said invocation and whether the said François had or received a response, he responded no, at least in terms of what he'd seen and heard.

Item, he stated and deposed that, this accomplished, he and the said François returned to Tiffauges, but they could not enter the castle before morning because it was shut; and they received hospitality in the village at someone's house where the said Eustache was waiting for them, who had his and their fires made and beds prepared. Moreover, he said that when the said François and he, the witness, were inside the circle, it rained heavily and a strong wind blew and a darkness fell that was so thick that they had difficulty returning.

Item, the said witness stated and deposed that last July the said Gilles, the accused, went to Vannes for an audience with the Lord Duke, and lodged with a man named Lemoine, outside the walls of the city of Vannes, opposite and near the episcopal palace, in a place commonly called La Mote; which André Buchet, abovementioned, handed over to Gilles de Rais a child of approximately ten, on whom the said Gilles committed and perpetrated his abominable sins of lust in the manner abovestated; which child was led to the house of a man named Boetden, where the squires of the said Gilles, the accused, were lodging, a house situated close to the marketplace of Vannes, and relatively near the house of the said Lemoine. The child was led there because there was no place secret enough at Lemoine's wherein to kill him; which child was killed in a room in the house of the said Boetden, his head having been cut off and separated from his body, then burned in the said room; as for the body, tied with the child's own belt, it was thrown into the latrines of the house of the said Boetden, where he, the witness, descended, with much pain and difficulty, in order to sink the body into the depths of the said latrines; and the witness added that the said Buchet knew all about this.

Item, he stated and deposed that the said Gilles, the accused, after cutting into a vein in the necks or throats of the said children, or into other parts of their body, and while they bled, and also after their decapitation, practiced as abovecited, would occasionally sit on their bellies and delight in watching them die thus, sitting at an angle the better to watch their end and death.

Item, he stated and deposed that occasionally and fairly often after the decapitation and death of the said children, effected thus and otherwise, as related above, the said Gilles delighted in looking at them and having them looked at by him, the witness, and others who were privy to his secrets; and he displayed to them the heads and members of the said slaughtered children, asking them which of these children had the most beautiful member, the most beautiful face, the most beautiful head; often he found joy in kissing one or another of these slaughtered children whose members were being examined, or one of those that had already been examined by someone and seemed to him to have the most beautiful face.

And such was the deposition of the witness. And he was enjoined to reveal nothing of it to anyone whomsoever, etc.


**4. Henriet Griart. October 17, 1440.**

HENRIET GRIART, originally from the parish of Saint-Jacques-de-la-Boucherie, in Paris, as he attests, aged about twenty-six, another witness produced in the case, admitted to swear to tell the truth, and excused under bail, on the aforesaid day, in the year of the aforesaid pontificate and general council, examined and submitted to investigation, interrogated on all points contained in the aforesaid articles, and on each of them, deposed in the nature of what follows.

And, first of all, that he has been a valet and servant of the said Gilles, the accused, for five or six years, and that three years after René de Rais, Lord de La Suze, the full brother of the said Gilles de Rais, the accused, took possession of the castle of Champtocé, the same René, Lord de La Suze, went to Machecoul and took possession of the castle of the said place; and it was there that the witness heard Charles du Léon, who was in the company of the said Lord de La Suze, say that the bodies and bones of two children had been found in the lower part of a tower of the said place of Machecoul; and the said Milord Charles asked the witness whether he knew anything; to which he, the witness, responded no, and he warranted that at this time, in fact, he knew nothing. But he said that after the said Gilles de Rais, the accused, recovered the said castle of Champtocé and arrived there to give and deliver it to the Lord Duke of Brittany, the said Gilles demanded an oath from him, the witness, not to reveal those secrets which he intended to reveal to him; and he commanded him, the witness, Étienne Corrillaut, also known as Poitou, Gilles de Sillé, Hicquet de Brémont, and Robin Romulart, servants of the said Gilles, to go into the tower of the said castle of Champtocé, where the bodies and bones of a large number of innocents were, put them in a coffer and, as secretly as possible, transport them to Machecoul. And he, the witness, and the others went into the said tower, and there they found the bones of thirty-six to forty-six children, which number he no longer precisely remembers. Which bones were desiccated; but they counted them by their heads, and in another way, so that they were certain of the number of children thrown there; which bones were put in a coffer tightly bound with cords and transported to Machecoul where they were burned in the room of the said Gilles de Rais, in his presence and in that of Gilles de Sillé, Étienne Corrillaut, also known as Poitou, Jean Rossignol, André Buchet, and him, the witness; and the dust or ashes of the said children were thrown into the pits or *moats*[19] of the castle of the said place of Machecoul. He said that they were not burned at Champtocé because the said Gilles, after having regained that castle from the said Lord de La Suze, held on to it for only two days, whereupon he handed its possession over, or had others hand it over, in his name and by his order, to the aforenamed Lord Duke, to whom he had already transferred the lordship of the said place.

Interrogated as to the reason the said bones were desiccated, he responded: because the said children were killed and thrown into the said tower before the taking of the said castle of Champtocé by the said Lord de La Suze, who held

[19] Translator's note: italicized in the French {*douves*}.

and kept it for nearly three years.[20]

Interrogated as to who killed them, and how and why they were killed, he responded that he did not know because when they were killed, he was not living with the said Gilles, the accused; but, at the same time, he says, the aforesaid Milord Roger de Briqueville, knight, and Gilles de Sillé were living with him, and the witness believed that they were well informed about it.

Moreover, he stated and deposed that he, the witness, the said Sillé, and Étienne Corriallaut, also known as Poitou, brought, gave, and handed over many boys and girls from Nantes, Machecoul, and especially Tiffauges, to the said Gilles de Rais in his room; according to him, as many as forty, on which the said Gilles, the accused, practiced his lascivious, unnatural passions: first by taking his virile rod in hand, stretching it, rubbing it, then agitating it, then by introducing it between the thighs of the said children so that, rubbing his said penis on the bellies of the said children, he took great delight, and got so excited that the sperm, criminally and in a way it ought not, spurted onto the bellies of the said children.

Item, he stated and deposed that the said Gilles, the accused, practiced his lust on each of the said children once or twice and, that done, sometimes killed the said children by his own hand, sometimes had them killed by the said Sillé, Corrillaut, also known as Poitou, or him, the witness, sometimes together, and sometimes separately.

Interrogated as to the manner of killing the said children, he responded that sometimes he severed the head and lopped off the members, sometimes he slit the throat, the head remaining attached to the body, sometimes he broke their necks with a cudgel, sometimes he cut into a vein in the neck or into another part of the throat, so that the said children bled, when sometimes the said Gilles de Rais would sit on the bellies of the said children, thus in the languor of death, and watch them die, leaning on them.

Item, he stated and deposed that sometimes when he intended to practice his criminal lusts on the said children, in order to stifle their wails or cries, the said Gilles, the accused, hung them or had him, the witness, Corrillaut, and Sillé, suspend them with cords around the neck, sometimes on a peg, sometimes on a crook or a small hook in his room, while threatening and frightening them, and then, when they were hurt and terrified by this treatment, cajoled them, telling them not to fear, assuring them that he only wanted to have fun with them, and finally practiced his lust on them, as abovecited.

Moreover, he stated and deposed that sometimes the said Gilles, the accused, practiced his debauchery on the said children before killing them, or before beginning to kill them, other times after it had begun and they were in the

---

[20] Probably three months. See p. 224.

languor of death, sometimes after they had been killed, their bodies still warm.

Interrogated as to what was done with their blood, he responded that it ran and spilt onto the ground, which was subsequently cleaned.

Interrogated as to what they did with the bodies and clothes, he said that they burned them in the room of the said Gilles, the accused.

Asked how, he said that they burned the clothes piece by piece in the fireplace of the said room, so that no one might smell the nasty odor; and that, to burn the said bodies, they laid them on thick logs on the andirons, on top of which they placed abundant faggots, and they were burned in this way.

Interrogated as to what they did with the ashes or dust of the said burned bodies, he responded that they threw them into secret places in the rooms where the aforesaid acts were committed, occasionally into the latrines, sometimes into the pits or other places which seemed fitting.

Interrogated as to the places where the things were done which he, the witness, was present for, he responded: in Nantes, in the said Gilles' house, commonly known as La Suze, and in the castles of Machecoul and Tiffauges.

Interrogated as to the location, he said in a certain room of the said house of La Suze, lying at the end of the building, near the parochial church of Saint-Denis, in the same city of Nantes, in which room the said Gilles regularly spent the night; and often at the entrance to the said castle of Machecoul.

Item, interrogated as to where he, the witness, snatched the said children whom he and the others, named by him, handed over to the said Gilles, he responded that the children handed over by him, the witness, were for the most part snatched among those asking for alms, as often at the residence of the said Gilles, the accused, as elsewhere.

Interrogated as to the number of children, he responded as above, namely that there were nearly forty handed over by him and the aforementioned others, fourteen or fifteen of whom were killed in Nantes, in the said house of La Suze, the others at Machecoul for the most part, and at Tiffauges and elsewhere.

Item, he deposed that Catherine, the wife of a painter named Thierry, then staying in Nantes, procured for and gave him, the witness, a brother of hers to be escorted to the house of the said Gilles, the accused, in the hope of his being made one of the choristers of the said Gilles; whom he led to Machecoul and brought into the room of the said Gilles, the accused. And after delivery of that child, the said Gilles, the accused, had the witness swear to reveal nothing of the secrets that he would make him privy to.

Interrogated as to the place where he took the said oath, he responded: in the church of the Sainte-Trinité at Machecoul.

Interrogated as to when, he responded that it had been about three years before. Moreover, he stated that after the said delivery of the said child he, the witness, went to Nantes, where he remained for three days without returning to Machecoul; and when, having returned to Machecoul after these three days, he sought the said child whom he could not find, he was told that he had left this world, in the same way as the others; and the said Corrillaut, also known as Poitou, made him understand that the said Gilles, the accused, had killed the said child by his own hand; and, like the others, the child had served him in his libidinous acts.

Item, he stated and deposed that the said Corrillaut, also known as Poitou, led a beautiful child from La Roche-Bernard to Machecoul, and gave him to the said Gilles, who abused him as he had the others abovenoted.

Item, he deposed that at Machecoul he saw a young and beautiful boy who was the page of Master François Prelati, and who had his throat cut, he does not know by whom, having been absent; and the said Gilles abused him like the others.

Item, he stated and deposed that during Pentecost in 1439, he, the witness, and the said Corrillaut, also known as Poitou, nabbed a very beautiful adolescent, about fifteen years old, who was living with a man named Rodigo in Bourgneuf, in the parish of Saint-Cyr-en-Rais, in the diocese of Nantes, and they led him to the said Gilles, the accused, and handed him over at the house of the Cordeliers in the said place of Bourgneuf, where he was staying; and after the said Gilles, the accused, had abused him lasciviously in the aforesaid manner, Henriet, the current witness, and Corrillaut killed him by order of the said Gilles de Rais and, consequently, brought the body of that young boy to Machecoul where they burned it in the room of the said Gilles.

Item, he deposed that about two and a half years previously, a man commonly called Princé, living in Nantes, had a very beautiful adolescent for a page, who was living with him and familiar with the witness, and who was given by the said Princé to the said Gilles, who promised to make him his valet in place of the said Corrillaut, also known as Poitou, this latter expressing a desire to leave Gilles' service; and immediately after the said Gilles had received this young boy, he abused him carnally and shamefully in his unnatural lusts; then he killed him by his own hand, and the said boy was about fourteen years old.

Item, he stated and deposed that a certain André Buchet, who had belonged to the chapel of the said Gilles de Rais, and who, at the time of the deposition, belonged to that of the Lord Duke, sent from the vicinity of Vannes to Machecoul a certain child dressed as a page, who was about nine years old and one of his servants, called Raoulet, and conducted him to the said Gilles, the accused. This child, after the said Gilles had carnally and criminally abused him, was killed and burned like the others, as related above. And the witness added that the said Gilles, the accused, paid the said Buchet for his services with a horse valued at sixty gold royals, which Pierre Heaume delivered to him.

Item, he deposed that he had heard the said Gilles, the accused, say that he took greater pleasure in murdering the said children, in seeing their heads and members separated, in seeing them languish and seeing their blood, than he did in knowing them carnally.

Item, he said that the said Gilles, the accused, had a sword, commonly called a *braquemard*,[21] with which to sever the heads of the said children and cut their throats, and he often delighted in looking at their severed heads and showed them to him, the witness, and Étienne Corrillaut, also known as Poitou, asking them which of the said heads was the most beautiful of those he was showing them, the head severed at that very moment, or that from the day before, or another from the day before that, and he often kissed the head that pleased him most, and delighted in doing so.

Item, he deposed that when the said Gilles, the accused, encountered two boys or girls, brothers or sisters, or other children living together, if one of them conformed to his taste and he did not want to know the other carnally, he had them both snatched together, and he dealt lasciviously with just the one; and, so that the other would not complain of the loss of the first, he had both their throats cut and each killed.

Item, he deposed that the said Gilles, the accused, exercised his debaucheries on girls and abused them in the same manner as he did the boys, disdaining and neglecting their sex.

Item, he deposed that he had heard the said Gilles, the accused, say that he was born under such a star that, in his view, nobody could know or understand the anomalies or illicit acts of which he was guilty.

Item, he deposed that sometimes the said Gilles, the accused, cut the throats of many of the said children, and cut off their members, or had others do so. And he said that he had heard Milord Eustache Blanchet, a priest and companion of the said Gilles, the accused, say that the said Gilles could not accomplish what he had begun to undertake without giving or offering the devil the feet, hands, or other members of the said children. And the witness added that he himself cut the throats of many of these children and carved them up in many and various ways, whose number he said he remembered as fewer than those about whom he had already deposed above.

Item, he deposed that the said Gilles, the accused, often chose from the boys and girls whom he saw asking for alms, according as they pleased him, and ordered that they be brought for the satisfaction of his evil pleasure.

Item, he deposed that he had heard the said Gilles de Sillé say to him, the witness, and the said Corrillaut, also known as Poitou, that it was lucky for the

---

[21] In French in the original Latin text.

said Gilles de Rais and him that he, Sillé, had carried off and removed the bones of nearly forty children from a certain tower near the castle of Mache-coul, as he said, and that less than a fortnight or three weeks before the said castle of Machecoul was taken by the said Lord de La Suze and Lord de Lohéac, and the witness said that it had now been occupied for the past two years; and that the said Sillé himself spoke these or similar words in French to the witness: "Wasn't Milord Roger de Briqueville a traitor to have asked Robin Romulart and me to watch Lady Jarville and Thomin d'Araguin through a slit when we removed the said bones? and his knowing full well everything that had been done?"[22]

Item, he said that the said Sillé told him, the witness, and the said Corril-laut, also known as Poitou, that he, Sillé, burned the said bones which, the witness asserted, had been there for as long as the said Sillé and Briqueville had been privy to the secrets of the said Gilles de Rais, the accused, and even before they had both exposed these secrets, namely Henriet, the present wit-ness, and Corrillaut, also known as Poitou.

Item, he deposed that when the said Gilles de Rais could not find children to his liking, he practiced his lust in the manner described above on the chil-dren in his chapel; but he did not kill them or have them killed, because they kept these things secret.

Interrogated as to those children in his said chapel with whom Gilles de Rais so acted, he responded: with Perrinet, son of Master Jean Briand, resident of Nantes, and with others whose names he could not remember; which Perrinet was the favorite of the said accused, whom he cherished more than the others.

Item, he stated and deposed that the said Milord Eustache Blanchet, above-mentioned, went to Italy to seek Master François Prelati and whom he brought back with him to the said Gilles de Rais, by order of the latter, to practice the art of alchemy and conjure demons. And that he heard him say these words in French: "that he would summon Master Aliboron."[23] More-over, he stated that he had heard the same Master Eustache say that for a jug of wine the said Master François Prelati would summon the devil and cause him to appear.

Item, he deposed that in the presence of the said Gilles de Rais, Master Eustache Blanchet, Étienne Corrillaut, also known as Poitou, and the witness, the said Master François Prelati made and composed a large circle with the tip

---

[22] In Old French in the original Latin text: "N'estoit pas messire Rogier de Briqueville bien traistre, qui nous faisoit regarder, Robin et moy, à la dame de Jarville et Thomin d'Araguin, par une fante quand nous oustions lesdiz ossemens, et savoit bien tout ce fait."

[23] In French {qu'il ferait venir M$^e$ Aliboron} in the original Latin text.

of a sword on the floor of the large hall of the castle at Tiffauges, in the four parts of which he inscribed crosses, signs, or characters in the manner of armories, by order of the said Gilles, the accused, and that he, the witness, the said Master Eustache Blanchet, and Étienne Corrillaut, also known as Poitou, carried in a large quantity of coal, incense, a lodestone or *pierre d'aimant*, torches or candles, tapers, an earthen pot and other things, which the said Gilles de Rais and Master François placed in a certain part of the said circle; and they lit a scorching fire in the said pot. Then the said François lit another fire at an angle to the door or at the entrance to the said hall, where they also made others signs in the manner of armories, near or on the walls of the said hall, near the last said fire; and not long afterwards the said Master François Prelati had the four windows of the said court opened, in the manner of a cross; that is, in such a way that the opening of the said windows or the action of opening them seemed to represent in some way the sign of the cross. This being done, the present witness, as well as Étienne Corrillaut, also known as Poitou, and Milord Eustache Blanchet, already mentioned, by order of the said Gilles, the accused, retired to his room on the floor above, thus dismissed by Gilles, the accused, and Master François, the only ones who remained in the said hall. Prior to and at the moment when the witness and the aforesaid Milord Eustache and Corrillaut, also known as Poitou, were withdrawing, Gilles, the accused, expressly forbade them ever to reveal to anyone whomsoever anything of what had gone on so far, or to come near in order to see or hear what he, Gilles, the accused, and Master François might be doing.

Item, he stated and deposed that after he had withdrawn as well as the said Milord Eustache and Corrillaut, also known as Poitou, and as soon as they entered the said room of the said Gilles, the accused, a certain period of time having elapsed, the witness and the said Milord Eustache heard the said Master François speaking aloud in the said room; but, as the witness asserted, he could not understand any of the things he was saying. And soon thereafter the witness and Milord Eustache heard a certain noise, like that made by a four-legged animal walking on the roof. Which animal, it seemed to them, approached near the dovecote of the said place, near where the said Gilles, the accused, and Master François were.

Interrogated to know whether the said Corrillaut, also known as Poitou, had heard anything of the preceding events gathered by the witness and Milord Eustache, as reported, he responded that he thought not; moreover, the witness believed that the same Corrillaut, also known as Poitou, was asleep by this time.

Interrogated as to the season or date, he responded that about a year had passed since these effects had been produced.

Interrogated as to the hour, he responded that the aforementioned things happened during the night, before midnight, and ended an hour later.

Interrogated as to the month and day, he responded that he did not know precisely anymore, but is certain that it was during the summer.

Item, the same witness, deposing in the case, added that the said Gilles de Rais, the accused, and Master François were alone at Machecoul for a period of five weeks, in a room of that same castle, a room whose key the said Gilles, the accused, always held; and the witness heard it said, he does not know by whom, that the figure or image of a hand, in a kind of wrought iron, had been discovered in the said room.

Item, he added and deposed, however, that the said Gilles de Rais, the accused, carried into his room in the castle at Tiffauges, a room that the same witness and Corrillaut, also known as Poitou, guarded, the hand and heart of a young boy who had been killed in the said place of Tiffauges by order of the said Gilles, the accused, perhaps by Gilles himself, and that the latter deposited them in a glass covered with a piece of linen, near the fireplace of the said room, namely on the upper part of the fireplace known in French as the *cyma*;[24] and he enjoined the witness and the said Corrillaut, also known as Poitou, to bolt the door of the said room.

Interrogated as to what was done with that hand and heart, he responded that he did not really know, but he thought Master François must have used them, and that the said accused Gilles must have entrusted them to him to perform his invocations, so that he might offer that heart and hand to the conjured demons.

And the witness was enjoined in the usual form to reveal nothing of his deposition to anyone, etc.


## II. Depositions concerning the violation of Church privileges.

### 1. Jean Rousseau, man-at-arms of the Duke of Brittany. October 19, 1440.

JEAN ROUSSEAU, man-at-arms of the Duke of Brittany, parishioner of Saint-Nicolas of Nantes, aged forty or thereabouts to the best of his belief, a witness, produced, received, and having sworn to bear witness to the truth, in the cases of this order, examined this October 19, 1440, in the year of the aforesaid pontificate and general council, submitted to inquiry and interrogated as to the content of Article XLII, beginning with: "Item, that two years ago, etc.," which mentions the violation of ecclesiastical immunity, deposed and stated

---

[24] In French {*la cimaise*} in the original Latin text. See p. 223, note 15.

that on the Monday following the past Pentecost, while this witness, as well as Jean Le Ferron and a certain Guillaume Hautreys, and several others, were in the parochial church of Saint-Étienne-de-Mermorte, in the diocese of Nantes, which parochial church was and is located near the castle of the said place; to which place the witness had gone on behalf of the Lord Duke in order to place a restraining order on the debtors of the royal treasury against discharging or paying over to Gilles, the accused, the rents, poll taxes, or other taxes of the place. And while the witness and the aforesaid others were there at the close of High Mass in the aforesaid parochial church, the witness saw the aforenamed Gilles, the accused, with a kind of sword, called in French a *gisarme*,[25] in his hand, followed by certain others of his men, enter the said church boisterously, and, addressing himself menacingly to the aforesaid Le Ferron and others then in the said church, but particularly to the aforesaid Ferron, cry out in a terrible voice, in French: "Outside! Outside!"[26] Then the witness saw a certain Lenano, Marquis de Ceva, an intimate of the said Gilles, the accused, who was also there, lead the aforesaid Le Ferron outside the said church behind the said Gilles, the accused, and his other men; and he believes that the said Le Ferron exited the said church then because he was terrified by the said accused's threats more than anything else. The witness intended to leave the said church then and would have done so had not someone in the retinue of the said Gilles, the accused, made a sign to the witness with his finger (and in making the said sign, he brought his finger to his nose and eyes similar to how one crosses oneself), and for this reason he remained in the aforesaid church.

He stated that he had heard several people say as well that at that very moment in a wood near the said place a company of men-at-arms, about sixty in all, were waiting for the said Gilles, who had them stationed there laying in ambush. He also stated that while he was in the said church, he caught sight of three or four men-at-arms, wearing capelines or sallets[27] on their heads, and other arms, going in front of the said church, and that he heard it said later that the said Le Ferron was brought to the aforesaid castle by the same Gilles, the accused, and his intimates, which castle the said Le Ferron restored or returned to the aforesaid Gilles, the accused, who incarcerated the said Le Ferron in the same place.

Interrogated as to whether, when the same Le Ferron left the said church, some other violence was perpetrated by the same Gilles, the accused, and his men, he responded that he neither saw nor knew anything else besides what

[25] In French {*jusarme*} in the original Latin text. Editor's note: this is a double-edged halberd.

[26] In French {*Dehors! dehors!*} in the original Latin text.

[27] Editor's note: two kinds of helmets.

was above noted. And the witness added that he had known the said Jean Le Ferron since his youth, and that, several years before he was thus conveyed and incarcerated, he had seen him in a cleric's habit, having received the clerical tonsure, and that he was commonly reputed to be a cleric.

And he was enjoined in the usual manner to reveal nothing of his deposition to anyone.

**2. Lenano, Marquis de Ceva, captain in the service of Gilles de Rais. October 19, 1440.**

LENANO DE CEVA, marquis, of the diocese of Alba,[28] forty or more to the best of his belief, a witness produced, examined the aforementioned day and year, submitted to inquiry and interrogated on the content of the article mentioning the violation of Church immunity, stated and deposed that the said Gilles de Rais, the accused, accompanied by Gilles de Sillé and Bertrand Poulein, arrived at the parochial and vicarial church of Sainte-Étienne-de-Mermorte during High Mass, after the elevation of the host and Communion; he did not remember the day, but he believed that it was on the solemnity of the previous Pentecost or the day following the feast; that the said Gilles, the accused, held a kind of sword, in French called a *gisarme*;[29] and that he said to the aforenamed Jean Le Ferron: "Ha, ribald, you beat my men, and extorted from them; come outside the church or I'll kill you on the spot!"[30] Whereupon the said Le Ferron, on his knees and pleading, indicated to him that he would do what he wanted. And, frightened by the said Gilles, the accused, he requested the witness to assist him and intercede for him, for fear of ill-treatment by the said accused. The witness made Le Ferron understand that if any harm should befall him, he would suffer it himself in like manner; and after a heated exchange of words, the said Le Ferron left the said church of his own volition, with the witness, following the same Gilles, the accused, toward the castle of Mermorte, which the said Gilles had previously sold to Geoffroy Le Ferron, and which the aforesaid Jean Le Ferron thereupon returned to the said accused; and the same Le Ferron remained a prisoner of the said Gilles, the accused.

Moreover, he said that the fifty or sixty men that the said Gilles, the accused, had assembled in a neighboring wood, laying in ambush, were to be

[28] In Piedmont.

[29] In French {*jusarme*} in the original Latin text.

[30] In Old French in the original Latin text: "Ha, ribault, tu as batu mes hommes, et leur as fait extorsion; viens dehors de l'eglise ou je te tueroy tout mort!"

charged with assaulting and invading the said castle if the said Le Ferron did not turn it over to the said Gilles, the accused. They were wearing mantles, which in French are called *paletots*,[31] capelines,[32] visored helmets, sallets[33] and other arms. But in fact, he said, none of those who entered the said church wore a capeline, a sallet, or a visored helmet.

And he added that he had seen the said Jean Le Ferron in a cleric's habit and tonsured, and that he was commonly held and well-known as a cleric.

And such was his deposition and he knew no more, except as public uproar would have it, which he said agreed with the facts deposed by him.

And he was enjoined in the usual manner to reveal nothing of his deposition to anyone.

### 3. Bertrand Poulein, man-at-arms in the service of Gilles de Rais. October 19, 1440.

BERTRAND POULEIN, of the diocese of Bayeux, originally from Cantelou, near Caen, in Normandy, about forty-five to the best of his belief, a witness produced and sworn in, examined this day in the aforementioned year, submitted to inquiry and interrogated on the content of Article XLII, which mentions the violation of Church immunity, said and deposed that he, the witness, in the company of the aforenamed Gilles de Rais, the accused, Gilles de Sillé, as well as many others, on the day of the solemnity of the previous Pentecost, or the day following that same feast, but he believed it was the day of the said solemnity, entered the parochial and vicarial church of Saint-Étienne-de-Mermorte, in the diocese of Nantes, in which church they found the aforenamed Jean Le Ferron hearing Mass: to which Jean Le Ferron the same Gilles, the accused, holding a kind of sword called a *gisarme*[34] in French, said in a rage, bursting with terrible threats upon the said Le Ferron, cried out in French: "Ha ribald, you beat my men, and extorted from them; come, come, outside the church, or I'll kill you on the spot!"[35] Whereupon the said Ferron, on his knees, said humbly to Gilles, the accused: "Do what you want."[36] And frightened by the said accused, the same Ferron asked the preceding witness to

---

[31] In French in the original Latin text.

[32] A kind of helmet.

[33] Another kind of helmet.

[34] In French {*jusarme*} in the original Latin text.

[35] See p. 242, note 30.

[36] Old French in the original: "Faictes ce que il vous plera."

assist him and intercede for him with the said accused, fearing ill-treatment by the latter. To whom the preceding witness said that there was nothing to fear from this same Gilles, the accused, and that if he had to suffer some harm, he himself, namely the preceding witness, would have to suffer as well. Then, after the preceding witness and Jean Le Ferron had exchanged heated words, the latter left voluntarily with the preceding witness; who, at the same time as he, the present witness, headed toward the said castle of Mermorte behind the said accused. Which castle the aforesaid Ferron restored or returned that same day to the said accused, as the preceding witness attested. And the same Jean Le Ferron was detained there by the said Gilles de Rais, the accused, who kept him incarcerated for some time, there and elsewhere. And he said that the ambush laid by fifty or sixty men-at-arms was prepared in the name of the said Gilles de Rais, the accused, in order to assail and invade the said castle, which the same Gilles would have invaded had the said Le Ferron not restored it to him. However, not one of those who were with the said Gilles, the accused, in the said church when the same Le Ferron left it was armed with a sallet, a visored helmet, or any other offensive arm, save swords and the aforesaid *gis-arme* borne by the aforenamed Gilles, the accused.

He stated, besides, that he had seen the said Jean Le Ferron in a cleric's habit and tonsured, and had known him to be commonly reputed to be a cleric.

And such was his deposition and he knew no more, except as rumor would have it, which he said agreed with the facts deposed by him.

And he was enjoined under oath to reveal nothing of his deposition to anyone.

**III. Depositions of fifteen witnesses on the subject of the public outcry. October 21, 1440.**

Venerable and circumspect Milord JACQUES DE PENCOETDIC, professor in both courts of law, aged forty; ANDRÉ SEGUIN, attorney of the ecclesiastical court of Nantes, aged forty; JEAN LORIENT, forty, attorney of the secular court; ROBIN RIOU, attorney of the secular court; Master JEAN BRIAND, fifty; JACQUES THOMICI, merchant of Lucanie, citizen of Nantes, forty-five; JEAN LE VEILL, merchant, forty; PIERRE PICARD, merchant, forty; GUILLAUME MICHEL, apothecary, aged forty; PIERRE DROUET, merchant, forty; EUTROPE CHARDAVOINE, apothecary, forty; JEAN LE TOURNOURS, apothecary, forty; PIERRE VIVIANI JUNIOR, notary public of the ecclesiastical court of Nantes, thirty-five; ROBIN GUILLEMET, surgeon, aged sixty; and JEAN AUDILAURECH, barber, all citizens of Nantes, witnesses produced, as above, admitted to take an oath to bear witness to the truth, and excused upon surety to depose in this affair or in the cases of this order, examined this October 21st in the aforesaid year, submitted to inquiry, at first separately and then together, and diligently interrogated on the content of the Fortieth and Forty-first Articles mentioning the public rumor; have said and deposed without discord or difference what public rumblings and clamor have spread and still spread in the city and diocese of Nantes, in the region of Machecoul and adjoining regions, namely that the said Gilles de Rais, the accused, had taken away many children, boys and girls, under false pretences, and caused others to do so, and regularly practiced with them the abominable sin of sodomy, in a vile, shameful, and dishonorable fashion, indulging in unnatural lust with them; that he had cut their throats, and had their throats cut, and that he had had their bodies and cadavers burned by his intimates Roger de Briqueville, knight, Gilles de Sillé, Étienne Corrillaut, also known as Poitou, and Henriet Griart, and by several others of his accomplices, abettors and assistants associated with him in this affair; and that, performing the dreadful invocations of demons, he had conjured evil spirits, and, contrary to our faith, had rendered the demons homage, offering them the members of children whom he had butchered, and had others make such offerings; and that he had regularly perpetrated other crimes and other villainies iniquitously and perversely; and that, for this, the same Gilles de Rais, the accused, was and is notoriously defamed among honest men.

And such was their deposition, and they knew no more, as they asserted, so far as these articles are concerned; and these same witnesses were enjoined, in the usual manner, to reveal nothing of their depositions.

« PART TWO »

# The
# Secular Court
# Trial[1]

---

[1] From the Old French of the "civil trial" transcript, dating from 1530; provenance of the Archives de la Trémoille, preserved in the National Archives, call number 1 AP 585. This unauthenticated copy is the oldest and the best.

# I

## SEMI-OFFICIAL REPORT OF
## THE COURT'S DISPATCH

### *Initial Complaints in the Appearance of the Accused*

What follows is the trial brought against Gilles de Rais and those of his men and servants, named below, before the exalted and prudent Pierre de L'Hôpital, President of Brittany, appointed to this by the Duke our Sovereign Lord and other men in the council of my said Lord, and thus appointed by him, on the complaint lodged by Jean Jenvret and his wife, Jeanne Degrépie, the widow of Regnaut Donete, Jean Hubert and his wife, Jeanne, the wife of Guibelet Delit, Agathe, the wife of Denis de Lemion,[1] Jeanne, the wife of Jean Darel, the wife of Perrot Couperie, Tiphaine, the wife of Éonnet Le Charpentier, Jean Magnet, Pierre Degrépie, and Jean Rouillé, living in the suburbs of Nantes or neighboring villages, and in several other places in the same diocese or elsewhere, declaring that they have lost their children and that they suppose that the said Lord and his men snatched them, or caused them to be taken, and put them to death; they say that the said Lord and his men are suspected of these crimes.

On this score, regarding the said complaint, an investigation and inquiry into the said complaint were made by the authority of my said Lord Duke and of Milord the aforesaid President, the tenor of which is provided below. The said plaintiffs requesting sorrowfully, with tears and loud cries, that justice be done, according to the necessity of the case, and the said inquiries having proven the guilt of Gilles de Rais, the latter being charged with the death of these small children and many others, authority was given to Jean Labbé and other subjects of our Sovereign Lord, if they could find the said Gilles de Rais,

---

[1] In the case of Agathe, the wife of Denis de Lemion, it is a question of her nephew, Colin Avril.

to seize him bodily. At which opportunity Jean Labbé and other subjects of my said Lord arrested Gilles de Rais in the province of Brittany, in the month of September, and previous to the present date, brought him to Nantes into the prisons of my said Lord. And it was stated and propounded to Gilles de Rais, on trial before the commissioners delegated by the prosecutor of Nantes, and by his lieutenant, that God's commandments and civil law forbade a person to kill his neighbor and, on the contrary, commanded him to love him as himself. However, the said Lord took many young children, and had them taken, not merely ten, nor twenty, but thirty, forty, fifty, sixty, one hundred, two hundred and more, such that the exact number can not be certified; he had sexual intercourse with them, taking his pleasure unnaturally and committing the detestable sin of sodomy, the horror and abomination of every good Catholic; not satisfied with that, he killed them or caused them to be killed and, upon their deaths, had their bodies burned and reduced to ashes. Moreover, the said Lord persevered in this evil, and considering that all power proceeds from God and every subject owes obedience to his prince, who is prince by the power of God, and that he was vassal and subject of our said Sovereign Lord and swore fidelity to the same, as other barons did; by virtue of this, he did not have the right to undertake anything by his own authority, by assault, in the province of my said Lord, without obtaining leave and permission from him; notwithstanding this, the said Gilles de Rais, deceiving my said Lord and taking no notice of his will, had men assembled and assaulted with offensive arms the aforenamed Jean Le Ferron, subject of my said Lord, guardian of the place and fortress of Saint-Étienne-de-Mermorte in the name of Geoffroy Le Ferron, his brother, to whom he had sold that place and his title of lordship by transference, and to whom he had given its possession; and he had the said Jean Le Ferron led before the said place, threatening him with decapitation on the spot, which obliged the said Jean Le Ferron to surrender the fortress to him. The said Lord took and held that place for a certain period of time, although he was ordered by my said Lord, and by his court, to abandon the premises and said place, and return it to the said Le Ferron with the goods he had taken, under pain of a penalty of fifty thousand gold crowns, which would be imposed by my said Lord in case of disobedience, refusal, or delay.

Which order the said Lord nowise obeyed, laying hands on the said Le Ferron and Guillaume Hauteris, a duty collector[2] for my said Lord, who was of his company, and he had them imprisoned, then conducted to Tiffauges, outside the duchy, where they were detained for a long time. And, since the imprisonment of the said Le Ferron, the said Lord had laid hands on Jean Rousseau, the sergeant-general of my said Lord, and had others do so, having

---

[2] Translator's note: The term in French is *foirage*, or *forage*, a "feudal term: the duty on wine and other drinks, imposed by a lord" (Littré II).

removed his dagger and committed other outrages. After which, at Machecoul he had other sergeants beaten, in his hatred of my said Lord, in proportion to his scorn for the restraining order brought by the latter on pain of a penalty of fifty thousand crowns, in reparation for the said outrages. The goods and possessions designated above being in the safekeeping of my said Lord, the said Lord transgressed that safekeeping and violated his oath of fidelity, showing himself rebellious and disobedient to my said Lord and his court.

And the said prosecutor presented his conclusions, according to which, in view of the said inquiries and said charge brought against him, he ought to be condemned to suffer corporal punishment with regard to justice. Furthermore, the possessions and lands he was holding from my said Lord Duke were to be confiscated; and the said penalties on his possessions were to be executed.

The said Lord de Rais acknowledged having assembled men to take the said place of Saint-Étienne-de-Mermorte by his own authority; and resorting to violence, having laid hands on the said Jean Le Ferron to deprive him of the said place; he acknowledged that the latter had given it to him for fear of having his head cut off on the spot; that he had held the place thereafter until my said Lord Duke had his men-at-arms recapture it; similarly, he acknowledged having had the said Jean Le Ferron brought to Tiffauges, where he was detained until his liberation through the Constable's intervention; he acknowledged further that my said Lord Duke had laid a restraining order on him, under the said penalty of fifty thousand crowns, to return the said place to Jean Le Ferron, which he had nowise obeyed. In view of which he would gladly conform to the will and order of my said Lord Duke, but he did not acknowledge having committed outrages upon the said sergeants, nor having had others commit them. Moreover, he disavowed the statements of the said prosecutor, who wanted evidence, which he was allowed to offer. Whereupon they had to ask the said Lord whether he would believe his servants, Henriet and Poitou, and whether he accepted them as witnesses. Which Lord responded that he would only tolerate honest men in his retinue and that, if he knew otherwise of them, he would be the first to see to their punishment. And he neither contested the witnesses nor gave his assent . . .[3]

---

[3] Hereafter, the manuscript of the Archives de la Trémoille reports on the ecclesiastical court events concerning the decision to torture (see p. 183), followed by what we provide here on the following pages. This kind of interpolation is characteristic of the free rendering of this portion of the manuscript.

# II

## INQUEST BY COMMISSIONERS
## OF THE DUKE OF BRITTANY

**From September 18 to October 8, 1440.**

*September 18, 1440.*

*Inquiry*[1] *and inquest with a view to proving, if possible, that the said Lord de Rais and his followers, his accomplices, conveyed away a certain number of small children, or other persons, and had them snatched, whom they struck down and killed, to have their blood, heart, liver, or other such parts, to make of them a sacrifice to the Devil, or to do other sorceries with, on which subject there are numerous complaints. This investigation was made by Jean de Touscheronde, appointed by the Duke, our Sovereign Lord.*

*Jean Colin* (sic) *is the first witness named that the Inquisitor received, September 18, 1440.*

PERONNE LOESSART, living in La Roche-Bernard, deposes under oath that two years ago this September the said Lord de Rais, returning from Vannes, came to lodge in the said place of La Roche-Bernard at the house of the said Jean Colin, and spent the night there. The witness was then living directly opposite the inn of the said Jean Colin. She had a ten-year-old child attending school, who attracted one of the servants of the said Lord de Rais, named Poitou. This Poitou came to speak with the said Peronne, requesting that she let the child live with him; he would clothe him very well and provide him with many advantages, while the child, for his part, would be the source of numerous benefits for Poitou as well. Whereupon the said Peronne told him that she had time to wait to benefit from her son, and that she was not going to take him out of school. The said Poitou assured her on this point and

---

[1] Titles and other information borne at the head of the inquest proper are rendered in italics.

solemnly promised that he would take her son and send him to school, and that he would give a hundred sous to this Peronne for a dress. Confident of his promise, she permitted him to take the child away.

Not long afterwards, Poitou brought her four pounds for the dress. She told him that twenty sous were missing; he denied this, saying that he had promised her only four pounds. She told him then that she knew by this that he would have difficulty keeping his other promises because he was already short twenty sous. He told her to stop worrying so much, that he would give her and her child plenty of other gifts. Then he led the said child away, conducting him to Jean Colin's, the innkeeper of the said Lord. And so, on the following day, as Gilles de Rais was leaving the said inn, this Peronne asked him for her said child, who was with him; but Lord de Rais did not respond at all. But he turned to the said Poitou, who was there, and said that the child had been well chosen, and that he was as beautiful as an angel. The said Poitou then responded that there had been no one but himself to make the choice, and the said Lord told him that he had not failed to choose well. Not long after this, the child left with the said Poitou in the company of the said Lord, riding on a pony that the said Poitou had bought from Jean Colin. Since then, this woman has had no more news of him; she has heard no word of where her said child might be, and she did not see him in the company of the said Lord who had since come through the said place of La Roche-Bernard. And she has not seen the said Poitou in the retinue of the said Lord since then. Those of the said Lord's men whom she asked where her son was told her that he was at Tiffauges or Pouzauges.

[Signed:] *De Touscheronde.*

JEAN COLIN and his wife,[2] and OLIVE, mother of the said Colin's wife, living at La Roche-Bernard, depose under oath that two years ago this September the said Lord de Rais, coming from Vannes, lodged at their inn and spent the night there. And that a fellow named Poitou, a servant of the said Lord, did so much for Peronne Loessart, who was living opposite their house then, that she entrusted him with her son, who was going to school, and who was one of the most beautiful children in the region, so that he might live with him; and the said Colin sold the said Poitou a pony he had for the sum of sixty sous, in order to take the said child away. And the said women said that, on the evening when the mother entrusted this Poitou with her son, he led him to the inn belonging to the witnesses, telling the other servants of the said Lord that this was his page; whereas these latter told him that he would not be there for him but that the said Lord, their master, would keep him for himself. And on the

---

[2] The first name of Jean Colin's wife is not given; Olive is her mother's first name.

following day, when the said Lord came out of the said inn to get going, these women heard the mother of the child ask for him of the said Lord, in the presence of the child and Poitou; whereupon the said Lord told Poitou that the child was well chosen; Poitou responded that there had been no one but himself to choose, and the said Lord told him that he had not been mistaken and that the child was as beautiful as an angel. Not long afterwards, the latter left, riding on the said pony with the said Poitou in the company of the said Lord. And the said Colin declares that two or three months later in Nantes, he saw someone other than the said child mount the said pony, which shocked him. And the aforenamed witnesses say that since then, they have not seen the said child nor heard where he was, save what the said women say, that when they had inquired of the Lord's men, some of them responded that he was at Tiffauges, others that he was dead: that while he was crossing over the bridges in Nantes, the wind had blown him into the river. Since then, she had not seen the said Poitou come through the said place of La Roche-Bernard in the retinue of the said Lord, although he had himself come through. And the last time he had come through, six weeks before, returning from Vannes, they heard it said by the said Lord's servants, whom they asked where the said Poitou was, in order to find out where the said child was, that Poitou had taken off in the direction of Redon; and they imagined that this was because of the shocking complaints that the said Perrone had made on the subject of her child; which complaints the said Poitou could have learned of through the said Lord's men.

[Signed:] *De Touscheronde.*

JEAN LEMEIGNEN and his wife, ALLAIN DULIS, PERROT DUPOUEZ, GUILLAUME GENTON, GUILLAUME PORTUYS, JEAN LEFEVRE, cleric, of Saint-Étienne-de-Montluc, depose under oath that about three years before, they saw a young child, the son of Guillaume Brice, a poor man of the said parish, frequent the borough of Saint-Étienne-de-Montluc, where his father lived, to ask for alms. This child was then about eight or nine years old; his father died over a year before around the beginning of Lent: this child was very beautiful and was called Jamet. The witnesses declare that, since last Saint John's Day, they have not seen him again or heard anything about where he might be found or what has become of him. Besides, this Dupouez says that some time around last Saint John's Day he ran into an old woman with a rosy face, fifty to sixty years old: she was coming from the direction of Coueron and he ran into her rather near the presbytery of Saint-Étienne; she was wearing a short linen tunic over her dress. And, on a previous occasion, he had seen her coming from Savenay and through the said (*sic*) wood of Saint-Étienne, working her way toward Coueron or Nantes. And on the day she was coming from the direction of Coueron, the witness saw the said child near the road where he had run into the said old woman, an arrow's flight above the said presbytery, so to speak, near which presbytery a man named Simon Lebreton lived. And the witness declares that since then, he has not seen the said child again nor heard anything said about where he might be. What is more, because he was friendless, there was no one in the region who might complain of his disappearance; and his mother, for her own part, was a beggar, daily begging for alms.

*The aforesaid witnesses were interrogated by Jean de Touscheronde, in the company of Jean Thomas, September 18, 1440.*

[Signed:] *De Touscheronde, Thomas.*

*September 27, 1440.*

*Part of the investigation and inquiry with a view to proving, if possible, that a certain number of children, or other persons, were conveyed and conducted to the castle at Machecoul, and there struck down and killed by the said Lord de Rais and his men, to have their blood, heart, liver, or other such parts, to make of them a sacrifice to the Devil, or to do other sorceries with. This investigation was made by Jean de Touscheronde, specially appointed by the Duke, assisted by Nicolas Chatau, notary public of the court of Nantes, September 27, 1440.*

GUILLAUME FOURAIGE and his wife, JEANNE, the wife of Jean Leflou, RICHARDE, the wife of Jean Gaudeau, of Port-Launay near Coueron, depose under oath that about two years previously, a young boy of approximately twelve, the son of the deceased Jean Bernard, their neighbor, of the said place of Port-Launay, and another young child of Coueron, the son of Jean Meugner, took off for Machecoul for the charity that was then customary there, with the intention of receiving alms; and from that day forward they had not seen the son of the said Bernard again and have had no news of him, save what they heard the son of Jean Meugner say, that after three days, he returned from the said place of Machecoul, and that one evening the son of Jean Bernard had told him to wait for him in a certain spot, beyond the houses, in the said place of Machecoul, and that he was going to find a place for them to stay; and with these words he departed, leaving the said Meugner in the spot where he had said and where the latter waited for him for over three hours, hoping that he would return, but since then, he had not seen him again nor heard any news. And the witnesses declare that they have since seen the mother of the said Bernard, who at present is harvesting grapes, complaining bitterly. Furthermore, the wife of the said Fouraige declared that for a year she had sometimes run into an old woman whom she did not know, wearing a paltry grey dress and black hood: this woman was small; once she had a young boy with her, and said that she was going to Machecoul, and went through Port-Launay with the said child; and not long afterwards, two or three days to be sure, the witness saw her returning without the child; therefore she asked her what had become of him, and this woman responded that she had placed him with a good master.

[Signed:] *De Touscheronde, Chatau.*

## September 28, 29, and 30, 1440.

*Another part of the investigation and inquiry touching on the aforesaid affair against the said Lord de Rais, his men and accomplices, led by Jean de Touscheronde, Michel Estrillart, and Jean Coppegorge Junior, appointed to this effect by the Duke, assisted by Nicolas Chatau, notary public of the court of Nantes, on September 28, 29, and 30, 1440.*

ANDRÉ BARBE, shoemaker, living at Machecoul, deposes under oath that since Easter he has heard that the son of Georges Le Barbier of Machecoul had been lost, that on a certain day he had been seen picking apples behind Rondeau's house and that he had never been seen since; certain neighbors of his had told Barbe and his wife that they ought to watch over their child, who was at risk of being snatched, and they were very frightened about him; in fact, the witness had even been at Saint-Jean-d'Angély, and someone asked him where he was from, and when he responded that he was from Machecoul, that person was shocked, telling him that they ate little children there.[3]

He further states that a child of Guillaume Jeudon, who was living with Guillaume Hilairet, a child of Jeannot Roussin, and another of Alexandre Chastelier, of Machecoul, had been lost. He also heard complaints of the loss of other children in the said place of Machecoul. He adds that nobody dared speak for fear of the men in Lord de Rais' chapel, or others of his men; those who complained risked imprisonment, or ill-treatment, should anyone report their complaints.

Furthermore, he states that he heard a man complaining in the church of the Trinité at Machecoul, whom he did not know, who was asking whether anyone had seen his child, whom he claimed was seven years old; and this about eight months earlier.

[Signed:] *De Touscheronde, Coppegorge, Chatau.*

---

[3] The Old French of the civil trial reads: "sur ce, l'on lui avait dit, en se merveillant, qu'on y mangeoit les petits enffants." {"as for that, someone had told him, marveling, that they ate small children there."}

## Document II — The Secular Court Trial

Jeannette, the wife of Guillaume Sergent, living in the parish of Sainte-Croix of Machecoul, in a hamlet called La Boucardière, declares that about a year ago last Pentecost, her husband and she had gone digging in a field to plant hemp. They had left one of their sons, eight years old, at home, to tend their little girl of one-and-a-half, but on their return they could not find the said child of eight, which greatly astonished and dispirited them; and they went to inquire about him in the parishes of Machecoul and elsewhere, but since then they have had no more news of him and have never heard that anyone had seen him.

[Signed:] *De Touscheronde, Coppegorge, Chatau.*

Georget [Le] Barbier, tailor,[4] living near the entrance to the castle of Machecoul, declares that he had a son named Guillaume, whom he had placed with Jean Peletier, tailor to Lady de Rais and Lord de Rais' men: he was learning the trade and living with him. Around last Saint Barnabas' Day this child, who was eighteen years old, was playing with a ball of thread at Machecoul; the said Lord and his men were then staying at the castle of Machecoul; and since that evening when his said child was playing thus with the ball of thread, the present witness had never seen him again, nor heard that anyone, no matter who, had spotted him, although he asked about his child many times. And he said that the tailor, his master, and the said child, his servant, were continually going to the castle and eating there.

Moreover, he states that he heard whispers that children were killed in the said castle.

Item, he declares that he heard it said that the page of Milord François,[5] who was living with the said Lord, had been lost as well.

Further he states that he had seen an endless procession of children go begging for alms at the castle of Machecoul, when the said Lord and his men were residing there.

[Signed:] *De Touscheronde, Coppegorge, Chatau.*

Guillaume Hilairet and his wife, Jeanne Hilairet, living at Machecoul, declare that they had heard that the son of the said Georget Le Barbier had disappeared around the aforesaid time, and since then they have not seen him again or heard that anyone had seen him. Moreover, the said Guillaume Hilairet recalls that, about seven or eight years previously, a twelve-year-old child, the son of Jean Jeudon, was living with him to learn the furrier's trade. And the said Guillaume Hilairet declares that in the presence of Roger de

[4] In Eustache Blanchet's deposition (p. 212), this Le Barbier is given as a pastry-cook.

[5] François Prelati.

258

Briqueville, around the aforesaid time, Gilles de Sillé requested that he lend him his said valet to carry a message to the said castle of Machecoul, and the said Hilairet lent him the valet and sent him to the said castle. And the said Guillaume and his wife declare that since then, they had not seen the said helper again nor heard that anyone else had seen him. And much later that same day the said Guillaume Hilairet asked the said Sillé and Briqueville what had become of his said valet: they told him that they did not know, unless he had had to go to Tiffauges, and into such a place, the said Sillé said, where thieves had snatched him to make him a page.

Item, the witnesses declare that they have heard many people say that a child of Jeannot Roussin and another of Alexandre Chastelier, the latter then living in front of the Trinité of Machecoul, the former in the vicinity of the village, had also been lost; they heard their father and mother complaining bitterly.

Item, the said Guillaume Hilairet declares that about five years before, he had heard a man named Jean du Jardin, then living with Milord Roger de Briqueville, state that a conduit filled with dead little children was found at the castle of Champtocé.

Item, this Guillaume Hilairet declares that he had previously heard one of Rais' women, whose name he did not know, complaining at Machecoul of the loss of a child of hers.

Item, the witnesses declare that it was public and common knowledge that children were put to death in the said castle, for which reason they presume that the aforesaid children had been killed and put to death there.

And since that time the aforesaid Jean Jeudon has appeared before us, the aforesaid commissioners, and declared that he had previously entrusted his son to the said Guillaume Hilairet to learn the furrier's trade; and his said child had been lost, he does not know how, and since the aforementioned time he has not seen him again nor heard any news. Furthermore, he says that he has heard complaints of the loss of other children.

[Signed:] *De Touscheronde, Coppegorge, Chatau.*

JEAN TIFOLOZ JUNIOR, JOUHAN AUBIN, CLÉMENT DORÉ, of Touvois, state that they had heard Mathelin Thouars complaining about and lamenting for one of his children, about whom he said he did not know what had become of him, about which he was very unhappy; and the witnesses say that Thouars was a poor man. And they heard him complaining about six months before. And the child was about twelve years old.

[Signed:] *De Touscheronde, Coppegorge, Chatau.*

JEAN ROUSSIN, of Machecoul, declares that about nine years previously, a child of his, nine years old, was to watch the animals one particular day, on which day he never returned home; he and his wife were greatly astonished by this, not knowing what had happened to him. And thereafter, after the complaints and outcry of his wife and family, two of his neighbors, who are now deceased, told him that they had seen Gilles de Sillé, wearing a tabard,[6] his face thinly veiled, speaking with the said child, and that the said child left for the castle, going through the back gate. What is more, he says that his said child, who was living close to the castle, knew the said Gilles de Sillé well and occasionally carried milk to the castle for those who wanted it. And he declares that he has heard no more talk of his said child since then.

He adds that the day before he lost his son he had heard complaints of the loss of the said Jeudon's son, who was living with the said Guillaume Hilairet. He also states that he heard other men complaining of the loss of their children.

[Signed:] *De Touscheronde, Coppegorge, Chatau.*

JEANNE, widow of Aimery Édelin and former wife of Jean Bonneau, living at Machecoul, states that she had a young boy aged eight, who went to school, and who was very beautiful, very fair, and clever. He was living with the mother of the said Jeanne across from the castle of Machecoul; and about eight years ago this child disappeared without anyone being able to find out what happened to him. And previously, a child of Roussin and another of Jeudon had also been lost. And about fifteen days later a child of Macé Sorin, whose wife was the aunt of this Jeanne, had also been lost; and, following on the complaints that they heard, these children were thought to have been taken to give to the English for the liberation of Milord Michel de Sillé, who was a prisoner of the English, so it was said; and the said Lord's men were supposed to have said that, for the ransom of the said Lord Michel, the stipulation was to furnish the English with twenty-four male children.

Item, she says that about two or three years before, she saw at Machecoul a man named Oran, who lived in the direction of Saint-Mesme, lamenting piteously and crying over the loss of a child; he was asking about him in the said place of Machecoul but so far as the said Jeanne knows, had no news of him.

Item, she says that after last Easter she heard a man named Aisé and his wife, living in the house of someone named Pinsonneau, at Machecoul, in the parish of Sainte-Croix, complaining of the loss of their child.

Item, she declares having heard that many other children had been lost, in Brittany and elsewhere, about which there was a great outcry. And, among others, she heard a man from around Tiffauges, whose name she has forgotten, say that for one child lost around Machecoul, seven were lost around

[6] Editor's note: A tunic or cape-like garment.

Tiffauges; they were taken in the country while watching the animals, and nobody knew what had happened to them or had become of them.

[Signed:] *De Touscheronde, Coppegorge, Chatau.*

MACÉ SORIN and his wife declare that around the same time indicated by the said wife of the said Édelin, the child of Édelin's wife was lost, without anyone's knowing what became of it; and right around the same time they had heard that a child of Alexandre Chastelier, another of someone named Roussin, and another of a man named Guillaume Jeudon, who was living with Guillaume Hilairet, had also been lost; and it was supposed then that they had been handed over to the English for the liberation of Milord de Sillé, their prisoner, given the rumor that his ransom and liberation required them to deliver up to a certain number of small children, of whom they would make pages.

Item, they state that a son of Georget Le Barbier, their close neighbor, has been lost since Easter, without anyone's knowing what had become of him. They heard great complaints of these and still other losses, but nobody dared to speak too much about it.

[Signed:] *De Touscheronde, Chatau, Coppegorge.*

PERRINE, the wife of Clément Rondeau of Machecoul, says that for a year already her husband has been so sick that he had received extreme unction and that they thought he was going to die. And before this time and earlier, Master François[7] and the Marquis de Ceva, both of them Lombards, who were in Lord de Rais' service,[8] were lodged in her house in an upper chamber, where they slept together; and on the day when her said husband received extreme unction, because of the tears and crying that her husband's state moved her to, this Perrine was installed in the evening in the room of Master François and the Marquis, who had gone to the castle of Machecoul, having left their pages in the said room to have supper. And when Master François and the Marquis returned, they were very irritated to find that Perrine had been allowed in and, showering her with insults, carried her, one by her feet, the other by her shoulders, to the staircase of the room, having decided to throw her from top to bottom; and with this in mind, the said François kicked her in the lower back; and she thinks she would have fallen had her nurse not caught her by the dress.

Item, she says that afterwards she heard the said Marquis announce to the said François that he had found a beautiful page for him from around Dieppe,

[7] François Prelati.

[8] The text reads: ". . . who were living with Lord de Rais."

about whom François said he was extremely delighted. And so it was that a young, very beautiful child, saying that he was from the Dieppe region and that he was of a good family, came to stay with the said François, and he remained with him for about fifteen days. Then this Perrine, shocked, asked herself what had become of him and posed the question to the said François: and where was his said page? François responded that he had cheated him royally, that he had taken off with his two crowns, getting them from him in exchange for worthless signatures.

Item, she says that afterwards this François and Master Eustache Blanchet went to stay in a small house at Machecoul, where a man named Perrot Cahu was living, whom they threw out and whom they relieved of the keys of the said house: this house is far from other habitations, in an isolated place, on an outside street with a well at the entrance; and in this small house, which is not a proper lodging for honorable men, the said François and Master Eustache slept; and the said Marquis, who frequently called on the said François and Master Eustache, slept in the house of the said Perrine and her husband.

Item, she says that after the arrest of the said Lord and aforenamed fellows, in the presence of Jean Labbé and others, she saw some ashes removed from the house of the said Cahu, said to have come from the children who were burned, and the small shirt of a bloody child, which stank so horribly that she was sick from having smelled it.

[Signed:] *De Touscheronde, Coppegorge, Chatau.*

André Bréchet, of the parish of Sainte-Croix of Machecoul, declares under oath that about six months previously, he was supposed to spy on the castle of Machecoul, but that after midnight he fell asleep; and, as he was sleeping, a small man he did not know appeared on the ramparts, who woke him and showed him his naked dagger, saying: "You're dead." However, because of the said André's pleas, this man did nothing to him, but continued on his way and took off. The said André was terrified, sweating all over. On the following day he ran into Lord de Rais, coming from the island of Boin, on his way to Machecoul. And thereafter he no longer dared to spy on the said castle.

[Signed:] *De Touscheronde, Coppegorge, Chatau.*

Perrot Pasqueteau, Jean Soreau, Catherine Degrépie, Guillaume Garnier, Perrine, the wife of Jean Veillart, Marguerite, the wife of Perrot Redinet, Marie, the wife of Jean Caeffin, Jeanne, the wife of Étienne Landais, of Fresnay, near Machecoul, declare under oath that one day after last Easter they heard Guillaume Hamelin and Ysabeau, his wife, sorrowfully complaining of the disappearance of two of their children, not knowing what had become of them. Since then, they had not heard whether anyone had seen these children or come upon them.

[Signed:] *De Touscheronde, Coppegorge, Chatau.*

YSABEAU, the wife of Guillaume Hamelin, living in the borough of Fresnay, where she and her husband had gone to live about a year before, from Pouancé, declares under oath that about seven days before the end of last year, she sent two of her children, two boys, the one aged fifteen, the other seven or thereabouts, to the village of Machecoul to buy bread with the money she had given them, and they did not return, and since then she has been unable to find out where they were. But the day after she had so dispatched them, Master François and the Marquis,[9] who were living with Lord de Rais,[10] whom she says she knows well and has seen many times, came to her house. The Marquis inquired whether she had recovered from the problem with her breast; in response to which she asked him how he knew she had been suffering, because, in fact, she had not. He told her that she had, after which he said that she was not from the region, but from Pouancé; and she asked him how he knew that, and he responded that he well knew it; then she acknowledged that he was right. Thereupon he cast a glance inside the house and asked her whether she were married, and she responded yes, but that her husband had come into their region looking for work. And as he saw two small children in the house, namely one girl and one boy, he asked her whether they were hers; she responded yes, whereupon he asked her whether she had only two children; to which she responded that she had two more, withholding the fact of their disappearance from him, which she dared not tell. Then they left and when they did she heard the Marquis say to the said Master François that two of the children had come from that house.

She says, besides, that about eight days earlier she had heard that Micheau Bouer and his wife, of Saint-Cyr-en-Rais, had also lost a child who had not been seen since.

[Signed:] *De Touscheronde, Chatau, Coppegorge.*

PERROT SOUDAN, of Fresnay, declares under oath that, around the time indicated by the said Ysabeau,[11] he saw the said Master François[12] and said

---

[9] François Prelati and the Marquis de Ceva.

[10] They were not actually living at the castle, but in the area. The wording implies only that they were in his service.

[11] Ysabeau Hamelin.

[12] François Prelati.

Marquis[13] speaking with the said Ysabeau in front of her house, but did not hear what they were saying because he was so far away that it simply would have been impossible. He had likewise heard Ysabeau complaining of the disappearance of her two children, and Micheau Bouer of another child, all of whom have not been seen by anyone insofar as he could discover.

[Signed:] *De Touscheronde, Coppegorge, Chatau.*

GUILLEMETTE, the wife of Micheau Bouer, of Saint-Cyr-en-Rais, declares under oath that seven days after last Easter her son, aged eight, who was beautiful and fair, had gone begging for alms at Machecoul and did not return, and she had not heard any news of him since, although her husband, the father of the said child, had made inquiries after him in various places; and on the following day, the day they distributed alms at Machecoul for the deceased Mahé Le Breton, as she was watching the animals, a large man dressed in black, whom she did not know, came to her and asked, among other things, where her children were, why they were not watching the animals. To which she responded that they had gone begging at Machecoul. Whereupon he left her and vanished.

[Signed:] *De Touscheronde, Coppegorge, Chatau.*

GUILLAUME RODIGO, also known as Guillaume de Guérande, and his wife, living at Bourgneuf-en-Rais, declare under oath that on last Saint-Bartholomew's Eve, Lord de Rais and his men, among them Master Eustache Blanchet and Poitou, came to lodge at Bourgneuf-en-Rais. And the said Lord supped at the house of Guillaume Plumet. At this Rodigo's then was a young boy aged fifteen, named Bernard Le Camus, from around Brest, who had been previously entrusted to one of his uncles and the *mancadre*[14] of Brest to learn French in his home. That same day the said Master Eustache and Poitou spoke with the said young man, who was very beautiful and very clever, the witnesses not knowing what they said to him, and the said Poitou came to their house as an agent for the said Lord, seeking to buy from the said Rodigo what he had to sell, saying that he had already closed the sale between the said Rodigo and the said Lord. And that same evening, around ten o'clock, the child left their house without his garment, shoes, or hood, unbeknownst to and in the absence of the said Rodigo and his wife. Their chamberlain told

---

[13] The Marquis de Ceva.

[14] Translator's note: A word whose exact meaning I have not been able to ascertain. However, Yves Le Gallo of the Centre de Recherche Bretonne et Celtique in France has access to the Old French civil trial document and offers three possible solutions: the word doesn't exist; it is a fabrication on the part of the adapter of the text; it is the name of a man from Lower Brittany, with article capitalized, viz. *Le Mancadre.*

them that before departing, the child had told him he was leaving and asked him to tend to and arrange the cups, whereupon he left the house; they have never seen the child again, or heard what happened to him, although the said Rodigo inquired of the said Lord and his men, and offered forty crowns to have him back. To which the said Poitou and Eustache responded that if they could find him, they would gladly bring him back, but they feared that he had not gone to Tiffauges to be a page.

MARGUERITE SORIN, of the parish of Saint-Aignan, chambermaid of the said Rodigo and his wife, declares under oath that at about the time indicated above, she and the said child being after supper in the house of the said Rodigo where they were playing together, the said Rodigo and his wife being not far away in another house of theirs, where they had supped, the said Poitou appeared, who asked them whether they played like that together. They answered yes, after which he took the child aside, laying one hand on his shoulder and holding his hat in the other, and spoke to him in a voice so low that she could not hear. Then, having thus spoken, the said Poitou left. Immediately, the present witness asked the child what Poitou had said to him, who responded that he had not said a thing; a little while later the child told her that he wanted to go away, and asked her to take care and arrange his affairs; then he left, unwilling to tell her where he was going even though she insisted. He left his garment, his shoes, and his hood, going out in his cloak. Since then, she has neither seen him again nor had any news of him.

[Signed:] *De Touscheronde, Coppegorge, Chatau.*

GUILLAUME PLUMET and his wife, MICHEL GÉRARD, of Bourgneuf-en-Rais, declare under oath that they saw quite a young boy named Bernard, originally from Lower Brittany, living with the said Rodigo. He had been there before the previous Saint-Bartholomew's Day, but, a short while before the said feast, Lord de Rais came to lodge and sleep at Bourgneuf; thereafter they heard the said Rodigo and his wife complaining bitterly of the loss of the said child, whom subsequently the witnesses never saw again, nor heard any more news of him.

[Signed:] *De Touscheronde, Coppegorge, Chatau.*

THOMAS AISÉ and his wife, living at Port-Saint-Père, declare under oath that for a year they lived at Machecoul, that they were still living there the previous Pentecost and that, being poor folk, around last Pentecost they had sent their son, aged about ten, to beg at the castle of Machecoul, where Lord de Rais was then residing; since that time they have not seen their child again, nor heard any news of him, with this exception: a small girl whose name and whose father she does not know told her that she had seen her son begging in front of the castle and that, first, alms had been given separately to the girls, then to the boys, and that after this second distribution she heard one of the castle servants say to the witnesses' son that he had not received any meat, that he should enter the said castle where he should be given some; and in fact, with these words, he was made to enter the said castle.

[Signed:] *De Touscheronde, Coppegorge, Chatau.*

JEANNETTE, the wife of Eustache Drouet, of Saint-Léger, near Port-Saint-Père, declares under oath that a year before the previous Christmas, about fifteen days before the feast, she had sent two of her boys, one aged ten, the other seven, to beg for alms in the village of Machecoul, because she had heard that Lord de Rais had them distributed there, and that, moreover, the men in that village willingly gave charity. And she states that her children stayed at Machecoul for several days, and that she had come upon some men who said they had seen them there; but afterwards, going there, she did not see them nor did she know what had become of them, although she and her husband asked about them numerous times.

[Signed:] *De Touscheronde, Coppegorge.*

**October 2, 1440.**

*Another inquiry and investigation made by Jean de Touscheronde and Étienne Halouart, appointed by the Duke, assisted by Nicolas Chatau, notary public of the court of Nantes, October 2, 1440.*

JEANNETTE DEGRÉPIE, [the widow of] Regnaud Donete, of the parish of Notre-Dame of Nantes, states and declares under oath that two years before, around Saint John's Day, Lord de Rais residing then at his house in Nantes, she lost a child of hers, aged twelve, who was attending school. And that she has not heard any news of him since then, except that fifteen days ago she heard Perrine Martin, detained in the Nantes prison, confess that she had led the said child to the said Lord in his room, in his house of La Suze, in the said place of Nantes, and that the said Lord had ordered her to take him to Machecoul and hand him over to the porter; she confessed, moreover, that she actually had conveyed the said child there.

Item, she says that Jean Hubert and Denis de Lemion, of the same place of Nantes, each lost his son,[15] whom she knew and whose loss she had heard

---

[15] With regard to Denis de Lemion, his nephew, not his son, was at issue.

them bemoaning; and since their complaints, she had not seen the children again.

Item, she says that given the complaint that she lodged with a fellow named Cherpy or with others of the said Lord's men, because [her child] sometimes frequented the house of La Suze, near which the said Perrine was living, this Cherpy and the said Lord's men told her that they thought he had gone to Machecoul to become a page.

[Signed:] *Étienne Halouart, De Touscheronde, Chatau.*


JEAN JENVRET and his wife, of Sainte-Croix-de-Nantes, declare under oath that two years ago, eight days before Saint John the Baptist's Day, Lord de Rais then residing in Nantes in his house, La Suze, they had lost their son, aged nine, who was attending school, and who sometimes frequented the said house of La Suze; and they had not had any news of him since then, except that three weeks before, they heard that Perrine Martin, detained in Nantes prison, confessed to having led the said child to Lord de Rais, in his castle at Machecoul.

[Signed:] *De Touscheronde, Étienne Halouart, Chatau.*


JEAN HUBERT and his wife, of Saint-Léonard of Nantes, declare under oath that two years previously, on the Thursday following Saint John the Baptist's Day, they lost a boy of thirteen, who was attending school; Lord de Rais then residing in his house in Nantes. Theretofore, this child, who had been employed for a week, lived with Princé, a member of the said Lord's retinue. Princé, on engaging him, was supposed to set the child up in the best conditions and had promised to do him and his parents much good, but he did not return them their child or even give them a reason for letting him go. The child told them that this Princé had a horse that he dared not mount for fear the horse would kill him. Whereupon his parents told him that he should return to school, but the child responded that there was a proper gentleman staying with Lord de Rais, who called himself Spadin, whom he had struck up a friendship with, and whom he desired to stay with, as he had promised to fit him out well, convey him to another region,[16] and do him much good. Trusting the child, the parents let him go, and he left, in fact, the very next day after his return from the said Princé, in fact, so that he spent only one night in their house. Subsequently, as he went to live at La Suze, where the said Lord was then, they saw their child there during the next seven days. But during this time, the said Lord was absent for four or five days, having left a party of his men and the said child at La Suze. And the day the Lord returned,

---

[16] The text reads: "en pays d'amont" ("in the region upriver").

the child came to his parents and told his mother that Lord de Rais was quite fond of him, that he had just cleaned his room and that his master had given him a round loaf of bread made for the said Lord, which he had brought her. Also he told her that a fellow named Simonnet, one of the said Lord's servants, had given him another round loaf of the same bread to take to a woman in town. And the witnesses say that since that time, they have not seen their child again nor had any news of him, even though they complained about it to the said Lord's men, who responded that a Scottish knight, who was quite fond of him, had taken him away. Also, a month before, they unsuspectingly complained in front of the wife of Master Jean Briand, and this woman accused the said Hubert's wife of claiming that the said Lord had killed her child. To which Hubert's wife responded that she had done nothing of the sort, but Briand's wife retorted that she had, and that she was going to regret it, she and the others.

Item, the witnesses say that after the loss of their child the said Lord stayed in Nantes about fifteen days, in the course of which Spadin sent for Hubert, so the latter says, and asked him where his child was; to which he responded that he did not know, but that he had entrusted him to Spadine[17] and that he was responsible: whereupon the said Spadine retorted that he was crazy and that he himself was responsible for the loss of his child. They also say that they heard Degrépie, [the widow of] Regnaud Donete, Denis de Lemion and his wife, and Jean Jenvret and his wife likewise grumbling about losing their children.

Item, the same Hubert declares that he said to Princé after the loss of his son, he had committed a mortal sin for not having really tended and governed the child: this Princé told him then that it was not his problem, and that he was undoubtedly with a proper gentleman, who would do him much good.

[Signed:] *De Touscheronde, Étienne Halouart, Chatau.*

AGAICE,[18] wife of Denis de Lemion, weaver, of the parish of Notre-Dame-de-Nantes, states that about a year and a half before, her nephew, the son of Colin[19] Avril, was living with her and her husband; he was eighteen years old and sometimes frequented La Suze. And that on or about one particular evening while Lord de Rais was living there, one of his servants requested that she entrust him with her child so as to show him the house of the Archdeacon of Merles, promising to give her a round loaf; she accepted, accompanied him,

---

[17] Editor's note: The French text offers both Spadine and Spadin.

[18] Editor's note: The French text offers both Agathe and Agaice.

[19] It is apparently the son Avril who is Colin; the father is named Guillaume. See pp. 160 and 269-270.

then returned; on the following day the said child returned to the house of La Suze, intending to receive the said round loaf; since then he has not returned, and she has had no news as to what could have become of him.

[Signed:] *De Touscheronde, Étienne Halouart, Chatau.*

JEANNE, the wife of Guibelet Delit, of Saint-Denis of Nantes, declares that a year ago last Lent she lost one of her children, aged seven, who frequented La Suze, where he had run into a man named Cherpy, cook for Lord de Rais, who was residing at the said place of La Suze when her child disappeared. And Master Jean Briand, who was living there, told her that he had seen the said child busy roasting meat, and according to him, had told the cook he was wrong to let him work in the kitchen like that; she has not seen the child again since nor had any news of him.

Item, she says that three or four months previously, she was complaining to the wife of the said Master Jean Briand, telling her how people were saying that Lord de Rais had small children caught to be killed; but two of the said Lord's servants, whose names she does not know, arrived as she was speaking, and this Briand's wife told them that the present witness claimed that the Lord was having small children killed, and the said woman told her that she and the others would regret it. The witness then excused herself to the said Lord's servants.

[Signed:] *De Touscheronde, Étienne Halouard, Chatau.*

JEAN TOUTBLANC, of Saint-Étienne-de-Montluc, declares that a year ago last Saint Julian's Day he went to Saint-Julien-de-Vouvantes, having left a young man of about thirteen at his house; the witness was the tutor of this boy, who lived at his house. But on returning from his trip, he discovered that the latter was gone, and he has not had any news of him since.

[Signed:] *De Touscheronde.*

JEAN FOUGERE, of the parish of Saint-Donatien, near Nantes, declares under oath that about two years ago he lost a son, aged about twelve, who was very beautiful; and since then he has been unable to find out what became of him.

[Signed:] *De Touscheronde.*

**October 2, 1440.**

JEAN FEROT, GUILLAUME JACOB, PERRIN BLANCHET, THOMAS BEAUVIS, ÉONNET JEAN, DENIS DE LEMION, of the parish of Notre-Dame-de-Nantes, declare under oath that they knew a son of Jean Hubert's, a son of Regnaud

Donete's, and a son of Guillaume Avril's who were living in the said parish of Notre-Dame, and they do not know what happened to these children, but they heard their fathers, their mothers, and their friends complaining bitterly about their disappearance. The witnesses have heard these complaints and verified this disappearance for two and a half years, without having had or heard news of them in these two and a half years, except that a year before they had heard that Lord de Rais and his men were taking children to be killed, and having them taken, and that there is public clamor (common report) on that score.

[Signed:] *De Touscheronde.*

NICOLE, the wife of Vincent Bonnereau, PHILIPPE, the wife of Mathis Ernaut, JEANNE, the wife of Guillaume Prieur, of the parish of Sainte-Croix of Nantes, declare under oath that they knew a son of Jean Jenvret and his wife, who was living with Monsieur d'Étampes.[20] This child was about nine years old, and they heard his father and mother complaining pitifully about his loss and disappearance. Since then, they have not seen the said child, nor heard any word of him. And they say that for six months they have heard it commonly said that Lord de Rais and his men were having little children taken and killed.

Item, they say that they knew a young boy, the son of the deceased Éonnet de Villeblanche, and heard his mother complaining for three months about his loss and disappearance, and that they have not seen him again since then.

Item, RAOULET DE LAUNAY, tailor, deposes that around last Assumption Day he made a doublet for the said child, who was living with Poitou then. And it was this Poitou, not the said Macée,[21] who haggled with him over the execution of this doublet, and who gave him twenty sous; he had not seen the child again.

[Signed:] *De Touscheronde.*

**October 6, 1440.**

JEAN ESTAISSE and MICHELE, the wife of the said Estaisse, of the parish of Saint-Clément, near Nantes, declare under oath that a son of the said Dagaie, named Perrot Dagaie, lived for two years or thereabouts with Master Gatien Ruis, and when he went to live with him, he could very well have been eleven years old. After having lived with him for these two years, he came home to his mother, where he remained one or two days and slept one night, to the witnesses' knowledge. And since then, that is about two years ago this coming All

---

[20] This appears to be Richard, Count d'Étampes, brother of Jean V, Duke of Brittany.

[21] Referring to the wife of Eonnet de Villeblanche (p. 281).

Saints' Day, the mother, the witnesses, and several of the neighbors were frightened one day to discover the disappearance of the said child; and to the witnesses' knowledge, he has never been seen in the said parish or elsewhere. And the witnesses have heard many times that the said child's mother was asking about him of the said Master Gatien, his men, and a fellow named Linache, living in Angers, lamenting and saying that she did not know what had become of him.

Likewise they have seen her asking about him while bewailing him to Tiphaine, the wife of Éonnet Le Charpentier, butcher, the sister of the said mother of the said child; which Tiphaine declared and reported it in the same manner.

Item, it was put to them whether they had heard it stated or claimed that the said Lord de Rais had taken this child or other children, or had them taken. They responded no, only since the arrest of the said Lord de Rais and his men; they also claim that up to the present, they had no knowledge of the said Tiphaine and Perrine,[22] presently held in prison.

**October 8, 1440.**

JEAN CHIQUET, parchment-maker, living outside the Sauvetout gate, deposes under oath that one month previously, or thereabouts, a man named Macé Drouet, haberdasher, from the vicinity of Chanteloup, near Rennes, came to lodge with him, the witness, and several other haberdashers with him. While they were talking together about the children who had been lost in the Rais region, the witness heard Drouet say that two other haberdashers and he had been to several fairs in the region of Rais, about a year before; he had left two children in the region of Rais, and he has not seen them again since; and he saw their father and mother again, who asked him for news, but he told them that he did not know what had become of the children.

[Signed:] *De Touscheronde.*

PIERRE BADIEU, haberdasher, of the said parish of Chanteloup, declares that a year ago, or thereabouts, he saw in the said region of Rais two young children, about nine years old; each had a pack and was going to the fairs, as the witness himself did; they were brothers, and the children of Robin Pavot of the said place. And he has never seen them again. Subsequently, he has been to the region from which they came and spoken to their parents and one of their

---

[22] Clearly Tiphaine, the widow of Robin Branchu, and Perrine Martin, called La Meffraie. This Tiphaine was produced as a witness together with Perrine Martin, but their depositions have not come down to us (see p. 129).

brothers; these latter asked him for news, and he told them that he has not seen the two children again since having seen them in the said region of Rais. He adds that he heard the brother say that he had gone into various regions in the hope of obtaining some news but could learn nothing.

[Signed:] *De Touscheronde.*

JEAN DAREL, of the parish of Saint-Séverin, near Nantes, declares that he has been living in this parish for three years now, or thereabouts; a year or so ago, when he was sick in bed, where he had to remain a long time, a child of his, who lived in the house with him, was picked up off Rue du Marché where he was playing with other children; he does not know who picked him up or whither he was taken, and he has been unable to obtain any news since then, although he has been to many regions hoping to learn something.

[Signed:] *De Touscheronde.*

JEANNE, the wife of the said Darel, declares that a year ago Saint Peter's Day she lost her son, named Olivier, then aged seven or eight, in the city of Nantes. And since that feast, she has not seen him again or had news of what could have become of him.

[Signed:] *De Touscheronde.*

JEANNE, the mother of the said wife of Jean Darel, declares that a year ago Saint Peter's Day, returning from Saint-Pierre-de-Nantes, where she was attending Vespers, she ran into the said child near the pillory and brought him just in front of Saint-Saturnin, thinking to bring him home with her, but lost him in a crowd of men in front of the church; she looked for him and asked in the church, but could not find him; and since then she has never seen him again nor had any news of him.

[Signed:] *De Touscheronde.*

ÉONNETTE, the wife of Jean Bremant, living in the market at the house in which the said Darels live, declares that she well knew the said Darels' child who went by the name of Olivier and was the age indicated above; she says that she is certain that at the time indicated above, the wife of the said Darel told her that she had lost her child and asked her whether she had seen him, and that she responded no; moreover, she says that to her knowledge, since that time the child never appeared in the house of his mother and father; and she has never heard that he had been found.

[Signed:] *De Touscheronde.*

NICOLE, the wife of Jean Hubert, of the parish of Saint-Vincent, in Nantes, having sworn to speak the truth, declares under oath that around two years ago last Saint John's Day she had a son named Jean, aged fourteen, whom she placed with a man named Mainguy, with whom he stayed only a short while because the said Mainguy died. Upon his decease, the said son came to live with her and his father; thereupon Lord de Rais, returning from Angers, came to stay in his house called La Suze, in Nantes. The son of the witness went to this house, where he made the acquaintance of a man named Spadine, who was living with the said Lord. This Spadine gave him a round loaf that the latter brought to the witness, saying that the former had given it to him and that he wanted the said child to live with him and ride in the company of the said Lord de Rais. The witness responded that that was fine. And once again her said son returned to La Suze, whence he returned shortly, bidding the witness goodbye several times, telling her that he was going to live with the said Spadine. And he left immediately, in fact, and since that time the witness has never seen him again nor learned anything whatsoever about what might have befallen him. Furthermore Jean Hubert, the husband of the witness and father of the child, declares that he showed up at La Suze afterwards, asking the said Spadine about his son, who told him twice that he did not know, that he had no choice but to leave and that the child was lost. And such is her deposition.

[Signed:] *De Touscheronde.*

JEAN BUREAU and his wife; JEANNE, wife of Thibaut Geffroi, and her daughter; GUILLAUME HEMERI, having sworn to speak the truth, declare under oath that they knew this Hubert and his wife well; also that they knew well the said Jean, their child; that they have seen them living in the parish of Saint-Léonard of Nantes for a long time and that they were still living there around two years before, last Saint John's Day. At this time the said Jean, their son, was living at home, and before and since that feast they had seen him in the house of his said mother and father. But a short while after this the child left or was led away; they did not know whither or in what direction, and never saw him again; after this, you could see his father and mother asking about him in this town and elsewhere. And such is their deposition.

[Signed:] *De Touscheronde.*

LA DEGREPIE, the wife of Regnaud Donete, living in the parish of Notre-Dame-de-Nantes, having sworn to speak the truth, testifies; interrogated, she declares under oath that two years ago last Saint John the Baptist's Day she and her husband were living in the house where they still live now. And one of their sons was living with them. Her husband hired himself out for a time to a man named Jean Ferot, baker, to learn the trade; and her said son often went with his father to put the bread in the oven. She declares, moreover, that before the designated time this son had met a certain number of Lord de Rais' men, whom she herself did not know, according to her deposition; as soon as the said Lord came into town, her son frequented his house, but she did not know what he did there. She says, finally, that at the time indicated above, namely two years before, last Saint John's Day, her son showed up at the house of the said Lord, and she has never seen him again since, and for all she knows he might be dead. As a result she betook herself to many places hoping for news, but has been unable to learn anything.

[Signed:] *De Touscheronde.*

JEAN FEROT and his wife declare under oath that two years previously last Saint John's Day, the now deceased Regnaud Donete had hired himself out to them to learn the baker's trade; and his son, aged twelve, often came with him to put the bread in the oven. But they noticed several times that after having prepared half an oven, if he saw or knew that the said Lord de Rais was in town, he abandoned the bread and went to the the said Lord's house, and they did not know what he did there. Now, in the period in question, although they cannot pin down the day, they saw him leave and have never seen him again since, and they do not know what became of him.

[Signed:] *De Touscheronde.*

PIERRE BLANCHET and GUILLAUME JACOB declare under oath that they live near the house of Regnaud Donete's widow; they are certain that two years ago last Saint John's Day the now deceased Donete and his wife had a child, whom they knew well; and as soon as Lord de Rais was in town he went to his house, and they do not know what he did there. But after this one day when he went there, they never saw him again, and they do not know what has become of him. Such is their deposition.

[Signed:] *De Touscheronde.*

# III

## RECORDS OF THE FINAL DAYS

### Confessions of Henriet and Poitou

**Henriet's confession**[1]

Let it be known that the said Henriet had been a servant and valet of the said Lord de Rais and that, when the said Lord de La Suze[2] took the castle and fortress of Machecoul, the said Henriet heard it said by Milord Charles du Léon that dead children had been found at the bottom of a tower of the said castle; and when the said Milord Charles asked him whether he knew anything about it, he told him no, because he did not know at that time. But he said that when Lord de Rais had recovered the garrison of Champtocé and gone there to give it to the Duke our Sovereign Lord, the said Lord made him take an oath to reveal nothing of the secrets he intended to confide in him. That oath taken, he ordered the said Henriet and Poitou, as well as a fellow named Petit Robin, now deceased, to go into the tower where the said dead children were, take them, and put them in a coffer to be carried to Machecoul. And in the said tower he had discovered thirty-six heads that were put in three trunks, which were bound with cords and taken across the water to the said place of Machecoul, where they were burned, and not in Champtocé, because the said Lord de Rais only stayed there a day or two after having recovered the said place from the said Lord de La Suze, his brother, by handing it over to my said Lord Duke's possession, to whom he had transferred it; and with that the said Lord de Rais betook himself to Machecoul where the said children were, who

---

[1] Henriet's confession before the secular court, especially at the beginning of the drafting of the deposition, is the same as before the ecclesiastical court (p. 232). It adds only a few details, such as the notion which struck Henriet, on his way to prison, to cut his own throat.

[2] René de Rais, Gilles' brother, Lord de La Suze.

were nearly totally putrefied, because they had been killed well before the said Lord de La Suze took the said place; and by diabolical temptation, while he was being conducted to prison in the city of Nantes, the said Henriet considered cutting his throat so as to not divulge what he knew.

Item, the said Henriet declared that the said Gilles de Sillé and Poitou had delivered many little children to the said Lord de Rais in his room, with whom the latter had intercourse, exciting himself and spilling his seed on their bellies; but he did not have his way with them but once or twice. Sometimes the said Lord himself cut their throats, sometimes Gilles de Sillé, Henriet, and Poitou slit them in his room; and they wiped up the blood that ran on the spot; and dead, the children were burned in the said room of the said Lord, after the latter had gone to lie down. The said Lord took greater pleasure in cutting their throats or watching their throats be cut than in knowing them carnally. And this Henriet, Gilles de Sillé, and a man named Rossignol had brought and handed over to him about forty, who were killed and burned in the same fashion. This Henriet nabbed those he delivered while they were begging, and the said Sillé, Poitou, and Rossignol burned them.

Item, the said Lord and Master François Prelati met alone for five weeks in a room at Machecoul to which the said Lord had the key. And the said Henriet heard that a hand of wax and a piece of iron had been found in it.

Item, he declared that Catherine, the wife of a man named Thierry, who was living in Nantes, gave him her child to be admitted as a chorister of the said Lord. And he, Henriet, led him to his room at Machecoul. And there the said Lord and Poitou made him swear to reveal nothing of their secret. The child delivered, the said Henriet returned to Nantes, where he remained for three days. But on returning to Machecoul, he did not see the child again and was told that he was dead. Henriet said that this was the first child that he had delivered to the said Lord; and he thinks that it was about four years previously.

Item, he said that he delivered to the said Lord, at his house, La Suze, in Nantes, a child of Guibelet Delit's, another of Jean Hubert's, another of one named Donete, another of one named Lemion, all four from Nantes. The said Lord had sexual intercourse with them in the said house, and they were killed and burned.

Item, he said that Hillary, a Breton, belonged to the said Lord's chapel, then left it, putting his brother in his place.

Item, he said that Poitou conveyed a beautiful child from La Roche-Bernard to the said Lord at Machecoul, who was likewise put to death.

Item, he said that children were taken to Nantes, and brought to the house of La Suze, where they were killed and burned in the room where the said Lord slept, who was in bed when they burned them; by his order, they placed large or long logs on the andirons in the fireplace, and two or three dry faggots on top of the logs, after which they placed the children; and the ashes of those burned were dispersed in various spots at Machecoul.

Item, he said that he had a beautiful page of Master François' killed at Machecoul.

Item, he said that a young and beautiful boy who was living with Rodigo at Bourgneuf-en-Rais had been brought by Poitou and killed at Machecoul, so Poitou told him. And Henriet said that he was not present at the death of the said child, but that he had heard it said by Poitou or by Gilles de Sillé that this child had been put to death like the others.

Item, he said that Prince delivered to Poitou a young page who was living with him, whom Henriet knew, who was put to death as well; he adds that the said murders of children had occurred in the room where the said Lord slept at Machecoul, or at the entrance, and that after burning their bodies, to move more quickly, they sometimes burned the garments and shirts of these children piece by piece in the flames, in such a manner that no one could detect the smoke.

Item, he said that Master François Prelati often went into the room of the said Lord and remained there an hour or two alone with him.

Item, he said that Master Eustache went looking for the said Master François and that he heard him say that he would summon Master Aliboron, that is, the devil; and that he heard Master Eustache say that Master François would make him come for a jug of wine.

Item, he heard that André Buchet, who belonged to the chapel of the said Lord, and presently belongs to that of the Duke, sent children from Vannes to the said Lord at Machecoul, and that his own servant, named Raoulet, brought him one who was put to death, and that this was around the time when the Duke paid the said Lord money due on Champtocé. He also said that the said Raoulet presently lives with Jamet Thomas of Nantes, and that the said André received from the said Lord a horse worth sixty royals.

Item, he said that Milord Roger de Briqueville, Gilles de Sillé, Poitou, and Rossignol knew about the aforementioned.

Item, he said that he had heard that he loved to see the children's heads cut off after having had sex with them on their bellies, their legs between his own; and sometimes he was on their bellies when the heads were separated from their bodies, other times he cut them behind the neck to make them languish, which he delighted in doing; and while they languished it happened that he had intercourse with them until their death, occasionally after they were dead, while their bodies were still warm; and there was a *braquemard* to cut their heads off with; and if occasionally the beauty of these children did not conform to his fantasy, he cut their heads off himself with the said cutlass, whereupon he occasionally had intercourse with them.

Item, he heard the said Lord say that there was no man alive who could ever understand what he had done, and it was because of his planet that he did such things.

Item, he said that occasionally the said Lord had the said children dismembered at the armpits and that he delighted in seeing the blood; and he heard Master Eustache Blanchet say that the said Lord could not accomplish what he had set out to do without offering up the feet, legs, and other members of the said children to the Devil; that he, Henriet, killed twelve by his own hand; and sometimes the said Lord asked Milord de Sillé, him, Henriet, and Poitou which of the slaughtered children had the most beautiful heads.

Item, he declared that he heard Gilles de Sillé say that since recovering the place, which had been seized by Lord de La Suze, in a room at Machecoul with hay in it, they had discovered forty dead children, who were dried out and had been burned; and he heard Lord de Sillé say that they were fortunate that the said children had not been discovered; [he further stated] that Milord Roger de Briqueville had a woman watch below, there where the said children were; and that when he noticed them he exposed the deed, in which he had not participated.

Item, he stated that one day at Tiffauges, he, Henriet, entered the said room of Lord de Rais', after the latter and Master François Prelati had remained there alone for a long time and then left, and that he noticed on the ground of the said room a large circle, inside of which were characters and crosses, the meaning of which he did not know.

Item, he said that the said Lord had a small book written in blood or red ink, but he is not certain which.

Item, he stated and confessed that to prevent the children from crying out when he intended to have intercourse with them, the said Lord de Rais had a cord put around their necks beforehand, and had them suspended about three feet off the ground in a corner of the room, and before they were dead he let them down or had them let down, asking them not to say a word, and he rubbed his penis in his hand, after which he spilled his seed on their belly; that done, he had their throats cut, having their heads separated from their bodies, and occasionally, after they were dead, asked which of these children had the most beautiful heads.

Item, he declared that the said Lord sometimes gave him two or three crowns for the said children; the said Lord chose them himself when they came begging, asking them where they were from and, when they were not from the region and said they had neither a father nor a mother, and they pleased him, he had them admitted to the castle of Machecoul. He then had the gates of the castle drawn apart.

Item, he said that occasionally the said Lord chose little girls, whom he had sex with on their bellies in the same way as he did with the male children, saying that he took greater pleasure in doing so, and had less pain, than if he had enjoyed them in their nature; thereafter these girls were put to death like the said male children.

Item, he stated that if two of the children were brothers, and if they were brought together, he took his pleasure with just one of them but kept them both in the castle, and so that he who remained would not reveal anything of his brother's fate they were both put to death.

Item, he stated that occasionally, when the said Lord did not have intercourse with the said children, he had it instead with those in his chapel, which was not the witness' concern, because he kept it a secret.

Item, he stated that on the last trip the said Lord made to Vannes, pretending to be waiting for money that the Duke owed him, and staying there two or three days, — and this was last July, it seems to the witness, — André Buchet led to the said Lord's lodging a child, who was killed, whose body was thrown into the latrines of the house, where the said Poitou descended by means of a cord to shove the said body down, whence Buchet and he, Henriet, who helped in the task, had difficulty removing him.

Such was the said Henriet's confession.


## Poitou's confession[3]

And as to that which concerns the said Étienne Corrillaut, also known as Poitou, he acknowledged and confessed the following without torture:

Firstly, that nearly ten years after he had come to stay with the said Lord de Rais — whose page he was for the first five years, when Milord Roger de Briqueville, knight, was looking after Rais' affairs, and whose child valet he was for the next five years — within about two or three months, he saw two dead children in the room of the said Lord, who wanted to kill him, but the said Milords Roger and de Sillé prevented him. That he was subsequently kept in a room by the said Milord Roger for four days, and, this done, they made him swear to conceal what he had seen and would see later; but before this oath, the said Lord had sex with the said Corrillaut on his belly.

Item, he said that Milords Roger and de Sillé ordered him to abduct children and lead them to the said Lord; and the aforesaid brought him many, whom the said Lord got excited over, holding his penis in his hand and spilling his seed onto their bellies; after which he had their throats cut; and sometimes while they were languishing he had intercourse with them. And it was five

---

[3] Poitou's confession differs more from his deposition before the ecclesiastical court than Henriet's did.

years before that he, Poitou, began to steer the said children to him and be his accomplice in crime.

Item, he said that since the day when the said Lord regained Champtocé from the said Lord de La Suze, his brother, which the latter had held for two years,[4] the said Lord went to Champtocé, where he stayed only one or two nights. The said Lord then told him, Poitou, Henriet, Petit Robin, and a man named Hicquet that for a long time there had been dead children in one of the towers, and that they had to be removed. Poitou and Robin went down, put them in a sack, and removed them. Henriet, Hicquet, and Sillé were on the lookout. They found forty-six that were put into coffers and transported to Machecoul and burned in a tower. The said children were dried out and rotten.

Item, he said that after the recovery of the place, which had been taken by Lord de La Suze and Lord de Lohéac, eighty dead children were found at Machecoul, who were likewise burned in the said place of Machecoul.

Item, he said that from the time of the deceased Lord de La Suze, the said Lord killed them in his room at the said place of Champtocé, according to what the said Poitou heard him say, and that it was about fourteen years before that the said Lord had begun to do so.

Item, he stated that occasionally he killed the children by opening their throats with a great *braquemard*; sometimes he kissed their heads after they had been severed, and he had intercourse with them; occasionally he killed them by his own hand, having had intercourse with them beforehand; he placed a cord around their neck that, with the help of a pole, he attached to a hook in his room.

Item, he stated that if there were two children who were brothers, the said Lord had them both snatched so that the one would not cry aloud about the other; and after having diverted himself with the one, he kept the other until his appetite returned.

Item, he stated that once the said Lord took the heart and hand of the said child, put them in his room, and ordered Poitou through a window to watch them; a little while later the said Lord tucked them up his sleeve, then went into the room of Master François, to whom he was bringing them; he does not know what they did with them, and the said heart was in a glass.

Item, he stated that the said Lord and François Prelati stayed one night in the said Lord's room at Machecoul, where they traced a large circle containing characters and crosses; they made a drawing on the wall in the manner of arms, which arms resembled a head; then they made him, Poitou, leave the room, and he went with the others into the hall and, eavesdropping, they heard a beast, like a dog, walking on the roof. After this the said Lord asked whether

---

[4] More likely "two months." See pp. 224 (note 10) and 234 (note 20).

they had heard anything, and he responded no.

Item, he stated that one night the said Lord sent him and Master François into a field close to Espérance, and the said François performed an invocation in a circle where he stood with Poitou. The said François lit a torch and called Barron and devils having other names, of which he, Poitou, was terrified. The said Lord and François had forbidden him to make the sign of the cross. But nothing came of it except for a strong rain, such that they could not leave.

Item, he said that Papelais, Guillemin le Portier, Guillemain Le Beille and Le Muet, Lord Gentelou, the prior of Chémeré, and the Marquis[5] knew nothing of the deaths of the said children; even a nephew of the said prior of Chémeré, whom the latter had entrusted to a fellow named Tabard to learn singing and writing, was killed like the other children.

Item, he said that once a man named Master Jean, an Englishman, and the said Lord went to perform invocations, and that before they went the first squeezed the pinky of the said Lord and then pricked its tip with a needle to make it bleed, and with the blood the said Lord signed a letter written in his own hand in ink. Thereafter, they left to perform the said invocation, and the latter returned as drenched as if he had fallen into a river. A man named Guillaume Cievaye had gone looking for the said Master Jean, who was English or a native of Picardy, and the latter told Lord de Rais before the said invocation that he should not cross himself or they would all be dead; and this took place in a field not far from Machecoul, that side of Espérance, near a house where someone named La Picarde lived. On another occasion the said conjuror returned wounded to such an extent that he could not speak; and after he left, Poitou heard it said by La Picarde that he was only faking it.

Item, he said that eleven or twelve had been killed in the house of La Suze, among them a young boy named Jenvret, from Nantes.

Item, he stated that on the last trip that the said Lord made to Vannes, pretending to be waiting for money that the Duke owed him, and staying there two or three days — this was last July, it seems to him — André Buchet led to the said Lord's lodging a child who was killed, whose body was thrown into the latrines of the house, where he, Poitou, descended by means of a rope to shove the said body down, whence Henriet and Buchet, who helped him with this piece of work, had difficulty removing him.

Item, he spoke of a beautiful child he brought from Roche-Bernard with the mother's approval; moreover, of another beautiful child, the son of the deceased Éonnet de Villeblanche, whose mother, living in Nantes, is named Macée: she entrusted her son to him to become a page, whom he, Poitou, outfitted; as well as a beautiful young child who was living at Bourgneuf with Guillaume Rodigo,

[5] The Marquis de Ceva.

whom he fetched away and brought to his master, and who was a page of the same age; also a page of Master François'; also a page of Prince's; and again, among others, a son of Georget Le Barbier, a tailor, living near the entrance of the said castle of Machecoul; the said Lord had sexual intercourse with them, and they were killed and burned. Finally, he spoke of many others whose mothers and fathers he did not know, many of whom were taken while begging for alms, as often at Machecoul as at Tiffauges and elsewhere.

Such was the said Poitou's confession, as it is contained in the preceding articles.

## Condemnations of Henriet and Poitou

After the confession of the said Henriet and Poitou, and on the advice of many people present, lawyers and others, in view of the cases and all things considered, it was judged and declared by my said Lord the President and Commissioner that the said Henriet and Poitou would be hanged and burned.

## Condemnation of Gilles de Rais

And afterwards, after the trial conducted and concluded by the ecclesiastical court against the said Lord, the latter was brought to Bouffay of Nantes on October 25th, where there was such a big crowd that the said Bouffay was practically filled. After the said prosecutor, by his deputy, had accused him of having committed the crimes indicated and laid out above, he acknowledged that he had committed them, and Monsignor the President asked him for a full confession, the shame he should experience in doing so before him equalling an alleviation of the punishment he would have to suffer in the next world; the said Lord then acknowledged before his judges that he had seized the place and fortress of Saint-Étienne-de-Mermorte by his own authority and with offensive arms, while Geoffroy Le Ferron was Lord of it and possessed it by a transfer that the said Lord had formerly made over to him; he acknowledged that in front of the said place he had constrained and obliged Jean Le Ferron to hand it over to him; and that at the said place of Saint-Étienne, he had abducted the person of Jean Le Ferron, and that he had had him led to Tiffauges, outside this duchy, where he had been detained a long time, until the day he was liberated through the intervention of Monsignor the Constable. Likewise he acknowledged that he had disobeyed the restraining orders placed on him by my said Lord Duke, who requested that he hand over and vacate the said place and release Jean Le Ferron under penalty of a fine of fifty thousand crowns. He further acknowledged, with a great show of remorse and grief, that he had killed a large number of small male children, whom he had burned and turned to ashes to eliminate any trace of his crimes and to avoid disclosures by the said children; and that, moreover, he had committed other crimes described in his confession; which was then read out to him and which he acknowledged and confessed to be true.

After this confession, my said Lord the President requested the advice of many upright men and council members present at the trial; the latter declared that he deserved to die, some asking that he suffer it one way, some that he suffer it another. After having taken counsel with the said men of probity and the witnesses, my said Lord the President and Commissioner of the Duke adjudged and declared, so far as the first case was concerned, that the said Lord had incurred the pecuniary penalties already mentioned, and that these should be paid in favor of Monsignor the Duke, and levied on the possessions and lands of the said Lord, with just moderation. Further, so far as the other crimes committed and confessed by the said Lord were concerned, my said Lord the President and Commissioner of the Duke adjudged and declared that the said Gilles de Rais was to be hanged and burned. After which he stated and declared that, so that he might beg God's mercy and prepare to die soundly with numerous regrets for having committed the said crimes, the said Gilles would be executed the following day at eleven o'clock. Then the said Lord thanked God and my Lord the President for having notified him of the hour of his death, and addressed this request to my Lord the President: he and the said Henriet and Poitou, his servants, having together committed the horrible and enormous crimes for which they were condemned to death, that it might please my said Lord the President that they be executed together, at the same hour of the same day, so that he, who was the principal cause of the misdeeds of his servants, might be able to comfort them, speak to them of their salvation at the hour of execution, and exhort them by example to die fittingly; he feared, he said, that were it otherwise, and the aforesaid servants did not see him die, that they should fall into despair, imagining that they were dying while he, who was the cause of their misdeeds, went unpunished; he hoped, on the contrary, with the grace of Our Lord, that he who made them commit the misdeeds for which they were dying would be the cause of their salvation.

My said Lord the President acceded to this request and, considering the said Gilles' profound contrition, accorded him this favor: the said execution carried out as abovestated, he will allow his body, having previously been opened and embraced by the flames, to be placed in a coffin and buried in this city of Nantes, in whatever church the said Gilles designates. For which the said Gilles thanked the said Lord the President, asking that his aforesaid body be buried in the church of the Carmelite monastery of Notre-Dame in Nantes.

My said Lord the President expressed satisfaction with this resolution. More-over, the said Gilles asked my said Lord the President to be so kind as to request the Bishop of Nantes and the men of his church to arrange a general procession in order to ask God to maintain in him and his said servants the firm hope of salvation; which was apparently accorded him by my said Lord the President.

Thus signed: *De Touscheronde.*

## The Executions of Lord de Rais, and Henriet and Poitou, his Servants

In the performance of the said sentences pronounced against the said Gilles de Rais, and against his servants Henriet and Poitou, they were led together to the place prepared for the said execution, in a field not far above the bridges of Nantes. And earlier that same day, at nine o'clock or thereabouts, a general procession took place wherein a great multitude of people prayed to God for the said condemned, who were present at the said place of execution; the said Gilles de Rais confessed and exhorted his aforesaid servants on the subject of the salvation of their souls, urging them to be strong and virtuous in the face of diabolical temptations, and to have profound regret and contrition for their misdeeds, but also to have confidence in the grace of God and to believe that there was no sin a man might commit so great that God in His goodness and kindness would not forgive, so long as the sinner felt profound regret and great contrition of heart, and asked Him for mercy with a great deal of perse-verance. And God was closer to forgiving and receiving the sinner in His grace than the sinner was to asking His forgiveness. And they should thank God for having shown them such a sign of love, He who required them to die in the fullness of their strength and memory, and did not permit them to be punished suddenly for their wrongs, and who gave them such an ardent love of Him and such great contrition for their misdeeds that they no longer had anything in this world to fear from death, which was nothing but a short death, without which one could not see God in all His glory. And they ought very much to desire to be out of this world, where there was nothing but misery, so as to enter into eternal glory. And thus, as soon as their souls left their bodies, those who had committed evil together would thereby meet each other again in glory, with God, in paradise. And he begged them to be sure to do as he asked, and to persevere in the little time remaining to them, lest they should lose the glory that never again would be lost to them. The said Henriet and Poitou then thanked the said Gilles de Rais for the good advice and warning he had given them on the salvation of their souls, his exhorting them to hold their deaths in this world as something agreeable, given the great desire that they had for God's grace and their certainty of entering paradise in His glory, praying to their master to seek for himself what he counseled them in. And after having exhorted them thus, Gilles got down on his knees, folding his hands together, begging God's mercy, praying to Him to be willing to punish them not according to their misdeeds, but, being merciful, to let them profit by the grace in which he put his trust, telling the people that as a Christian, he was their brother, and urging them and those among them whose children he had killed, for the love of Our Lord's suffering to be willing to pray to God for him and to forgive him freely, in the same way that they themselves intended God to forgive and have mercy on themselves. Recommending himself to holy Monsignor Jacques, whom he had always held in singular affection, and also to holy Monsignor Michel, begging them in his hour of great need to be willing to help him, aid him, and pray to God for him, despite the fact that he had not obeyed them as he should have. He further requested that the instant his soul left his body, it might please holy Monsignor Michel to receive it and present it unto God, whom he begged to take it into His grace, without punishing it according to its offenses. And the said Gilles then made beautiful speeches and prayers to God, recommending his soul to Him. And then, so as to set his aforesaid servants a good example, he wished to die first. Just before his death, his said servants told him and implored him to be a strong and valiant knight in the love of God, asking him to remember His suffering, which had been for our Redemption. Which Gilles de Rais died repentant. And before the flames could open his body and entrails, it was drawn away and his body placed in a coffin and carried inside the Carmelite church of Nantes, where it was buried. And immediately the said Henriet and Poitou were hanged and burned, such that they were reduced to ashes. And they had felt much contrition and regret for their misdeeds, and they had persevered in this contrition and this regret to the end.

Thus signed: *De Touscheronde.*

# BIBLIOGRAPHY

BOSSARD, Abbot Eugène. *Gilles de Rais, Maréchal de France.* 8 vols. Paris, 1886.

BOURDEAUT, Abbot A. *Chantocé, Gilles de Rays et les Ducs de Bretagne.* 8 vols. Rennes, 1924. Reprinted from *Mémoires de la Société d'Histoire et d'Archéologie de Bretagne*, 1924, pp. 41-150.

FLEURET, Fernand. See HERNANDEZ, Lodovico.

GABORY, Emile. *La Vie et la Mort de Gilles de Raiz, dit à tort Barbe-Bleue.* Paris, 1926.

HERNANDEZ, Lodovico. *Le Procès inquisitorial de Gilles de Rais, Maréchal de France*, with an *Essai de Réhabilitation.* 8 vols. Paris, 1922. [A literal translation of the canonical trial, and a recreation of the civil trial.]

HUYSMANS, Joris-Karl. *Là-Bas.* Paris, 1891.

REINACH, Salomon. "Gilles de Rais." *Cultes, Mythes et Religions.* 8 vols. Paris, 1912. Vol. 4: 267-299. First published in *Revue de l'Université de Bruxelles*, (December 1904): 161-182.

VILLENUEVE, Roland. *Gilles de Rays. Une grande Figure diabolique.* Paris, 1955.